MARITIME BOUNDARY

Publications on Ocean Development

Volume 9

A series of studies on the international, legal, institutional and policy aspects of ocean development

General editor: Shigeru Oda

1. Anand, R.P.: Legal regime of the seabed and the developing countries. ISBN 90-286-0616-5
2. Papadakis, N.: The international legal regime of artificial islands. ISBN 90-286-0127-9
3. Oda, S.: The law of the sea in our time I — New developments, 1966–1975. ISBN 90-286-0277-1
4. Oda, S.: The law of the sea in our time II — The United Nations Seabed Committee, 1968–1973. ISBN 90-286-0287-9
5. Okidi, C.O.: Regional control of ocean pollution: legal and institutional problems and prospects. ISBN 90-286-0367-0
6. Rembe, N.S.: Africa and the international law of the sea: a study of the contribution of the African states to the Third United Nations Conference on the Law of the Sea. ISBN 90-286-0639-4
7. Anand, R.P.: Origin and development of the law of the sea: history of international law revisited. ISBN 90-247-2617-4
8. Post, A.M.: Deepsea mining and the law of the sea. ISBN 90-247-3049-x
9. Jagota, S.P.: Maritime boundary. ISBN 90-247-3133-X

Maritime Boundary

S.P. JAGOTA

1985 **MARTINUS NIJHOFF PUBLISHERS**
a member of the KLUWER ACADEMIC PUBLISHERS GROUP
DORDRECHT / BOSTON / LANCASTER

Distributors

for the United States and Canada: Kluwer Academic Publishers, 190 Old Derby Street, Hingham, MA 02043, USA
for the UK and Ireland: Kluwer Academic Publishers, MTP Press Limited, Falcon House, Queen Square, Lancaster LA1 1RN, UK
for all other countries: Kluwer Academic Publishers Group, Distribution Center, P.O. Box 322, 3300 AH Dordrecht, The Netherlands

Library of Congress Cataloging in Publication Data


```
Jagota, S. P.
   Maritime boundary.

   (Publications on ocean development ; v. 9)
   Bibliography: p.
   1. Economic zones (Maritime law)  2. Territorial
waters.  I. Title.  II. Series.
JX4131.J34  1985       341.4'48        85-3040
ISBN 90-247-3133-X
```

ISBN 90-247-3133-X (this volume)
ISBN 90-247-2616-6 (series)

Copyright

PRINTED IN THE NETHERLANDS

To my parents

Preface and acknowledgements

This study on maritime boundary is an updated and more comprehensive version of the lectures delivered by the author at The Hague Academy of International Law, The Hague, in August 1981. It deals with the outer limits of maritime zones, as well as with the delimitation of maritime zones between States with opposite or adjacent coasts. The latter aspect has been covered more comprehensively, with emphasis on three areas, namely (a) State practice reflected in treaties and agreements concluded between States, (b) judicial, arbitral and other decisions, and (c) developments at the Third United Nations Conference on the Law of the Sea (1973 – 1982), leading to the adoption of the United Nations Convention on the Law of the Sea, 1982.

The period of time covered in this study is between 1945 and 1983. Only the concluded agreements and the decided cases have been covered. Thus the agreements still under negotiation, or the cases pending in the International Court of Justice or in other forums have not been covered.

The developments in the three segments covered in this study have been divergent, and yet coordination may emerge in current and forthcoming State practice and in judicial and other decisions, as shown in Part Five of this study, Conclusions.

The author is grateful to The Hague Academy of International Law for permission to publish this study, as well as to the Government of India, Ministry of External Affairs, with whom he had the honour to work from 1963 to 1983, and from where he retired as Additional Secretary and Legal Adviser in September 1983. The basic research work for this study was completed in India. The concluding work was done at Dalhousie University, Halifax, N.S., Canada, with the library and research facilities made available by the Dalhousie Law School Library and the Dalhousie Ocean Studies Programme, to whom the author is grateful. The author has also benefited from the numerous studies which have been made of different aspects of the subject-matter covered in this study by many scholars, as well as from the basic documents collected and analysed by their authors. He acknowledges his debt to these scholars and their studies, as well as to these facilities. The responsibility for the views expressed in this study remains that of the author alone.

It is hoped that the study will be found useful by those who may need to look into these developments in the law on delimitation of maritime boundaries as a whole, particularly by government officials and scholars and students of international law.

S.P. JAGOTA
April 7, 1984

Contents

X

PART FOUR: MARITIME BOUNDARY AT THE
THIRD UNITED NATIONS CONFERENCE
ON THE LAW OF THE SEA, 1973 – 1982

List of charts

Abbreviations

A/CONF.62 . . .	refers to a document of the Third United Nations Conference on the Law of the Sea, 1973 – 1982
AJIL	American Journal of International Law
Art./Arts.	Article/Articles
BYBIL	The British Year Book of International Law
CS	Continental Shelf
EE	Eastern Europe (Socialist) States
EEZ	Exclusive Economic Zone
FRG	Federal Republic of Germany
GDR	German Democratic Republic
Ibid.	*ibidem* – in the same place
ICJ	International Court of Justice
ICNT	Informal Composite Negotiating Text
i.e.	*id est* – that is
ILC	International Law Commission
km./kms.	kilometre/kilometres
MB	Maritime Boundary
n./f.n.	note/footnote
NG	Negotiating Group
op. cit.	*opus citatum* – in the work cited
p./pp.	page/pages
Rev.	Revision
RSNT	Revised Single Negotiating Text
SNT	Informal Single Negotiating Text
UAE	United Arab Emirates
UK	United Kingdom of Great Britain and Northern Ireland
UNCLOS	The Third United Nations Conference on the Law of the Sea, 1973 – 1982
US/USA	United States of America
USSR	Union of Soviet Socialist Republics

Footnotes have been numbered Part-wise, that is, in Parts One, Two, Three, Four, Five and Six respectively. Cross-reference to a note is therefore to a note in the same Part, unless indicated otherwise in the reference.

PART ONE

Scope, limits of maritime zones, technical aspects

CHAPTER 1

Introduction

Scope

The term 'maritime boundary' has two main implications. It refers to the seaward *outer limits* of the maritime zones of a coastal State, such as the territorial sea, the exclusive economic zone and the continental shelf. It also refers to the *limits* of the maritime zones of States with opposite or adjacent coasts, in order to avoid an overlap. The latter is popularly called 'delimitation of maritime boundary'. Although both aspects of maritime boundary will be covered in this Part, the rest of this study will concentrate on the *limits* of maritime zones of States with opposite or adjacent coasts.

The study also concentrates on the analysis and the development of international law relating to maritime boundary since 1945, with greater emphasis on developments since 1958. It is during this period that the development of the law has crystallised concerning the maritime zones over which a coastal State has sovereignty, sovereign rights or jurisdiction in specified matters. These zones extend to long distances from the shores, such as the 200-nautical mile exclusive economic zone, or the continental shelf which may in some cases extend beyond 200 nautical miles. The extended coastal State jurisdiction necessitated a review and crystallisation of the principles or rules of maritime delimitation.[1]

The study examines and analyses the development of the law relating to maritime boundary with reference to three main aspects: State practice reflected in agreements concluded between States; judicial and arbitral decisions; and developments at the Third United Nations Conference on the Law of the Sea (1973 – 1982). These are dealt with in Parts Two, Three and Four of this study, respectively. Where observed, the interaction of these main sources of the applicable law has also been referred to. The study has not dealt with the pending agreements or the pending disputes.

The term 'maritime boundary' has also been used in this study as having a comprehensive connotation. It covers 'territorial sea boundary', 'exclusive economic zone boundary', 'continental shelf boundary', or boundary with respect to any other maritime zone.

Maritime boundary, like territorial or land boundary, is a politically sensitive subject, because it affects the coastal State's jurisdiction concerning the fishery, petroleum and other resources of the sea as well as concerning the other uses of the sea. Its sensitivity will be manifest particularly from observing the time-consuming and laborious efforts made at the Third United Nations Conference on the Law of the Sea between 1974 and 1982 to crystallise the delimitation criteria and deal with the other related matters. These are covered in Part Four of the study below.

Part Five deals with the conclusions reached from this study, the main conclusion being that a maritime boundary agreement, a decision of a court or an arbitral tribunal, or the rules of international law, to be durable and of value, must establish or lead to the establishment of a boundary which is fair and equitable to the parties.

The subject is thus of interest to students of international law, researchers and experts, statesmen and negotiators, and counsel, arbitrators and judges handling concrete cases.

Part One will now deal with the background to the subject, the limits of maritime zones, and the technical aspects.

Background

The sea covers about five-sevenths of the globe. Human knowledge about the sea and its resources and its diverse uses has increased with the passage of time. Traditionally the sea was used mainly for navigation, transportation and fishing. During the past four hundred years or so, the sea was used for the discovery, conquest and the maintenance of colonies and the development of the colonial economy. During the present century, newer uses have come to light, such as the recovery of petroleum and gas from the continental shelf through vertical and directional drilling from the sea, hard minerals from near the coast, and polymetallic nodules from the deep ocean floor. With increased knowledge, innovation, technology and capability, the traditional uses of the sea, including fishing and shipping, have also undergone a new phase. The sea is also being used now for the generation of power from tides, winds and ocean thermal energy conversion, for the establishment of offshore terminals, installations, artificial islands, and seabed storages, for the conducting of marine scientific research, for newer forms of recreation, and for national and global security.

Historically, the rulers along the coast and the others had exercised some form of maritime jurisdiction over the ports and the adjoining sea in respect of access of ships to the ports, trade and commerce, prohibition of piracy at sea, control over contraband vessels, and State security. But the open sea beyond the marginal belt and the oceans were free. Alexandrowicz, who examined the Asian State practice in the 16th, 17th and 18th centuries, concluded as follows:

It is therefore possible to assume that Grotius in formulating his doctrine of the freedoms of the sea found himself encouraged by what he learned from the study of the Asian maritime custom.[2]

The European State practice was however contradictory and the jurisdiction was determined by whoever ruled the waves in their respective zones. The Papal Bull of 1493 had divided the jurisdiction of Spain and Portugal in the oceans of the world along the Meridian. Grotius had however interpreted this claim of Papal donation by Portugal as merely settling the internal dispute between them. According to Grotius, 'the decision of the Pope will of course not affect the other peoples of the world'.[3]

Grotius' views prevailed. The concept of a small belt of territorial sea, initially justified as extending up to the reach of a cannon shot and limited in many cases to 3 nautical miles from the baselines along the coast, in which the coastal State enjoyed sovereignty, became generally recognised. Beyond the belt of the territorial sea were the high seas, open to all nations. The freedoms of the high seas became accepted and established as a part of international custom, and included the freedoms of navigation, overflight, fishing and the laying of submarine cables and pipelines.

The questions of the outer limits of the territorial sea and the fishing rights of coastal States in a contiguous zone were discussed at The Hague Codification Conference which was convened by the League of Nations and which met at The Hague from March 13 to April 12, 1930. Although certain draft articles were provisionally approved, no convention could be adopted by the Conference.[4]

With the discovery of the petroleum resources of the continental shelf, the question of the coastal State jurisdiction relating thereto arose. In the first case reported, the United Kingdom and Venezuela entered into an agreement in February 1942 dividing the submarine area outside the territorial sea in the Gulf of Paria, recognizing each other's claims to the respective areas and its resources, and providing for mutual abstention from exercising any right across the boundary line. The legal doctrine justifying this action was thus discovery and effective occupation, and the expected acquiescence from the other States. After the conclusion of the agreement, the submarine area of the Gulf of Paria on their side of the boundary line was in fact annexed to form part of the British dominions and 'attached to the Colony of Trinidad and Tobago for administration purposes'.[5]

The general question of the coastal State jurisdiction was, however, also being examined in the United States, both with respect to the petroleum resources of the continental shelf and the protection of the fishery interests of the United States in areas beyond the territorial sea. Two Proclamations were issued by the

President of the United States, Harry S. Truman, on September 28, 1945, one concerning the continental shelf adjacent to its territorial sea, which was regarded as 'an extension of the land-mass of the coastal nation', and whose natural resources were regarded as 'appertaining to the United States, subject to its jurisdiction and control', and the other concerning the establishment of conservation zones for the protection of fisheries in certain areas adjacent to its territorial sea where the United States fishermen might have fished exclusively or along with the nationals of other States.[6] Both these Proclamations had a generatin effect on the evolution of international customary law. The first led to the crystallisation of the concept of the continental shelf. The second followed a different course and led to the evolution of an exclusive fishery zone and exclusive economic zone.

The continental shef Proclamation also provided that 'In cases where the continental shelf extends to the shores of another State, or is shared with an adjacent State, the boundary shall be determined by the United States and the State concerned in accordance with equitable principles'.[7]

The Truman Proclamation on the Continental Shelf, which was followed in extensive State practice, was given a pride of place in the evolution of the concept of the continental shelf and the rules of maritime delimitation by the International Court of Justice in the *North Sea Continental Shelf* cases, 1969.

The subject of the law of the sea was extensively discussed by the International Law Commission between 1949 and 1956, and a set of 73 articles was prepared by it. These articles constituted the basic proposal for consideration by the First United Nations Conference on the Law of the Sea which met in Geneva from February 24 to April 27, 1958. The 1958 Conference led to the adoption of the following four Conventions:
1. Convention on the Territorial Sea and the Contiguous Zone;
2. Convention on the High Seas;
3. Convention on Fishing and Conservation of the Living Resources of the High Seas;
4. Convention on the Continental Shelf.[9]

Along with these Conventions, an Optional Protocol concerning the Compulsory Settlement of Disputes was adopted by the 1958 Conference. These Conventions and the Optional Protocol entered into force between 1962 and 1966.

The questions of the precise outer limits of the territorial sea and of the exclusive fishing rights of a coastal State, which were not settled in the 1958 Conventions, were taken up by the Second United Nations Conference on the Law of the Sea held in March – April 1960, but without success.

The 1958 Conventions had not dealt with the question of the exploitation of the mineral resources of the deep seabed. The discovery of the commercially exploitable polymetallic nodules from the deep seabed which could yield valuable minerals such as nickel, copper, cobalt and manganese and the increasing mili-

6

tary uses of the seabed, led to the demand that the resources of the international seabed area beyond the limits of national jurisdiction should be regarded as 'the common heritage of mankind', and that the seabed should be used exclusively for peaceful purposes. An item dealing with these aspects was inscribed in the agenda of the United Nations General Assembly in 1967 by Malta. A seabed committee was established forthwith. On December 17, 1970, the United Nations General Assembly adopted two resolutions — one containing the Declaration of Principles concerning the resources of the international seabed area (Resolution 2749(XXV)), and the other concerning the convening of the Third United Nations Conference on the Law of the Sea in 1973 to review the law of the sea and establish an international regime and machinery for regulating the exploitation of the resources of the international seabed area (Resolution 2750C (XXV)). The military aspects of the uses of the seabed were taken over by the Committee on Disarmament, Geneva, and a Treaty on the Employment of Nuclear Weapons and Other Weapons of Mass Destruction on the Seabed and the Ocean Floor and in the Subsoil Thereof was adopted in 1971.

The membership of the United Nations Seabed Committee was enlarged in 1970, and it acted as the preparatory committee for the Third United Nations Conference on the Law of the Sea (hereafter abbreviated as UNCLOS). The UNCLOS held eleven sessions between December 1973 and December 1982. In the absence of a basic proposal prepared by the International Law Commission or completed by the United Nations Seabed Committee, and with a view to reconciling all important interests and reaching decisions by consensus in conformity with a gentleman's agreement on procedure, the UNCLOS devised the mechanism of preparing negotiating texts in its move towards the adoption of a convention on the law of the sea. The first Informal Single Negotiating Texts (SNT) were presented by the Chairmen of the three Main Committees and the President[10] in May and June 1975. The Revised Single Negotiating Texts (RSNT) were prepared in May 1976. The negotiating texts were consolidated into an Informal Composite Negotiating Text (ICNT) in July 1977, which was given its first revision in April 1979, its second revision in April 1980, and its third revision in August 1980. The third revision of ICNT in August 1980 was also called the Draft Convention on the Law of the Sea (Informal Text), which was formalised as an official document and the basic proposal for UNCLOS in 1981 and appeared as document A/CONF.62/L.78 of August 28, 1981. The Draft Convention, along with four resolutions including those relating to the establishment of the Preparatory Commission and Preparatory Investment in Pioneer Activities Relating to Polymetallic Nodules, was adopted as a package by UNCLOS on April 30, 1982 by a recorded vote of 130 delegations in favour, 4 against (Israel, Turkey, United States, and Venezuela), and 17 abstentions. In September 1982, the final recommendations of the Drafting Committee concerning the text of the Convention were accepted by UNCLOS, the text of the

Final Act of UNCLOS was approved, and it was decided to designate the Convention as the United Nations Convention on the Law of the Sea.

The concluding part of the eleventh session of UNCLOS was held in Montego Bay, Jamaica, from December 6 to 10, 1982. The Convention and the Final Act were opened for signature on December 10, 1982. The United Nations Convention on the Law of the Sea was signed by 117 States, apart from the Cook Islands and the Council for Namibia. It was also ratified by Fiji. By December 1983, the Convention had been signed by 131 States and ratified by 9 States. It shall enter into force 12 months after it has been ratified by 60 States.

The Final Act of the Conference,[11] which contains the text of the Resolutions on Preparatory Commission and Preparatory Investment in Pioneer Activities, was signed on December 10, 1982, by 150 States.

Since more than 50 States had signed the Convention, the Preparatory Commission was convened and held its first session in two parts in Kingston, Jamaica, in March – April and August – September 1983. It will, *inter alia*, take preparatory steps for the establishment of the International Seabed Authority and the International Tribunal for the Law of the Sea, and implement the resolution on preparatory investment in pioneer activities.

The United Nations Convention on the Law of the Sea, 1982[12] is a comprehensive document. It consists of 320 Articles and 9 Annexes. It deals with all aspects of the law of the sea, including those covered in the four 1958 Conventions mentioned above. The Convention also expressly provides that it 'shall prevail, as between States Parties, over the Geneva Conventions on the Law of the Sea of 29 April 1958'.[13]

In summary, the 1982 Convention establishes a 12-mile territorial sea, a 24-mile contiguous zone, a 200-mile exclusive economic zone, precise outer limits for the continental shelf, right of transit passage through international straits, regime of archipelagic States, regime of islands, regime of the high seas, protection of the interests of the landlocked States and the geographically disadvantaged States, delimitation of maritime zones, and so forth.[14] The Convention also establishes a comprehensive regime and machinery for the exploitation of the resources of the international seabed area, which are 'the common heritage of mankind', the interim arrangements relating to which are contained in the resolutions relating to the preparatory commission and the preparatory investment in pioneer activities.[15] The Convention also deals with the protection and preservation of the marine environment, marine scientific research, and development and transfer of marine technology.[16] It contains comprehensive provisions concerning the settlement of disputes, including the establishment of the International Tribunal for the Law of the Sea.[17] Finally, it makes some general provisions, including a provision on fulfilment of obligations in good faith and in a manner which would not constitute an abuse of right,[18] and contains the final provisions,[19] which deal *inter alia* with the entry into force of the Convention and provide that 'No reservations or exceptions may be made to this Convention unless expressly permitted by other articles of this Convention'.[20]

This study will concentrate on the outer limits of the maritime zones of a coastal State and the delimitation of maritime bundary between States with opposite or adjacent coasts. The development of these concepts, including the relevant provisions of the Geneva Conventions of 1958 and the United Nations Convention on the Law of the Sea, 1982, will now be dealt with below.

Notes

1. For a comprehensive review of State practice between 1648 and 1939, including judicial and arbitral decisions, treatment in Conferences and research institutions, and the views of experts and publicists, see Sang-Myon Rhee, 'Sea Boundary Delimitation Between States Before World War II', *American Journal of International Law* (hereafter cited as AJIL), Vol. 76, No. 3 (July 1982), pp. 555-588.
2. C.H. Alexandrowicz, *An Introduction to the Study of the Law of Nations in the East Indies*, Oxford, London, 1967, at p. 65. For his reference to Kautilya's *Arthasastra*, written in about 300 B.C., and the jurisdiction of the 'Superintendent of Ships' and the 'Superindendent of Mines' along the Indian Coast, see pp. 61 and 62.
3. *Ibid.*, at p. 47.
4. C. John Colombos, *The International Law of the Sea*, Sixth Edition (1967), pp. 103-106.
5. See below at pp. 101-102.
6. Marjorie M. Whiteman, *Digest of International Law*, Vol. 4, pp. 756-757 and 954-955. See also Ann L. Hollick, 'U.S. Oceans Policy: The Truman Proclamations', *Virginia Journal of International Law*, Vol. 17: 1 (1976), pp. 23-55.
7. Whiteman, n. 6, at p. 757.
8. For an exhaustive paper on the state of the law of the sea in 1950, see A/CN.4/32 of 14 July 1950 in *Year Book of International Law Commission*, 1950, Vol. II, pp. 67-113. For text of the 73 articles prepared by the Commission, along with the commentary thereon, see *Year Book of International Law Commission*, 1956, Vol. II, pp. 256-301.
9. For text of these Conventions, see *The Work of the International Law Commission*, United Nations, New York, Third Edition (1980), pp. 140-166.
10. The three Main Committees dealt with the following subjects: the First Committee dealt with the international seabed area and its resources; the Second Committee dealt with the other law of the sea questions, including the territorial sea, the exclusive economic zone, the continental shelf, and the high seas; the Third Committee dealt with the questions of marine environment, marine scientific research, and transfer of marine technology. The President was the chairman of the informal plenary meeting of UNCLOS which dealt with the question of the settlement of disputes and the final clauses.
11. For text of Final Act, see A/CONF.62/121 and Corr. 1-8. The symbol A/CONF.62 refers to the documents of the Third United Nations Conference on the Law of the Sea, 1973 – 82.
12. For text of the Convention, see A/CONF.62/122 and Corr. 1-11.
13. Article 311(1).
14. Articles 2-132; Annexes I and II.

15. Articles 133-191; Annexes III, IV and VII (Articles 14, 35-40). Final Act, A/CONF.62/121, Annex I, Resolutions I and II.
16. Articles 192-278.
17. Articles 279-299; Annexes V, VI, VII and VIII.
18. Articles 300-304; Article 300 deals with good faith and abuse of rights.
19. Articles 305-320.
20. Article 309.

CHAPTER 2

Outer limits of maritime zones

A. Pre-1949 position

The designation of maritime zones and the determination of their seaward outer limits have had a chequered history. We have already noted in Chapter 1 that the Asian State practice in the pre-colonial period had supported the concept of coastal State jurisdiction in ports and in a small belt of the adjoining sea, the sea and the ocean beyond which were open and free for all, and that despite the then contrary European State practice, the concepts of a small belt of the territorial sea and of the high seas had emerged and received a broad support.

However, the adequacy of a 3-mile territorial sea was questioned with reference to the exploitation of fisheries, and suggestions were made even in the late nineteenth century in India that the territorial sea should be extended to 12 miles. In 1903, the Madras High Court considered the question whether an Indian ruler could have traditional fishery jurisdiction (concerning *chanks* on the seabed) in the Palk's Bay between India and Ceylon (Sri Lanka) and whether the unauthorised and dishonest taking away of such resources by a person other than the licensee would constitute theft, and decided it in the affirmative and in favour of the licensee.[21] This and other similar cases and developments led to Sir Cecil Hurst's article in 1923 entitled 'Whose is the Bed of the Sea?'[22] The British Government was however reluctant either to extend the limits of the territorial sea beyond 3 nautical miles or to recognise historical or prescriptive rights beyond that limit, lest it affect their interests in other areas, such as in relation to Norway.

One of the important topics considered at *The Hague Codification Conference of 1930* was the question of territorial waters, the other topics being nationality and responsibility of States. The term 'territorial sea' was preferred to the more commonly used term 'territorial waters'. The Conference was divided on the question of the outer limits of the territorial sea and the contiguous zone, the latter being considered from the point of view of fishing rights of coastal States and their security interests. The Conference was attended by delegations from 47 States. Twenty States supported a 3-mile territorial sea, 12 States supported a 6-mile territorial sea, whereas the Nordic States wanted a 4-mile territorial sea. The support for the contiguous zone was also varied. The Conference did not consider the question of delimitation of the territorial sea boundary between States with opposite or adjacent coasts. No Convention was adopted by the Conference.[23]

The Truman Proclamations of September 28, 1945 on the continental shelf and on coastal fisheries led to a further review of the limits of national jurisdiction and to claims for new maritime zones, apart from the territorial sea and the contiguous zone.

B. International Law Commission: 1949 – 1956

It was against this background that, in 1949, the International Law Commission included the topics of 'the regime of the high seas' and 'the regime of the territorial sea' in the list of topics whose codification it considered necessary and feasible. The Commission gave priority to the former and included therein the concepts of the fishery resources of the seas, the contiguous zone, and the continental shelf. In 1951, upon the recommendations of the United Nations General Assembly, the Commission took up the subject of the regime of the territorial sea.

On the question of the maritime zones and their outer limits, the major developments which influenced the work of the International Law Commission were the following:

(i)   Pursuant to the *Truman Proclamation* on the Continental Shelf, 1945, which was followed in State practice by Mexico, Argentina, Chile, Peru, Costa Rica, Honduras, Ecuador, Nicaragua, Venezuela, Saudi Arabia and others,[24] it became apparent that the concept of the continental shelf had to be recognised and developed with a sound legal basis and with appropriate outer limits.

(ii)   Pursuant to the *Truman Proclamation* on coastal fisheries, 1945, the question of the recognition of the fishery interests of the coastal States received further stimulus.

(iii)   The realisation that the continental shelf of a coastal State up to 200 metre depth of water may extend from 1 to 800 miles[25] led to a demand by the short continental shelf States for an extended national maritime zone, which was justified on grounds of equity. The initiative for this was taken by some Latin American States (Chile, Peru and Ecuador) and led to the adoption of *the Santiago Declaration* in August 1952, which proclaimed a 200-mile national maritime zone. The material part of the Santiago Declaration read as follows:

12

. . . the Governments of Chile, Ecuador, and Peru, being resolved to preserve for and make available to their respective peoples the natural resources of the areas of sea adjacent to their coasts, hereby declare as follows:

(I)   Owing to the geological and biological factors affecting the existence, conservation and development of the marine fauna and flora of the waters adjacent to the coasts of the declarant countries, the former extent of the territorial sea and contiguous zone is insufficient to permit of the conservation, development, and use of those resources, to which the coastal countries are entitled.

(II)   The Governments of Chile, Ecuador, and Peru therefore proclaim as a principle of their international maritime policy that each of them possesses sole sovereignty and jurisdiction over the area of sea adjacent to the coast of its own country and extending not less than 200 nautical miles from the said coast.

(III)   Their sole jurisdiction and sovereignty over the zone thus described includes sole sovereignty and jurisdiction over the sea floor and subsoil thereof.

(IV)   The zone of 200 nautical miles shall extend in every direction from any island or group of islands forming part of the territory of a declarant country. The maritime zone of an island or group of islands belonging to one declarant country and situated less than 200 nautical miles from the general maritime zone of another declarant country shall be bounded by the parallel of latitude drawn from the point at which the land frontier between the two countries reaches the sea . . .[26]

The Santiago Declaration protected the innocent and inoffensive passage of vessels of all nations through the aforesaid 200-mile zone.

(iv)   The Judgment of the International Court of Justice in the *Anglo-Norwegian Fishery Case*, 1951[27] upheld the straight baselines drawn by Norway in 1935 joining the outermost points on its coastal islands and low-tide elevations as compatible with international law, and also approved its claim for a 4-mile exclusive fishing zone and territorial sea measured from these baselines.

Both these aspects of the *Judgment* influenced the International Law Commission's deliberations on the questions of the baselines and the outer limits or breadth of the territorial sea.

(v)   On the question of the outer limits of the continental shelf, the *Resolution of Ciudad Trujillo* of March 1956, adopted by the Inter-American Specialized Conference on 'Conservation of Natural Resources: The Continental Shelf and Marine Waters', held in Ciudad Trujillo (Dominican Republic), provided a depth-cum-exploitability criteria for these outer limits as follows:

> The Inter-American Specialized Conference on 'Conservation of Natural Resources: The Continental Shelf and Marine Waters',

13

I. *Resolves:*

To submit for consideration by the American states the following conclusions:

1. The sea-bed and subsoil of the continental shelf, continental and insular terrace, or other submarine areas, adjacent to the coastal state, outside the area of the territorial sea, and to a depth of 200 meters or, beyond
that limit, to where the depth of the superjacent waters admits of the exploitation of the natural resources of the sea-bed and subsoil, appertain exclusively to that state and are subject to its jurisdiction and control.

2. Agreement does not exist among the states here represented with respect to the juridical régime of the waters which cover the said submarine
areas, nor with respect to the problem of whether certain living resources
belong to the sea-bed or to the superjacent waters . . .[28]

The substance of paragraph 1 of the Resolution of Ciudad Trujillo was accepted by the International Law Commission in 1956, and later adopted by the 1958
United Nations Conference on the Law of the Sea and included in the Convention on the Continental Shelf, 1958.

Briefly, despite intensive efforts between 1952 and 1956, the Commission was
unable to decide about the outer limits of the *territorial sea*. Concerning the
contiguous zone, the outer limits were fixed at 12 miles from the appropriate
baselines. No outer limits were specified for protecting the special interests of
coastal States in *fisheries* adjacent to their territorial sea. Finally, on the question of the *continental shelf*, the Commission adopted the depth-cum-
exploitability criteria in 1956.

The developments in this regard item-wise may be summarised hereunder.

(1) As to the *outer limits of the territorial sea*, the Commission's Report for
1954, when it discussed the matter intensively, contains an elaborate summing
up of the various suggestions made in its sessions. Para. 68 of that Report reads
as follows:

On the question of the breadth of the territorial sea, divergent opinions
were expressed during the debates at the various sessions of the Commission. The following suggestions were made:

(1) That a uniform limit (three, four, six or twelve miles) should be
adopted;

(2) That the breadth of the territorial sea should be fixed at three miles
subject to the right of the coastal State to exercise, up to a distance of
twelve miles, the rights which the Commission has recognized as existing
in the contiguous zones;

(3) That the breadth of the territorial sea should be three miles, subject
to the right of the coastal State to extend this limit to twelve miles, provided
that it observes the following conditions:

14

(i) Freedom of passage through the entire area must be safeguarded;

(ii) The coastal State may not claim exclusive fishing rights for its nationals beyond the distance of three nautical miles from the base line of the territorial sea. Beyond this three-mile limit the coastal State may prescribe regulations governing fisheries in the territorial sea, though the sole object of such regulations must be the protection of the resources of the sea;

(4)   That it should be admitted that the breadth of the territorial sea may be fixed by each State at a distance between three to twelve nautical miles;

(5)   That a uniform limit should be adopted for all States whose coasts abut on the same sea or for all States in a particular region;

(6)   That the limit should vary from State to State in keeping with the special circumstances and historic rights peculiar to each;

(7)   That the basis of the breadth of the territorial sea should be the area of sea situated over its continental shelf;

(8)   That it should be admitted that the breadth of the territorial sea depends on different factors which vary from case to case, and it should be agreed that each coastal State is entitled to fix the breadth of its own territorial sea in accordance with its needs;

(9)   That the breadth of the territorial sea, in so far as not laid down in special conventions, would be fixed by a diplomatic conference convened for this purpose.[29]

In view of the above, the Commission did not include any text in the Article on 'Breadth of the territorial sea', and invited the States to indicate their attitude to this question and suggest as to how it could be resolved.

The position in 1955 also remained inconclusive. Accordingly, the Article on the 'Breadth of the territorial sea' only recognised that the international practice on the subject was not uniform, that international law did not justify the extension of the territorial sea beyond 12 miles, and that the Commission, without taking any decisions as to the breadth of the territorial sea, considered that international law did not require States to recognise a breadth beyond 3 miles.[30]

In 1956, the International Law Commission completed its work on the law of the sea and prepared 73 Articles, which included Article 3 on the 'Breadth of the territorial sea'. This Article read as follows:

Breadth of the territorial sea

Article 3

1.   The Commission recognizes that international practice is not uniform as regards the delimitation of the territorial sea.

2.   The Commission considers that international law does not permit an extension of the territorial sea beyond twelve miles.

15

3. The Commission, without taking any decision as to the breadth of the territorial sea up to that limit, notes, on the one hand, that many States have fixed a breadth greater than three miles and, on the other hand, that many States do not recognize such a breadth when that of their own territorial sea is less.

4. The Commission considers that the breadth of the territorial sea should be fixed by an international conference.[31]

This text was similar to the one adopted by the Commission in 1955, with some minor amendments. Para. 4 was new. In the commentary to the Article, the Commission referred to five sets of opinion, among the States and in the Commission, relating to the subject, namely, (i) that 'it was for each coastal State, in the exercise of its sovereign powers, to fix the breadth of its territorial sea', (ii) that 'international practice was not uniform . . . but would not authorise an extension of the territorial sea beyond twelve miles', (iii) that every coastal State may establish a territorial sea between 3 and 12 nautical miles, and the actual limit claimed should either be based on long usage or should recognise 'that interest of the other States in maintaining the freedom of the high seas and the breadth generally applied in the region', (iv) that a State may fix a limit between 3 and 12 miles 'in accordance with its economic and strategic needs . . . subject to the recognition by States maintaining a narrower belt', and (v) that a greater limit than 3 miles, but not exceeding 12 miles, 'should be recognised if based on customary law', but the higher limit could not be invoked against an objecting State or a State which had not adopted an equal or greater breadth.[32]

None of these proposals secured a majority in the Commission, which accepted, by a majority vote, the text of Article 3 cited above.

The Commission concluded as follows:

As regards the right to fix the limit between three and twelve miles, the Commission was obliged to note that international practice was far from uniform. Since several States have established a breadth of between three and twelve miles, while others are not prepared to recognize such extensions, the Commission was unable to take a decision on the subject, and expressed the opinion that the question should be decided by an international conference of plenipotentiaries.[33]

(2) As to *baselines*, from which the breadth of the territorial sea is to be measured, after an extensive examination the Commission adopted in 1956 Articles on the normal baseline, the straight baseline, the bay closing line, islands, and the related matters. Article 4 defined the normal baseline as the 'low-water line' along the coast, as marked on large-scale charts officially recognised by the coastal State.

Article 5 dealt with the straight baselines, where the Commission was influenced by the Judgment of the International Court of Justice in the Anglo-

16

Norwegian Fisheries Case, 1951,[34] which had upheld the validity of the Norwegian straight baselines along the islands off the Norwegian coast (*Skjaergaard* – rock rampart), and by the Report of the Committee of Experts consulted by it in April 1953.[35] A straight baseline was described in Article 5 in terms of the circumstances necessitating a special regime. The essential circumstances and conditions were that 'the coast is deeply indented or cut into', or that 'there are islands in its immediate vicinity'. However, 'the drawing of such baselines must not depart to any appreciable extent from the general direction of the coast, and the sea areas lying within the lines must be sufficiently closely linked to the land domain to be subject to the regime of internal waters'. Account may be taken, where necessary, of 'economic interests peculiar to a region, the reality and importance of which are clearly evidenced by a long usage'. Baselines shall not be drawn to or from 'drying rocks and drying shoals'. If a straight baseline enclosed as internal waters areas which formerly were part of the territorial sea or the high seas, the right of innocent pasage will continue to apply.

In 1954, the Commission provided that the maximum length of a straight baseline shall be 10 miles and the maximum distance of such a line from the coastline shall be 5 miles. These provisions were dropped by the Commission in 1955, as some Governments had regarded these limits as arbitrary and not in conformity with the ICJ Judgment in the Anglo-Norwegian Fisheries case, 1951. These limits were not included in the 1956 text by the Commission.

Article 7 of the 1956 text prepared by the Commission dealt with bays. A bay was distinguished from an indentation or a mere curvature of the coast if it enclosed an area which is 'as large as, or larger than, that of the semi-circle drawn on the mouth of that identation'. Thus the enclosed area should extend to a distance which is at least half of the bay closing line. Paragraph 2 of Article 7 provided that the line drawn across the mouth of the bay shall not exceed 15 miles measured from the low-water line. In 1955, the Commission had adopted a 25-mile bay closing line, which was reduced to 15 miles in 1956.

Articles 8 and 9 dealt with the harbour works in ports and roadsteads, making the former as part of the coast and the latter as included in the territorial sea.

Article 10 defined an island as 'an area of land, surrounded by water, which in normal circumstances is permanently above high-water mark', and provided that 'Every island has its own territorial sea'. Article 11 allowed the use of drying rocks and drying shoals, which are wholly or partly within the territorial sea, for measuring the extension of the territorial sea.

Finally, Article 13 referring to the baselines at the mouth of a river, provided as follows:

1. If a river flows directly into the sea, the territorial sea shall be measured from a line drawn *inter fauces terrarum* across the mouth of the river.

2.   If the river flows into an estuary the coasts of which belong to a single State, article 7 shall apply.[36]

(3)   As to the *outer limits of the contiguous zone*, Article 66 as adopted by the International Law Commission in 1956 read as follows:

2.   The contiguous zone may not extend beyond twelve miles from the baselines from which the breadth of the territorial sea is measured.

It was clarified in the commentary to this Article that the Commission was not willing 'to recognize any exclusive right of the coastal State to engage in fishing in the contiguous zone'.[37]

As to the relations between the 12-mile contiguous zone and the breadth of the territorial sea, the Special Rapporteur had clarified it in his Report of 27 January 1956 as follows:

A State which claims a territorial sea twelve miles broad has no right, in the Commission's view, to claim any further contiguous zone, as it can exercise within that territorial sea all the rights which the Commission intended to concede to States in contiguous zones.[38]

Endorsing this, the Commission's commentary to Article 66 stated that 'States which have claimed extensive territorial waters have in fact less need for a contiguous zone than those which have been more modest in their delimitation.[39]

(4)   As to *fisheries*, in Article 54, adopted by the Commission in 1956, it did recognise that 'A coastal State has a special interest in the maintenance of the productivity of the living resources in any area of the high seas adjacent to its territorial sea'. Even if its nationals did not carry on fishing there, a coastal State had an equal right to participate in any system of research and regulation therein. It could also adopt unilateral measures of conservation in case of urgent need, but such measures must be based on appropriate scientific findings and must be non-discriminatory. Any dispute relating thereto would be subject to a binding decision of an arbitral commission.[40]

These Articles were based on the recommendations of an international technical conference held in 1955 at the headquarters of the United Nations Food and Agriculture Organization in Rome, which were accepted by the Commission in 1955. The commentary to the 1956 Articles clarified that 'the Commission did not wish to imply that the "special" interests of the coastal State would take precedence *per se* over the interests of the other States concerned'.[41]

Thus the recognition of the special fishery interests of a coastal State in the area adjacent to its territorial sea were non-exclusive, non-jurisdictional, and only regulatory, subject to the dispute settlement procedure.

Neither the breadth of the territorial sea nor the outer limits of such area of special fishery interests of a coastal State were specified by the International Law Commission in 1956, although in 1953 the figure of 100 miles was mentioned in a restricted context.[42]

(5)   As to the *outer limits of the continental shelf*, the International Law

Commission switched its position between fixing these limits in relation to (i) the exploitability of the natural resources of the shelf, and (ii) the edge of the geological continental shelf, that is, where the gradient changes substantially in the declivity of the shelf towards the deep ocean floor. This edge was considered to be at an average depth of 100 fathoms, or alternatively approximately 200 metre depth of water.[43] Later the Commission combined the two provisions and adopted a depth-cum-exploitability criteria in 1956.

The first definition of the outer limits of the continental shelf adopted in 1951, which mentions the exploitability criterion, reads as follows:

> As here used, the term 'continental shelf' refers to the sea-bed and subsoil of the submarine areas contiguous to the coast, but outside the area of territorial waters, where the depth of the superjacent waters admits of the exploitation of the natural resources of the sea-bed and subsoil.[44]

In its commentary to this Article, the Commission indicated that it had not adopted the 200-metre depth criterion because 'such a limit would have the disadvantage of instability. Technical developments in the near future might make it possible to exploit resources of the sea-bed at a depth of over 200 metres. Moreover, the continental shelf might well include submarine areas lying at a depth of over 200 metres but capable of being exploited by means of installations erected in neighbouring areas where the depth does not exceed this limit'. The Commission also said that 'It follows that areas in which exploitation is not technically possible by reason of the depth of the waters are excluded from the continental shelf here referred to'.[45]

In 1953, in order to promote certainty in definition, the Commission adopted the depth criterion in the definition of the continental shelf, which reads as follows:

> As used in these articles, the term 'continental shelf' refers to the sea-bed and subsoil of the submarine areas contiguous to the coast, but outside the area of the territorial sea, to a depth of two hundred metres.[46]

In its commentary, the Commission considered that the 200-metre depth limit for the continental shelf would at present be sufficient for all practical purposes and probably for a long time to come. A fixed limit would also have an advantage concerning the delimitation of the continental shelf between States with opposite or adjacent coasts.[47]

In 1956, following the recommendations adopted by the Latin American States in paragraph 1 of the 'Resolution of Ciudad Trujillo, 1956'[48] the Commission adopted the following compromise definition of the continental shelf in Article 67:

> For the purposes of these articles the term 'continental shelf' is used as referrng to the sea-bed and subsoil of the submarine areas adjacent to the coast but outside the area of the territorial sea, to a depth of 200 metres (approximately 100 fathoms) or beyond that limit, to where the depth of

the superjacent waters admits of the exploitation of the natural resources of the said areas.[49]

In its commentary to the Article, the Commission recalled the history of its consideration of the question in 1951 and 1953, and justified the adoption of the depth-cum-exploitability criteria on the ground that if the exploitation of the natural resources of the seabed beyond 200 metres of depth became a practical possibility, 'the right to exploit should not be made subject to prior alteration of the limit'. The adoption of the geographical text, rather than geology, for the legal definition of the continental shelf was also justified on the ground that otherwise a distinction may be made between an 'inner shelf' and an 'outer shelf'. 'Thus, if, as is the case in the Persian Gulf, the submarine areas never reach the depth of 200 metres, that fact is irrelevant for the purposes of the present article', the Commission said in the commentary. Nor did the Commission agree to substitute the term 'submarine areas' in place of the 'continental shelf' because the latter term was in current use. The Commission also clarified that the term 'continental shelf' 'also covers the submarine areas contiguous to islands'.[50]

Summing up, the International Law Commission was unable to settle the breadth of the territorial sea, and left it to be determined by an international conference. It made elaborate provisions concerning the baselines. It specified a 12-mile limit for the contiguous zone. It did not prescribe any outer limits of the area adjoining the territorial sea, in which a coastal State may have special fishery interests. It adopted the depth-cum-exploitability criteria for the outer limits of the continental shelf.

C. The 1958 Conference and the Geneva Conventions

The First United Nations Conference on the Law of the Sea, which was convened by the United Nations General Assembly by Resolution 1105 (XI) adopted on February 21, 1957, met in Geneva from February 24 to April 27, 1958. It was attended by 86 States.

The State practice was changing concerning the breadth of the territorial sea. By 1958, '21 nations claimed a 3-mile territorial sea, 17 claimed 4 to 6 miles, 13 claimed 7 to 12 miles, and 9 nations claimed the sea above the continental shelf for varying distances'.[51]

Despite intensive efforts, the 1958 Conference could not resolve the questions of the *breadth of the territorial sea and the limits of a fishery zone*. These subjects were first considered in the First Committee of the Conference, later in its plenary session. In the First Committee, some 13 proposals were made, some of which were withdrawn in favour of other proposals or compromises, and later reintroduced. The two questions got intermingled, and the thrust of the delegations appeared to favour the coastal State jurisdiction up to 12 nautical miles, whether as outer limits of the territorial sea, or as part of a dual regime, namely, partly as territorial sea and the balance as a fishery zone. Initially, the proposals concerning the fishery zone were linked to the Article on the contiguous zone. Later the two aspects were considered as part of a single proposal. In the First Committee, initially the proposals by the United States, Canada and Greece supported a 3-mile territorial sea. Both USA and Canada also proposed the coastal State fishing rights in the 12-mile contiguous zone. With the United Kingdom, Sweden, Italy and Ceylon (Sri Lanka) proposing a 6-mile territorial sea, the United States and Canada also revised their separate proposals for a 6-mile territorial sea and an additional 6-mile fishery zone, the US proposal protecting the traditional fishing rights in the 6-mile fishing zone. India and Mexico, in a joint proposal, supported a territorial sea of up to 12 miles. Later they withdrew this proposal in favour of a joint proposal by Canada, India and Mexico, which proposed a 6-mile territorial sea, protected a higher limit for a territorial sea of up to 12 miles for a State which had proclaimed it prior to February 24, 1958, and proposed a 6-mile exclusive fishery zone. When this compromise appeared unacceptable, it was withdrawn, and Canada, India and Mexico reintroduced their own respective proposals. The USSR proposal allowed a State to determine the breadth of its territorial sea within the limits of 3 to 12 miles.

In the vote in the First Committee, which was held on April 9, 1958, all proposals concerning the breadth of the territorial sea were defeated. Only the second paragraph of the Canadian proposal was adopted by 37 votes in favour, 35 against, and 9 abstentions. This paragraph read as follows:

> A State has a fishing zone contiguous to its territorial sea, extending to a limit twelve nautical miles from the baseline from which the breadth of its territorial sea is measured, in which it has the same rights in respect of fish-in and the exploitation of the living resources of the sea as it has in its territorial sea.[52]

In the plenary, this Canadian proposal was defeated in the vote held on April 25, 1958. The vote was 35 in favour, 30 against, and 20 abstentions. It did not receive the requisite two-thirds majority for adoption. Earlier, three other proposals had been introduced in the plenary: *one* by the United States repeating its proposal in the First Committee, namely, a 6-mile territorial sea and an additional 6-mile fishing zone, subject to traditional fishing rights exercised during the five years preceding the date of signature of the convention in the area having a continuous baseline;[53] *another* by 8 States from Asia, Africa and Latin America proposing a 12-mile territorial sea, and if a lesser territorial sea was claimed, an exclusive fishery zone for the balance of the 12 miles;[54] and a *third* by the USSR repeating its proposal in the First Committee.[55] No proposal was made proposing a 3-mile limit for the territorial sea.

In the vote held on April 25, 1958, in the plenary, all these three proposals were also defeated. The US proposal was not adopted, although it received the best vote, namely, 45 in favour, 33 against, and 7 abstentions. The 8-Power proposal received 39 votes in favour, 38 against, and 8 abstentions. The USSR proposal received 21 votes in favour, 47 against, and 17 abstentions.[56]

Thus the 1958 Conference did not succeed in settling the questions of the breadth of the territorial sea or the fishery limits.[57] It adopted a resolution on April 27, 1958, requesting the United Nations General Assembly to convene another conference of plenipotentiaries 'for further consideration of the questions left unsettled by the present Conference'.[58]

The 1958 Conference adopted detailed provisions on *baselines*, as recommended by the International Law Commission. It also adopted the provision on the *contiguous zone* with a 12-mile outer limit.

Having failed to resolve the question of the limits of the fishery zone, no limits were prescribed for the limits to a zone of *coastal fishery interests* adjacent to its territorial sea.

As to the outer limits of the *continental shelf*, the Conference accepted the recommendations of the International Law Commission concerning the depth-cum-exploitability criteria. It also adopted the proposal by the Philippines to include a separate paragraph in the definition to the effect that the term 'continental shelf' will apply also 'to similar submarine areas adjacent to and surrounding the coasts of islands'. As mentioned above, this application to islands had already been clarified by the International Law Commission in its commentary to Article 67 in 1956.

Several other amendments were proposed concerning the outer limits of the continental shelf in the Fourth Committee, where the matter was first considered. These swung from the deletion of the exploitability test (France and Lebanon) to the deletion of the 200-metre depth test (Republic of Korea) in the draft Article on the definition of 'continental shelf' proposed by the International Law Commission, and included the substitution of 550 metres depth (India), or shelf edge or 550 metres depth (Canada), or a limit by distance (Yugoslavia), or shelf and slope (Panama). None of these amendments was adopted.

Thus the Article as proposed by the International Law Commission, and as amended by the Philippines proposal, was reported to the plenary of the Conference, with minor drafting changes. In the plenary, Yugoslavia again proposed that the outer limits of the continental shelf should not exceed 100 miles measured from the outer limits of the territorial sea. The extension of this distance to 200 miles was orally proposed by the Netherlands. The Yugoslav proposal was defeated. The Article on the limits of the continental shelf, as reported by the Fourth Committee, was then adopted by vote held on April 22, 1958, with 51 votes in favour, 5 against, and 10 abstentions, after a separate favourable vote was taken on the portion thereof dealing with the exploitability test.[59]

As to the breadth of the *territorial sea*, no provision was made in the Geneva Convention on the Territorial Sea and the Contiguous Zone, 1958. Article 6 of this Convention provided as follows:

> The outer limit of the territorial sea is the line every point of which is at a distance from the nearest point of the baseline equal to the breadth of the territorial sea.

This was a provision intended to indicate the method of constructing the outer limits of the territorial sea, such as by the application of the envelope line.

This Convention did however provide for the establishment of a *contiguous zone* beyond the territorial sea in which the coastal State may exercise jurisdiction in matters relating to customs, fiscal, immigation or sanitary regulations. Article 24 of this Convention provided that 'the contiguous zone may not extend beyond twelve miles from the baseline from which the width of the territorial sea is measured'. Accordingly, the territorial sea and the contiguous zone of a coastal State taken together could not extend beyond 12 nautical miles measured from the applicable baseline.

The 1958 Convention on the Territorial Sea and the Contiguous Zone also made detailed provisions concerning the *baselines* from which the breadth of the territorial sea will be measured.[60] Broadly the recommendations of the International Law Commission, summarised above, were accepted. The Article on normal baselines (Article 3) was basically the same as proposed by the Commission, with minor drafting changes. The Article on straight baselines (Article 4) was slightly modified. Straight baselines could not be drawn to and from low-tide elevations, unless lighthouses or similar installations which were permanently above sea level had been built on them. The economic interests peculiar to a region were given a subsidiary role. These could be taken into account in determining particular baselines, if the method of straight baselines was first applicable to the area under Article 4.

The Article on bays (Article 7) was also simplified in drafting. The bay closing line was not to exceed 24 miles. The International Law Commission had in its 1956 draft recommended 15 miles. The provisions on harbour works (Article 8), roadsteads (Article 9), and islands (Article 10) were basically the same as proposed by the Commission.

The terms 'drying rocks and drying shoals' were changed to 'low-tide elevation' in Article 11, which could be used by a coastal State for measuring the breadth of its territorial sea, if it was situated wholly or partly within its territorial sea. But if it was situated wholly outside the territorial sea, 'it has no territorial sea of its own'.

Finally, Article 13 provided that if a river flows directly into the sea, the baseline shall be a straight line across its mouth between the points on the low-tide line of its banks. However, the reference to the application of the bay regime to a river flowing into an estuary, as recommended by the Commission, was deleted.[61]

As to *fisheries*, Article 6(1) of the Geneva Convention on Fishing and Conservation of the Living Resources of the High Seas, 1958, recognised the special fishing interests of the coastal State as follows:

A coastal State has a special interest in the maintenance of the productivity of the living resources in any area of the high seas adjacent to its territorial sea.

It could accordingly participate on an equal footing in any system of research and regulation for the conservation of these resources, 'even though its nationals do not carry on fishing there' (Article 6(2)).

The coastal State could also adopt unilateral measures of conservation in case of urgent need, but these should be based on appropriate scientific findings and should not 'discriminate in form or in fact against foreign fishermen' (Article 7(2)(c)).

Any disputes relating to these provisions shall, at the request of any party, be submitted to a special commission under Article 9 of the Convention, whose decision shall be binding on the States concerned.

It will thus be observed that no outer limits of the area adjacent to the territorial sea were prescribed in the Convention. Nor were the fishing rights of the coastal State exclusive therein.

However, the 1958 Conference also adopted a resolution on April 26, 1958, which recognised the preferential requirements of a State whose people are overwhelmingly dependent on coastal fisheries for their livelihood or economic development, or who engage in local fishing in small boats and are dependent on coastal fisheries for the animal protein of their diet. If a limitation on the total fish catch in an area of the high seas adjoining the territorial sea of a coastal State became necessary for the purpose of conservation of the resource, the Resolution provided that the preferential requirements of the coastal State shall be recognised in adopting the necessary measures, while having regard to the interests of the other States. No limits of this area were specified.[62]

As to the *outer limits of the continental shelf*, Article 1 of the Geneva Convention on the Continental Shelf, 1958, provided as follows:

For the purposes of these articles, the term 'continental shelf' is used as referring (a) to the seabed and subsoil of the submarine areas adjacent to the coast but outside the area of the territorial sea, to a depth of 200 metres or, beyond that limit, to where the depth of the superjacent waters admits of the exploitation of the natural resources of the said areas; (b) to the seabed and subsoil of similar submarine areas adjacent to the coasts of islands.

24

The questions of the breadth of the territorial sea and the fishery limits, which could not be resolved at the 1958 Conference, were considered at the Second Conference which met in Geneva from March 17 to April 26, 1960, pursuant to UN General Assembly Resolution 1307 (XIII) adopted on December 10, 1958. The 1960 Conference was attended by 88 States.

The updated paper prepared by the Secretariat concerning State practice showed that by February 1960, *as to the breadth of the territorial sea*, 26 States claimed between 3 and 5 miles territorial sea, the 3-milers being 22 in number, and 25 States claimed between 6 and 12 miles territorial sea, the 6-milers being 10 and the 12-milers 13 in number. Two States claimed 50 km and 200 miles territorial sea, respectively. Five States claimed to establish their territorial sea 'in accordance with international law'. *As to fishery limits*, 12 States claimed from 3 to 5 miles, 15 States from 6 to 12 miles, and 9 States beyond 12 miles.[63]

At the 1960 Conference, the division was between the 6-miler and the 12-miler claimants of the territorial sea. No proposal was made at the Conference limiting the territorial sea to 3 miles. As to the fishery zone, the controversy was about the extent of the coastal State's rights therein, the protection or the phasing-out of the traditional rights, and the relations between the fishery zone and the territorial sea.

Procedurally, the questions were discussed first in the Committee of the Whole and later in the plenary session of the Conference. In the Committee, a number of proposals were made, which included the proposals concerning the entitlement of a coastal State to establish the breadth of its territorial sea up to 12 miles, and if its territorial sea was less than 12 miles to establish an exclusive fishing zone for the balance distance up to 12 miles (USSR, Mexico, 16-Power proposal by Asian, African and Latin American States, 18-Power proposal), preferential fishing rights adjacent to the exclusive fishing zone (Argentina, Iceland), a 6-mile territorial sea with another 6-mile exclusive fishing zone (Canada), and a 6-mile territorial sea, with another 6-mile fishing zone subject to traditional fishing rights of other States whose vessels have fished in that zone for 5 years preceding January 1, 1958 (USA).[64]

The 12-mile territorial sea – exclusive fishing zone proposals were amalgamated into a single 18-Power proposal, which was defeated in the Committee on April 13, 1960, with 36 votes in favour of the proposal, 39 against and 13 abstentions.[65]

The separate proposals of Canada and the United States were combined into a single joint proposal which provided for a 6-mile territorial sea and a 6-mile fishing zone with protection of traditional fishing rights for ten years with effect from October 31, 1960. This proposal was adopted by the Committee by 43 votes in favour, 33 against and 12 abstentions.[66]

In addition, the Icelandic proposal, which provided for the preferential rights of a coastal State in the areas adjacent to the coastal fisheries zone when the total fish catch is to be limited therein and the coastal State is dependent for its livelihood or economic development on such coastal fisheries, was also adopted by the Committee by 31 votes in favour, 11 against and 46 abstentions.[67]

Thus the proposals to be considered by the plenary session of the 1960 Conference were the joint proposal of Canada and USA and the proposal of Iceland. Intensive diplomatic activity followed. It appeared that the 6-mile territorial sea plus 6-mile fishery zone, with a provision on the phasing out of the traditional fishing rights in ten years, and with an appropriate recognition of the preferential rights of a coastal State in the fishery resources of the area adjacent to its exclusive fishery zone, would receive the two-thirds majority of the members present and voting necessary for the adoption of a proposal in the plenary, and activity was concentrated in that direction.

Ten Asian, African and Latin American States supporting a territorial sea up to 12 miles proposed a draft resolution which would request the UN General Assembly to convene, at an appropriate date, another United Nations Conference to examine the question of the breadth of the territorial sea, request the participating States which had declared their independence prior to 24 October 1945 not to extend the present breadth of their territorial sea, and without prejudice to the question of the breadth of the territorial sea and pending the consideration of the question by the UN General Assembly, allow any coastal State to establish a 12-mile exclusive fishery zone.[68]

On the preferential fishery rights, draft resolutions were proposed by Peru and Cuba. On the lines of the 1958 Conference Resolution, Brazil, Cuba and Uruguay proposed an amendment to the joint Canada – US proposal protecting the preferential fishing rights of a coastal State 'in any area of the high seas adjacent to its exclusive fishing zone' if because of its economic development or the feeding of its population, the coastal State was dependent on the living resources of this area, and the total fish catch was being limited in the interests of conservation. The disputes relating to such claim, and the extent and the duration for preferential fishing rights, would be determined by the special commission provided for in the 1958 Convention on Fishing and Conservation of the Living Resources of the High Seas.[69] Iceland proposed an amendment to the Canada – US joint proposal to the effect that the protection of the traditional fishery rights will not apply 'to the situation where a people is overwhelmingly dependent upon its coastal fisheries for its livelihood or economic development'.[70]

In the meantime, the joint Canada – US proposal was also amended by its sponsors to clarify *inter alia* that the fishing zone beyond the 6-mile territorial sea will be 'a fishing zone *in the high seas* contiguous to its territorial sea', that the term 'mile' means 'a sea mile (1,852 metres)', that disputes relating to traditional fishing rights shall be resolved with reference to Articles 9 and 11 of the 1958 Convention on Fishing and Conservation of the Living Resources of the High Seas, and that the existing or future bilateral or multilateral agreement regulating matters of fishing shall not be affected by the present proposal.[71]

The voting in the plenary was held on April 26, 1960. Of the two proposals adopted by the Committee of the Whole, the Icelandic proposal was rejected by the plenary. Iceland's amendment to the Canada – US proposal moved in the plenary was also rejected. The amendment on coastal preferential fishing rights moved by Brazil, Cuba, and Uruguay was adopted in the plenary by 58 votes in favour, 19 against and 10 abstentions. The United States and Canada voted in favour of this amendment. The joint Canada – US proposal, as amended by the proposal of Brazil, Cuba, and Uruguay, was then put to the vote, and was not adopted, the vote being 54 in favour, 28 against and 5 abstentions. Thus the proposal of a 6-mile territorial sea, another 6-mile fishing zone subject to traditional fishing rights for 10 years, and preferential fishing rights beyond the fishing zone, was also not adopted by the plenary. The vote was, as Arthur H. Dean, chairman of the United States Delegation described it correctly, 'one negative vote short of a two-thirds majority', that is, if one negative vote cast had been an abstention, the proposal would have been adopted. Thereafter, the draft resolution proposed by 10 Asian, African and Latin American States allowing the interim establishment of a 12-mile exclusive fishery zone, referred to above, was put to the vote and was lost, with a vote of 32 in favour, 38 against and 18 abstentions. A motion by the United States for reconsideration of the joint Canada – US proposal was also defeated, with 50 votes in favour, 29 against and 8 abstentions.[72]

Thus the 1960 Conference did not succeed in settling the questions of the breadth of the territorial sea and the fishery limits.[73]

In view of the above, the only outer limits of the maritime zones specified in the 1958 Conventions related to the 12-mile contiguous zone and the depth-cum-exploitability criteria for the outer limits of the continental shelf.

D. The Third United Nations Conference on the Law of the Sea (UNCLOS): 1973 – 1982

The failure of the 1960 Conference on the Law of the Sea in settling the questions of the breadth of the territorial sea and the fishery limits led to a further upsurge in State practice towards a 12-mile territorial sea and a larger exclusive fishery zone. It was calculated that by March 1, 1972, out of 103 States covered in the survey, 49 had adopted a 12-mile territorial sea, 6 claimed a territorial sea of between 18 and 130 miles, and 10 claimed a 200-mile territorial sea. As to the fishery zone, out of 105 States covered in the survey, 66 claimed a limit of 12 miles, 7 claimed between 18 and 130 miles, and 11 claimed 200 miles, apart from 2 other specified zones claimed by the Maldives and the Philippines.[74]

Both the United States and the USSR were also agreed in the mid-1960s, it appeared, to a package proposal of a 12-mile territorial sea, transit passage through the international straits, and coastal fishery rights adjacent to the 12-mile territorial sea.

In the meantime, between 1958 and 1970, the exploitability criterion in the definition of the outer limits of the continental shelf had also raised the apprehension that with the development of the requisite technology concerning the recovery of oil and gas from the continental shelf and the polymetallic nodules from the deep ocean floor, it could be worked to divide up the seas and the deep ocans between the States with opposite or adjacent coasts.[75]

Shigeru Oda, writing in 1962, and referring to the exploitability criterion in the definition of the outer limits of the continental shelf, stated that:

> . . . the concept of exploitability must be interpreted each time in terms of the most advanced standards of technology and economy in the world. . . .
> It is inferred that all the submarine areas of the world have been theoretically divided among the coastal States by this Geneva Convention.[75a]

We have already referred to the Maltese initiative of 1967 in the United Nations General Assembly seeking, *inter alia*, the establishment of an international regime and machinery for the exploitation of the resources of the international seabed area, which were described as the common heritage of mankind. The regime required the definition of the international seabed area, and the definition of the limits of national jurisdiction, including the outer limits of the continental shelf. That is how the questions of the outer limits of the territorial sea and of the fishery zone and the precise limits of the continental shelf became relevant and closely interrelated, and the United Nations General Assembly decided in December 1970 to convene the Third United Nations Conference on the Law of the Sea (UNCLOS) in 1973 to review the entire law of the sea.[76]

The UNCLOS met between December 1973 and December 1982 and held 11 sessions. After prolonged negotiations, it succeeded in resolving the questions of the maritime zones and their outer limits, and approved a 12-mile territorial sea, a 24-mile contiguous zone, and a 200-mile exclusive economic zone, and settled the precise outer limits of the continental shelf. The related problems were also dealt with. These decisions were embodied in the Draft Convention on the Law of the Sea, which was adopted by UNCLOS by a vote of 130 in favour, 4 against, and 17 abstentions on April 30, 1982. The Convention so adopted was named as the United Nations Convention on the Law of the Sea in September 1982. It was opened for signature at Montego Bay on December 10, 1982 and has so far been signed by 131 States and ratified by 9 States.

The outcome of the negotiations in UNCLOS will be referred to in the next section which deals with the 1982 Convention and the maritime zones.

28

E. The 1982 Convention and the outer limits of maritime zones

The outer limits of maritime zones, as settled in the United Nations Convention on the Law of the Sea, 1982, and the related matters may be summarised as follows:

(1) Territorial sea

As to the territorial sea, the limits were fixed as extending up to 12 nautical miles. Articles 3 and 4 of the 1982 Convention read as follows:

Article 3

Breadth of the territorial sea

Every State has the right to establish the breadth of its territorial sea up to a limit not exceeding 12 nautical miles, measured from baselines determined in accordance with this Convention.

Article 4

Outer limit of the territorial sea

The outer limit of the territorial sea is the line every point of which is at a distance from the nearest point of the baseline equal to the breadth of the territorial sea.

The controversy about the breadth of the territorial sea and the fishery limits, which could not be resolved by the International Law Commission and the 1958 and the 1960 Conferences on the Law of the Sea, was resolved in UNCLOS in a package compromise of a 12-mile territorial sea and a 200-mile exclusive economic zone. The United States and other maritime States linked up the question of the 12-mile territorial sea with the right of transit passage through international straits. The developing States of Asia, Africa and Latin America were agreeable to a 12-mile territorial sea as part of a package with the 200-mile exclusive economic zone. Although the claims of a 3-mile territorial sea by the United States, and of a 200-mile territorial sea by some 11 States, organised in UNCLOS as 'territorialists', continued to be expressed throughout, the 12-mile territorial sea as part of the aforesaid package was a dominant trend since 1974. The Chairman of the Second Committee referred to it in his statement of August 28, 1974 in that Committee as follows:

> The idea of a territorial sea of 12 miles and an exclusive economic zone beyond the territorial sea up to a total maximum distance of 200 miles is, at least at this time, the keynote of the compromise solution favoured by the majority of the States participating in the Conference, as is apparent from the general debate in the plenary meetings and the discussions held in our Committee.[77]

The 12-mile territorial sea was included in all negotiating texts, namely, the Informal Single Negotiating Text, May 1975 (Article 2), the Informal Composite Negotiating Text (ICNT), July 1977 (Article 3), and its three revisions. The third revision of ICNT was formalised as the official document of the conference in August 1981, and became the Draft Convention on the Law of the Sea.[78]

None of the 31 amendments proposed to the Draft Convention by April 13, 1982 related to the breadth of the territorial sea. In the vote on the Draft Convention in the plenary on April 30, 1982, when 130 delegations voted in favour, almost all the 'territorialists' voted in favour of the Draft Convention, except Ecuador which did not take part in the vote.[79] The Convention was also signed by most of the 'territorialists' on December 10, 1982, except Ecuador and Peru.

Ecuador, Peru, Colombia and Chile, however, addressed a letter to the President of UNCLOS on April 28, 1982, which pointed out the universal recognition of the rights of sovereignty and jurisdiction of the coastal State within the 200-mile limit provided for in the Draft Convention was in accordance with the basic objectives stated in the Santiago Declaration of 1952.[80]

The representative of Chile in his statement of April 1, 1982 in the plenary, summed up the position as follows:

> The pivotal point of the new law of the sea was, in all probability, the concept of the exclusive economic zone extending up to 200 miles, to which his country was unalterably bound since it had been the first ever to declare the concept in July 1947. Its *sui generis* legal character, distinct from both the territorial sea and the high seas, had been specified in the draft Convention, which clearly recognised the sovereign rights of the coastal States over all economic activities within a distance of 200 miles, without prejudice to freedom of navigation and overflight.[81]

It may, therefore, be expected that with the signing of the 1982 Convention and its entry into force, the 12-mile territorial sea is the established outer limit of the territorial sea.

(2) Baselines

Since the starting point for measuring the breadth of the territorial sea and the other maritime zones extending by distance from the coastline is the baseline, the 1982 Convention contains detailed provisions in Articles 5 to 14 relating thereto. These provisions have in most respects been based on the corresponding provisions of the 1958 Convention on the Territorial Sea and the Contiguous Zone, with some modifications. These were reviewed by a small working group of experts from the delegations at the Third Session of UNCLOS held in Geneva in 1975.

Normal baselines and related provisions

The normal baseline is 'the low-water line along the coast as marked on large-scale charts officially recognised by the coastal State' (Article 5). In the case of islands situated on atolls or of islands having fringing reefs, the baseline is the seaward low-water line of the reef (Article 6).[82] In the case of a river flowing directly into the sea, 'the baseline shall be a straight line across the mouth of the river between points on the low-water line of its banks' (Article 9). If a low-tide elevation is situated wholly or partly within the territorial sea, 'the low-water line on that elevation may be used as the baseline for measuring the breadth of the territorial sea' (Article 13(1)). If a low-tide elevation is wholly situated outside the territorial sea, it has no territorial sea of its own (Article 13(2)).

It has also been clarified that the outermost permanent harbour works which form an integral part of the harbour system or a port are regarded as forming part of the coast for measuring the breadth of the territorial sea. However, off-shore installations and artificial islands shall not be considered as permanent harbour works.[83] Later the 1982 Convention further clarifies that although offshore installations and structures, and artificial islands, established by a coastal State within its territorial sea, exclusive economic zone or the continental shelf for the exploitation of their resources or for other purposes, will be within its exclusive jurisdiction to which it may extend its laws and regulations relating *inter alia* to customs, fiscal, health, safety and immigration matters, and the coastal State may establish safety zones not extending a distance of 500 metres around them, the offshore installations and structures and artificial islands 'do not possess the status of islands. They have no territorial sea of their own, and their presence does not affect the delimitation of the territorial sea, the exclusive economic zone or the continental shelf'.[84]

In connection with the ports, it has also been clarified that roadsteads which are normally used for the loading, unloading and anchoring of ships, and which would otherwise be situated wholly or partly outside the outer limit of the territorial sea, will be included in the territorial sea.[85] Thus they cannot be used to extend the outer limits of the territorial sea or other maritime zones.

Bays

Article 10 deals in detail with the internal bays, that is bays the coasts of which belong to a single State, and which are *not historic bays*. A bay has been distinguished from an indentation which is 'a mere curvature of the coast'. A bay would enclose waters whose area comes within or exceeds 'that of the semi-circle whose diameter is a line drawn across the mouth of that indentation'. If because of the presence of islands, an indentation has more than one mouth, the semi-circle shall be drawn on a line as long as the sum total of the lengths of the lines across the different mouths. Islands within an indentation shall be included as if they were part of the water area of indentation.

The area of the bay is measured from the low-water mark around the indentation and a line joining the low-water marks of its natural entrance points. The closing line of the bay should not exceed 24 nautical miles.

The Article is thus identical to Article 7 of the Geneva Convention on the Territorial Sea and the Contiguous Zone, 1958.

Straight baselines

Detailed provisions have been made in Article 7 of the 1982 Convention about straight baselines, based mainly on the corresponding provisions of the 1958 Convention on the Territorial Sea and the Contiguous Zone, which had been influenced mainly by the decision of the International Court of Justice in the *Anglo-Norwegian Fisheries Case*, 1951. Thus straight baselines may be drawn by a coastal State by joining appropriate points in localities where the coastline is deeply indented and cut into, or if there is a fringe of islands along the coast in its immediate vicinity, such as the coastal archipelago or the Norwegian 'Skjaergaard'.

New provisions have also been made to meet the concerns expressed by deltaic States, like Bangladesh, in some measure. For a deltaic State whose coastline is highly unstable, the appropriate points for drawing straight baselines may be selected along the furthest seaward extent of the low-water line and 'notwithstanding subsequent regression of the low-water line, the straight baselines shall remain effective until changed by the coastal State in accordance with this Convention'.[86] 'Straight baselines must not depart to any appreciable extent from the general direction of the coast, and the sea areas lying within the lines must be sufficiently closely linked to the land domain to be subject to the regime of internal waters'.[87] Straight baselines shall not be drawn to and from low-tide elevations, unless lighthouses or similar establishments are built thereon 'or except in instances where the drawing of such baselines to and from such elevations has received general international recognition'.[88] Where the method of straight baselines is applicable, account may be taken, in determining particular baselines, 'of the economic interests peculiar to the region concerned, the reality and importance of which are clearly evidenced by long usage'.[89] The straight baselines shall not cut off the territorial sea of another State from the high seas or an exclusive economic zone.[90]

The 1982 Convention specifically allows a coastal State to use a combination of methods for determining baselines to suit different conditions (Article 14).

Thus it may have normal baselines in one sector or region of its coast, and straight baselines in another, or a combination of the two.

The waters on the landward side of the baseline, normal, straight, bay-closing line or other, form part of the internal waters of the coastal State, and are subject to its sovereignty. The right of innocent passage of foreign vessels does not apply in these waters. Exceptions have however been made in respect of archipelagic waters mentioned below. However, if the drawing of straight baselines encloses as internal waters areas which had not previously been considered as such, a right of innocent passage shall exist in such waters.[91]

Archipelagic baselines

In respect of an archipelagic State, which means 'a State constituted wholly by one or more archipelagos and may include other islands',[92] and which reflected a major development of the law in UNCLOS, detailed provisions have been made regarding the drawing of archipelagic baselines enclosing the archipelagic waters, which have been given a specified legal regime. Within its archipelagic waters, the archipelagic State may, like any other coastal State, draw closing lines across the mouth of a river, the mouth of a bay or the outermost harbour works, for the delimitation of its internal waters.[93] The archipelagic State enjoys sovereignty over the archipelagic waters, their bed and the subsoil, and the resources contained therein, as well as over the air space above those waters.[94] However, existing agreements, traditional fishing rights and existing submarine cables have been protected, as well as the right of innocent passage for all ships through the archipelagic waters. The archipelagic State may designate sea lanes and air routes thereabove for regulating the passage of foreign ships and aircraft through or over its archipelagic waters and the adjacent territorial sea.[95]

The breadth of the territorial sea and other maritime zones of an archipelagic State shall be measured from the archipelagic baselines.[96]

As to archipelagic baselines, which are a special category of straight baselines and were not dealt with in the 1958 Convention, an archipelagic State may draw 'straight archipelagic baselines joining the outermost islands and drying reefs of the archipelago provided that within such baselines are included the main islands and an area in which the ratio of the area of the water to the area of the land, including atolls, is between 1 to 1 and 9 to 1'.[97] The length of such baselines shall not exceed 100 nautical miles, although up to 3 per cent of the total number of such baselines may go up to 125 nautical miles.[98] The other provisions concerning the nature of such baselines, including the use of low-tide elevations, is similar, *mutatis mutandis*, to the nature of the straight baselines mentioned above (Articles 47(3-5)). In order to meet some concerns, such as those of Malaysia with the two parts of its State separated by the sea in which

Indonesia may have its archipelagic baselines, the following paragraph was included in the 1982 Convention:

> If a part of the archipelagic waters of an archipelagic State lies between two parts of an immediately adjacent neighbouring State, existing rights and all other legitimate interests which the latter State has traditionally exercised in such waters and all rights stipulated by agreement between those States shall continue and be respected.[99]

The archipelagic baselines shall be shown on charts of an appropriate scale, or the lists of geographical coordinates of points, specifying the geodetic datum, may be substituted. These shall be given due publicity, and copies thereof shall be deposited with the Secretary-General of the United Nations.[100]

The text of Articles 5 to 14 and 47 relating to baselines and the archipelagic baselines, respectively, are reproduced in Annex III to this study.

Importance of baselines

The baselines, whether normal or straight or archipelagic, or bay closing lines, have a direct bearing on the outer limits of maritime zones, when these are to be determined with reference to distance thereforem. Where other criteria for determining the outer limits have evolved, such as in relation to the continental shelf, baselines may not be relevant except to the extent that a distance is to be measured therefrom, such as the limit of 350 miles for the outer limits of the continental shelf in certain cases.

As to its impact on the maritime boundary between States with opposite or adjacent coasts, the direct reference to baselines is only in relation to the territorial sea boundary in Article 15 of the 1982 Convention, when a median or equidistance line is to be drawn as the boundary. Article 15 reads as follows:

> Where the coasts of two States are opposite or adjacent to each other, neither of the two States is entitled, failing agreement between them to the contrary, to extend its territorial sea beyond the median line every point of which is equidistant from the nearest points on the baselines from which the breadth of the territorial seas of each of the two States is measured. The above provision does not apply, however, where it is necessary by reason of historic title or other special circumstances to delimit the territorial seas of the two States in a way which is at variance therewith.

In practice, a median or equidistance line as the territorial sea boundary may be drawn with reference to specified basepoints on the coastline or the islands as controlling points, without any reference to baselines, or by adopting *ad hoc* baselines.

As to the delimitation of the exclusive economic zone and the continental shelf, no direct reference is made to the median or equidistance line in Articles

74 and 83 of the 1982 Convention. The use and relevance of proper baselines in such cases will therefore be an element of equity. In the maritime boundary agreements concluded between India and its neighbouring States (Sri Lanka, Maldives, Indonesia and Thailand) between 1974 and 1980, no reference was made to baselines, although the boundary line generally reflected a median or equidistance line.

In the *Case Concerning the Continental Shelf* between Tunisia and Libya (Judgment of February 24, 1982),[101] the International Court of Justice made no ruling 'as to the validity or opposability to Libya of the straight baselines' adopted by Tunisia in 1973 for measuring the outer limits of its territorial sea. Nor did it pass on the question of historic rights as justification for the Tunisian baselines. The Court also tested the equitableness of its proposed boundary lines in the first and the second sectors by the criterion of proportionality in the delimitation area, which was computed from the shorelines of the two States rather than from the straight baselines.[102]

(3) Contiguous zone

In a zone contiguous to the territorial sea, the coastal State may exercise control for preventing and punishing infringement of its laws and regulations relating to customs, fiscal, immigration or sanitary matters, as well as concerning the removal of archaeological and historical objects found at sea.

The *outer limits* of the contiguous zone 'may not exceed beyond 24 nautical miles from the baselines from which the breadth of the territorial sea is measured'.[103]

With the trends supporting the compromise of a 12-mile territorial sea and a 200-mile exclusive economic zone, the need for a contiguous zone beyond the territorial sea became controversal in 1974. India had taken the initiative in pressing the need for a contiguous zone, since the jurisdiction in fiscal, anti-smuggling and other matters will not otherwise be available to a coastal State in the exclusive economic zone. Originally, the Indian delegation proposed an 18-mile contiguous zone beyond the territorial sea (30 miles from the baselines).[104] The concept gained a general acceptance and was included in the Informal Single Negotiating Text with a 12-mile limit beyond the territorial sea (24 miles from the baselines),[105] as well as in later texts.

(4) Exclusive economic zone

The exclusive economic zone was among the major developments in the law of the sea emerging from UNCLOS. The concept reconciled the divergent claims and proposals relating to a 200-mile territorial sea, a 200-mile patrimonial sea, a 200-mile exclusive fishery zone, a 200-mile exclusive economic zone, a pollution control zone, and so forth. In the exclusive economic zone as ultimately accepted by UNCLOS and included in the 1982 Convention, the coastal State has sovereign rights over the exploitation of its living and non-living resources, such as fisheries, oil and gas, and over other economic activities, such as the production of energy from the water, currents and winds. It also has specified jurisdiction with respect to the establishment and use of artificial islands, installations and structures, marine scientific research, the protection and preservation of the marine environment, and some other matters.[106]

As to the *outer limits* of the exclusive economic zone, the 1982 Convention provides as follows:

> The exclusive economic zone shall not extend beyond 200 nautical miles from the baselines from which the breadth of the territorial sea is measured.[107]

Thus the baselines continue to be relevant not only for the outer limits of the territorial sea and the contiguous zone but also for the exclusive economic zone. The 1982 Convention does not prescribe the detailed manner for fixing these outer limits, except to say that these shall be shown on charts of a scale or scales adequate for ascertaining their position, or that where appropriate lists of geographical coordinates of points, specifying geodetic datum, may be substituted therefor. Due publicity shall be given to the charts or the coordinates, and a copy thereof shall be deposited by the coastal State with the Secretary-General of the United Nations.[108]

(5) Continental shelf

The question of the outer limits of the continental shelf involved intensive and prolonged negotiations at UNCLOS between 1974 and 1980. On the one side was the question of removing the flexibility from the depth-cum-exploitability criterion of the definition of continental shelf in the 1958 Convention on the Continental Shelf in relation to the precise definition of the international seabed area; on the other side was the need to make a distinction between the outer limits of the exclusive economic zone and the outer limits of the continental shelf. Upon the wider acceptance in UNCLOS of the 200-mile exclusive economic zone, it was maintained by the landlocked and geographically disadvantaged States, the Arab States, many African States, and initially by the USSR, France and Japan, that the outer limits of the continental shelf should also not exceed 200 nautical miles from the appropriate baseline. The broad margin States, including Ireland, the United Kingdom, Australia, Canada, Norway, the USA, Argentina, India, and some others, and often known as the

'Margineers', maintained that since the continental shelf was the natural prolongation of the land territory of a coastal State, its outer limits should extend up to the outer edge of the continental margin, and that this was also supported by existing international law.

At the Caracas Session of UNCLOS in 1974, a number of proposals were made concerning the outer limits of the continental shelf. These included a continental shelf extending (a) up to 200 nautical miles, (b) up to 500 metres or 200 nautical miles, (c) up to the outer edge of the continental margin, and (d) up to the outer edge of the continental margin or up to 200 nautical miles where the continental margin did not extend up to that distance. These proposals were summarised by the Chairman of the Second Committee, Andres Aguilar, in the form of *Main Trends*.[109]

The proposal which influenced the further developments in this regard was a working paper sponsored by Canada, Chile, Iceland, India, Indonesia, Mauritius, Mexico, New Zealand and Norway.[110] Article 19(2) of this proposal defined the outer limit of the continental shelf as follows:

2.   The continental shelf of a coastal State extends beyond its territorial sea to a distance of 200 miles from the applicable baselines and throughout the natural prolongation of its land territory where such natural prolongation extends beyond 200 miles.

The contents of this proposal, with reversed redrafting of its text, were embodied in Article 62 of the Informal Single Negotiating Text in May 1975, which read as follows:

Article 62

The continental shelf of a coastal State comprises the sea-bed and subsoil of the submarine areas that extend beyond its territorial sea throughout the natural prolongation of its land territory to the outer edge of the continental margin, or to a distance of 200 nautical miles from the baselines from which the breadth of the territorial sea is measured where the outer edge of the continental margin does not extend up to that distance.[111]

Although this text continued to be embodied in the subsequent negotiating texts, and is included in Article 76 of the 1982 Convention, the determination of the precise outer limits of the continental margin did consume a lot of time and attention in Negotiating Group 6 between 1978 and 1980, before a solution could be worked out.[112] The broad conclusions reached therein and accepted by the plenary were embodied in Article 76 and the related provisions of the United Nations Convention on the Law of the Sea, 1982. These provisions may now be analysed, and their evolution briefly explained, as follows:

(i)   Since every coastal State is entitled to establish an exclusive economic zone extending up to 200 nautical miles measured from the appropriate baseline, in which it has sovereign rights over the living and *non-living* resources of the zone, it shall also be entitled to a 200-mile continental shelf. Thus every State is entitled to a 200-mile continental shelf except those States whose continental margin extends beyond 200 nautical miles from the appropriate baselines. This is how one segment of the controversy was resolved as early as 1975.

Article 76, paragraph 1, of the 1982 Convention defines the continental shelf as follows:

> The continental shelf of a coastal State comprises the sea-bed and subsoil of the submarine areas that extend beyond its territorial sea throughout the natural prolongation of its land territory to the outer edge of the continental margin, or to a distance of 200 nautical miles from the baselines from which the breadth of the territorial sea is measured where the outer edge of the continental margin does not extend up to that distance.

(ii)   As to the precise outer limits of the continental shelf of a coastal State where it extends beyond 200 nautical miles measured from the appropriate baseline, a solution was found first by developing a combination of what were popularly known as *the Hedberg formula*[113] and *the Irish formula*,[114] and later by modifying the same. Hedberg, whose views had been adopted by the US National Petroleum Council in 1974, had suggested that the outer limits of the continental shelf should be fixed by a coastal State within an area located between the *base* of the continental shelf, which was described as the most natural and identifiable limit of the continental shelf, and a fixed distance beyond, the width of which may be internationally agreed, say at UNCLOS. The precise limits should be fixed by a coastal State by drawing straight lines joining the points with geographical coordinates within this extended zone, rather than by following a bathymetric contour. The Hedberg formula was thus a depth-cum-distance formula. The Irish formula, also known as the Gardiner formula, which was first circulated at UNCLOS in March 1976, accepted the Hedberg formula which was defined to extend up to 60 nautical miles beyond the *foot* of the continental slope, and added thereto the alternative concept of the outer limits of the continental shelf extending up to points at each of which the thickness of the sedimentary rocks underlying the seabed was at least 1 per cent of the shortest distance from the foot of the continental slope. The coastal State could fix the outer limits of its continental shelf with reference to either formula or by combining the two formulas in different sectors. The outer limits shall be drawn by joining the geographical points by straight lines not extending beyond 60 nautical miles.

It will be observed that in either case the point of reference for the outer limits of the continental shelf became the foot of the slope rather than the baseline, which was the starting point for the outer limits of the territorial sea, the contiguous zone, and the exclusive economic zone, which were to be determined by the distance from the shore. Hedberg and Gardiner had also expressed differences on whether or not the continental rise should be treated as part of the continental margin. The rise was the basis of the sedimentary thickness alternative in the Irish formula, the rationale of which has been explained by Gardiner in his stand referred to earlier.[115] This was supported by States like India for whom the foot of the slope plus 60 nautical miles alone might fall short of 200 miles in the Bay of Bengal, which however had a unique basin with thickness of sedimentary rocks on the seabed varying from 18 km in the north to 8 km in the middle and tapering to 3 and later 1 km in the southern part of the Bay of Bengal. Hedberg however was of the view that the foot of the slope was the natural outer edge of the continental margin, and his own proposal of a zone, covering the rise beyond the foot of the slope, had been justified for simplifying the fixing of the outer limits as well as for political reasons for meeting the concerns of those who had a short continental shelf.[116].

Critics were also apprehensive as to whether the foot of the slope itself was a reliable criterion and could be easily identified without controversy. In April 1979 the USSR delegation illustrated the point with reference to the maps exhibited by them informally at UNCLOS. Earlier, at the request made at UNCLOS in June 1977, the Conference Secretariat prepared a map of the world with the assistance of experts from Lamont Doherty Geological Observatory of Columbia University (United States), the International Hydrographic Organisation and the Inter-Governmental Oceanographic Commission of UNESCO, indicating the limits of the 200-mile line, a line showing the 500-metre isobath, a line showing the outer edge of the margin and the foot of the slope, and lines illustrating the effects of the Irish formula. This map was distributed to the delegations at UNCLOS in April 1978, and corrections were made thereto in August 1978.[117]

In 1978, the delegations of France, Japan and the Federal Republic of Germany changed their positions and supported the Irish formula. The USSR was also agreeable to let the continental shelf extend up to 300 nautical miles from the applicable baselines.[118] Later in 1978, the delegations of the United Kingdom and the USSR developed a compromise, which was popularly known as the 'bisquits formula', since neither party wanted to be named as its sponsor and both agreed to ascribe it to the bisquits on the table instead. According to this formula, the outer limits of the continental shelf shall not extend beyond 100 nautical miles from the 2,500 metre isobath, if the depth-cum-distance criterion was relied on, and not beyond 350 nautical miles from the baselines from which the breadth of the territorial sea was measured, if the sedimentary thickness alternative was relied on.

After considerable discussion at the Eighth Session of UNCLOS held in Geneva in March/April 1979, the Chairman of the Second Committee, Andres Aguilar, proposed on April 26, 1979 the inclusion of the substance of the 'Irish formula' and the 'bisquits formula' in Article 76 of the ICNT. Despite some reservations, Aguilar's proposals received widespread support, and Article 76 was appropriately amended with the addition of new paragraphs 4 and 5, and included in ICNT/Rev. 1 in April 1979.[119] To the revised Article were added two footnotes, one concerning the ocean ridges, and the second concerning the suggestion of Sri Lanka. Discussions on these points were continued in 1979 and 1980.

During these further negotiations, the USSR insisted that the outer limits of the continental shelf of a coastal State should not include oceanic ridges by going around them at the 2,500 metre isobath, but later agreed that on submarine ridges the outer limits of the continental shelf shall not exceed 350 nautical miles, and that this limitation will not apply to 'submarine elevations which are the natural components of the continental margin, such as its plateaux, rises, caps, banks and spurs'.

Accordingly, the mid-oceanic ridges were excluded from the definition of the continental margin in paragraph 3 of Article 76. The application of the 350-mile limit to the submarine ridges was accepted along with the exclusion therefrom of submarine elevations, and a new paragraph 6 of Article 76 was drafted accordingly. These changes were included in ICNT/Rev. 2, prepared at UNCLOS in April 1980.[120].

The delegation of Sri Lanka had suggested in 1979 that an exception should be made to the application of the Irish formula in the southern part of the Bay of Bengal, where because of the unique geomorphological features of the seabed, the outer limits of the continental margin of a coastal State should extend up to points where the thickness of the sedimentary rocks was not less than 1 km. The exception would apply both to Sri Lanka and to India.

The Sri Lanka suggestion was accepted by the plenary session of UNCLOS on August 29, 1980, and it was decided that a Statement of Understanding to this effect would be appended to the Final Act of the Conference on the Law of the Sea.[121]

Article 76 of the 1982 Convention, as finally adopted, embodies the aforementioned outer limits of the continental shelf where these exceed 200 nautical miles from the appropriate baseline, namely, the alternative of the foot of the slope and 60 nautical miles beyond with a limit at the 2,500-metre isobath and 100 nautical miles beyond, the alternative of the sedimentary thickness formula with a limit of 350 nautical miles from the appropriate baselines, the exclusion of mid-oceanic ridges, and the applicability of the 350-mile limit to submarine ridges with the exclusion of the natural submarine elevations.[122] Article 76 also indicates the manner in which the outer limits shall be delineated by joining geographical points not more than 60 miles apart.[123]

The Statement of Understanding concerning the exception applicable to the southern part of the Bay of Bengal was included in the Final Act of UNCLOS which was signed by 150 States on December 10, 1982.[124] A reference to the Statement was also included in Article 3(1)(a) of Annex II to the 1982 Convention, dealing with the Commission on the Limits of the Continental Shelf.

The texts of Article 76 of the 1982 Convention as well as of the Statement of Understanding referred to above and Article 3 of Annex II to the 1982 Convention are reproduced in Annex III to this study.

(iii)   The establishment of a 21-member Commission on the Limits of the Continental Shelf has been provided for in the 1982 Convention. The 21 experts will be elected within 18 months from the entry into force of the Convention. The Commission shall receive information submitted to it by a coastal State concerning the limits of its continental shelf beyond 200 nautical miles, and shall make recommendations thereon. The limits of the continental shelf established by a coastal State on the basis of these recommendations shall be final and binding. The Commission may also provide scientific and technical advice to a coastal State during the preparation of the data at its request.[125]

(iv)   Another part of the compromise relating to the outer limits of the continental shelf concerned the payments to be made by a coastal State regarding the exploitation of the non-living resources of its continental shelf beyond 200 nautical miles from the appropriate baselines. The basic compromise on this point was also included in Chairman Aguilar's proposal of April 1979 and included in ICNT/Rev. 1.[126] The 1982 Convention provides that a coastal State shall make such payments or contributions in kind. After the first five years of production at site, the rate of payments or contributions will be 1 per cent of the value or volume of production at that site which will increase to 7 per cent in the twelfth year of production, and will remain constant thereafter. The developing States which are net importers of that mineral resource are exempted from making payments. These payments and contributions shall be made through the Internatonal Seabed Authority which shall distribute them among States on the basis of an equitable sharing formula, taking into account the interest and needs of developing States, particularly the least developed States and the landlocked among them.[127]

(v)   The 1982 Convention makes another distinction between the conducting of marine scientific research on the continental shelf within and beyond the 200 nautical miles from the appropriate baselines. The coastal State may within its discretion withhold its consent to the conducting of marine scientific research *within the 200-mile continental shelf* if such research project 'is of direct significance for the exploration and exploitation of natural resources, whether living or non-living'.[128] The coastal State may however not exercise this discretion in respect of research projects to be undertaken on the *continental shelf beyond 200 miles* 'outside those specific areas which coastal States may at any time publicly designate as areas in which exploitation or detailed exploratory operations focused on those areas are occurring or will occur within a reasonable period of time.'[129]

In connection with the provisions on the continental shelf, the 1982 Convention recognises 'the right of coastal States to exploit the subsoil by means of tunnelling, irrespective of the depth of water above the subsoil'.[130]

(6) Islands

Article 121 of the 1982 Convention, which expressly refers to the regime of islands and their maritime zones and makes a restrictive provision concerning certain types of rocks in paragraph 3, reads as follows:

Article 121
Régime of islands
1. An island is a naturally formed area of land, surrounded by water, which is above water at high tide.
2. Except as provided for in paragraph 3, the territorial sea, the contiguous zone, the exclusive zone and the continental shelf of an island are determined in accordance with the provisions of this Convention applicable to other land territory.
3. Rocks which cannot sustain human habitation or economic life of their own shall have no exclusive economic zone or continental shelf.

As regards the archipelagic States, as already mentioned above, the 1982 Convention expressly provides that the breadth of their territorial sea and other maritime zones shall be measured from the archipelagic baselines.[131]

Summing up

Thus in so far as the *outer limits* of the maritime zones are concerned, the review of their evolution since 1945 shows that by 1982 a 12-mile territorial sea, a 24-mile contiguous zone, a 200-mile exclusive economic zone, and the continental shelf with precise outer limits have emerged as part of the international law of the sea. These limits apply to the mainland territory of the coastal States as well as to their islands, and to archipelagic States. These limits have been included in the United Nations Convention on the Law of the Sea, 1982, which was negotiated with the active participation of all the interests involved. Although the 1982 Convention has not yet entered into force, it has been signed by 131 States by now, which will therefore be under an obligation to ensure that their actions are not incompatible with the Convention. The widespread evidence of State practice in conformity with the Convention will further strengthen the normative character of the outer limits of the maritime zones as provided in the Convention, and give them the status of both conventional and customary rules of international law.[132]

Notes

21. Annakumaru Pillai v. Muthupayal, *The Indian Law Reports* (Madras Series), Vol. XXVII (1904), pp. 551-576.
22. *The British Year Book of International Law* (BYBIL), 1923 – 24, pp. 34-43.
23. Colombos, n. 4, pp. 103-106. For other reviews of the 1930 Conference, see Manley O. Hudson, 'The First Conference for the Codification of International Law', *AJIL*, Vol. 24 (1930), pp. 447-466; Jesse S. Reeves, 'The Codification of the Law of Territorial Waters', *ibid.*, pp. 486-499; Hunter-Miller, 'The Hague Codification Conference', *ibid.*, pp. 674-693; and S. Whittemore Boggs, 'Delimitation of the Territorial Sea', *ibid.*, pp. 541-555.
24. Colombos, n. 4, pp. 74-75.
25. R.W. Mouton, *The Continental Shelf*, 1952, pp. 22-32 (Section 5. The Width of the Continental Shelf), where he cites the opinions of a number of geologists.
26. Shigeru Oda, *The International Law of the Ocean Development*, Basic Documents, 1972, p. 345. The Santiago Declaration later led to the demands for a 200-mile patrimonial sea, a 200-mile exclusive fishery zone, and a 200-mile exclusive economic zone.
27. *ICJ Reports 1951*, p. 115. For analysis and review, see Professor C.H.M. Waldock, 'The Anglo-Norwegian Fisheries Cases', *BYBIL*, 1951, pp. 114-171.
28. Shigeru Oda, n. 26, at p. 346.
29. *Yearbook of the International Law Commission*, 1954, Vol. II, p. 153.
30. *Ibid.*, 1955, Vol. II, p. 35 (Article 3).
31. *Ibid.*, 1956, Vol. II, p. 265.
32. *Ibid.*, p. 266.
33. *Ibid.*, p. 266.
34. *ICJ Reports 1951*, p. 116.
35. A/CN.4/61/Add.1/Annex, *Yearbook of the International Law Commission*, 1953, Vol. II.
36. For text of Articles 4, 5, 7, 8, 9, 10, 11 and 13 adopted by the International Law Commission in 1956 and the commentary thereto, see *ibid.*, 1956, Vol. II, pp. 266-272.
37. *Ibid.*, p. 295.
38. *Ibid.*, p. 5 (Document A/CN.4/97).
39. *Ibid.*, p. 295.
40. *Ibid.*, p. 262 (Articles 54, 55, 57 and 58).
41. *Ibid.*, p. 288.
42. In 1953, the Commission adopted Article 2 on Fisheries which read as follows:
    > In any area situated within one hundred miles from the territorial sea, the coastal State or States are entitled to take part on an equal footing in any system of regulation, even though their nationals do not carry on fishing in the area.
    Ibid., 1953, Vol. II, p. 218.
43. Mouton, n. 25, pp. 12-16, where he cites opinions of various geologists. The average depth at the edge is estimated at 130 metres.
44. *Yearbook of the International Law Commission*, 1951, Vol. II, p. 141 (Article 1 and commentary thereto).
45. *Ibid.*
46. *Ibid.*, 1953, Vol. II, p. 212 (Article 1). For commentary on the Article, see pp. 213-214.
47. *Ibid.*
48. See n. 28 above.
49. *Yearbook of the International Law Commission*, 1956, Vol. II, p. 264.
50. *Ibid.*, pp. 296-297.
51. Aaron L. Shalowitz, *Shore and Sea Boundaries*, Vol. I (1962), p. 269 and footnote 150.
52. A/CONF.13/C.1/L.77/Rev.3. For *Report of the First Committee* (A/CONF.13/L.28/

Rev.1), which refers to all proposals made therein, see *United Nations Conference on the Law of the Sea*, 1958, *Official Records*, Vol. II, pp. 115-125. For the text of the proposals, see *ibid.*, Vol. III, Annexes.

53. A/CONF.13/L.29. For text, see *ibid.*, Vol. II, pp. 125-126.
54. A/CONF.13/L.34 (Proposal by Burma, Colombia, Indonesia, Mexico, Morocco, Saudi Arabia, United Arab Republic, and Venezuela). For text, see *ibid.*, Vol. II, p. 128.
55. A/CONF.13/L.30. For text, see *ibid.*, Vol. II, p. 126.
56. For record of vote in the plenary, see *ibid.*, Vol. II, pp. 35-42 (14th Meeting – 25 April 1958).
57. For a comprehensive review of the work of the 1958 Conference on this subject, see Arthur H. Dean, 'The Geneva Conference on the Law of the Sea: What was Accomplished', *AJIL*, Vol. 52 (1958), pp. 607-628. Arthur Dean, who was chairman of the US Delegation to the Conference, said that the US was opposed to the 12-mile territorial sea for security and commercial reasons, *ibid.*, pp. 610-613. See also K.P. Misra, 'Territorial Sea and India', *Indian Journal of International Law*, Vol. 6 (1966), pp. 465-482.
58. For text of the Resolution, see *Official Records*, n. 52, Vol. II, p. 145.
59. For discussion and vote in the plenary, see *ibid.*, Vol. II, pp. 11-13 (8th plenary meeting – April 22, 1958). For *Report of the Fourth Committee*, A/CONF.13/L.12, and *Report of the Drafting Committee*, A/CONF.13/L.13, see *ibid.*, pp. 89-93.
    For comments and appraisal, see Marjorie M. Whiteman, 'Conference on the Law of the Sea: Convention on the Continental Shelf', *AJIL*, Vol. 52 (1958), pp. 629-659 at p. 634; and J.A.C. Gutteridge, 'The 1958 Geneva Convention on the Continental Shelf', *BYBIL*, 1959, pp. 102-123, at pp. 106-110.
60. Articles 3-5, 7-11, and 13. For text of these Articles, see *United Nations Conferences on the Law of the Sea*, 1958, *Official Records*, Vol. II, pp. 132-133; Lay, Churchill, Nordquist, *New Directions in the Law of the Sea*, 1973, Vol. I, pp. 2-5.
61. For a review of the work of the 1958 Conference on this topic, see Sir Gerald Fitzmaurice, 'Some Results of the Geneva Conference on the Law of the Sea – Part I – The Territorial Sea and Contiguous Zone and Related Topics', *International and Comparative Law Quarterly*, Vol. 8 (1959), pp. 73-121 at pp. 76-90.
62. For text of the Resolution (Resolution VI), see *United Nations Conference on the Law of the Sea*, 1958, *Official Records*, Vol. II, p. 144.
63. Document A/CONF.19/4 (8 February 1960) – Synoptical table concerning the breadth and juridical status of the territorial sea and adjacent zone. For text, see *Second United Nations Conference on the Law of the Sea*, 1960, *Official Records*, Vol. I (A/CONF.19/8), pp. 157-163.
64. For text of the proposals before the Committee of the Whole, see *Official Records*, n. 63, pp. 164-169.
65. Report of the Committee of the Whole, A/CONF.19/4. *Ibid.*, pp. 169-171 at p. 170. For text of the 18-Power Proposal (A/CONF.19/C.1/L.2/Rev.1, see *ibid.*, at pp. 165-166. For vote, see *ibid.*, p. 151.
66. *Ibid.*, at p. 170. For text of the Canadian – US proposal (A/CONF.19/C.1/L.10), see p. 169. For vote, see *ibid.*, p. 152.
67. *Ibid.*, at p. 170. For text of the proposal of Iceland (A/CONF.19/C.1/L.7/Rev.1), see p. 169. For vote, see *ibid.*, p. 151.
68. A/CONF.19/L.9. For text, see *ibid.*, p. 172.
69. A/CONF.19/L.12. For text, see *ibid.*, p. 173.
70. A/CONF.19/L.13. For text, see *ibid.*, p. 174.
71. A/CONF.19/L.11. For text, see *ibid.*, p. 173.
72. For a record of the vote on all proposals and amendments in the plenary, see *ibid.*, pp. 29-32.
73. For a detailed review of the 1960 Conference, see Arthur H. Dean, 'The Second Conference

on the Law of the Sea: The Fight for Freedom of the Seas', *AJIL*, Vol. 54 (1960), pp. 751-789; 'The Second United Nations Conference on the Law of the Sea — A Reply', by Alfonso Garcia Robles, Chairman of the Mexican Delegation to that Conference, *ibid.*, Vol. 55 (1961), pp. 669-675, and Arthur H. Dean's Response, at pp. 675-680; D.W. Bowett, 'The Second United Nations Conference on the Law of the Sea', *International and Comparative Law Quarterly*, Vol. 9 (July 1960), pp. 415-435; K.P. Misra, 'Territorial Sea and India', *Indian Journal of International Law*, Vol. 6 (1966), pp. 465-482.

As to the 'one negative vote short' for the adoption of the joint Canadian — US proposal, Arthur Dean referred to Ecuador, which was expected by them to abstain rather than cast a negative vote. Bowett said that the change of abstention in the Committee of the Whole to a negative vote in the plenary by India was 'one of the enigmas in the Conference'. India had expressed its views clearly in the Committee on March 31, 1960 and in the plenary on April 25, 1960 (before the vote). It was in favour of a 12-mile territorial sea, having cosponsored a proposal with Mexico to that effect in 1958. Having adopted a 6-mile territorial sea for itself in 1956, India could also support a 6-mile territorial sea and a 6-mile fishery zone with freedom of navigation and overflight in the latter zone, but with the assured protection of its security and fishery interests (see *Official Records*, n. 72, at pp. 76-77 and 22-23, respectively). There were other changes of votes also: Japan voted for the Canadian — US proposal in the Committee but abstained in the plenary; Iran and El Salvador voted against it in the Committee but abstained in the plenary; Finland, France, Ghana, Guatemala, The Holy See, Sweden, Argentina, Belgium and Cuba changed their votes from abstention in the Committee to a favourable vote in the plenary; and Jordan, Lebanon and Tunisia which had voted against the proposal in the Committee voted in favour in the plenary. Thus there were gains and losses in the vote — more gains, few losses for the Canadian — US joint proposal.

74. Shigeru Oda, *The International Law of Ocean Development*, Basic Documents, 1972, Part VI — Delimitation of Maritime Jurisdiction, pp. 368-372.

75. Arthur H. Dean, in his article in 1960, had referred to Dr. Columbus Iselin's remarks at the close of the International Oceanographic Congress, 1959, concerning the possibility of mining manganese nodules from the deep sea bed of the ocean, that, in his judgment, the economic, social and political problems involved in serious exploitation seemed 'more formidable than the remaining unsolved scientific problems'. Arthur H. Dean, n. 73, p. 786, footnote 154.

75a. Shigeru Oda, *International Control of Sea Resources*, Sijthoff, Leiden, 1963, p. 167. See also pp. 174-176 for similar views of other authors.

These views were repeated by him in his comprehensive Hague Lectures delivered in 1969: Shigeru Oda, 'International Law of the Resources of the Sea', Académie de Droit International, *Recueil des cours*, 1969 (II), pp. 355-484, at p. 442. Noting the developments at the UN Seabed Committee since 1967, he said that the resources of the area 'beyond the limits of present national jurisdiction', which should be utilised 'in the interests of mankind', are of the area beyond the outer limits of the continental shelf, which will need to be precisely defined. *Ibid.*, pp. 460-464.

76. Resolution 2750C adopted by the United Nations General Assembly on December 17, 1970. In its preamble, the Resolution stated that the General Assembly was '*Conscious* that the problems of ocean space are closely interrelated and need to be considered as a whole'.

77. A/CONF.62/C.2/L.84. *Third UNCLOS, Official Records*, Vol. III, p. 243.

78. A/CONF.62/L.78.

79. For Ecuador's reservation, see A/CONF.62/SR.182, p. 9 (April 30, 1982). The Ecuador representative had earlier indicated his intention of not participating in the consensus on the adoption of the Draft Convention in his statements on March 31, 1982 (A/CONF.62/SR.161, pp. 30-32) and April 16, 1982 (A/CONF.62/SR.172, p. 15), and in his letter of April 13, 1982 to the President of UNCLOS (A/CONF.62/L.128).

80. A/CONF.62/L.143.

81. A/CONF.62/SR.164, p. 30.

82. This is a new provision and was not included in Article 10 of the 1958 Convention on the Territorial Sea and the Contiguous Zone. It was included in the Informal Single Negotiating Text (SNT) in May 1975, and is expected to apply to tropical and subtropical atolls and islands possessing fringing reefs. See Robert D. Hodgson and Robert W. Smith, 'The Informal Single Negotiating Text (Committee II): A Geographical Perspective', *Ocean Development and International Law*, Vol. 3, No. 3 (1976), pp. 225-259 at pp. 229-230.

83. Article 11.

84. Article 60.

85. Article 12.

86. Article 7(2).

87. Article 7(3).

88. Article 7(4). The words within quotation marks are new, that is, these were not contained in Article 4(3) of the 1958 Convention on the Territorial Sea and the Contiguous Zone, and were proposed by Norway whose baselines drawn from low-tide elevations had been approved by the International Court of Justice in the *Anglo-Norwegian Fisheries Case*, 1951, but were not covered by the provisions of the 1958 Convention. See Hodgson and Smith, n. 82, at p. 239.

89. Article 7(5).

90. For a brief review of the straight baselines drawn by 39 coastal States by the end of 1982, see Lewis M. Alexander, 'Baseline Delimitations and Maritime Boundaries', *Virginia Journal of International Law*, Vol. 23, No. 4 (Summer 1983), pp. 503-536, at pp. 517-519.

91. Article 8.

92. Article 46(a).

93. Article 50.

94. Article 49.

95. Articles 51-54.

96. Article 48.

97. Article 47(1). In computing the land – water ratio, the waters within the fringing reefs of islands and atolls and other similar lagoons as explained in Article 47(7) will be treated as land areas.

98. Article 47(2). The length of the archipelagic baselines was 80 nautical miles in SNT, 1975 (Article 118(2)) and RSNT, 1976 (Article 119(2)). It was raised to 100 nautical miles in ICNT, July 1977 (Article 47(2)). Similarly the percentage for the application of the 125 nautical mile baseline was 1 in RSNT, 1976, which was raised to 3 in ICNT, July 1977.

99. Article 47(6). For background, see Malaysian statements in the 35th meeting of the plenary on July 10, 1974 (Third *UNCLOS, Official Records*, Voll. I, pp. 144-145), and in the 25th and 37th meetings of the Second Committee on August 5 and 12, 1974 (*ibid.*, Vol. II, pp. 198 and 270, respectively), and their proposal in A/CONF.62/C.2/L.64 of August 16, 1974 (*ibid.*, Vol. III, pp. 233-234). The matter was resolved and a paragraph was included in SNT in May 1975 (*ibid.*, Vol. IV, p. 169, Article 118(7)).

100. Article 47(8 and 9).

101. *ICJ Report 1982*, p. 18, paragraphs 97 to 105.

102. For a comprehensive treatment of baselines, and their relevance to maritime boundary, see Lewis M. Alexander, 'Baseline Delimitations and Maritime Boundaries', *Virginia Journal of International Law*, Vol. 23, No. 4 (Summer 1983), pp. 503-536.

103. Article 33(2). See also Article 303(2).

104. See Indian statements in the plenary on July 3, 1974 (*Official Records*, n. 99, Vol. I, 27th Meeting, p. 96), and in the Second Committee on July 19, 1974 (*ibid.*, Vol. II, p. 121).

105. *Ibid.*, Vol. IV, p. 150 – Article 33.

106. Article 56.

107. Article 57.
108. Article 75(1) and (2).
109. A/CONF.62/C.2/WP.1 (15 October 1974), *Main Trends*, Provisions 68 and 81.
110. A/CONF.62/L.4 (26 July 1974). For text, see *Official Records*, n. 99, Vol. III, pp. 81-83. A similar proposal was also made by the US Delegation on 8 August 1974 which referred to 'the limit of the economic zone' rather than to 200 miles. A/CONF.62/C.2/L.47, *ibid.*, Vol. III, pp. 222-225.
111. A/CONF.62/WP.8/Part II, *ibid.*, Vol. IV, p. 162.
112. After the Informal Composite Negotiating Text (ICNT) was prepared at UNCLOS in July 1977, further negotiations continued in UNCLOS on the remaining outstanding issues, and seven negotiating groups were established in 1978 to deal with these issues. Negotiating Group 6 dealt with the question of the outer limits of the continental shelf and the related matters.
113. Hollis D. Hedberg, 'Relations of Political Boundaries on the Ocean Floor to the Continental Margin', *Virginia Journal of International Law*, Vol. 17, No. 1 (Fall 1976), pp. 57-75.

    For his earlier study, see 'National – International Jurisdictional Boundary on the Ocean Floor', Occasational Paper No. 16, 1972, Law of the Sea Institute, University of Rhode Island, also published in *Ocean Management*, 1 (1973), pp. 83-118.
114. Piers D. Gardiner, 'Reasons and Methods of Fixing the Outer Limit of the Legal Continental Shelf beyond 200 Nautical Miles', *Geological Survey of Ireland*, Dublin, January 1978, pp. 1-24.
115. See n. 114. Hedberg had also cited references from geological and oceanograpic literature on the definition of 'continental margin', which included the rise. See his 1976 article, n. 113, pp. 73-75.
116. Commenting on the subject in the light of the provision (Article 62) in SNT prepared in UNCLOS in May 1975 (n. 111 above), Hodgson and Smith stated as follows:

> Some physical scientists restrict the use of the term 'continental margin' to the continental shelf and the slope. Others included the rise, or at least that part which is continentally derived, within the margin. Thus a serious ambiguity lies in the very heart of the definition. It is assumed, although no concrete evidence is available, that the definition is intended to cover the shelf, the slope and the rise.

Hodgson and Smith, n. 82, at pp. 254-255.

    The authors supported the Hedberg formula, stated that the base of the slope was 'one of the most pronounced geographic features in the oceans', recognised some exceptions thereto, and added the following:

> In the case of the Ganges, the actual break in the slope occurs rather close to the shore, whereas the fan extends hundreds of kilometers southwards beyond Sri Lanka. It is possible that in these particular and few instances an alternative provision would have to be written into the Convention because the fans represent natural prolongations of continental sediments of great depths.

Ibid., at p. 256.

Hedberg maintained his position even after the precise formula for the outer limits of the continental shelf was negotiated by 1980 and the Draft Convention was adopted by UNCLOS in April 1982. See his 'A Critique of Boundary Provisions in the Law of the Sea Treaty', originally written in August 1981 and updated in *Ocean Development and International Law*, Vol. 12 (1983), pp. 337-342, and the exchange of comments with V.E. McKelvey, who supports the provisions in the Convention, at pp. 343-348.
117. A/CONF.62/C.2/L.98 and Adds. 1-3. For text, see *Official Records*, n. 99, Vol. IX, pp. 189-191.
118. C.2/Informal Meeting/14, April 27, 1978. For text and discussion, see Bernard H. Oxman, 'The Third United Nations Conference on the Law of the Sea: The Seventh Session (1978)', *AJIL*, Vol. 73 (1979), at pp. 20-21.

119. For text of Aguilar's proposals, see A/CONF.62/L.37. For text of revised Article, see ICNT/Rev.1 − A/CONF.62/WP.10/Rev.1 (27 April 1979), Article 76.
120. A/CONF.62/WP.10/Rev.2 (11 April 1980).
121. A/CONF.62/SR. 141; *Official Records*, n. 99, Vol. XIV, pp. 83-84.
122. Article 76(4), (5), (3) and (6), respectively.
123. Article 76(7).
124. A/CONF.62/121, Annex II.
125. Article 76(8) and Annex II to the Convention.
126. See n. 119 above.
127. Article 82.
128. Article 246(5).
129. Article 246(6). See also Article 246(7).
130. Article 85. This is similar to Article 7 of the Geneva Convention on the Continental Shelf, 1958.
131. Article 48.
132. Smith has mentioned that 'As of February 1982, ninety-two States, or 67 percent of the independent coastal states, presently claim 200-mile resource zones; 56 states claim 200-mile economic zones, while another 36 states claim 200-mile fishery zones'. Robert W. Smith, 'A Geographical Primer to Maritime Boundary-Making', *Ocean Development and International Law*, Vol. 12 (1982), pp 1-22 at p. 6. See also *National Claims to Maritime Jurisdictions, Limits in the Seas*, No. 36, 4th Revision, US Department of State, May 1, 1981, pp. 8-13.

CHAPTER 3

Delimitation between States with opposite or adjacent coasts

A. Pre-International Law Commission

Prior to 1945, the delimitation between States with opposite or adjacent coasts had been restricted to the territorial sea and to straits, gulfs, bays and lakes, except the Agreement of February 26, 1942 between the United Kingdom and Venezuela concerning the boundary in the Gulf of Paria. In a comprehensive study of the subject between 1648 and 1939, Sang-Myon Rhee has reached the broad conclusions that the boundary in the lakes, straits, gulfs, bays and the territorial sea between States with *opposite* coasts had generally, but not always, followed the median line, but that between the States with *adjacent* coasts, the boundary line had been varied and had followed a perpendicular line from the terminal point of the land boundary at sea, or a perpendicular to the general direction of the coastline, or a latitude or a longitude, or an equidistance line modified to remove the distorting effect of small islands or coastal projections. In the latter case, he concluded that 'Indeed, there is no basis to suppose that the equidistance method should have been adopted as a general rule of delimitation'.[133]

The Hague Codification Conference of 1930 had not dealt with the question of delimitation between States with opposite or adjacent coasts. It was concerned mainly with the questions relating to the territorial sea, including the breadth of the territorial sea and the measurement thereof, and the question of the contiguous zone.

In the Proclamation concerning the continental shelf issued by the President of the United States, Harry S. Truman, on September 28, 1945, the delimitation criteria referred to the equitable principles as follows:

> In cases where the continental shelf extends to the shores of another State, or is shared with an adjacent State, the boundary shall be determined by the United States and the State concerned in accordance with equitable principles.[134]

In an article published in 1951, S. Whittemore Boggs explained at some length the principles and techniques concerning the median or equidistance line as the boundary between the States with opposite or adjacent coasts, and expressed the view that these were of 'universal applicability' and independent of the width of the belts of waters claimed, including the contiguous zones and the continental shelf.[135]

B. International Law Commission: 1949 – 1956

The International Law Commission started its work in 1949 by giving priority to the regime of the high seas, which included the continental shelf. In 1951, the Commission, pursuant to a recommendation by the United Nations General Assembly, decided to initiate work on the regime of the territorial sea. The Special Rapporteur for both these items was J.P.A. Francois of the Netherlands. In the Draft Articles on the Continental Shelf and Related Subjects, adopted by the Commission in 1951, it was suggested that the continental shelf boundary should be established by agreement between the parties, failing which by reference to arbitration *ex aequo et bono*. Article 7 of these Draft Articles and the Commentary thereto read as follows:

Article 7

Two or more States to whose territories the same continental shelf is contiguous should establish boundaries in the area of the continental shelf by agreement. Failing agreement, the parties are under the obligation to have the boundaries fixed by arbitration.

1. Where the same continental shelf is contiguous to the territories of two or more adjacent States, the drawing of boundaries may be necessary in the area of the continental shelf. Such boundaries should be fixed by agreement among the States concerned. It is not feasible to lay down any general rule which States should follow; and it is not unlikely that difficulties may arise. For example, no boundary may have been fixed between the respective territorial waters of the interested States, and no general rule exists for such boundaries. It is proposed therefore that if agreement cannot be reached and a prompt solution is needed, the interested States should be under an obligation to submit to arbitration *ex aequo et bono*. The term 'arbitration' is used in the widest sense, and includes possible recourse to the International Court of Justice.

2. Where the territories of two States are separated by an arm of the sea, the boundary between their continental shelves would generally coincide with some median line between the two coasts. However, in such cases the configuration of the coast might give rise to difficulties in drawing any median line, and such difficulties should be referred to arbitration.[136]

In 1952, the Special Rapporteur in his first report on the regime of the territorial sea drafted an Article on the delimitation of the territorial sea of the two adjacent States which would generally apply the median line.[137] The Commission, however, decided to consult the States about their practice and suggested that the Special Rapporteur might consult some experts for clarification of certain technical aspects of the problem.[138] The Special Rapporteur accordingly reserved the provision on the territorial sea delimitation in his Second Report on the subject.[139]

It was against this background that the Special Rapporteur presided over a meeting of the *Committee of Experts* held at The Hague between April 14 and 16, 1953, who were consulted in their personal capacity on the technical aspects of territorial sea delimitation between States with opposite or adjacent coasts. The questions posed to the Committee of Experts and their answers thereto as embodied in their Report were as follows:

VI

How should the international boundary be drawn between two countries, the coasts of which are opposite each other at a distance of less than 2 T miles? To what extent have islands and shallow waters to be accounted for?

An international boundary between countries the coasts of which are opposite each other at a distance of less than 2 T miles should as a general rule be the median line, every point of which is equidistant from the baselines of the States concerned. Unless otherwise agreed between the adjacent States, all islands should be taken into consideration in drawing the median line. Likewise, drying rocks and shoals within T miles of only one State should be taken into account, but similar elevations of undetermined sovereignty, that are within T miles of both States, should be disregarded in laying down the median line. There may, however, be special reasons, such as navigation and fishing rights, which may divert the boundary from the median line. The line should be laid down on charts of the largest scale available, especially if any part of the body of water is narrow and relatively tortuous.

VII

How should the (lateral) boundary line be drawn through the adjoining territorial sea of two adjacent States? Should this be done

A.   by continuing the landfrontier?

B.   by a perpendicular line on the coast at the interaction of the landfrontier and the coastline?

C.   by a line drawn vertically on the general direction of the coastline?

D.   by a median line? If so, how should this line be drawn? To what extent should islands, shallow waters and navigation channels be accounted for?

1.   After thoroughly discussing different methods the Committee de-

cided that the (lateral) boundary through the territorial sea — if not already fixed otherwise — should be drawn according to the principle of equidistance from the respective coastlines.

2. In a number of cases this may not lead to an equitable solution, which should be then arrived at by negotiation.

Remark regarding the answers to VI and VII:

The Committee considered it important to find a formula for drawing the international boundaries in the territorial waters of States, which could also be used for the delimitation of the respective continental shelves of two States bordering the same continental shelf.[140]

The Commission decided to be guided by the recommendations by the Committee of Experts concerning the territorial sea boundary, but embodied them first in Article 7 on the continental shelf boundary in 1953 in a simpler and elastic manner as follows:

Article 7

1. Where the same continental shelf is contiguous to the territories of two or more States whose coasts are opposite to each other, the boundary of the continental shelf appertaining to such States is, in the absence of agreement between those States or unless another boundary line is justified by special circumstances, the median line every point of which is equidistant from the base lines from which the width of the territorial sea of each country is measured.

2. Where the same continental shelf is contiguous to the territories of two adjacent States, the boundary of the continental shelf appertaining to such States is, in the absence of agreement between those States or unless another boundary line is justified by special circumstances, determined by application of the principle of equidistance from the base lines from which the width of the territorial sea of each of the two countries is measured.[141]

In 1954, the Commission adopted two separate Articles, namely, Articles 15 and 16, on the territorial sea boundary between States with opposite or adjacent coasts, respectively, guided by the recommendations of the Committee of Experts. These articles read as follows:

Article 15

Delimitation of the territorial sea of two States the coasts of which are opposite each other

The boundary of the territorial sea between two States the coasts of which are opposite each other at a distance less than twice the breadth of the territorial sea is, in the absence of agreement of those States, or unless another boundary line is justified by special circumstances, the median line every point of which is equidistant from the base lines from which the width of the territorial sea of each country is measured.

Article 16

Delimitation of the territorial sea of two adjacent States

The boundary of the territorial sea between two adjacent States is drawn, in the absence of agreement between those States or unless another boundary line is justified by special circumstances, by application of the principle of equidistance from the base lines from which the width of the territorial sea of each of the two countries is measured.[142]

After further consideration, and in the light of the comments of States, the Commission decided to combine the Articles on the boundary in straits and the territorial sea boundary between States with opposite coasts into a single Article, which thus also dealt with the assimilation of small resulting enclaves. However, two separate Articles on the territorial sea boundary between States with opposite and with adjacent coasts respectively were maintained. The drafting was also similar to the Article on the continental shelf boundary, which stated that the boundary, in the absence of agreement between those States or unless another boundary line was justified by special circumstances, 'is the median line' in the case of States with opposite coasts, or is drawn 'by the application of the principle of equidistance' in the case of States with adjacent coasts.

By 1956, the Commission completed its study of the law of the sea and prepared a set of 73 Articles with commentaries, and recommended that these be now considered by a plenipotentiary international conference. The Articles dealing with the maritime boundary concerning the territorial sea and the continental shelf between States with opposite or adjacent coasts read as follows:

Delimitation of the territorial sea in straits and off other opposite coasts
Article 12

1. The boundary of the territorial sea between two States, the coasts of which are opposite each other at a distance less than the extent of the belts of territorial sea adjacent to the two coasts, shall be fixed by agreement between those States. Failing such agreement and unless another boundary line is justified by special circumstances, the boundary line is the median line every point of which is equidistant from the nearest points on the baselines from which the breadths of the territorial seas of the two States are measured.

2. If the distance between the two States exceeds the extent of the two belts of territorial sea, the waters lying between the two belts shall form part of the high seas. Nevertheless, if, as a consequence of this delimitation, an area of the sea not more than two miles in breadth should be entirely enclosed within the territorial sea, that area may, by agreement between the coastal States, be deemed to be part of the territorial sea.

3. The first sentence of the preceding paragraph shall be applicable to cases where both coasts belong to one and the same coastal State. If, as a consequence of this delimitation, an area of the sea not more than two

miles in breadth should be entirely enclosed within the territorial sea, that area may be declared by the coastal State to form part of its territorial sea.

4.   The line of demarcation shall be marked on the officially recognized large-scale charts.

Delimitation of the territorial sea of two adjacent states
Article 14

1.   The boundary of the territorial sea between two adjacent States shall be determined by agreement between them. In the absence of such agreement, and unless another boundary line is justified by special circumstances, the boundary is drawn by application of the principle of equidistance from the nearest points of the baseline from which the breadth of the territorial sea of each country is measured.

2.   The boundary line shall be marked on the officially recognized large-scale charts.

Article 72

1.   Where the same continental shelf is adjacent to the territories of two or more States whose coasts are opposite to each other, the boundary of the continental shelf appertaining to such States shall be determined by agreement between them. In the absence of agreement, and unless another boundary line is justified by special circumstances, the boundary is the median line, every point of which is equidistant from the baselines from which the breadth of the territorial sea of each country is measured.

2.   Where the same continental shelf is adjacent to the territories of two adjacent States, the boundary of the continental shelf shall be determined by agreement between them. In the absence of agreement, and unless another boundary line is justified by special circumstances, the boundary shall be determined by application of the principle of equidistance from the baselines from which the breadth of the territorial sea of each of the two countries is measured.[143]

In its commentary to Article 12 above, the Commission recognised that special circumstances would probably necessitate frequent departures from the mathematical median line, but 'it thought it advisable to adopt, as a general rule, the system of the median line as the basis for delimitation'.[144] In its commentary to Article 14, it referred to the other possible lines of delimitation, such as the extension of the land frontier out to the sea as far as the outer limits of the territorial sea, a line at right angles to the coast at the land frontier point, a geographical parallel, or a line at right angles to the general direction of the coastline, and agreed with the Committee of Experts of 1953 in disapproving of them, and in upholding the equidistance line. However, it considered 'that this rule should be very flexibly applied'.[145] In its commentary to Article 72, the Commission said that it had adopted the same principles for the continental shelf delimitation as for the territorial sea in Articles 12 and 14, and added the following:

> As in the case of the boundaries of the territorial sea, provision must be made for departures necessitated by an exceptional configuration of the coast, as well as the presence of islands or of navigable channels. This case may arise fairly often, so that the rule adopted is fairly elastic.[146]

No separate provisions were made by the International Law Commission for the delimitation of the contiguous zone between the States concerned.

C. The 1958 Conference and the Geneva Conventions

The First United Nations Conference on the Law of the Sea, 1958, accepted the draft Articles proposed by the International Law Commission, with small changes. It combined them into a single Article for the territorial sea boundary, deleted the reference to straits and enclaves, drafted the median line negatively as a residual rule, and added a reference to 'historic title' in addition to 'special circumstances' for varying the application of the median line. It also added a separate Article on the delimitation of the contiguous zone boundary. It kept the Article on the continental shelf boundary with separate paragraphs dealing with the States with opposite and those with adjacent coasts.

As to the continental shelf boundary, several amendments were proposed, including one by *Iran* to ignore the islands located within an enclosed sea between States with opposite coasts and to delimit the continental shelf boundary with reference to the coastlines of the States concerned, another by *Yugoslavia* to delete references to special circumstances, and a third by *Venezuela* suggesting that the boundary between the States concerned may be settled by agreement or by other means recognised in international law. None of these amendments was accepted.[147]

The following provisions on delimitation were included in the 1958 Conventions:

Regarding the delimitation of the *territorial sea, Article 12* of the Geneva Convention on the Territorial Sea and the Contiguous Zone, 1958, provided as follows:

> 1.   Where the coasts of two States are opposite or adjacent to each other, neither of the two States is entitled, failing agreement between them to the contrary, to extend its territorial sea beyond the median line every point of which is equidistant from the nearest points on the baselines from which the breadth of the territorial seas of each of the two States is measured. The provisions of this paragraph shall not apply, however, where it is necessary by reasons of historic title or other special circumstances to delimit the territorial sea of the two States in any way which is at variance with the provision.

2.   The line of delimitation between the territorial seas of the two States lying opposite to each other or adjacent to each other shall be marked on large-scale charts officially recognised by the coastal States.

Regarding the *contiguous zone* delimitation, *Article 24* of the same Convention provided as follows:

3.   Where the coasts of two States are opposite or adjacent to each other, neither of the two States is entitled, failing agreement between them to the contrary, to extend its contiguous zone beyond the median line every point of which is equidistant from the nearest points on the baselines from which the breadth of the territorial seas of the two States is measured.

No reference was made here to historic title or other special circumstances.

Regarding the delimitation of the *continental shelf*, *Article 6* of the Geneva Convention on the Continental Shelf, 1958, provided as follows:

1.   Where the same continental shelf is adjacent to the territories of two or more States whose coasts are opposite each other, the boundary of the continental shelf appertaining to such States shall be determined by agreement between them. In the absence of agreement, and unless another boundary line is justified by special circumstances, the boundary is the median line, every point of which is equidistant from the nearest points of the baselines from which the breadth of the territorial seas of each State is measured.

2.   Where the same continental shelf is adjacent to the territories of two adjacent States, the boundary of the continental shelf shall be determined by agreement between them. In the absence of agreement, and unless another boundary line is justified by special circumstances, the boundary shall be determined by application of the principle of equidistance from the nearest points of the baselines from which the breadth of the territorial sea of each State is measured.

3.   In delimiting the boundaries of the continental shelf, any lines which are drawn in accordance with the principles set out in paragraphs 1 and 2 of this article should be defined with reference to charts and geographical features as they exist at a particular date, and reference should be made to fixed permanent identifiable points on the land.

Although there was an element of nuance between the delimitation criteria for the territorial sea and the continental shelf, and in the latter case separate paragraphs made reference to States with opposite coasts and States with adjacent coasts, the basic criterium for the maritime boundary embodied in the 1958 Convention was the median or equidistance line unless another boundary line was justified by special circumstances.

There was not much controversy about the general application of the provisions of the 1958 Convention on the Territorial Sea and the Contiguous Zone on the delimitation of the territorial sea boundary, and these were by and large accepted and applied in State practice as well as in UNCLOS and have been embodied in the United Nations Convention on the Law of the Sea, 1982.

Whether the rule embodied in Article 6 of the 1958 Convention on the Continental Shelf was a conventional rule, or a rule of customary international law applicable to all States whether or not parties to the Convention, became a matter of contention before the International Court of Justice and other tribunals as well as a subject of intensive controversy and negotiations at the UNCLOS since December 1973. These aspects will be dealt with in Parts Three and Four respectively.

D. The UNCLOS and the 1982 Convention

The question of the delimitation of the maritime boundary between States with opposite or adjacent coasts became an intensely controversial one at the UNCLOS between 1974 and 1982, particularly concerning the exclusive economic zone and the continental shelf. The principal controversy was concentrated on the delimitation criteria. A large group of delegations supported the delimitation criteria as embodied in the 1958 Conventions, giving a pride of place to the principle of the median or the equidistance line. Another large group of delegations supported the view expressed by the International Court of Justice in the *North Sea Continental Shelf* cases, 1969, and gave a pride of place to the equitable principles in settling the delimitation of the maritime boundary. Various attempts were made to combine the two criteria, particularly in Negotiating Group 7 on maritime boundary between 1978 and 1980, but without much success. Ultimately, a solution was arrived at in August 1981 which was supported by both the equity group and the equidistance group of delegations at UNCLOS and embodied in the Draft Convention on the Law of the Sea, which was adopted at UNCLOS by vote in April 1982 and opened for signature and ratification in December 1982. The solution was, however, strongly objected to by some States, including Turkey and Venezuela who voted against the Draft Convention in April 1982 and did not sign the Convention in December 1982.

As mentioned above, there was not much controversy about the delimitation criteria for the territorial sea boundary, and by and large the provisions of the 1958 Convention on the Territorial Sea and the Contiguous Zone were followed.

No provision was made concerning the delimitation of the contiguous zone boundary.

Regarding the delimitation of the exclusive economic zone and the continental shelf boundary, no distinction was made between the two concerning the delimitation criteria. Nor was any distinction made between States with opposite or adjacent coasts.

Apart from the delimitation criteria, the questions of the provisional or interim arrangements pending the conclusion of a delimitation agreement, and of the settlement of delimitation disputes, were also discussed extensively at UNCLOS, and solutions were arrived at.

The developments in UNCLOS concerning the delimitation between States with opposite or adjacent coasts, leading to the adoption of the 1982 Convention, will be covered in Part Four of this study.

Notes

133. Sang-Myon Rhee, 'Sea Boundary Delimitation Between States Before World War II', *AJIL*, Vol. 76, No. 3 (July 1982), pp. 555-588 at p. 588.
134. Marjorie M. Whiteman, *Digest of International Law*, Vol. 4, p. 757.
135. 'Delimitation of Seaward Areas under National Jurisdiction', *AJIL*, Vol. 45, No. 2 (April 1951), pp. 240-266. Boggs added that 'The method here suggested would provide the "adequate principles" for accord between the United States and a neighbour state which are referred to in Presidential Proclamation No. 2667, signed September 28, 1945'. *Ibid.*, at p. 262, footnote 34. He also noted that the various decrees and laws of other States since 1945 also call for accord on the basis of equitable principles.
136. Report of the International Law Commission, Third Session, 16 May – 27 July 1951, *Yearbook of the International Law Commission*, 1951, Vol. II, at p. 143.
137. Document A/CN.4/53, Article 13, *Yearbook of the International Law Commission*, 1952, Vol. II, p. 38.
138. *Ibid.*, at p. 68.
139. A/CN.4/61 (19 February 1953), Article 13, *Yearbook of the International Law Commission*, 1953, Vol. II, at p. 70.
140. Annex to A/CN.4/61/Add.1 (18 Mary 1953), *ibid.*, at p. 19. Also cited in Whiteman, *Digest of International Law*, Vol. 4, pp. 316-317 and 325-326. The words 'less than 2T' mean 'less than twice the breadth of the territorial sea'.
141. *Yearbook of the International Law Commission*, 1953, Vol. II, p. 213. For commentary, see p. 216.
142. *Ibid.*, 1954, Vol. II, pp. 157 and 158.
143. *Ibid.*, 1956, Vol. II, pp. 257, 258 and 264.
144. *Ibid.*, at p. 271.
145. *Ibid.*, at p. 272.
146. *Ibid.*, at p. 300.
147. For a summary review of these amendments, see Marjorie M. Whiteman, 'Conference on the Law of the Sea: Convention on the Continental Shelf', *AJIL*, Vol. 52 (1958), pp. 629-659 at pp. 651-654.

CHAPTER 4

Technical aspects

Maritime boundary in both its aspects, namely, seaward *outer limits* of maritime zones and *limits* of maritime zones between States with opposite or adjacent coasts, has technical aspects and needs the assistance and advice of hydrographers, geographers and geologists.

The *outer limits* of maritime zones may be determined either with reference to a specified distance from the appropriate baseline, such as a 12-nautical mile territorial sea or a 200-nautical mile exclusive economic zone, or with reference to a depth-cum-distance or a sedimentary-thickness ratio formula, such as in relation to the continental shelf of a coastal State. As already indicated in Chapter 2 above, the starting point for the distance related zone will be the baseline, which may be a normal baseline, that is the low-water line along the coast, or a straight baseline, which may be a line enclosing a deeply indented or cut into coast, a deltaic coast, or a fringe of islands along the coast, or a line closing the mouth of a bay, or an archipelagic baseline. Since the baseline is used for measuring the outer limits of maritime zones, its accurate marking on large-scale charts officially recognised by a coastal State is necessary. This will require the technical assistance of hydrographers or geographers since the low-water line or other depths of water shown on the chart will be based on a vertical or chart datum, that is the water level from which the depths shown on a chart are measured. In the case of straight baselines joining long distances between islands, including archipelagic baselines, the geodetic datum and the spheroid will provide the precision in determining the locations by taking into account the curvature of the earth. The availability of geodetic satellites for checking the precise location of the geographical points may also be useful.

The technical aspects of fixing the outer limits of the territorial sea, extending up to 12 nautical miles, are fairly simple and well-known. Article 4 of the United Nations Convention on the Law of the Sea, 1982, like the 1958 Convention on the Territorial Sea and the Contiguous Zone, defines the outer limits as the line 'every point of which is at a distance from the nearest point of the baseline equal to the breadth of the territorial sea'. In normal cases, this would imply the application of the envelope line which follows the major sinuosities of the coast. If the baseline is a straight basline or a bay-closing line, the outer limit may be the envelope line or the replica line and both will produce the same result as the strictly parallel line.[148]

The technical aspects of fixing the outer limits of the exclusive economic zone and of the continental shelf raise complex questions.[149] Because of the extensive breadth of the exclusive economic zone, the nature and scale of the chart and the curvature of the earth may become more relevant, particularly in higher latitudes. The United Nations Convention on the Law of the Sea, 1982, does not specify the manner in which the outer limits of the exclusive economic zone will be determined, except to say that the zone 'shall not extend beyond 200 nautical miles from the baselines from which the breadth of the territorial sea is measured',[150] and that these limits 'shall be shown on charts of a scale or scales adequate for ascertaining their position',[151] and 'where appropriate, lists of geographical coordinates of points, specifying the geodetic datum, may be substituted for such outer limits lines . . .'.[152]

The determination of the outer limits of the continental shelf beyond 200 nautical miles, under the United Nations Convention on the Law of the Sea, 1982, is more complex, since it involves the determination of the foot of the continental slope, the thickness of sedimentary rocks, the nature of the ridges, the drawing of straight lines 'not exceeding 60 nautical miles in length, connecting fixed points, defined by coordinates of latitude and longitude' for determining such outer limits, and so forth.[153] A Commission on the Limits of the Continental Shelf, consisting of 21 experts in geology, geophysics and hydrography, has also been established under the Convention, whose functions in relation to these limits have already been described in Chapter 2 above.[154] The coastal State shall deposit the charts and the relevant information, including geodetic datums, permanently describing the outer limits of its continental shelf with the Secretary-General of the United Nations and the Secretary-General of the International Seabed Authority,[155] since beyond the limits of national jurisdiction lies the international seabed area and an elaborate regime for the exploration and exploitation of the area and its resources has been set out in the United Nations Convention on the Law of the Sea, 1982.[156]

The technical aspects have been considered more intensively with reference to the determination of the *limits* of maritime zones between States with opposite or adjacent coasts. Initially, the median or equidistance line was regarded as an equitable maritime boundary, particularly when it extended to short distances.[157] Its application to the delimitation of the maritime boundary be-

tween States with adjacent coasts sometimes created inequitable situations arising from the concavity or convexity of the coasts, the presence of islands, the
length of the boundary line and the relevant special circumstances, and led to
the adoption of a modified median or equidistance line, or a separate negotiated line. A lot of literature has appeared on the technical aspects of delimiting
the maritime boundary extending to long distances.[158]

In either case, namely, whether the boundary relates to States with opposite
coasts but extends to long distances or to States with adjacent coasts, attention
has been drawn to some technical aspects which must be borne in mind by negotiators, counsel, conciliators, arbitrators and judges. The more important of
these technical aspects may be summarised as follows:

Since the maritime boundary settles the question of jurisdiction of the parties
in the maritime zone, it must conform precisely to the intention of the parties,
if a decision has been reached on the alignment thereof. Thus the delimitation
area of the sea in question, the precise location of the terminal and turning
points, the nature of the lines joining these points, and the angle or direction
of the segment or segments of the boundary line must be clearly ascertainable
or recoverable from the maritime boundary line as agreed to or intended by the
parties. The parties may, while negotiating, certainly engage in a 'give and take'
or other adjustments, whatever be the method or principle used in settling the
maritime boundary, but a political or negotiated 'give and take' is different
from a gain or loss arising from a technical error, such as by using a wrong chart
projection, or by using the different geodetic datums (horizontal and vertical)
of the parties as the basis of locating points with geographical coordinates or
the sea level near the shore, or by using a high-water mark in place of a low-
water mark for the baseline.

It will thus always be useful and even necessary to have the assistance of
qualified technical experts in geography, hydrography, and, where appropriate, geology and geophysics, while negotiating a maritime boundary agreement, drafting the clauses relating to the description of the boundary line and
preparing the chart delineating the boundary.

Scale of charts

The chart to be used for delineating the boundary should be of a large scale and
should, if possible, cover the entire boundary line. The degree of accuracy of
the boundary line on a small-scale chart may be small. The United Nations study has illustrated the point by indicating that 'a limit depicted on a chart of scale
1:500,000 by a line 0.3 mm thick will represent a line on the sea's surface nearly
1/10 of an international nautical mile (185 metres) in width',[159] and suggested
that the range of charts for maritime boundary may lie between 1:50,000 and

1:200,000.[160] The territorial sea limits between States should be developed on charts in the 1:20,000 to 1:40,000 range.[161]

If, on the other hand, the boundary line is long and the parties intend to show the entire boundary on a single chart, only a small-scale chart with its limitations will have to be used. Smith states that in the Treaty between the USA and Venezuela to delimit their Caribbean maritime boundary (1978), the scale of the chart used is '1:1,800,000 at 15° north latitude. At this scale, one inch equals approximately 28 miles. The width of the line itself used to depict the boundary would be about 0.7 miles (about 1100 metres). It is noted in Article 3 of the treaty that the chart has been used "for illustrative purposes only".'[162]

Chart projection

For the boundary line in the higher latitudes, say above 15° latitude, the chart projection should preferably be conformal so as to divide the area in question in conformity with the actual distances and area on the spheroidal earth. The Mercator Projection charts, which are used for navigation, emphasise the direction rather than the area. The measurement or length of a straight line joining two points on a Mercator Projection chart, which is technically known as a loxodrome or a rhumb line and makes the same angle with the meridians throughout, may be different from a geodetic line joining the same two points on a conformal chart which takes into account the curvature of the earth. The latter is shorter. Hodgson and Cooper illustrated it by drawing the arcs of a 200-nautical mile equidistance line boundary between two adjacent States, one on a Mercator Projection chart and the other on Lambert Conformal Projection, and showed that the area in between the two lines measured more than 700 sq. nautical miles.[163]

Nature of lines

It will thus be useful if the nature of the lines joining the turning and terminal points of the boundary line is also described in the agreement or agreed to between the parties, namely, whether these will be loxodromes or geodesics or arcs of Great Circles, etc. 'A straight line on the three-dimensional, spheroidal earth can be rendered in at least nine different ways on a two-dimensional chart', say Hodgson and Cooper, although they advise that 'the geodesic is the most accurate line and, as a result, should be preferred in any delimitation involving the use of "straight" line'.[164]

The same will apply to the recommendations or a decision of a conciliation commission, a Court of Arbitration, or the International Court of Justice. In

62

the *English Channel Arbitration Case between the United Kingdom and France*, 1978, the United Kingdom had urged the Court of Arbitration to correct the error in the delimitation of the boundary between Points M and N in the Western Approaches to the English Channel in the Decision rendered by it in 1977. The boundary line in this sector was 'to be determined by the equidistance method by giving half-effect to the Scillies'. The Court's Expert had drawn this line as a 'loxodrome' or a straight line on the Mercator Projection chart, which had been approved by the Court. Such a line would not take into account the curvature of the Earth and would not be equidistant from the two coasts. Accordingly, the United Kingdom argued that the true equidistance line should be drawn on a Transverse Mercator Projection chart which would push the terminal Point N (located some 170 nautical miles from Point M) four nautical miles toward France. The discrepancy would increase to six miles if the boundary line were extended to 200 nautical miles, and would be larger if the boundary line were extended to the outer edge of the continental margin.

The Court of Arbitration held that the use of a Mercator Projection chart was not against the general practice of States concerning delimitation, and that such review now would reopen the question of basepoints and other issues and would not be within the scope of the interpretation of its Decision of 1977.[165]

Geodetic datum and spheroid

For precision in locating the course of the maritime boundary, and identifying a point, line or area in relation thereto, which may be useful in avoiding a controversy about the location of a drilling site in the continental shelf or about other aspects of the uses of the maritime zone, it is necessary to ensure the accuracy of the geographical positions or coordinates from which the boundary line is measured or derived. If the parties use different geodetic datum and reference spheroid, these should be harmonised and a common or single geodetic datum and reference spheroid used which assumes certain spheres and dimensions of the earth (radius of the major axis, degree of flattening, etc) which are relevant to the boundary area. 'The introduction of satellite position fixing methods allows the geographical position of any chosen site to be determined on a single global geodetic datum', says the UN study.[166] Smith refers to the World Geodetic System, developed by the United States, under which 'all major geodetic systems could be unified and the coordinates of points anywhere on the earth would be compatible', and which was used by the United States in their maritime boundary agreements with the Cook Islands and New Zealand (Tokelau).[167]

Expert advice on the geodetic datum and the spheroid to be used, and on the availability of satellite imagery, should therefore be sought before concluding

63

the maritime boundary delimitation. If possible, reference to the geodetic datum and the spheroid used may also be included in the maritime boundary agreement. This information is also required to be submitted to the Secretary-General of the United Nations under the UN Convention on the Law of the Sea, 1982, in relation to the geographical coordinates used for the boundary delimitation of the territorial sea, the exclusive economic zone and the continental shelf.[168]

A sample of a detailed technical clause used in the Agreement between Australia and Papua New Guinea, 1978, is as follows:

> 2. Where for the purposes of this Treaty it is necessary to determine the position on the surface of the Earth of a point, line or area, that position shall be determined by reference to the Australian Geodetic Datum, that is to say, by reference to a spheroid having its centre at the centre of the Earth and a major (equatorial) radius of 6,378,160 metres and a flattening of 100/29,825 and by reference to the position of the Johnson Geodetic Station in the Northern Territory of Australia. That station shall be taken to be situated at Latitude 25°56′54.5515′′ South and at Longitude 133°12′30.0771′′ East and to have a ground level of 571.2 metres above the spheroid referred to above.[169]

Conversely, the technical points referred to above may cause, and have caused, variations in the location of boundary points in the agreement, apart from the interpretation dispute between the United Kingdom and France referred to above. Thus the geographical coordinates of points in USSR charts are different from those on the US Naval Oceanographic charts. The distances between the turning and terminal points of the boundary line in some Agreements have also been calculated differently in the maps prepared in the United States. The use of computer-developed programmes has however helped precise computations.

To conclude, the boundary line, as agreed to between the parties, or as determined by the Court or the Tribunal, should be drawn on an appropriate chart, with a scale which can depict the full course of the boundary line therein. The geodetic datum with reference to which the geographical points, directions and the area are identified, indicated and computed should be made uniform and specified in the agreement or the decision. The nature of the lines joining the turning or other points of the boundary line should also be specified. The agreement in question should describe the course of the boundary line with reference to the geographical coordinates, which would be delineated on a chart enclosed with the agreement. The agreement may provide as to how the physical location or recovery of a point may be agreed to between the parties or their experts, and as to how a discrepancy between the description in the agreement and the line shown on the chart will be resolved, such as by the description in the agreement having a prevailing effect.

Greater attention to the technical aspects of maritime delimitation is already in evidence in State practice.

As mentioned at the outset of this Part, this study will concentrate on the delimitation of maritime boundary between States with opposite or adjacent coasts. The substance of this question is examined in the following Parts as follows:

Part Two deals with State practice in concluding agreements on the maritime boundary. A sample of 100 agreements, organised region-wise, will be analysed.

Part Three deals with the major judicial, arbitral or other decisions concerning the maritime boundary.

Part IV deals with the developments at UNCLOS between 1973 and 1982 leading to the adoption of the United Nations Convention on the Law of the Sea, 1982.

The conclusions of the study will be summed up in Part Five.

Literature

A select bibliography arranged Part-wise has been added to the study at the end.

Notes

148. For technical aspects, see S. Whittemore Boggs, 'Delimitation of the Territorial Sea', *AJIL*, Vol. 24 (1930), pp. 541-555, and 'Delimitation of Seaward Areas Under National Jurisdiction', *AJIL*, Vol. 45, No. 2 (April 1951), pp. 240-266; Aaron L. Shalowitz, *Shore and Sea Boundaries*, Vol. I (1962), pp. 169-172, and p. 72, footnote 12; Marjorie M. Whiteman, *Digest of International Law*, Vol. 4, pp. 195-207.

149. For background information on the technical issues involved, see D.C. Kapoor, 'The delimitation of the exclusive economic zones', *Maritime Policy and Management* (1977), 4, pp. 255-263; 'Methods and Basis of Seaward Delimitation of Continental Shelf Jurisdiction', Note by Frederic A. Eustus III, *Virginia Journal of International Law*, Vol. 17 (1976 – 77), pp. 107-130.

    See also *Study on the Future Functions of the Secretary General Under the Draft Convention and on the Needs of Countries, especially developing countries, for information, advice and assistance under the new legal regime*, prepared by the (UN) Secretary-General in his capacity as Secretary-General of the Third United Nations Conference on the Law of the Sea, Doc. A/CONF.62/L.76 (18 August 1981), at pp. 4-5 and 42-45.

150. Article 57.
151. Article 75.
152. Article 75.
153. Article 76.
154. See p. 41 above.
155. Articles 76(9) and 84(2).
156. Part XI, Articles 133-191.

157. See Boggs, n. 148, *AJIL*, Vol. 45, No. 2 (April 1951), pp. 240-266, who regarded the principles and techniques concerning the median or equidistance line as of 'universal applicability', and independent of the width of the belts of waters claimed, including the contiguous zones and the continental shelf.

    See, however, Sang-Myon Rhee, 'Sea Boundary Delimitation Between States Before World War II', *AJIL*, Vol. 76, No. 3 (July 1982), pp. 555-588 at pp. 580-588.

    For technical aspects of constructing a median or equidistance line, see also Shalowitz, n. 148, Vol. I, pp. 230-235; Whiteman, n. 148, Vol. 4, pp. 328-333.

158. See, for example, Robert D. Hodgson and E. John Cooper, 'The Technical Delimitation of a Modern Equidistant Boundary', *Ocean Development and International Law*, Vol. 3, No. 4 (1976), pp. 361-388; Robert D. Hodgson and Robert W. Smith, 'Boundary Issues Created by Extended National Marine Jurisdiction', *Geographical Review*, published by the American Geographical Society, January 1979, pp. 423-433; 'Delimitation of Continental Shelf Jurisdiction Between States: The Effect of Physical Irregularities in the Natural Continental Shelf', Note by Gary R. Feulner, *Virginia Journal of International Law*, Vol. 17 (1976 – 77), pp. 77-105; *Limits to National Jurisdiction over the Sea*, University of Virginia Press, 1974; Robert W. Smith, 'A Geographical Primer to Maritime Boundary-Making', *Ocean Development and International Law*, Vol. 12 (1982), pp. 1-22. See also Document A/CONF.62/L.76 (18 August 1981), at n. 149 above.

159. A/CONF.62/L.76, n. 149, at p. 43.

160. *Ibid.*

161. Hodgson and Cooper, n. 158, p. 377.

162. Smith, n. 158, *Ocean Development and International Law*, Vol. 12 (1982), at p. 16.

163. N. 158, p. 374. See also p. 380. For details of map projections, see pp. 371-376.

164. *Ibid.*, pp. 378-379.

165. For details, see pp. 159-161 below.

166. A/CONF.62/L.76, n. 149, p. 44. For information on geodetic datums (horizontal and vertical) and the different spheroids, see Hodgson and Cooper, n. 158, pp. 369-70 and 377-78 and A/CONF.62/L.76 at p. 44. See also Smith, n. 158, pp. 17-20. For detailed information about the United States practice, see Shalowitz, n. 148, Vol. Two, 1964, Parts I and II.

167. Smith, n. 158, at pp. 19-20.

168. Articles 16, 75 and 84.

169. *New Directions in the Law of the Sea*, Vol. VIII, 1980, at p. 221 (Art. 1(2)).

PART TWO

Treaties and agreements

CHAPTER 5

Introduction

Treaties on the maritime boundary between States with opposite or adjacent coasts or with features of both, whether multilateral or bilateral, are a source of international law. Their study is of importance from many angles; their provisions will be a source of general or particular international law binding on the parties to those treaties; their provisions may be evidence of existing customary law, or may crystallise the emerging custom on the point, or may be the source of development of custom in that direction. They also constitute a significant part of State practice which may be relevant to the development of international law at a Plenipotentiary Conference, like the recently concluded Third UN Conference on the Law of the Sea. State practice may also be relevant in determining the applicable law among the parties either during negotiations for settling the maritime boundary between them or during the settlement of a dispute by arbitration or adjudication or by other peaceful means.

In this Part a total of 100 Agreements,[1] which have been collected from the available records, will be analysed.[2] Most of these Agreements are bilateral; a few are trilateral. The multilateral conventions have been covered in Part One or will be covered in Part Four.

A list of these Agreements is given in the Annex.[3]

The main sources of the texts of these Agreements have been the following:

(1)   The publication entitled *International Boundary Study, Series A, Limits in the Seas*, published by the US Department of State, Office of the Geographer, since January 1970. To date, 100 issues have been published in this series, which include the texts of 65 Agreements covered in this Part. These issues give the text of the Agreement in question, add an analysis thereof, and enclose a chart of the boundary, which is often plotted on the United States Naval Oceanographic Chart rather than on the chart used by the parties to the Agreement, which in some cases, because of the change in the scale of the chart, geodetic datum or other technical reasons, may lead to divergence in location of points, their geographical coordinates, and the computation of distances.

(2) *National Legislation and Treaties relating to the Law of the Sea, United Nations Legislative Series*, ST/LEG/SER.B/16(1974); ST/LEG/SER.B/18 (1976); and ST/LEG/SER.B/19(1980). Texts of registered Agreements are also published in the *United Nations Treaty Series*.

(3) Churchill, R., Nordquist, M. and Lay, H., *New Directions in the Law of the Sea, Documents*, Vol. I (1973), V (1977), and Nordquist, M., and Lay, H., Vol. VIII (1980).

(4) *International Legal Materials*, American Society of International Law, Volumes 1 to 22.

(5) Oda, Shigeru, *The International Law of the Ocean Development*, Basic Documents, Volumes I and II, Sijthoff/Leyden, 1972 and 1975 (updated).

In addition to the above sources, a few unpublished texts of Treaties and Agreements have also been relied upon for this Part.

The following preliminary observations on the source material used for this Part may be made at the outset:

(1) Although efforts have been made to collect the comprehensive source material up to the moment of writing, it may not be complete. For the lectures delivered on the subject by the author at The Hague Academy of International Law in August 1981, 75 Agreements were surveyed. To that list 25 Agreements have been added. Out of the total of 100 Agreements, 9 may not have yet been ratified, although they have been formally signed and no doubts have been expressed about any reservations relating thereto.

(2) The source material has been organised and analysed on a regional group basis rather than on a geographical group basis. The regional group classification has been used from the practice followed in the United Nations and in the Third United Nations Conference on the Law of the Sea. The regional groups are Asia, Africa, Latin America, Western Europe and Other States (WEO), including the USA, and Eastern Europe (Sociast) States. This has been done to make the study pragmatic and systematic rather than to examine or develop the concept of a regional custom. In fact not all Agreements could be divided into the aforementioned regional groups. Twenty-six Agreements out of the total of 100 had parties belonging to different regional groups. For example, the Agreements between the USA and Mexico, the USA and Cuba, the USA and Venezuela, the USSR and Turkey, the USSR and Norway, the USSR and Finland, Australia and Indonesia, Australia and Papua New Guinea, Italy and Tunisia, Italy and Yugoslavia, France and Mauritius, and France and St. Lucia, would appear to fall in the category of inter-regional Agreements. However, they have also been analysed along with the relevant regional groups.

These Agreements have the regional and inter-regional distribution shown in Table 1.

(3) Over three-fourths of the Agreements reflect the State practice after

Table 1.

Asia	28 + 8 = 36
Africa	4 + 2 = 6
Latin America	14 + 8 = 22
Western Europe and Others	25 + 3 = 28
Eastern Europe (Socialist)	3 + 5 = 8
Total	74 + 26 = 100

Table 2.

	Asia	Africa	Latin America	WEO	EE	Inter-regional	Total
Pre-1969 Agreements	6	1	4	7	3	3	24
Post-1969 Agreements	22	3	10	18	0	23	76

Table 3.

	Asia	Africa	Latin America	WEO	EE	Inter-regional	Total
Territorial sea boundary	2	1	0	5	1	3	12
Continental shelf boundary	23	3	14	20	2	22	84
Joint or common zone	3*					1**	4

* including one concerning the territorial sea (Kuwait – Saudi Arabia), and two concerning the continental shelf (Japan – Republic of Korea; Malaysia – Thailand).

** concerning the seabed beyond the territorial sea and 1,000 metre isobath (Saudi Arabia – Sudan).

1969, that is from about the time when the *Judgment in the North Sea Continental Shelf Cases* was delivered by the International Court of Justice. The distribution is shown in Table 2.

The earliest Agreements included in this study are the territorial sea boundary Agreement between Denmark and Sweden of 1932 and the Agreement between Trinidad & Tobago and Venezuela of 1942 concerning submarine areas in the Gulf of Paria.

(4) Of the 100 Agreements, 12 deal with the territorial sea boundary between the parties, whereas 84 establish the continental shelf boundary, including in an increasing number of cases the boundary in the fishery or exclusive economic zone. In addition, 4 Agreements establish joint or common zones, 3 in Asia and 1 in an inter-regional Agreement, without settling the maritime boundary. Their distribution is shown in Table 3.

(5)   Sixty-four of the 100 Agreements relate to States with opposite coasts whereas 36 Agreements relate to States with adjacent coasts. In three Agreements, the parties have adjacent coasts but the boundary is determined as if their coasts were opposite (Italy – Yugoslavia, 1968; Norway – Sweden, 1968; USSR – Turkey, 1978). The region-wise distribution of the Agreements is shown in Table 4.

Table 4.

	Asia	Africa	Latin America	WEO	EE	Inter-regional	Total
Opposite coasts	22	1	6	19	0	16	64
Adjacent coasts	6	3	8	7	3	9	36

(6)   In some regions, the Agreements related to a particular area or sub-region. Thus, among the 28 Agreements from the Asian region, 8 related to the Gulf, 9 to Agreements between India and the neighbouring States, 9 to Southeast Asia, and 2 between Japan and the Republic of Korea. Similarly, of the 14 Agreements in Latin America, 6 related to South America, 3 to Central America and 5 to the Caribbean Sea. Out of the 25 Agreements relating to WEO, 11 Agreements related to the North Sea, and 14 related to other areas. There was no special regional distribution for Agreements in Africa or Eastern Europe (Socialist) States.

Of the 26 inter-regional Agreements, the USA is party to 6, the USSR and France to 5 each, Australia to 4, Italy to 2, the Netherlands to 1, 1 Agreement is between Sweden and the GDR, 1 Agreement is between the FRG and the GDR, and 1 Agreement is between Saudi Arabia and Sudan. Five of these 26 Agreements relate to the Caribbean Sea, 3 to the South Pacific, and the others relate to the Baltic Sea, the Mediterreanean, the Indian Ocean, the Gulf of Mexico, the Red Sea, and other areas.

A brief analysis will now be made of these Agreements region-wise in the following chapters, and their main features will be summed up accordingly. The broad conclusions of the study of State practice as a whole will be attempted towards the end of this Part.

Notes

1. Robert W. Smith has calculated that by June 1, 1982, out of 376 potential global maritime boundaries 'approximately 90, or 23.9 percent, have been negotiated; of these 69 (18.3 percent) have actually entered into force and the remaining 21 await ratification. Over 285 boundaries have yet to be negotiated'. See his article, 'A Geographical Primer to Maritime-

Boundary Making', *Ocean Development and International Law*, Vol. 12 (1982), p. 3. See also Table 1 on p. 4, where he has tabulated maritime boundaries region-wise into 13 regions. The highest number of potential boundaries are in the Caribbean (81), Indian Ocean and Periphery (57), Western and Central Pacific (51), Mediterranean and Black Seas (43), Southeast Atlantic (36), and East Asian Seas (30).

Earlier Smith had calculated as follows: 'There may be approximately 331 potential maritime boundaries required by a universal claim to 200-nautical mile zones. The United States may have to negotiate approximately thirty maritime boundaries that will account for approximately 10 percent of the total maritime boundaries in the world.' Robert W. Smith, 'The Maritime Boundaries of the United States', *The Geographical Review*, Vol. 71, No. 4 (October 1981), pp. 395-410 at p. 397. See also Robert D. Hodgson and Robert W. Smith, 'Boundary Issues Created by Extended National Jurisdiction', *The Geographical Review*, January 1979, at pp. 426-427.

2. The State practice covered in this Part relates to Agreements concluded after the Second World War, except the Agreement between the UK (Trininad and Tobago) and Venezuela concerning the Gulf of Paria, 1942, and the Agreement between Denmark and Sweden, 1932.

For a comprehensive review of State practice between 1648 and 1939, including judicial and arbitral decisions, treatment in conferences and research institutions, and the views of experts and publicists, see Sang-Myon Rhee, 'Sea Boundary Delimitation Between States Before World War II', *AJIL*, Vol. 76, No. 3 (July 1982), pp. 555-588.

3. See Annex I.

CHAPTER 6

Asian Agreements

Twenty-eight Agreements between Asian States will be surveyed in this Chapter.[4] Eight of these relate to the countries around the Gulf; 9 were concluded between India and the neighbouring States; 9 relate to the South-East Asian region; and 2 were Agreements between Japan and the Republic of Korea. Another set of 8 inter-regional Agreements comprising 1 Agreement between Saudi Arabia and Sudan relating to the Red Sea, 4 Agreements between Indonesia, Papua New Guinea and Australia, and 3 relating to the South Pacific will also be covered in the Chapter.[5]

The main features of these Agreements may be dealt with hereunder.

A. The Gulf

The Gulf is an enclosed sea which opens out into the Gulf of Oman and the Arabian Sea through the Strait of Hormuz. The depth of water in the Gulf is less than 50 fathoms. At its widest point it is 150 nautical miles along the meridian; at the Strait of Hormuz it is 28 nautical miles wide. The Gulf as a whole is located in the northwest and southeast direction and the coastline around it has been computed to be around 2300 nautical miles long. There are a number of islands, and a few are located near the middle. Controversies have existed and still exist concerning claims to sovereignty over some islands. Some of these have been resolved in the maritime boundary Agreements reviewed in this Chapter. The Gulf has resources of oil and gas, apart from the living resources. The northern and northwestern side of the Gulf belongs to Iran; the rest of the Gulf coast belongs to Iraq, Kuwait, Saudi Arabia, Bahrain, Qatar, the UAE and Oman.

Between 1958 and 1974, seven Agreements on the continental shelf boundary, and one concerning a joint zone, were concluded.

Of these 8 Agreements, Iran was party to five. Two Agreements were between Bahrain and Saudi Arabia, 1958 and Abu Dhabi and Qatar, 1969. One Agreement was between Kuwait and Saudi Arabia, 1965. Agreements among other States surrounding the Gulf, such as between Iran and its neighbouring States, have yet to be concluded.[6]

Six out of the 8 Agreements concerning the boundary in the Gulf are between States with opposite coasts, two are between States with adjacent coasts (Abu Dhabi – Qatar, 1969; Kuwait – Saudi Arabia, 1965).

The first seven Agreements relate to the continental shelf boundary. None of the States in question are parties to the Convention on the Continental Shelf, 1958. Therefore, their practice may indicate evidence of customary law on the point.

As to the applicable principles, the Agreement between Bahrain and Saudi Arabia, 1958, mentioned the 'middle' or the median line. In another Agreement, reference was made to the determination of the boundary 'in a just and accurate manner' (Iran – Saudi Arabia, 1968). Similarly, in four other Agreements, reference was made to establishing the boundary line in a 'just, equitable and precise manner' (Iran – Qatar, 1969; Iran – Bahrain, 1971; Iran – Oman, 1974; Iran – UAE, 1974). In the Agreement between Qatar and Abu Dhabi, 1969, no reference was made to the principle followed.

In general, the median line was followed for delimiting the boundary. The boundary line was, however, modified in relation to the solution of the islands question. The special feature of the Agreements relating to the Gulf is the treatment of islands. In one Agreement, all the islands on either side were ignored (Iran – Qatar, 1969). In another Agreement, islands were ignored in some sectors, but those located in the middle were used to establish points for the boundary line (Bahrain – Saudi Arabia, 1958). In one Agreement, an island located near the median line was given a territorial sea arc of 3 nautical miles and the boundary line was adjusted accordingly (Abu Dhabi – Qatar, 1969 – the island of Dayyinah was recognised to be part of the territory of Abu Dhabi. The Agreement also recognised that the islands of Al Ashat and Shara'iwah were part of the territory of Qatar). In another Agreement, an island was given a 12-mile territorial sea, which constituted points 9 and 10 on the boundary line (Iran – Oman, 1974).

In another Agreement (Iran – Saudi Arabia, 1968), which replaced the earlier unratified Agreement of 1965, two islands were located near the boundary line, namely, Farsi and Al-Arabiya. Settling the controversy, sovereignty of Iran over Farsi and of Saudi Arabia over Al-Arabiya was recognised. The main boundary line in this area was adjusted by giving to each island an arc of 12 nautical miles territorial sea, establishing a 'local' median line between them, and moving the main boundary line along these arcs on either side of the 'local' median line, respectively. Again, an Iranian island, namely Kharg, located about 17 nautical miles from its coast, was given half-effect in delimiting the boundary line between Iran and Saudi Arabia in the northern sector.

The other special feature of the Gulf Agreements related to the treatment of known or expected petroleum and gas resources. In the Agreement between Qatar and Abu Dhabi, 1969, a boundary point (point B) was located on a known petroleum field, Al Banduq, which was to be under Abu Dhabi's jurisdiction but revenues from which were to be equally shared by the parties. In the Agreement between Bahrain and Saudi Arabia, 1958, although a specified area (Fasht Abu Safah Hexagon) was exclusively under the sovereignty and administration of Saudi Arabia, half of the net revenues from the exploitation of its resources were to be given to the other party, namely, Bahrain.

As for the clause on unity of resources extending across the boundary line, four out of seven Agreements contained such clauses, providing that in such circumstances both parties should use their best endeavours to reach agreement as to the manner in which the operations on both sides of the boundary line could be coordinated or unitised. In one Agreement it was provided that no drilling would take place within 500 metres of its side of the boundary line, including directional drilling from outside that limit (Iran – Saudi Arabia, 1968). In four Agreements the prohibition on drilling was restricted to 125 metres from the boundary line (Iran – Qatar, 1969; Iran – Bahrain, 1971; Iran – Oman, 1974; Iran – UAE, 1974).

A typical clause read as follows:

If any single geological petroleum structure or petroleum field, or any single geological structure or field of any other mineral extends across the boundary line set out in Article 1 of this Agreement and the part of such structure or field which is situated on one side of that boundary line could be exploited wholly or in part by directional drilling from the other side of the boundary line then:

(a) No well shall be drilled on either side of the boundary line as set out in Article 1 so that any producing section thereof is less than 125 metres from the said boundary line except by mutual agreement between the two contracting Parties.

(b) If the circumstances considered in this Article shall arise both Parties hereto shall use their best endeavours to reach agreement as to the manner in which the operations on both sides of the boundary line could be coordinated or unitized.[7]

Commenting on the inter-relationship of these aspects, namely, the effect given to islands, the location of known petroleum resources and the prohibition on drilling in fields straddling across the boundary, S.H. Amin, analysing the Iran – Saudi Arabia Agreement of 1968, states as follows:

The issues related to the effects of islands on continental shelf boundaries, including the case of Kharg, are of great significance. Kharg received a partial effect. The legal basis for such an arrangement was the concept of 'equitable division of the oil in place'. Having cautiously estimated the disputed oil deposits, Iran and Saudi Arabia agreed by the 1968 Agreement to draw a boundary line which would divide the deposits into two equal parts. The prevailing boundary is half-way between the lines constructed with Kharg as national base points and lines otherwise constructed. Furthermore, to avoid the capture problem, both parties agreed not to drill within 500 metres of each side of the boundary line.[8]

The Gulf Agreements had a short text and were written in simple language. The boundary was described in relation to terminal and turning points and their geographical coordinates were indicated. These points were to be joined by geodetic lines. Direction of the boundary was also indicated in terms of the azimuth angle, where necessary.

The sample of Gulf Agreements will thus indicate that although the boundary was generally a median line, it was modified where considerations of fairness and equity so required it. The special circumstances necessitating such modification related to the position of islands or the location of known resources.

By the eighth Agreement in the Gulf, namely, the Agreement between Kuwait and Saudi Arabia, 1965, the overland Neutral Zone, over which the two States had joint sovereignty, was partitioned into two equal zones which were to be annexed by either State as part of its sovereign territory. The equal rights of the parties to the natural resources (oil, etc.) of the whole of the Partitioned Zone were, however, to continue. The same dual regime was to continue in the respective territorial waters adjoining the Partitioned Zone, which was restricted for the purposes of exploiting the natural resources to not more than six marine miles. Article VII of the Agreement provided that 'the two Contracting Parties shall agree to determine the boundary line which divides the territorial waters which adjoin the Partitioned Zone'. The northern boundary of the submerged area adjoining the Partitioned Zone was to be delineated 'as if the Zone has not been partitioned and without regard to the provisions of this Agreement' (Article VIII). Beyond the aforesaid six miles also, the parties were to exercise their equal rights in the submerged area 'by means of joint exploitation, unless the two Parties agree otherwise' (Article VIII).

Thus a joint maritime zone, adjoining the Partitioned Zone, for exploiting its natural resources was established by the 1965 Agreement. Whether the northern boundary of the submerged area, and the boundary dividing the respective territorial waters for purposes other than the exploitation of the natural resources, which were to be determined later on, have since been agreed to and delimited is not known. The regime of the joint maritime zone for the exploitation of the natural resources will however not be affected by the alignment of the maritime boundary.[9]

B. India and the neighbouring States

India has seven neighbouring States for maritime boundary purposes, namely, Pakistan, Maldives, Sri Lanka, Bangladesh, Burma, Thailand and Indonesia. With five of them, the coasts are opposite, namely, Maldives, Sri Lanka, Burma, Thailand and Indonesia, although in some respects the coasts appear to be adjacent. The other two States are located on the same coast adjacent to India, namely, Pakistan and Bangladesh.

India has between 1974 and 1979 concluded nine Agreements with four of its neighbours, namely, Sri Lanka, Maldives, Indonesia and Thailand. The boundary negotiations with Burma commened in March 1976 and have not yet been concluded. The boundary negotiations with Bangladesh commenced in October 1974 and have also not yet been concluded. Maritime boundary talks with Pakistan have not yet commenced.

Although it is still an incomplete story, it may be of interest to refer to and briefly analyse the nine Agreements concluded by India with its neighbouring States.

These Agreements were concluded between the States concerned in stages. The first Agreement between India and Sri Lanka was concluded in 1974 and related to the boundary in the historic waters of the Palk's Bay. In 1976, the boundary line was extended both into the Gulf of Manaar and into the Bay of Bengal. Later during the same year, an Agreement between India, Sri Lanka and Maldives fixed the trijunction point between the three countries which, by a strange and perhaps unique coincidence, was located at a distance of about 200 nautical miles from the Indian, Sri Lanka and Maldives coasts. Thereafter, a third Agreement between India and Sri Lanka extended the terminal point of the boundary in the Gulf of Manaar to the trijunction point between India, Sri Lanka and Maldives.

Towards the end of December 1976, an Agreement between India and Maldives on the maritime boundary was also signed in New Delhi.

Similarly, with Indonesia, the first Agreement which was concluded in 1974 settled the boundary between Great Nicobar (India) and Sumatra (Indonesia). The distance between the two is about 90 nautical miles. The boundary line settled by this Agreement extended to about 48 nautical miles. In 1977, this boundary line was extended both into the Indian Ocean and into the Andaman Sea by another Agreement.

In 1977, the boundary between India and Thailand in the Andaman Sea was negotiated, and an Agreement was signed in June 1978 which entered into force in December 1978.

In February 1978, the trijunction point between India, Indonesia and Thailand was settled at official level in Jakarta. The Agreement was signed in June 1978 and came into force in March 1979.

Thus, by early 1979, India's boundary with Sri Lanka, the Maldives, Indonesia and Thailand was in large measure concluded. All these Agreements have entered into force.

The negotiations with Sri Lanka were prolonged because of two special questions, namely, (i) the controversy concerning ownership of and sovereignty over the island of Kachchativu in the Palk's Bay, and (ii) Sri Lanka's claim of historic fishing rights in the Wadge Bank located south of Cape Comorin. The first question was resolved in the 1974 Agreement by developing a package solution which comprised: (a) Sri Lanka's sovereignty over the island, (b) the right of Indian fishermen and pilgrims to visit Kachchativu as hitherto, without the requirement of travel documents or visas for these purposes, and (c) the boundary line in the Palk's Bay would run one mile from the island of Kachchativu. The vessels of India and Sri Lanka would also enjoy in each other's waters such rights as they have traditionally enjoyed therein.

On the second question, namely, the Wadge Bank, the 1976 Agreement between India and Sri Lanka acknowledged each other's sovereign rights and exclusive jurisdiction over its respective continental shelf and the exclusive economic zone falling on its own side of the boundary. The Wadge Bank, being located within India's exclusive economic zone and partly within its territorial sea, was thus acknowledged to be under India's sovereign rights and exclusive jurisdiction. Letters were, however, exchanged along with the Agreement on March 23, 1976, which allowed Sri Lanka to fish in the Wadge Bank for a period of three years from the date of establishment by India of its exclusive economic zone. This was done by India, as well as by Sri Lanka, on January 15, 1977. After the expiry of three years therefrom, it was agreed in these letters that the Government of India will provide annually to Sri Lanka, at their request, 2,000 tonnes of fish of a quality and species and at a price to be mutually agreed upon between the two Governments. This supply was to be for a period of five years. The boundary line between India and Sri Lanka followed the median line, except as adjusted in the Palk's Bay in relation to the settlement on the question of the island of Kachchativu.

Another small adjustment was made in the Andaman Sea in the Agreement between India and Thailand of 1978 to simplify the boundary line for convenience to navigation.

Bearing in mind the aforementioned special features, the main features of the Agreements concluded between India and its neighbouring States until now may be summarised as follows:

(1) There is some variation in the Agreements regarding the title. Thus the 1974 Agreement between India and Sri Lanka refers to 'the boundary in historic waters' between the two countries. The 1976 Agreements between India and Sri Lanka and between India and the Maldives refer to 'maritime boundary', thereby implying that the boundary settled therein will apply not only to the respec-

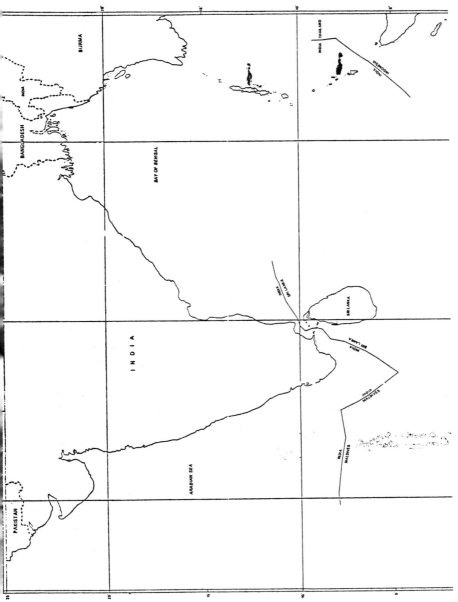

Chart 1. India and its neighbouring States

81

tive continental shelf but also to the respective exclusive economic zone, and where applicable to the territorial sea also. The Agreements between India and Indonesia of 1974 and 1977 refer to 'continental shelf boundary'. The Agreement between India and Thailand of 1978 refers to 'seabed boundary'. It was, however, agreed both with Indonesia and with Thailand that when they established their own exclusive economic zone, respectively, the boundary settled by these Agreements would also apply to the respective exclusive economic zone. Thailand established its exclusive economic zone on February 23, 1981. Indonesia established its exclusive economic zone on March 21, 1980.

(2)   In the Agreements concluded between India and Sri Lanka in 1974 and 1976 and India and Maldives in 1976, a comprehensive provision was included which related to mutual recognition of sovereignty over islands falling on the respective side of the boundary, recognition of sovereign rights and exclusive jurisdiction over the respective maritime zones, and rights relating to navigation. The text in Article IV of the Agreement betwee India and Maldives reads as follows:

(1)   Each Party shall have sovereignty over all islands falling on its side of the aforesaid boundary, as well as over the territorial waters and the air space above them.

(2)   Each Party shall have sovereign rights and exclusive jurisdiction over the continental shelf and the exclusive economic zone as well as over their resources, whether living or non-living, falling on its own side of the aforesaid boundary.

(3)   Each Party shall respect rights of navigation through its territorial sea and the exclusive economic zone in accordance with its laws and regulations and the rules of international law.

(3)   Although the parties did discuss between themselves the applicable principles before drawing the boundary, no reference has been made in any of the Agreements to these principles. The boundary has been described with reference to points, whose positions by latitudes and longitudes have been indicated in the Agreement in question. These points will be joined by shortest straight lines, or by 'arcs of great circles', as provided in the Agreements between India and Sri Lanka, 1974 and 1976. The actual location at sea and on the seabed of these positions will be determined by a method to be mutually agreed upon between the competent authorities of the parties.

Barring the adjustment made in the Palk's Bay due to the settlement of the question of Kachchativu, and in a minor way in the Andaman Sea between India and Thailand, the boundary line in all other cases has been drawn on the basis of the median line between the opposite coasts or, where the boundary extends laterally into the sea, the equidistance line from the adjoining coasts of the two countries.

India not yet having notified their baselines, in no Agreement were baselines used for establishing the turning points of the boundary line. These turning points were determined with reference to the relevant controlling points on the respective coast, as agreed to between the technical officers of the parties concerned. The only exception to this procedure was the 1974 Agreement between India and Sri Lanka in the historic waters of the Palk's Bay, where the 1921 unratified fishing boundary line was appropriately adjusted to settle the boundary.

(4) All Agreements contained a clause requiring cooperative handling of exploitation of any resource of a geological, petroleum, gas or natural field or other deposit, which extended across the boundary. This ensured the unity of the resource and the development of cooperative and equitable procedures for its exploitation and for the distribution of the proceeds derived therefrom.

(5) Any disputes relating to the interpretation or implementation of the Agreements were to be settled peacefully by consultation or negotiation between the parties.

(6) The Agreements were short and simple in language. They were subject to ratification by the parties.

Chart 1 indicates the maritime boundary settled in these Agreements.

C. Southeast Asia

Nine of the Asian Agreements related to Southeast Asia, six of which related to the Straits of Malacca and the Andaman Sea, the seventh and eighth were the Agreements between Malaysia and Thailand in the Gulf of Thailand, and the ninth was the Agreement between Burma and Thailand.

Two of the six Agreements concerning the Straits of Malacca related to the territorial sea boundary (Indonesia – Malaysia, 1970; Indonesia – Singapore, 1973), the other four related to the continental shelf boundary. In both cases, the baselines were used to determine the boundary. Generally, the median line was followed between the baselines, except where modified by negotiation. The applicable principle was not mentioned in any Agreemnt. The Agreements were short and simple. They specified the turning and terminal points with their geographical coordinates. These points were to be joined by straight lines to constitute the boundary. All the Agreements included a clause on unity of resource extending across the boundary line, a common phrase being that 'the two Governments shall seek to reach agreement as to the manner in which the structure shall be most effectively exploited'. In the territorial sea boundary between Singapore and Indonesia, the relevant islands and low-tide elevations were used for base points.

An interesting Agreement in this sample was the Agreement between Indonesia, Malaysia and Thailand, signed on December 21, 1971. This Agreement settled the common point between the three countries in the Strait of Malacca, extended the Indonesia – Malaysia continental-shelf boundary settled in the Agreement of 1969 to a common point (trijunction point between Indonesia, Malaysia and Thailand), settled the Malaysia – Thailand continental-shelf boundary as adjacent States, and settled the Indonesia – Thailand continental-shelf boundary in the Strait of Malacca and the Andaman Sea concerning which an Agreement had alredy been signed on December 17, 1971. This last-mentioned boundary line was further extended up to a point near the trijunction point between Indonesia, India and Thailand by an Agreement concluded between Indonesia and Thailand on December 11, 1975.

Although generally the median line was followed in these Agreements, in the determination of (a) the common point between Indonesia, Malaysia and Thailand in December 1971, (b) the lateral continental shelf boundary between Malaysia and Thailand, and (c) the extended continental shelf boundary line between Indonesia and Thailand between 1971 and 1975, a negotiated line was settled as the boundary line. The special circumstances appear to be the geomorphological features obtaining in the area. No reference was made in these Agreements to any special treatment of islands.

The Gulf of Thailand

Two Agreements were concluded between Malaysia and Thailand in the Gulf of Thailand in the form of Memorandums of Understanding, shown in Table 5.

Table 5.

	Date of signature	Date of entry into force
1. Memorandum of Understanding between Malaysia and the Kingdom of Thailand on the Delimitation of the Continental Shelf Boundary Between the Two Countries in the Gulf of Thailand	October 24, 1979	July 15, 1982
2. Memorandum of Understanding between the Kingdom of Thailand and Malaysia on the Establishment of Joint Authority for the Exploitation of the Reserves of the Seabed in a Defined Area of the Continental Shelf of the Two Countries in the Gulf of Thailand	February 21, 1979	July 15, 1982

By the first Agreement, a short continental shelf boundary was settled between the two adjacent countries in the Gulf of Thailand comprising straight lines joining three points whose geographical coordinates were specified therein. This boundary followed the equidistance line, although the principle followed was not stated in the Agreement. The Agreement contained a clause concerning the exploitation of a resource which extends across the boundary line.

84

Beyond the agreed line, there were differences between the two countries and opposite claims were advanced by them. In the preamble to the second Agreement,[10] the two Governments recognised that 'it is in the best interest of the two countries to exploit the resources of the seabed in the overlapping area as soon as possible', and that 'such activities can be carried out jointly through mutual cooperation'. Accordingly, the area comprising the overlapping claims made by the two countries was defined with reference to geographical coordinates (Article I). For the exploration and exploitation of the non-living resources of the seabed and sub-soil in the overlapping area, a 'Malaysia – Thailand Joint Authority' was established for a period of 50 years from the date the Agreement came into force (Article III).[11]

In the meantime, the parties agreed to continue to resolve the problem of delimitation of the continental shelf boundary between them (Article II). If they settled this boundary prior to the expiry of the said 50-year period, the Joint Authority would be would up and all its assets and liabilities would be equally shared and borne by both parties. However, a new arrangement may also be concluded between them if they so decide (Article VI). If, however, no satisfactory solution was found to the question of delimitation of the boundary of the continental shelf within the said 50-year period, the existing arrangements would continue after the expiry of that period (Article VI).

The arrangements for the joint exploitation of the overlapping area were thus without prejudice to the question of delimitation. The two parties would also continue to exercise their rights in the overlapping area in matters of fishing, navigation, research, pollution control and other matters. The overlapping area was however divided into two zones for the purposes of the exercise of criminal jurisdiction. This division also appeared to be on a half-and-half basis, although the dividing line itself would not constitute the continental shelf boundary between the two countries. The geographical coordinates of the zone of criminal jurisdiction of Malaysia and Thailand, respectively, were also specified in the Agreement (Article V).

The second Agreement also contained a provision concerning the resources extending across the lines constituting the joint development area, similar to the provisions in the first Agreement.

The second Agreement constitutes a unique example of interim or provisional arrangements as well as of cooperation between the two neighbouring countries in exploiting the resources of an area, the precise exclusive jurisdiction relating to which is a matter of controversy. It followed in some respects the precedent of the Japan – Republic of Korea Agreement of 13 January 1974, referred to in the next section.

Articles 74(3) and 83(3) of the United Nations Convention on the Law of the Sea, 1982, do encourage the States concerned, in a spirit of understanding and cooperation, to make every effort to enter into provisional arrangements of a practical nature, pending agreement on the delimitation of the exclusive economic zone or the continental shelf, as the case may be. During this transitional period, the States concerned shall not jeopardise or hamper the reaching of the final Agreement. Such provisional arrangements shall also be without prejudice to the final delimitation.

The history of these provisions shows that during their crystallisation, views were expressed that such provisional arrangements should be transitional or shortlived and that such arrangements should not constitute a moratorium on either party for exclusively exploiting the resources of the overlapping area.

The second Malaysia – Thailand Agreement, while coming within the scope of the principles embodied in the above-mentioned Articles of the UN Convention, would provide an example of unique cooperation of a practical nature. Its smooth working may therefore be of interest to other countries having similar problems.

It may also be recalled that the International Court of Justice in its Judgment in the *North Sea Continental Shelf* cases, 1969, had, while indicating the principles and the rules of international law applicable to the delimitation of the continental shelf boundary of States, clearly specified that 'if . . . the delimitation leaves to the Parties areas that overlap, these are to be divided between them in agreed proportions or, failing agreement, equally, unless they decide on a regime of joint jurisdiction, user, or exploitation for the zones of overlap or any part of them.'[12]

The second Agreement between Malaysia and Thailand would thus also provide an example of the application of the principle set out by the International Court of Justice in 1969.

Agreement between Burma and Thailand

An Agreement on the delimitation of the maritime boundary between Burma and Thailand in the Andaman Sea was signed on July 25, 1980, and entered into force on April 12, 1982, on ratification. In the preamble, the Agreement refers to the desire of the parties to establish the maritime boundary between them in the Andaman Sea, and to settle permanently the limits of the areas within which the respective Governments shall exercise sovereignty and sovereign rights. Article 1 of the Agreement states that the maritime boundary between Burma and Thailand in the Andaman Sea is an equidistance line formed by a series of straight lines connecting 9 points, the geographical coordinates of which have been specified therein. Points 1 to 5 constitute the territorial sea boundary, points 5 to 9 constitute the continental shelf boundary. It is however added that 'in the event that Thailand establishes her exclusive economic zone, this same line shall also constitute the boundary between the exclusive economic zone of

Burma and the exclusive economic zone of Thailand'.[13] The extension of the boundary from point 9 up to the maritime boundary trijunction point between Burma, Thailand and India will be the subject of a subsequent Agreement.

The Agreement is a short one and does not contain a clause on the exploitation of a resource extending across the boundary line.

D. Other Agreements

Japan and the Republic of Korea

Finally, the Asian sample included two Agreements concluded between Japan and the Republic of Korea on January 30, 1974. The first related to the continental shelf boundary in the northern part of the sea between them, the second related to the establishment of a Joint Development Zone in the southern part of the continental shelf adjacent to the two countries.[14]

The parties have opposite coasts. The first Agreement established a 35-point boundary line which follows the median line except at one point (point 3) where the boundary appears to be closer to the Republic of Korea than to Japan. The Takeshima island to the north, title to which was disputed between the parties, was ignored.

The second Agreement did not establish the boundary line. In fact it is stated to be without prejudice to the question of sovereign rights over the area of the Joint Development Zone or to the question of the delimitation of the continental shelf (Article XXVIII). This Agreement established a Joint Development Zone, the initiative for which was taken by the Republic of Korea in September 1977.[15] The area of the zone is about 24,092 square nautical miles, most of which appears to be on the Japanese side of the median line between Japan and the Republic of Korea and Japan and China.[16] This is to be jointly exploited by concessionaires from both parties.

The second Agreement contained detailed provisions about the joint exploration and exploitation of the zone and its subzones, and referred to the appointment of concessionaires by either party, the appointment of the operator and the conclusion of the operating agreement, work requirements, relinquishment of the area, liability for compensation, 50:50 share of resources and of costs, and the application of the laws and regulations of the parties. The Zone was not divided for the purpose of application of the respective criminal jurisdiction.

A detailed clause on the unity of resource was included which required consultation between the concessionaires to agree on the most effective method of exploiting the structure or field, failing which it was to be resolved by consultations between the two parties (Article XXIII). A Joint Commission has been established to ensure the cooperative and effective implementation of the Agreement. The settlement of disputes will initially be through diplomatic channels, failing which by resort to compulsory arbitration. The arbitration board may in urgent cases issue a provisional order. The arbitral award will be binding on the parties. The Agreement is valid for 50 years and shall continue beyond that period, unless it is terminated, by a 3-year notice, either at the end of the initial 50-year period or at any time thereafter (Artcile XXXI).

The People's Republic of China protested to Japan about the signing and ratification of the second Agreement.[17]

In the Asian sample of 28 Agreements, the principle followed has generally been that of the median or equidistance line. The median line has been modified or a negotiated line has been agreed to in some cases where special circumstances so required it. The special circumstances included the position of islands (the Gulf Agreements) and geomorphology (Agreements in the Straits of Malacca and the Andaman Sea). In two cases (Japan – Republic of Korea, 1974; Malaysia – Thailand, 1980), long-term provisional arrangements were made for a joint development zone or area, without prejudice to the conclusion of an Agreement on maritime boundary. The Agreement between Kuwait and Saudi Arabia, 1965, established a 6-mile joint maritime zone adjacent to the Partitioned Zone. The inclusion of a clause on unity of resource extending across the boundary line, which should be exploited by mutual consultation, was a common feature of the Asian Agreements.

E. Inter-regional Agreements

Agreement between Sudan and Saudi Arabia

By the Agreement between Sudan and Saudi Arabia relating to the resources of the Red Sea in the Common Zone, which was signed on May 16, 1974, and which entered into force on August 26, 1974, the two Governments recognised each other's exclusive sovereign rights in the area of the seabed adjoining their respective coasts up to the 1,000-metre isobath, and established a Common Zone comprising the seabed of the Red Sea between the exclusive sovereign rights areas. Article V provided that

> The two Governments have equal sovereign rights in all the natural resources of the Common Zone, which rights are exclusive to them. No part of the territorial sea of either Government shall be included in the Common Zone.

A Joint Commission, representative of the two Governments, was established to facilitate the exploitation of the natural resources of the Common Zone. The

Joint Commission shall be charged with the function, *inter alia*, 'to establish, delimit and demarcate the boundaries of the Common Zone' (Article VII(a)).

Agreements between Indonesia, Papua New Guinea and Australia

Four Agreements were concluded between Indonesia, Papua New Guinea and Australia between 1971 and 1978. In form, they may be described as inter-regional Agreements, since one party to them was Australia. However, they relate to the common sea or seabed between them. They also include the boundary between Indonesia and Papua New Guinea, which has continued to be in force after the attainment of independence by Papua New Guinea on September 16, 1975.

These four Agreements may be summarised as follows:

(1)   The first Agreement was concluded between Indonesia and Australia on May 18, 1971, which came into force on November 8, 1973. It defined the boundary in the Arafura Sea between points A-1 and A-12 following the median line. The line was extended towards the land boundary up to point B-1. The line joining points A3-A2-A1-B1 constitutes the southern boundary between Indonesia and Papua New Guinea. In addition, the boundary between Indonesia and Papua New Guinea on the northern coast was also settled by this Agreement to consist of 2 points, namely C-1 and C-2, being at a distance of about 27 nautical miles. The line was drawn on the basis of the principle of equidistance.

(2)   In October 1972 another Agreement was concluded between Indonesia and Australia supplementary to the Agreement of 1971. It came into force on November 8, 1973, that is, along with the 1971 Agreement. By this Agreement the boundary between Indonesia and Australia in the area of the Timor and Arafura Seas was extended and settled. The extension consists of two parts, namely, one, the boundary line joining points A-12 of the 1971 Agreement to A-16, and two, the boundary line joining points A-17 to A-25. The gap between points A-16 and A-17 south of Timor has been left undemarcated.

The extension of the boundary line in these two segments does not follow the median line. The boundary line has been settled between the true median line and the deepest channel in the sea near the Indonesian coast. The settlement of the boundary line is thus negotiated, the relevant factors being the geomorphological features of the seabed favouring Australia and the petroleum concessions already awarded by Australia. The Agreement also contains a provision enabling the existing holder of a permit or licence granted by Australia in the area of the seabed which lies to the north of the boundary line to apply within nine months to Indonesia for an appropriate production-sharing contract in accordance with Indonesian law.

The boundary in the two Agreements is called the seabed boundary, although the term seabed has been understood to imply the seabed and the subsoil and is equivalent to the continental shelf. Both Agreements also include a clause on the exploitation of the resources located across the boundary line.

(3) The third Agreement was signed between Indonesia and Australia on 12 February, 1973, which came into force on November 26, 1974. This Agreement settled the boundary between Indonesia and Papua New Guinea, which was still the trust territory of Australia. By this Agreement, the boundary in the southern coast of Indonesia and Papua New Guinea was extended from point B-1, settled in the 1971 Agreement, to points B-2 and B-3, B-3 being the intersection of the land boundary line with the mean low-water line on the southern coast of the island of Irian. A provision was made for the adjustment of this point, if it becomes necessary. The Agreement also confirmed the boundary between Indonesia and Papua New Guina as settled in the 1971 Agreement. The entire boundary has been drawn on the basis of equidistance. Indonesia and Papua New Guinea are adjacent States.

(4) The fourth Agreement was a Treaty concluded between Australia and Papua New Guinea after Papua New Guinea became independent on September 15, 1975. The Treaty was signed on December 18, 1978, by the Prime Ministers and Foreign Ministers of the two States. It has yet to be ratified. The Treaty is a comprehensive one and consists of 32 Articles and 9 Annexes. It deals with the question of sovereignty over islands, maritime boundaries concerning the respective continental shelf and the fishery zone, establishment of a Protected Zone for protecting traditional rights and for regulating commercial fishing by both parties, and related matters. Point A-3 settled in the 1971 Agreement between Indonesia and Australia has been made the starting point of the boundary between Australia and Papua New Guinea. In other words, the boundary between Papua New Guinea and Indonesia will, in the southern sector, comprise the line joining points A-3, A-2, A-1, B-1, B-2 and B-3.

The main features of the Treaty between Australia and Papua New Guinea may be summarised as follows:

The Treaty lists 15 Australian islands which lie to the north of the seabed jurisdiction line. Australia's sovereignty over these islands, and Papua New Guinea's sovereignty over 3 specific islands, namely, Kawa Island, Mata Kawa Island and Kussa Island, have been mutually recognised (Article 2). These islands have been given a 3-mile territorial sea around them, except in the area of overlap in the north close to the mainland of Papua New Guinea where the territorial sea boundary follows the median line.

The Treaty establishes the seabed jurisdiction line in the area between the two countries extending to approximately 1200 miles. The seabed boundary line is a modified median line.

In the Torres Strait, the Treaty establishes a fisheries jurisdiction line, which

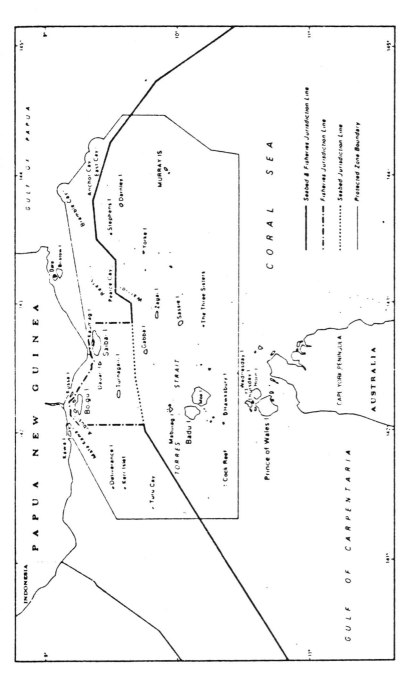

Chart 2. Central Torres Strait area

Source: H. Burmester, 'The Torres Strait Treaty: Ocean Boundary Delimitation by Agreement', *AJIL*, April 1982, at p. 335. (published with permission)

diverges from the seabed boundary line and skirts the inhabited and other Australian islands north of the seabed jurisdiction line. Thus there are two separate boundary lines in this area, one for seabed jurisdiction and the other for fisheries jurisdiction (Article 4(2)). The other Australian islands outside the dual line area are enclaves, with a 3-mile territorial sea around them, north of the seabed jurisdiction line on the Papua New Guinea side. The residual jurisdiction in the Torres Strait, such as in matters concerning marine pollution, marine scientific research, and production of energy from water, shall be settled by mutual agreement (Article 4(3)).

The Treaty establishes a Protected Zone cutting across the fishery and seabed jurisdiction lines for protecting the rights of traditional fishing and free movement of traditional inhabitants (Article 10), and for regulating the exploitaton and sharing of commercial fisheries (Articles 20-28). For the exploitation of commercial fisheries, the allowable catch is to be determined jointly and the share of the party in the zone within its own jurisdiction, including the 3-mile territorial sea, will be 75% as against 25% for the other party, whereas in the territorial sea around the uninhabited Australian islands north of the seabed jurisdiction line, it will be 50:50 (Article 23). Enforcement of the provisions of the Treaty concerning the Protected Zone remains with the State of nationality of the ships or persons. A Joint Advisory Council has been established with advisory functions to promote cooperation. The Treaty prohibits mining or drilling for petroleum and gas or for other mineral resources of the Protected Zone for a period of 10 years from the date of its entry into force (Article 15), thereby emphasising concentration on exploitation of the living resources of the Zone. The Treaty also provides for the freedoms of navigation and overflight on and over the waters of the Protected Zone.

The special features of this Treaty thus relate to the establishment of two boundary lines in the Torres Strait, one for the seabed and subsoil and the other for fisheries. This has been described as 'the area of divergence' or the 'top hat',[18] and along with the Protected Zone for protecting the traditional fishing and movement rights of the traditional inhabitants, and for regulating and sharing of commercial fishing, it resolves the question of islands and the interests of the islanders as well as of the two neighbouring States (see chart 2).

This subsample thus shows that the boundary line between Indonesia and Papua New Guinea follows the median line. The boundary line between Indonesia and Australia is a combination of a median line and a negotiated line, the latter comprising a larger sector. During these negotiations, the geomorphology of the area and the existing concessions appear to have been taken into account. The seabed jurisdiction line between Papua New Guinea and Australia follows the median line, modified in relation to the islands.[19] In the Torres Strat, the fisheries jurisdiction line skirts the inhabited and other Australian islands north of the seabed jurisdiction line. A Protected Zone enclosing the fisheries jurisdiction line and cutting across the seabed jurisdiction line protects the mutual interests of the parties and of the islanders. Drilling in the Protected Zone for petroleum and gas or mining for other mineral resources has been prohibited for a period of 10 years.

Agreements in the South Pacific

During 1980, three Agreements were concluded concerning the States or Territories in the South Pacific, namely, the Convention between France and Tonga, and the Treaties between the United States and the Cook Islands, and the United States and New Zealand (Tokelau).[20]

The Convention between France and Tonga, 1980, settled the principle of delimiting the exclusive economic zone between Tonga and the French islands of Wallis and Futuna as the median or equidistance line, which France regarded as equitable, and the parties agreed to draw up the relevant cartographic documents by mutual agreement as soon as possible.

The Treaty between the United States and the Cook Islands, 1980, was a case of the practical application of the principle embodied in Article 305 of the United Nations Convention on the Law of the Sea signed in Jamaica on December 10, 1982, namely, the competence of self-governing associated States in matters concerning the law of the sea and their treaty-making capacity. The Cook Islands are an associated State of New Zealand since 1965. It had enacted the Territorial Sea and Exclusive Economic Zone Act of 1977. The Treaty of 1980 refers to this Act as well as to the US Fishery Conservation and Management Act, 1976, and records the recognition by the United States of sovereignty of the Cook Islands over the islands of Penrhyn, Pukapuka, Manihiki and Rakahanga, despite earlier US claims thereto, and settles the maritime boundary between the Cook Islands and American Samoa by following the median line, after settling the question of the datum and the charts, although the principle followed has not been referred to in the Treaty.[21]

The Treaty between the United States and New Zealand (for Tokelau), 1980, appears to be the first case of anticipatory application of the principle embodied in Resolution III, adopted by the Third United Nations Conference on the Law of the Sea on April 30, 1982. This Resolution was later embodied in the Final Act of the Conference which was signed by more than 150 delegations in Montego Bay, Jamaica, on December 10, 1982. This Resolution relates to non-self-governing territories and declares that the UN Convention on the Law of the Sea shall be implemented for the benefit of the people of the territory concerned with a view to promoting their well-being and development. Tokelau is still a non-self-governing territory, pending exercise by the people of Tokelau of their right of self-determination in accordance with the United Nations Declaration on the granting of independence to colonial countries and peoples.

The Treaty notes the Tokelau Territorial Sea and Exclusive Economic Zone Act of 1977, records the recognition by the United States, despite their earlier claims to the contrary, that sovereignty over the islands of Atau, Nukunonu and Fakaofo is vested in the people of Tokelau[22] and is exercised on their behalf by the Government of New Zealand pending an act of self-determination in accordance with the Charter of the United Nations, settles the maritime boundary between the Tokelau Islands and American Samoa by following the median line, although no reference is made to the principle followed in the Treaty. The Treaty was also described in the preamble as having been concluded 'with the concurrence of the people of Tokelau'.

The three inter-regional Agreements in the South Pacific involving islands opposite to each other, thus follow the median line for delimiting the maritime boundary between them, and also settle the question of sovereignty over some islands. They also involve a non-self-governing territory (Tokelau) and an associated State (Cook Islands).

Notes

4. For a list of these Agreements, see Annex I, items 1-28.
5. For a list of these Agreements, see Annex I, items 75-82.
6. For a comprehensive treatment of these Agreements, along with a chart, see *Limits in the Seas*, No. 94 (September 1981). For historical and analytical study of these Agreements, see S.H. Amin, 'Customary Rules of Delimitation of the Continental Shelf: The Gulf States Practice', *Journal of Maritime Law and Commerce*, Vol. II, No. 4 (July 1980), pp. 509-526; and 'Law of the Continental Shelf Delimitation: The Gulf Example', *Netherlands International Law Review* (1980), pp. 335-346. See also *Maritime Boundaries in the Western Indian Region*, Research Memorandum No. 1/252(81), October 1981, Office of National Assessment, Canberra, pp. 11-12, 15-18; Richard Young, 'Equitable Solutions for Offshore Boundaries: The 1968 Saudi Arabia – Iran Agreement', *AJIL*, Vol. 64 (1970), pp. 152-157.

   Besides these Agreements, an offshore boundary Agreement had also been concluded between Dubai and Abu Dhabi on 18 February 1968. Since both constitute parts of the United Arab Emirates (UAE) since December 1971, this Agreement has not been included as a separate Agreement in this study.

   It has been estimated that, ignoring internal UAE boundaries, 9 maritime boundaries remain to be negotiated. See *Limits in the Seas*, No. 94 (1981), p. 1.
7. Agreement between Bahrain and Iran, 1971, Article 2, *Limits in the Seas*, No.58; and Agreement between Iran and Oman, 1974, Article 2, *Limits in the Seas*, No. 67.
8. 'Customary Rules of Delimitation of the Continental Shelf: The Gulf States Practice', n. 6, at p. 517; see also Richard Young, n. 6, at pp. 154-155.
9. For background and analysis of the Agreement, see Sayed M. Hosni, 'The Partition of the Neutral Zone', *AJIL*, Vol. 60 (1966), pp. 735-749.
10. For text, see Annex II, pp. 347-351 below.
11. The joint development area, which is a pentagon measuring about 2100 n m², has been divided

94

by a single line to separate the Thai and Malaysian areas of criminal jurisdiction – J.R.V. Prescott, *Maritime Jurisdiction in Southeast Asia: A Commentary and Map*, Research Report No. 2, East-West Environment and Policy Institute, East-West Centre, Honolulu, Hawaii, January 1981, at p. 10.

12. *North Sea Continental Shelf, Judgment, ICJ Reports*, 1969, paragraph 101.
13. Article 1(3). Thailand established its exclusive economic zone on February 23, 1981. Burma had established its exclusive economic zone on April 9, 1977.
14. For reference to these Agreements, see Annex I, items 27 and 28.
    For historical analysis and comments, see Shigeru Oda, 'The Continental Shelf Agreements between Japan and the Republic of Korea, 1974', *The Law of the Sea in Our Time I – New Developments 1966 – 1975*, Sijthoff, 1977, pp. 250-265; Chi Young Park, 'The Continental Shelf between Korea, Japan and China', *Marine Policy Reports*, University of Delaware, Newark, USA, Vol. 4, No. 5 (June 1982).
15. Chi Young Park, *op. cit.*, p. 2.
16. *Limits in the Seas*, No. 75, September 1977, p. 11.
17. For text of the protest made on June 13, 1977, and its background, see People's Republic of China Mission to the United Nations, New York, Press Release No. 49 (June 13, 1977). The substance of the protest read as follows: 'The East China Sea continental shelf is the natural extension of the Chinese continental territory. The People's Republic of China has inviolable sovereignty over the East China Sea continental shelf. It stands to reason that the question of how to divide those parts of the East China Sea continental shelf which involve other countries should be decided by China and the countries concerned through consultations. The so-called Japan – South Korea Agreement on Joint Development of the Continental Shelf signed by the Japanese Government with the South Korean authorities unilaterally behind China's back is entirely illegal and null and void'.
18. H. Burmester, 'The Torres Strait Treaty: Ocean Boundary Delimitation by Agreement', *AJIL*, Vol. 76, No. 2 (April 1982), pp. 321-349, at 337-338. This Article makes a detailed historical and analytical study of the Treaty. Its author was a member of the Australian team for negotiating the Treaty.
19. *Ibid.*, p. 336.
20. For reference to these Agreements, see Annex I, items 80, 81 and 82.
21. Mark B. Feldman and David Colson, 'The Maritime Boundaries of the United States', *AJIL*, Vol. 75, No. 4 (October 1981), pp. 729-763, at p. 749. See also *Limits in the Seas*, No. 100 (1983), p. 9.
22. *Ibid.*, at p. 749. The boundary line puts Swains Island on the US side.

CHAPTER 7

African Agreements

Only a small sample of 6 African Agreements[23] will be surveyed in this Chapter. Two of these Agreements are in fact inter-regional Agreements.

The first Agreement is between Guinea-Bissau and Senegal, which was concluded on April 26, 1960, by an Exchange of Notes between their metropolitan powers, namely, Portugal and France. Senegal became independent on August 20, 1960. Guinea-Bissau became independent on September 20, 1975. The boundary is presumed to be still in force. The maritime boundary is defined as a straight line following the 240° azimuth from the intersection of the extension of the land boundary and the low-water mark. The States are adjacent. The outer limits of the boundary are not specified.

The second Agreement was concluded by an Exchange of Notes between Kenya and Tanzania and entered into force on July 9, 1976. It defines the territorial sea boundary between the two countries which is an equidistant boundary measured from the specified baselines. The existing fishing rights of local fishermen within 12 nautical miles on either side of the boundary line have been protected. To the north and east of Pemba Island, the boundary follows the specified latitude. The terminal points will vary, since Kenya claims a 12-mile territorial sea while Tanzania claims a 50-mile territorial sea. The boundary line is thus partly a median line and partly a negotiated line.

The third Agreement is between Gambia and Senegal, which was signed on June 4, 1975, and which entered into force on August 27, 1976. Since Gambia is surrounded on three sides by Senegal and has a coastal front of 32 nautical miles, two boundary lines have been drawn, one in the north and the other in the south. The northern boundary follows the specified latitude from the land boundary terminal point. The southern boundary has a small jog or kink near the shore but thereafter follows the specified latitude. The outer limits of the boundary lines are not specified. Gambia claims a territorial sea of 50 miles; Senegal claims a territorial sea of 150 miles. Both States are adjacent States.

The fourth Agreement is between Mauritania and Morocco, which was signed on April 14, 1976, and does not appear to have been ratified yet. Against the background of the Advisory Opinion of the International Court of Justice concerning the Sahara of October 16, 1975, and the transfer by Spain of joint interim administration over the Sahara to Morocco and Mauritania, the two Governments concluded this Agreement and settled a land boundary as well as the continental shelf boundary between them. The continental shelf boundary follows the 24th Parallel North from the terminus of the land boundary on the coast.

The fifth Agreement, which is an inter-regional Agreement, is between Italy and Tunisia. This Agreement settles the continental shelf boundary between the two countries and follows the median line measured from the appropriate baselines, taking into account the islands, islets and low-tide elevations of the respective countries, with the exception of four islands of Italy. For these four islands, namely Pantelleria, Lampione, Lampedusa and Linosa, which are located near or across the median line between the two countries, a specified maritime zone is given and the median line is adjusted accordingly. The island of Lampione is given a maritime zone of 12 nautical miles around it, whereas the other three islands are given a maritime zone of 13 nautical miles each around them. Thus, in so far as these islands are concerned, they get a territorial sea of 12 nautical miles and in three cases a continental shelf of one nautical mile. Their maritime zones are connected with the median line. The Agreement between Italy and Tunisia follows the precedents of the Agreement between Italy and Yugoslavia, 1968, on the one hand and of Iran and Saudi Arabia, 1968, and Qatar and the UAE, 1969, on the other. In this Agreement, the situation of islands is thus recognised as a special circumstance and the median line is adjusted by a negotiated line in this sector.

The sixth Agreement, which is also an inter-regional Agreement, is between France and Mauritius and was signed on April 2, 1980, and entered into force on the same date. It settled the exclusive economic zone boundary between the islands of Reunion and Mauritius on the basis of the median line, which was referred to in the Agreement as being equitable. The boundary line crosses the depth of water ranging from 3300 to 5000 metres.[24]

Thus, the limited African State practice is varied. In three cases, either a straight line at a specified angle or the latitude were followed as the boundary. In one case it was a negotiated boundary line. In another case, the boundary line was the median line but, because of the location of islands on or across the median line, it was appropriately adjusted. In another case, the boundary line was the median line. The different outer limits of the territorial sea of the parties also created a question about the denomination of the boundary line in relation to the maritime zones of the parties.

98

Notes

23. For a list of these Agreements, see Annex I, items 29-32 and 83-84.
24. *Limits in the Seas*, No. 95 (1982), p. 3.

CHAPTER 8

Latin American Agreements

A total of 14 Agreements on Latin America, and 8 inter-regional Agreements, will be surveyed in this Chapter.[25] Of the 14 Agreements, both parties to which are from Latin America, 6 are amongst States of South America, 3 have a party from Central America, and 5 relate to the Caribbean Sea. Of the 8 inter-regional Agreements, 1 has a party from South America, 2 are between the USA and Mexico and 5 relate to the Caribbean Sea. Out of the total of 22 Agreements, 13 have opposite coasts and 9 have adjacent coasts. Only one Agreement relates to the territorial sea boundary, whereas the others relate to the continental shelf boundary, the exclusive economic zone boundary, or both. From the documents consulted, it was not clear whether 4 of them, which had been signed subject to ratification, had entered into force. Most of the Agreements have been concluded since 1970 and therefore reflect the current developments in international law following the Judgment of the International Court of Justice in the *North Sea Continental Shelf* cases, 1969, and the developments at the Third United Nations Conference on the Law of the Sea.

These Agreements will now be surveyed briefly subregion-wise.

South America and Central America

Of the 9 Agreements relating to South America and Central America, the first accord on maritime delimitation was between the UK and Venezuela relating to the Gulf of Paria in 1942. In this Agreement, the seabed and the subsoil outside the territorial sea and underneath the Gulf of Paria was called a 'submarine area' which was divided between the parties partly by following the median line and partly by a negotiated line. The legal status of the continental shelf as the natural prolongation of the land territory had not yet emerged in international law. Accordingly, the 1942 Agreement appears to regard the submarine area as *res nullius*, which could be claimed by effective occupation. In fact, following the Agreement, the British Government annexed their side of the area in the

Gulf of Paria to form part of the British dominions and 'attached to the Colony of Trinidad and Tobago for administrative purposes'.[26] The Agreement provides for the mutual recognition of each other's claims to the submarine areas outside the territorial sea and mutual abstention from exercising any rights across the boundary line.

On August 28, 1962, Chile, Peru and Ecuador signed the Santiago Declaration on the Maritime Zone claiming 'as a principle of their international maritime policy', sole sovereignty and jurisdiction over at least a 200-nautical mile area, including the seabed and subsoil. The maritime boundary between the parties to this Declaration was to follow the parallel of latitude drawn from the point where the land frontier between them reached the sea. This principle and practice were followed in South America in the Maritime Boundary Agreements between Chile and Peru (1954), Peru and Ecuador (1954), and Colombia and Ecuador (1975). A combination of latitude and longitude was also followed for settling the boundary in the Agreement between Colombia and Costa Rica (1977). In the Agreement between Colombia and Panama (1976), the boundary line followed in part the median line and in part a latitude and longitude in a step-like formation in the Caribbean Sea due to the location of Colombian islands in the area. In the Pacific, the boundary between Colombia and Panama followed first a simplified median line and later a perpendicular to the general direction of the coastline.

In the Treaty between Costa Rica and Panama (1980), settling the boundary in the respective 'marine areas' in the Caribbean Sea and the Pacific Ocean, the boundary line is described as the median line (Article I), although it consists of straight one-segment lines in either sector and is akin to a perpendicular to the general direction of the coastline.

On the eastern side of South America, the Agreements between the adjacent States, namely Argentina and Uruguay (1973) and Brazil and Uruguay (1972), determined the boundary line by drawing a perpendicular from a predetermined point. In the Argentina – Uruguay Agreement, this point was the mid-point of the straight line enclosing the mouth of the Rio de la Plata. In this Agreement, the boundary is defined 'by an equidistant line, determined by the adjacent coasts method' (Article 70).

Thus the State practice in Latin America reflected in these Agreements is varied. The States which follow the provisions of the 1952 Santiago Declaration have established their maritime boundary along a latitude or longitude starting from the international land boundary point. In other cases, generally the median or equidistance line has been followed either in its entirety or with some simplification or modification as by drawing a perpendicular from a point along the general direction of the coastline. In some cases the median line and the parallel or the meridian have also been used in combination.

No distinction has been made between the States with opposite or adjacent coasts, or between the territorial sea boundary, the continental shelf or the economic zone boundary, regarding the applicable delimitation principles.

The following special provisions have also been made in these maritime boundary Agreements:

(1) In the Agreement between Argentina and Uruguay (1973) the parties established a common fishing zone comprising a 200-mile arc drawn from the respective terminal points of the closing baseline on the Rio da la Plata. Provisions were also made regarding the regulation of joint fisheries in this zone.

In the same Agreement, a pollution control zone was also established.

(2) In the Agreements following the latitude as the boundary line, a zone comprising 10 nautical miles on either side of the boundary line was also established. This zone was, however, not a common fishing zone. Exclusive fishery rights in the zone on either side of this boundary line remained with the State concerned. The zone was established only to ensure that accidental trespassers will not be punished for violation of the respective maritime zones.

A word may also be mentioned about the title and scope of the Agreements. Following the 1942 Agreement between the UK and Venezuela, Colombia has throughout continued to refer to 'marine and submarine areas' in its boundary Agreements rather than to the fishery zone, the exclusive economic zone or the continental shelf even when the other party called it the exclusive economic maritime zone and the continental shelf boundary (Colombia – Haiti, 1978). The Treaty between Costa Rica and Panama (1980) also refers to the delimitation of 'marine areas'.

The Caribbean Sea

In the five Agreements relating to the Caribbean Sea, the maritime boundary was either among Island States or involved an Island State. The boundary line was determined in all cases on the basis of the median line, although the principle was mentioned in the Agreement in a variety of ways. Thus the Agreements between Mexico and Cuba, 1976, Colombia and Haiti, 1978, and Colombia and the Dominican Republic, 1978, referred to the median line principle directly as the basis for the boundary line. In the Agreement between Venezuela and the Dominican Republic, 1979, the preamble refers to delimiting the boundary 'justly, accurately, and on the basis of equitable principles'. In the Agreement between Haiti and Cuba, 1977, delimitation is to be made 'on the basis of the principle of equidistance or equity, as the case requires' (Article 1).

Inter-regional Agreements

Of the 8 inter-regional Agreements, one related to South America, 2 were between the USA and Mexico and 5 related to the Caribbean Sea.

The Agreement between France and Brazil, 1981, settled the maritime boundary between French Guiana and Brazil by following from certain specified points 'the loxodromic curve of the true azimuth forty one degrees and thirty minutes (41°31′)', i.e. by the shortest straight line along a specified angle. The starting point of the boundary line was the intersection of the boundary in the Bay of Oyapock with the outer limits of the Bay, both of which had been settled earlier by a Mixed Commission of the two Governments on boundary delimitation. The Agreement referred to the history of these earlier negotiations. The boundary line settled by the Agreement was also thus a negotiated line.

Mexico and the USA

Two Agreements have been concluded between Mexico and the USA. The first Agreement of November 23, 1970, settled the boundary in the territorial sea of the adjacent States both in the Gulf of Mexico and in the Pacific Ocean, and followed the equidistance line. The second Agreement of May 4, 1978, recalled the background of the establishment by Mexico and the USA of an exclusive economic zone and a fishery conservation zone under their respective legislation in 1976, and the notes exchanged between them on November 24, 1976, provisionally recognising the maritime boundary between the two countries between 12 and 200 nautical miles seaward in the Gulf of Mexico and in the Pacific Ocean, and agreed to formalise the provisional maritime boundary. The boundary line established by the second Agreement thus extends to 200 nautical miles and establishes the economic zone/fishing zone boundary. It is 'a simplified equidistance line, with equal area trade-offs, giving full effect to islands'.[27] It was realised that in the middle of the Gulf of Mexico, the 200-mile arc drawn from the Louisiana coast of the US and the Mexican islands north of the Yucatan would leave a 'gap', which has been computed to be approximately 129 nautical miles.[28] The boundary has not covered this gap. Accordingly, the second Agreement settles the points of the maritime boundary in three sectors outside the territorial sea, namely in the western Gulf of Mexico, the eastern Gulf of Mexico and the Pacific Ocean.

Thus both the Agreements between Mexico and the USA follow the equidistance line. In the first Agreement, reference was made to equidistance in accordance with Articles 12 and 24 of the Geneva Convention on the Territorial Sea and the Contiguous Zone, 1958. In the second Agreement, the provisional maritime boundary which was formalised by the Agreement was called 'practical and equitable'. The official view of the United States has been that maritime boundaries between adjacent and opposite States are to be determined by agreement in accordance with equitable principles.[29]

The Caribbean Sea

Of the 5 inter-regional Agreements related to the Caribbean Sea, 3 followed the median line (USA – Cuba, 1977; USA – Venezuela, 1968; France – Saint Lucia, 1981) and 2 followed a negotiated line (Netherlands – Venezuela, 1978; France – Venezuela, 1980).

In the Agreement between the USA and Cuba signed on December 6, 1977, no reference was made to the principle followed in delimiting the maritime boundary between them. The boundary line is a simplified median line.[30] The Agreement was simple. It protected their respective positions on the law of the sea. It was subject to ratification but was provisionally applied for a period of two years from January 1, 1978, which was later extended for another two years.

In the Agreement between the USA and Venezuela, 1978, reference has been made to 'the need to establish precise and equitable maritime limits', and 'according to international law'. The boundary line, which extends from points 1 to 22 between Puerto Rico and Venezuela, is a median line, and gives full effect to the Aves Island of Venezuela.[31]

In the Agreement between France and Saint Lucia of March 4, 1981, which determined the maritime boundary between Martinique and Saint Lucia, it was noted in the preamble that 'the equidistance method provides an equitable means of delimitation in the present case'. The Agreement was a simple one and did not contain any unity of resource clause.

On the other hand, in the Agreement between France and Venezuela, 1980, the maritime boundary between the French islands of Martinique and Guadaloupe and the Venezuelan islands was drawn on the basis of equitable principles and ran along the meridian 62 degrees 48 minutes 50 seconds.

The Treaty between the Netherlands and Venezuela, 1978, was a comprehensive one and dealt with the maritime boundary between the Netherlands Antilles and the Venezuelan mainland and islands. The boundary line which extended from points 1 to 16 was drawn in four sectors: sector A joined points 3, 2 and 1 and comprised the boundary between the west of Aruba and the Venezuelan territory (Monges Archipelago); sector B extended it from point 3 to point 11 and comprised the boundary between the Leeward Islands of the Netherlands Antilles (Aruba, Bonaire and Curaçao) and the northern coast of Venezuela; sector C extended it from point 11 to point 13 and comprised the bound-

105

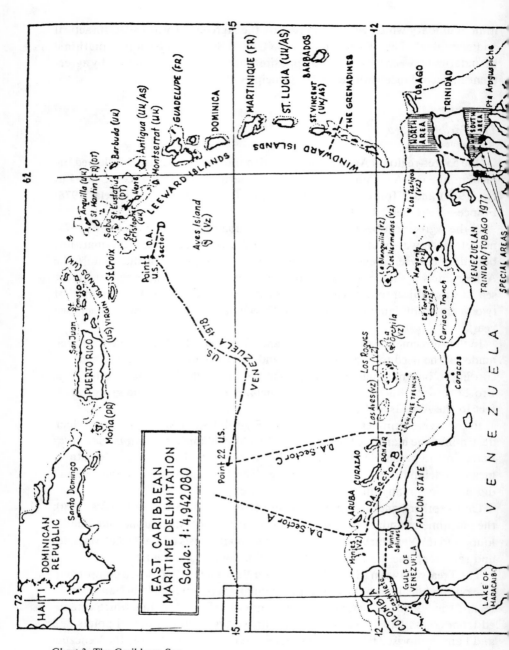

Chart 3. The Caribbean Sea
Source: Kaldone G. Nweihed, 'EZ (Uneasy) Delimitation in the Semi-enclosed Caribbean Sea:
Recent Agreements between Venezuela and Her Neighbours',
Ocean Development and International Law (1980), p. 5 (enlarged)
(published with permission)

106

ary between Bonaire and the Venezuelan territory; and sector D joined points 14, 15 and 16 and comprised the boundary between the Venezuelan islands of Aves and the Netherlands islands of Saba and St. Eustatius (see Chart 3). The gap between points 13 and 14 of the boundary line in the present Agreement constituted the maritime boundary line between the USA and Venezuela settled in their Agreement of 1978.[32] The Treaty refers to the delimitation of their respective marine and submarine areas in a manner which is 'just, precise and based on equitable principles'. The boundary line in sectors A, B and C is a negotiated line, whereas in sector D it is the median line. The Treaty contains a provision on the unity of a structure or field extending across the boundary line (Article 6), prohibits drilling by either party up to one nautical mile from the boundary line (Article 7), makes detailed provisions on the 'right of transit passage' for Venezuelan ships and aircraft if the Netherlands Antilles were to extend the limits of their 3-mile territorial sea (Article 4), requires that the establishment of artificial islands and installations in the respective zone shall not affect navigation (Article 5), and promotes cooperation in matters concerning the protection of the marine environment (Articles 4 and 9), the conduct of marine scientific research (Article 11), and the conservation and exploitation of the living resources in the adjacent waters of both countries (Article 10). Disputes concerning Articles 4, 5 and 6 (navigation, unity of resource clause), unless otherwise resolved, shall be referred to a three-member Commission of Experts whose decision shall be binding (Article 12).

It will thus be seen that of the 8 inter-regional Agreements, 3 adopted a negotiated boundary line, whereas 5 followed the median or equidistance line.

Looking at the Latin American geographical region as a whole, the maritime boundaries between the South American States were mainly among adjacent States, and for historical and practical reasons these followed either a latitude or a meridian or a straight line along a specified angle. In the three Agreements of Central America, the boundary line was a simplified or modified median line. In the Caribbean Sea, where the boundary was either between island States or between States one of whom was an island State, 8 out of the 10 Agreements followed the median line and 2 a negotiated line.[33] In the 2 Agreements between the USA and Mexico, the equidistance line was followed.

Despite the differences regarding the applicable principle, say between Venezuela and Colombia or between France and the island States, the approach followed in the concrete delimitations was practical. The Latin American State practice is varied and does not appear to suggest a regional approach or custom in delimitation, although in a majority of cases the median line was followed, particularly in the Caribbean and between Mexico and the USA.

Notes

25. For a list of these Agreements, see Annex I, items 33-46 and 85-92.

26. For comments on the 1942 Agreement between the UK and Venezuela, see Francis A. Vallat, 'The Continental Shelf', *The British Year Book of International Law*, 1946, pp. 333-338; J.A.C. Gutteridge, 'The 1958 Geneva Convention on the Continental Shelf', *ibid.*, 1959, at pp. 102-103, 116; and Kaldone G. Nweihed, 'Venezuela's Contribution to the Contemporary Law of the Sea', *San Diego Law Review*, 1974, pp. 603-632.

27. Mark B. Feldman and David Colson, 'The Maritime Boundaries of the United States', *AJIL*, Vol. 75, No. 4 (October 1981), at p. 743.

28. *Ibid.*, p. 743; Robert W. Smith, 'The Maritime Boundaries of the United States', *The Geographical Review*, Vol. 71, No. 4 (October 1981), pp. 395-410 at p. 403.

29. Feldman and Colson, n. 27, pp. 731 and 738. Reviewing the 6 Agreements signed by the US so far (4 covered in the present study in this Chapter and 2 in Chapter 6), the authors sum up the position as follows: 'Although the U.S. maritime boundary position is based on the concept of "equitable principles", the boundaries that have been negotiated to date generally have been based on the equidistance method to one degree or another, giving full effect to islands. This approach has been adopted, not because the equidistance method has any special merit, but because its application in the particular circumstances served U.S. interests and the interests of our treaty partners' − at p. 749. They add that in two important cases, the United States has determined that the equidistance method would not protect US interests and does not conform to international law, namely the boundary in the Atlantic Ocean in the Gulf of Maine/Georges Bank area between the USA and Canada, and the potential boundary with the Bahamas − at p. 750.

30. Smith has explained that the boundary line was drawn first as a median line between the artificial 'construction lines' along Florida and the straight baselines of Cuba, then between the relevant basepoints on the coasts of the two countries and finally by dividing equally the area between them. 'The final boundary represented a negotiated settlement based on equitable principles', he concluded. Smith, n. 28, at p. 402.

31. *AJIL*, n. 27, p. 747. See also Kaldone G. Nweihed, 'EZ (Uneasy) Delimitation in the Semi-enclosed Caribbean Sea: Recent Agreements Between Venezuela and Her Neighbours', *Ocean Development and International Law*, Vol. 8 (1980), pp. 1-33 at 20-23. Smith notes that 'Interestingly the resultant boundary from point 13 to point 22 was developed between the United States and non-Venezuelan territory, the Dutch island of Bonaire'. Smith, n. 28, at p. 407.

32. These two Agreements were in fact signed within a span of a few days − the Agreement between the USA and Venezuela was signed on March 28, 1978, and the Agreement between the Netherlands and Venezuela was signed on March 30, 1978.

33. Nweihed feels that 'In the particular case of the Caribbean, some help may be derived by determining the horizontal axis or general median line that would separate the waters adjacent to the northern coast of South America (*costa firme*) from those of the Greater Antilles (Cuba, Hispaniola and Puerto Rico), roughly along Latitude 15°N, allowing for bulges and curves when insular territory projects the sovereignty of a State across the opposite side of such a line'. *Op. cit.*, n. 31, at p. 4.

CHAPTER 9

Agreements between Western European and other States

Twenty-eight Agreements, including 3 inter-regional Agreements, concluded between Western European and other States, will be surveyed in this Chapter.[34] Eleven of these Agreements relate to the North Sea, 14 relate to other areas, and 3 are inter-regional Agreements.

These Agreements may be reviewed as follows:

The North Sea

The Agreements relating to the continental shelf boundary in the North Sea, which may also be applicable to other maritime zones of the respective parties, have made their own contribution, both through negotiations and adjudication, to the development of international law and State practice in maritime delimitation. With unusual speed between 1964 and 1968, the five States surrounding the North Sea, namely the United Kingdom, Norway, Denmark, the Federal Republic of Germany and the Netherlands, concluded a series of Agreements between them delimiting the continental shelf which was regarded as appertaining to the respective parties. The Agreement between the United Kingdom and Norway was signed on March 10, 1965, which was based on the median line disregarding the Norwegian trough or trench. Similarly, the Agreement between Norway and Denmark was signed on December 8, 1965, on the basis of the median line, disregarding the Norwegian trench. The 1965 Agreement between Norway and Denmark was amended by an Exchange of Notes on April 24, 1968, correcting the geographical coordinates of one point. All these Agreements are in force.

Simultaneously, negotiations for the maritime boundary between the Netherlands and the FRG on the one hand, and Denmark and the FRG on the other, led to the conclusion of partial Agreements in coastal areas between them. Differences, however, arose on the further alignment of the boundary in the North Sea. The FRG insisted that the equidistance line was not equitable to it whereas the Netherlands and Denmark stuck to the equidistance line as the applicable rule for maritime delimitation. The Netherlands, the FRG and Denmark are States with adjacent coasts. The partial boundary Agreement between the FRG and the Netherlands was signed on December 1, 1964, which extended the existing terminal point further into the sea up to 26 nautical miles. This was done on the basis of the equidistance line. Similarly, the Agreement settling the partial boundary between Denmark and the FRG was signed on June 9, 1965, which settled the boundary up to a point of 26 nautical miles into the North Sea on the basis of the equidistance line. While the aforementioned differences concerning the extension of the partial boundary subsisted, the Netherlands signed an Agreement with the United Kingdom on October 6, 1965, and Denmark signed an Agreement with the United Kingdom on March 3, 1966. With these Agreements, the boundary line in the middle of the North Sea was completed from the north to the south, segments of which comprised the boundary between the UK and Norway, the UK and Denmark, and the UK and the Netherlands.

In addition, Denmark and the Netherlands also signed an Agreement on March 31, 1966, settling the maritime boundary between the two countries starting from the trijunction point between the UK, the Netherlands and Denmark, which extended south-eastwards up to a distance of 85 nautical miles to a point where the maritime boundaries between the Netherlands and the FRG, and Denmark and the FRG, if drawn on the basis of the equidistance line, would meet.

All the aforementioned Agreements were ratified and entered into force.

Soon thereafter, in 1967, an Agreement was reached between the FRG, the Netherlands and Denmark to refer the dispute regarding the extension of their partially settled boundaries into the North Sea to the International Court of Justice for indicating the applicable principles of international law on delimitation of the continental shelf boundary between them. The Court delivered its Judgment on February 20, 1969, indicating the equitable principles as the applicable principles.

Pursuant to this Judgment, further negotiations were held between the FRG, Denmark and the Netherlands which led to the conclusion of five new Agreements in 1971 apart from the cancellation of the Agreement between Denmark and the Netherlands of March 31, 1966.

These new Agreements became necessary because the negotiations between the FRG, Denmark and the Netherlands led to the FRG having access to the common line of delimitation with the United Kingdom in the middle of the North Sea.

The conclusion of the new Agreements was synchronised. Thus the Agreements between the FRG and Denmark, and the FRG and the Netherlands, were signed on January 28, 1971. A new Agreement was signed between Denmark and the UK on November 25, 1971, replacing the 1966 Agreement. A Protocol amending the Agreement of 1965 between the Netherlands and the UK was also signed on November 25, 1971. Finally, the Agreement between the FRG and the UK, which gave to the FRG an 8-nautical-mile boundary line with the UK in the North Sea, was also signed on November 25, 1971.

All these five Agreements came into force on a single date, namely December 7, 1972.

A study of the 10 Agreements concluded between 1964 and 1972 in the North Sea will reveal a useful and instructive combination of State practice, applicable law, and assessment of special circumstances during negotiations for finding an equitable solution. The eleventh Agreement between Norway and the United Kingdom, 1978, will be dealt with a little later in this section.

The Agreements between the United Kingdom and Norway, and Norway and Denmark, which are in force, established the boundary on the basis of the median line. The same was true of the Agreement between the United Kingdom and the Netherlands, 1965, which was later modified by a Protocol in 1971. The 5 Agreements of 1971 resulted from the need to negotiate a new boundary line between the Netherlands and the FRG, and Denmark and the FRG, due to the special circumstances arising from the concavity of the FRG's coast. The two coastal area Agreements between the FRG and the Netherlands (1964) and the FRG and Denmark (1965) based on the equidistance line have not been disturbed. The first turning point on the maritime boundary line determined both between the FRG and the Netherlands, and between the FRG and Denmark, in 1971, are also equidistance points. The rest of the 1971 boundary lines between the three countries are negotiated lines. It is not quite clear as to what factors or special circumstances obtaining in the area were taken into account during these negotiations. A record of such negotiations has not been published. However, it appears that the Federal Republic of Germany was eager to reach the common boundary line with the United Kingdom in the middle of the North Sea, and regarded this as justified by the principle that the continental shelf was the natural prolongation of the land territory of a coastal State. Once this was conceded by the other parties, negotiations appear to have been conducted in settling the lateral lines between the FRG and the Netherlands on the one hand and the FRG and Denmark on the other. In these negotiations, it appears that the unity of the known resources or structures for which exploration licences had already been granted by the Netherlands or Denmark were taken into account and protected. However, certain licensed areas still had to fall on the FRG-side of the boundary line. Accordingly, a provision was made in both these Agreements to allow the existing enterprises operating in the area to apply for a fresh licence for the area in question to the FRG Government within a period of 12 months after the entry into force of the Agreement (Article 4). Detailed provisions have also been made regarding the unity of resource

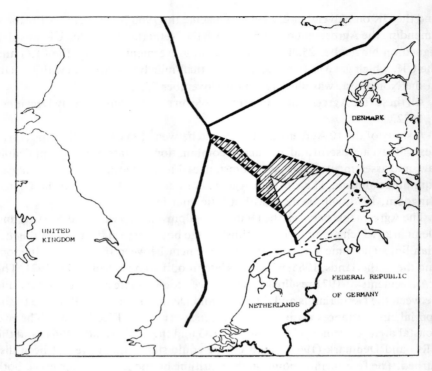

Continental Shelf boundaries in the North Sea

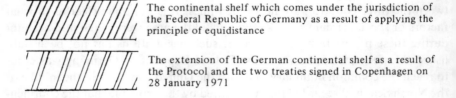

The continental shelf which comes under the jurisdiction of the Federal Republic of Germany as a result of applying the principle of equidistance

The extension of the German continental shelf as a result of the Protocol and the two treaties signed in Copenhagen on 28 January 1971

Chart 4. North Sea boundary Agreements, 1971.

clause, where it extends across the boundary line (Article 2). Any dispute relating to this shall be settled by arbitration, detailed provisions for which have been made in both Agreements (Articles 2 and 5).

The Agreement between the FRG and the UK, signed on November 25, 1971, which was consequential from the above developments and established an 8-nautical-miles boundary between the two countris, has already been referred to above. This boundary was obviously not equidistant from the UK and the FRG; it is closer to the UK by 20 nautical miles. The boundary line is 178 nautical miles from the FRG coast.[34a]

The Agreements between Denmark and the UK (1966) and the Netherlands and the UK (1965) were also accordingly amended in 1971 and the extent of their boundary lines was reduced. The residual boundary lines between them, however, remained equidistant. (For the resulting boundary between the FRG, Denmark, the Netherlands and the UK, see Chart 4).

By these Agreements, the FRG gained about 12,000 sq. kms (5,000 sq. kms from the Netherlands and about 7,000 sq. kms from Denmark) in relation to the area which it would have otherwise got had the boundary between the three countries been settled on the basis of the equidistance line.[35]

Finally, the eleventh Agreement relating to the North Sea was a Protocol, signed on December 22, 1978, by which the United Kingdom and Norway extended the boundary line established under the Agreement of March 10, 1965, in the northern and north-western direction from point 8 thereof to point 26. Point 26 was equidistant from Norway, Denmark (Faroe Islands) and the United Kingdom, and this position was to be 'subject to acceptance by the Government of the Kingdom of Denmark' (Article II(3)). The accepted boundary line was the median line, and the principle was mentioned in the Protocol with reference to the 1965 Agreement.

To conclude, this sub-sample of 11 Agreements relates mainly to the determination of the continental shelf boundary among the States adjoining the North Sea, although it may also apply to the respective fishing or economic zones. Most of them are opposite States, except in the area where the FRG, the Netherlands and Denmark are adjacent States. Among the opposite States, the maritime boundary has been determined on the basis of the median line. Among the adjacent States, the coastal areas boundary has also been drawn on the basis of the equidistance line. Due to the special circumstances arising from the concavity of the coast of the FRG in relation to the coast of the Netherlands and Denmark, the further delimitation between the three countries led to a negotiated line, pursuant to the Judgment of the International Court of Justice in the *North Sea Continental Shelf* cases, 1969. The negotiations appear to have taken into account the location of known structures or resources. In the remaining area of the North Sea, no other special circumstances appear to have played a part in maritime delimitation, such as islands. The Norwegian trough or trench which is between 20 and 81 nautical miles wide and has a depth of up to 371 fathoms and lies close to the Norwegian coast, both towards the west and in the south, was ignored for the purpose of delimitation in the Agreements between Norway and the United Kingdom (1965) and Norway and Denmark (1965). The boundary line was established on the basis of the median line. The northern and north-western extension of the boundary line between the UK and Norway by a Protocol signed in 1978 was also done on the basis of the median line.

The State practice in the North Sea would thus support the application of the median line between the States with opposite coasts and of the equitable principles between the States with adjacent coasts.

WEO Agreements in other areas

The WEO Agreements relating to areas other than the North Sea are 14 in number, in addition to 3 inter-regional Agreements. These relate to the Baltic Sea, the Bay of Biscay, the Atlantic Ocean, the Mediterranean Sea, and in one case the Coral Sea and the Indian Ocean. Out of these 14 Agreements, 7 are between States with opposite coasts and 7 with adjacent coasts. Three of the 14 Agreements relate to the territorial sea boundary, 10 of them relate to the continental shelf boundary which in most cases may also apply to their other maritime zones, including the exclusive economic zone, and one Agreement relates to the boundary in the fishery zone and the exclusive economic zone (Denmark – Norway (Faroes), 1979). The Agreement establishing the territorial sea boundary between Denmark and Sweden, 1932, is the oldest delimitation Agreement covered in this Part. The other Agreements were concluded between 1968 and 1981. One of them was signed in 1965 but ratified in 1977 (Denmark – Federal Republic of Germany (Baltic)), the delay being perhaps due to the controversy between Denmark and the FRG over the extension of their maritime boundary line in the North Sea concerning which the International Court of Justice delivered its Judgment in 1969.

In the four Agreements concerning the Baltic Sea, the boundary line was determined on the basis of the median line, whether it related to the territorial sea or to the continental shelf. In the Agreement between Finland and Sweden, 1972, the boundary line followed the Convention on the Aaland Islands, 1921.

In the territorial sea and contiguous zone boundary Agreement between France and Spain in the Bay of Biscay, 1974, the boundary line followed the median line. Under the second Agreement of 1974, the continental shelf boundary between them followed partly the equidistance line and partly the negotiated line. In the negotiated line sector, the relevant length of the coastlines in the

114

Bay of Biscay measured from specified points was taken into account.

In the Agreement between Portugal and Spain, 1976, the boundary line in the Atlantic followed a parallel, namely, Latitude 41 degrees 50 minutes 57 seconds North, whereas the boundary line in the Mediterranean followed the meridian, namely Longitude 7 degrees 23 minutes 48 seconds West. The parties to this Treaty were both parties to the Convention on the Continental Shelf, 1958, but they agreed that the Treaty would be modified in the light of later developments, namely if a new international Convention on the Law of the Sea, to which both States were parties, so required it.

In the Agreement between Italy and Spain in the Mediterranean Sea, 1974, and the Agreement between Italy and Greece, 1977, the boundary line was drawn on the basis of the median line.

In the North Atlantic, in the Agreement between Norway and Denmark (Faroes), 1979, the boundary line was drawn on the basis of the median line, starting from point 26 in the Agreement between the UK and Norway, 1978, which was equidistant from Norway, the UK and Denmark (Faroes), and whose location was subject to acceptance by Denmark.

On the other hand, in the Agreement between Iceland and Norway (Jan Mayen), signed on October 22, 1981, which was in implementation of the Arbitration Commission's recommendations of May 1981, the parties agreed that the exclusive economic zone of Iceland would extend up to 200 miles from its coastline, although the distance between Iceland and Jan Mayen Island of Norway was 270 nautical miles. The Agreement also provided that the continental shelf boundary between the two countries would be the same as for the exclusive economic zone (Article 1). It then established a specified area for joint and cooperative exploration and exploitation of mineral resources. The details of the area and of the cooperative research and exploration were set out in the Agreement (Articles 3 to 9). The area cut across the boundary line and comprised 32,750 square kms on the Norwegian side and 12,720 square kms on the Iceland side, in each of which the other party would be entitled to a 25 per cent share in costs and profits. The terms of the cooperative understanding were more favourable to Iceland in conformity with the recommendations of the Arbitration Commission. Thus, the Agreement established a negotiated boundary line as well as a specified area for joint exploitation.

In the Agreement between Canada and Denmark (Greenland), 1973, the larger part of the boundary line was established on the basis of the median line, but a little more than one-third of the boundary line in the northern part is a negotiated line. Because of the problem of sovereignty and the effect to be given to Hans Island, it was ignored for purposes of delimitation, except that the boundary points were joined to the island on either side.[36]

Similarly, in the territorial sea boundary Agreement between Canada and France (St. Pierre and Miquelon), 1972, the boundary line was located on a

Canadian island and an islet, although it was generally drawn on the basis of the median line.

Finally, the Agreement between France and Australia, 1980, determined the maritime boundary between New Caledonia and Chesterfield Islands of France and the Norfolk Islands of Australia in the Coral Sea, and the Kirguelen Islands of France and MacDonald and Heard Islands of Australia in the Indian Ocean. The boundary line was drawn on the basis of the median line and extended up to 200 nautical miles. It was provided in the Agreement that for the purpose of the continental shelf boundary, the boundary may be extended later.

In the light of the above brief analysis, the main features of the WEO Agreements in other areas may be summed up as follows:

(1) In 11 of the 14 Agreements, generally the median line was followed for settling the maritime boundary, whether it related to the territorial sea or to the continental shelf. In some cases, the median line has been modified for reasons of the position of or the controversy about an island, or for historical reasons, or for other special circumstances. As indicated above, in the case of the Agreement between Canada and Denmark (Greenland), 1973, although the larger part of the boundary line followed the median line, the northern one-third part was a negotiated line.

In three Agreements, the maritime boundary was established on the basis of a negotiated line. In the Agreement between Portugal and Spain, 1976, the boundary line was a parallel in one sector and a meridian in another. In the Agreement between Iceland and Norway, 1981, the boundary line was not a median line but a negotiated line. In the continental shelf boundary Agreement between France and Spain, 1974, the boundary line was mainly a negotiated line, although for a minor part it was the median line.

(2) The treatment of *islands* was varied. In the Agreement between Canada and Denmark (Greenland), 1973, the boundary line joined Hans Island on either side, in view of the problem of sovereignty and the effect to be given to this island. Similarly, in the Agreement between Canada and France (St. Pierre and Miquelon), 1972, the boundary line was located on a Canadian island and an islet on points 4 and 5.

In the Agreement on the territorial sea boundary between Denmark and Sweden, 1932, the presence of offshore islands was ignored, particularly the island of Ven.

(3) Almost all Agreements, particularly those relating to the continental shelf boundary, contained a clause on resources extending across the boundary line which should be exploited by cooperation between the parties concerned. Even the territorial sea boundary Agreement between Denmark and Sweden, 1932, added such a clause to the Agreement by a Protocol. The only Agreements which did not contain such a clause were the Agreement between France

and Spain on the territorial sea boundary, 1974, the Agreement between Finland and Sweden, 1972, and the Agreement between Denmark and Norway (Faroes), 1979.

(4) The Agreement between France and Spain on the continental shelf boundary, 1974, established a common zone, the resources of which were to be divided equally between the parties (Article 3). This zone crosses the boundary line in the Bay of Biscay in that portion where it was not the median line. This arrangement appears to be part of the equitable utilisation of the resources of the area in relation to the negotiated boundary line.

Similarly, the Agreement between Iceland and Norway (Jan Mayen), 1981, established a specified area for joint exploitation, details of which were set out in the Agreement.

(5) Although the views of States regarding the applicable principles of delimitation were known to be different, these did not create difficulty in their concluding Agreements between them. An example of this was the Agreement between Spain and France in the Bay of Biscay, 1974, on the one hand, and Spain and Italy in the Mediterranean Sea, 1974, on the other. Spain and Italy support the median or equidistance line. France supports equitable principles as the basic criteria for maritime delimitation. Thus, in the Agreement between Spain and France no principle was mentioned and the boundary also reflects a line which was partly the equidistance line and partly the negotiated line. On the other hand, in the Agreement concluded between Spain and Italy within a month of the Agreement between Spain and France, the two parties indicated the applicable principle as the median line (Article 1) and the boundary line between them was also established on the basis of the median line.

The Agreement between Italy and Greece, 1977, referred expressly to the application of the principle of the median line. The Agreement between France and Australia recognised that the application of the equidistance line for the maritime boundary Agreement between them was equitable.

This subsample thus shows that in most cases, whether the boundary related to the territorial sea or to the continental shelf or to other maritime zones, the parties have followed the median line as the applicable rule. Where the special circumstances so required it, the median line was modified, particularly in relation to the location of islands. Where, however, because of geographical, geological or other reasons, the median line was not regarded as appropriate or equitable, a negotiated line was agreed to between the parties. Sometimes the boundary line was in part the median line and in part the negotiated line, the latter being determined in some cases in relation to the length of the coastlines of the parties, supplemented by a zone cutting across the boundary line for joint exploitation. In the Agreement between Iceland and Norway (Jan Mayen), 1981, a larger zone for joint exploitation was established on the recommendation of the Arbitration Commission. It was more favourable to Iceland.

Inter-regional Agreements

There were 3 inter-regional Agreements. In the territorial sea boundary Agreement between the Federal Republic of Germany and the German Democratic Republic, 1974, the boundary line which is just short of 8 nautical miles was inclined towards the GDR and in fact followed an established navigation route rather than the median line.

In the Agreement between Italy and Yugoslavia, 1968, although the continental shelf boundary followed the median line, the line was adjusted to give a 12-mile area around the islands of Pelagruz and Kajola between points 34 and 36 of the boundary line. The median line was not drawn between these islands and the Italian main coast. Similarly, the island of Jabuka (Yugoslavia) was also given limited effect. However, all the islands along the coast of Yugoslavia were given full effect in drawing the boundary line as a median line.[37] A similar treatment of islands has also been made in the Agreements between Qatar and Abu Dhabi, 1969, Saudi Arabia and Iran, 1968, and Italy and Tunisia, 1971. The Agreement between Italy and Yugoslavia was also referred to in the Arbitration Case between the United Kingdom and France, 1977.

In the Agreement between Sweden and the German Democratic Republic, which was signed on June 22, 1978, the continental shelf boundary between the two States was settled on the basis of the principle of the median line (Article 1). The boundary consists of three points, which were joined by geodetic lines. The geographical coordinates of these 3 points varied since the parties used their own respective charts. A unity of resource clause was included in the Agreement, which requires prior negotiations and agreement on the conditions concerning the extraction of natural resources straddling across the boundary line (Article 3).

Notes

34. For a list of these Agreements, see Annex I, items 47-71 and 93-95.
34a. *Limits in the Seas*, No. 10 − Revised, 1974, p. 24.
35. Keesing's Contemporary Archives, 24-31 July 1971, p. 24718.
36. *Limits in the Seas*, No. 72, p. 8.
37. *Limits in the Seas*, No. 9, pp. 4-7.

CHAPTER 10

Eastern Europe (Socialist) Agreements

In this Chapter, 8 Agreements will be surveyed, 3 among the Eastern Europe (Socialist) States and 5 inter-regional Agreements to which the USSR was a party.[38]

Five of these Agreements were among States with adjacent coasts. In the remaining 3 Agreements between the USSR and Finland, and the USSR and Turkey, although the States were adjacent, the boundary was drawn between their coasts which are in effect opposite.

In two cases the boundary related to the territorial sea (USSR – Poland, 1958; USSR – Turkey, 1973). In 3 other cases, the Agreements related to the comprehensive boundary including the territorial sea boundary and the continental shelf boundary (USSR – Norway, 1957; USSR – Finland, 1965; and GDR – Poland, 1968). Three Agreements related only to the continental shelf boundary, since they extended the existing territorial sea boundary line (USSR – Finland, 1967; USSR – Poland, 1969; and USSR – Turkey, 1978).

Generally the median line has been followed in all these Agreements, whether they relate to the territorial sea boundary or to the continental shelf boundary. However, in the Agreement between the USSR and Norway, 1957, the terminal point of the territorial sea segment of the boundary line is 4 nautical miles from the Norwegian baseline and 12 nautical miles from an unnamed cape along the coast of the USSR, reflecting the outer limits of the territorial sea of the parties. The territorial sea boundary between the USSR and Poland, 1958, is a perpendicular line from the common land boundary terminal. The territorial sea boundary between the USSR and Turkey, 1973, runs along the 290° azimuth from the common land boundary terminal point. Despite these variations of description, these boundary lines are by and large equidistant.

All continental shelf boundary lines, however, follow the median or equidistance line. The Agreements between the USSR and Poland, 1969, and between the GDR and Poland, 1968, specifically refer to the median or equidistance line principle (Article 1 in both Agreements). The Agreement between the USSR and Turkey, 1978, refers to equitable principles as the basis of demarcation of the continental shelf boundary, which was an extension of the territorial sea boundary settled by the Protocol of April 17, 1973. The boundary line appears to be the median line.

In this sample, no special circumstances requiring the modification of the median or equidistance line appear to have played any part. Barring Norway and Turkey all other States were parties to the Geneva Convention on the Continental Shelf, 1958.

Notes

38. For a list of these Agreements, see Annex I, items 72-74 and 96-100.

CHAPTER 11

Treaties and Agreements: summary

The broad features of the sample of 100 Agreements covered in this study were indicated at the outset of this Part. The sample is not comprehensive. It is based on Agreements whose texts were available to the author. Three-fourths of the Agreements were concluded after 1969. Eighty-four of the Agreements deal with the continental shelf, seabed or maritime boundary, which may also be applicable to other maritime zones, like the fishery zone and the exclusive economic zone; 12 deal with the territorial sea; and 4 establish the joint or common zones, without settling the maritime boundary. Sixty-four of the Agreements relate to States with opposite coasts, 36 relate to States with adjacent coasts. The special features of the Agreements in each region and subregion have already been indicated in the Chapters in this Part.

From the the sample of 100 Agreements as a whole, the following broad conclusions may be drawn:

(1) The main controversy concerning maritime delimitation during negotiations among the parties to an Agreement, at the Third United Nations Conference on the Law of the Sea, among the parties before a court or an arbitrator, and among the writers on the subject, relates to the question whether the applicable principles of international law are 'the equitable principles' or 'the median or equidistance line' or a combination of the two in an acceptable form.

Any analysis of the concluded Agreements among States must presume that the Agreement in question was fair and equitable to the parties concerned who have signed it freely and without duress.

The overall conclusion which one draws from this study is that in a large majority of cases States have been satisfied that the median or equidistance line leads to an equitable solution or result. They have also been ready to negotiate an equitable solution by modifying the median or equidistance line or by adopting a new line if special circumstances obtaining in the area so required it. In some cases, the parties have followed a principle of their own, like the boundary line along a latitude or a meridian, particularly among States adhering to the Santiago Declaration of 1952, and in some other regions also. In four cases, joint or common zones were established, without settling the maritime boundary.

Table 6 will show the overall position on this point.

Table 6. Criteria in delimitation Agreements

Region	Median/equi-distance line (whether true or simplified)	Modified median line	Negotiated line	Joint or common zone	Total
Asia	19	5	1	3	28
Africa	2	1	1	—	4
Latin America	7	4	3	—	14
WEO	16	4	5	—	25
EE	3	—	—	—	3
Inter-regional	17	4	4	1	26
Total	64	18	14	4	100

(2)   An analysis of State practice in relation to the parties to the Geneva Conventions of 1958 is not very helpful or categorical. The 100 Agreements were concluded among 59 States. Of these 22 States were parties to the relevant 1958 Geneva Convention, whereas 37 were non-parties. Of the 100 Agreements, 24 were concluded before 1969, whereas 76 Agreements were post-1969. Of the 76 post-1969 Agreements, only 17 Agreements were concluded between States both of whom were parties to the relevant 1958 Convention. Of these 17 Agreements, 14 followed the median or equidistance line, and 3 adopted a negotiated boundary line. In the remaining 59 Agreements, either both States or one of them was not a party to the 1958 Convention. This point is clarified in Table 7.

Thus, in view of the inadequacy of the number of parties to the 1958 Conventions being parties to the maritime boundary agreements, for general conclusion the analysis indicated in point (1) above may be more helpful.

(3)   The conclusion mentioned in point (1) is generally applicable whether the coasts of the States concerned are opposite or adjacent, or whether the boundary relates to the territorial sea or to the continental shelf or other maritime zones. The Agreements restricting themselves to the territorial sea boundary have, however, mainly followed the median line, although there are exceptions, such as the Agreement between the Federal Republic of Germany and the German Democratic Republic, 1974.

In the Agreement between Australia and Papua New Guinea, 1978, a dual boundary was established in the Torres Strait, one for fisheries and the other for seabed jurisdiction.

122

Table 7

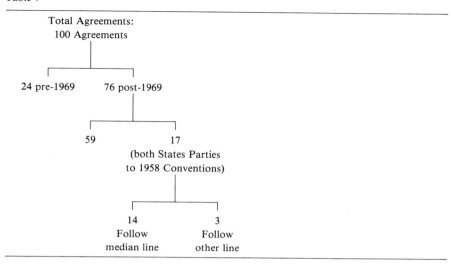

(4)   The special circumstances leading to the adoption of a modified median line or a negotiated line have been the following:

(i)   islands, particularly if title thereto is disputed or if they are located on or near the median line or across the median line (Agreements in the Gulf area, Agreements between Italy and Yugoslavia, 1968, Italy and Tunisia, 1971, India and Sri Lanka, 1974, Australia and Papua New Guinea, 1978);

(ii)   the concavity of the coast (Agreements concerning the North Sea between the FRG and Denmark, the FRG and the Netherlands, and the FRG and the UK, 1971);

(iii) comparable length of coast in the delimitation area (Agreement between France and Spain, 1974);

(iv)   geomorphology (Agreements between Australia and Indonesia, 1972, Indonesia and Thailand, 1975);

(v)   location of resources and structures, and extent of existing licences or contracts (Agreements between Australia and Indonesia, 1972, the FRG and Denmark, 1971, the FRG and the Netherlands, 1971); and

(vi)   traditional fishing rights or rights under an existing Agreement (Agreement between Denmark and Sweden, 1932).

(5)   To promote goodwill and cooperation between the parties, particularly when they hold different views on the principles of maritime delimitation, the Agreements have, while setting the boundary line, also established joint zones for exploitation in some areas (Agreements between France and Spain, 1974, Argentina and Uruguay, 1973, Iceland and Norway (Jan Mayen), 1981), or provided for sharing of proceeds from specified structures or fields (Saudi Ara-

bia and Bahrain, 1958, Qatar and Abu Dhabi, 1969), or recognised traditional fishing rights (Australia and Papua New Guinea, 1978, Kenya and Tanzania, 1975).

In four cases, the parties have established joint or common zones, pending the conclusion of a delimitation agreement or without settling the maritime boundary or unaffected by the alignment of the boundary line (Agreements between Japan and the Republic of Korea, 1974, Malaysia and Thailand, 1979, Kuwait and Saudi Arabia, 1965, and Saudi Arabia and Sudan, 1974).

(6) Most of the Agreements contain a clause protecting the unity of resources extending across the boundary line. Sometimes drilling is prohibited within a specified limit from the boundary line, such as 500 metres in the Agreement between Iran and Saudi Arabia, 1968, or 125 metres in the Agreements between Iran and Qatar, 1969, Iran and Bahrain, 1971, and Iran and Oman, 1974. The Agreement between Venezuela and the Netherlands (Netherlands Antilles), 1978, prohibits drilling by either party up to one nautical mile from the boundary line. In all these Agreements, mutual consultation or agreement of the parties is required before exploitation of such resources.

(7) The Agreements have generally specified the direction of the boundary line or the geographical coordinates of the starting, turning and terminal points of the boundary line, which are to be joined by straight lines, or geodesic lines, or arcs of Great Circle, as may be specified therein. The practical problem of physically locating these points at sea or on the seabed is generally left to the technical experts of the parties concerned. The Agreements have generally indicated the datum relied on for determining the geographical coordinates of the turning and terminal points and plotted them on the charts enclosed with them.

(8) As to the procedure followed, in many cases the parties have negotiated the Agreement on maritime boundary through technical and legal experts, who adopted a Memorandum of Understanding, which was later embodied into a formal Agreement signed at the political level (most of the Agreements concluded by India, and the Southeast Asian Agreements). In some cases, the parties have adopted a provisional Agreement through exchanges of letters or notes and later concluded a formal Agreement on that basis (Agreements between Mexico and the USA, 1977 and 1978), or concluded an Agreement subject to ratification but provisionally applied it for a specified period (Agreement between the USA and Cuba, 1977).

PART THREE

Judicial, arbitral and other decisions

CHAPTER 12

Judicial, arbitral and other decisions

In this Chapter decisions by the International Court of Justice, Courts of Arbitration or other forums relating to the subject of maritime boundary since 1969 will be reviewed.[1] The main cases to be covered will be the following:

1. *North Sea Continental Shelf* cases (Federal Republic of Germany/Denmark; FRG/Netherlands), Judgment of 20 February 1969.
2. Arbitration between the United Kingdom of Great Britain and Northern Ireland and the French Republic on the Delimitation of the Continental Shelf – Decisions of the Court of Arbitration dated 30 June 1977 and 14 March 1978.
3. Controversy concerning the Beagle Channel Region (Chile/Argentina) – Decision of Court of Arbitration dated 18 February 1977 – Award dated 2 May 1977.
4. *Aegean Sea Continental Shelf* case (Greece v. Turkey), Judgment of 19 December 1978.
5. Report of the Conciliation Commission on the Continental Shelf Area between Iceland and Jan Mayen (Norway).
6. *Case concerning the Continental Shelf* (Tunisia/Libyan Arab Jamahiriya), Judgment of 24 February 1982.

A. North Sea Continental Shelf cases, 1969

These are the leading cases decided by the International Court of Justice on the principles and rules of international law applicable to delimitation of the continental shelf among adjacent States. Denmark and the Netherlands, which were recognised as parties in the same interest in these cases, are parties to the Geneva Convention on the Continental Shelf, 1958. The Federal Republic of Germany (FRG) had signed the Convention but did not ratify it. The FRG and the Netherlands entered into a partial boundary Agreement on 1 December 1964, covering the boundary in the North Sea up to 26 miles from the existing terminal point. The FRG and Denmark entered into an Agreement on 9 June 1965 settling a partial boundary in the North Sea up to 26 miles. Both these Agreements followed the equidistance line. Denmark and the Netherlands also concluded an Agreement on 31 March 1966 settling the boundary line between them beyond the notional equidistance line boundaries between them and the FRG in the North Sea. This was also drawn on the basis of an equidistance line.

Differences arose between the parties regarding the alignment of the boundary beyond the partial boundary Agreements of 1 December 1964 and 9 June 1965, respectively. By two Special Agreements of 2 February 1967, the parties agreed to refer the question of the applicable principles and rules of international law to the International Court of Justice and further agreed to negotiate the remaining boundary in the light of the decision of the Court.

In the written memorials and in oral pleadings, the FRG submitted that the basic principle of delimitation is that 'each coastal State is entitled to a just and equitable share' and contended that keeping in mind the nature of the North Sea as a quasi-enclosed sea, the FRG should be entitled to a proper share of the continental shelf area in the North Sea on the basis of the length of its coastline or the 'coastal front' or facade and that its continental shelf should converge in the North Sea towards a central point situated on the median line of the whole seabed rather than be 'cut off' by the strict application of the equidistance line due to the concavity of its coast. The method of equidistance was not a rule of customary international law, and its application in the North Sea between them 'would not lead to an equitable apportionment'. Alternatively, if the equidistance method was applicable to the area, the concave configuration of the FRG coast should constitute a 'special circumstance' to justify a departure therefrom.

The Netherlands and Denmark submitted that the principles of delimitation for the maritime boundary between them and the FRG in the North Sea would be those which were expressed in the 'equidistance – special circumstances' rule embodied in Article 6, paragraph 2, of the Geneva Convention on the Continental Shelf, 1958, namely that in the absence of agreement, and unless another boundary was justified by special circumstances, the boundary between them and the FRG is to be determined by the application of the principle of equidistance. Alternatively, the boundary is to be determined on the basis of the exclusive right of each Party over its continental shelf adjacent to its coast and should leave to each Party 'every point of the continental shelf which lies nearer to its coast than to the coast of the other Party'.

Article 6 of the Geneva Convention on the Continental Shelf, 1958, reads as follows:

1. Where the same continental shelf is adjacent to the territories of two or more States whose coasts are opposite each other, the boundary of the continental shelf appertaining to such States shall be determined by agree-

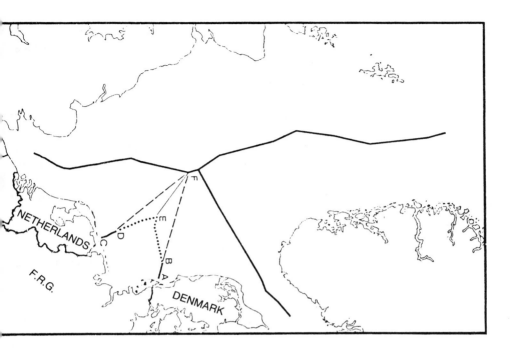

Chart 5. North Sea Continental Shelf cases – claims by the Parties

Note: Lines AB and CD were established by the Agreements reached between the FRG and Denmark on 9 June 1965 and between the FRG and the Netherlands on 1 December 1964, respectively. Line EF was settled between Denmark and the Netherlands by the Agreement reached on 31 March 1966. Lines BE and DE reflect the lines claimed by Denmark and the Netherlands in their negotiations with the FRG on the basis of equidistance. Lines BF and DF reflect the claims of the FRG on the basis of equitable apportionment. The other solid lines in the North Sea reflect the boundary lines established by the existing Agreements between the UK, Norway, Denmark and the Netherlands.
Source: ICJ Judgment 1969, at p. 16 (without the note)

ment between them. In the absence of agreement, and unless another boundary line is justified by special circumstances, the boundary is the median line, every point of which is equidistant from the nearest point of the baselines from which the breadth of the territorial sea of each State is measured.

2. Where the same continental shelf is adjacent to the territories of two adjacent States, the boundary of the continental shelf shall be determined by agreement between them. In the absence of agreement, and unless another boundary line is justified by special circumstances, the boundary shall be determined by application of the principle of equidistance from the nearest points of the baselines from which the breadth of the territorial sea of each State is measured.

The comparative length of the coasts of the FRG, the Netherlands and Denmark were 152, 189 and 203 nautical miles respectively.

The Court confined the Judgment to indicating the delimitation principles applicable to adjacent States for the continental shelf boundary, as distinct from the delimitation principles applicable to States with opposite coasts or for the lateral territorial sea boundary.

At the outset, addressing itself to the FRG contention, the Court said that 'its task in the present proceedings relates essentially to delimitation and not to apportionment of the areas concerned, or their division into converging sectors'.[2]

With reference to the contentions advanced by Denmark and the Netherlands, the main question considered by the Court was thus the following:

Does the equidistance – special circumstances principle constitute a mandatory rule, either on a conventional or on a customary international law basis, in such a way as to govern any delimitation of the North Sea continental shelf areas between the Federal Republic and the Kingdoms of Denmark and the Netherlands respectively?[3]

The Judgment dealt with this question exhaustively. It recognised that the equidistance method has the combination of practical convenience and certainty of application, but added: 'Yet these factors do not suffice of themselves to convert what is a method into a rule of law, making the acceptance of the results of using that method obligatory in all cases in which the parties do not agree otherwise, or in which "special circumstances" cannot be shown to exist'.[4] Under certain circumstances, the equidistance line can produce results which are 'extraordinary, unnatural or unreasonable'. The Court added: 'The plea that, however this may be, the results can never be inequitable, because the equidistance principle is by definition an equitable principle of delimitation, involves a postulate that clearly begs the whole question at issue.'[5]

In the first place, the Court decided that Article 6 of the 1958 Convention, as a conventional rule, was not applicable or opposable to the FRG in the present case, because the FRG was not a Party to that Convention, and if and when it decided to become a Party, the FRG could enter into reservations relating to that Article. The conduct of the FRG did not amount to its assumption or acceptance of the conventional rule in Article 6, nor its recognition as a generally applicable rule. Nor did the FRG conduct create a situation of estoppel because, relying thereon, Denmark or the Netherlands did not change their position detrimentally or suffer prejudice. Nor did the Court consider it appropriate to interpret Article 6 to indicate the stage of the application of equidistance. It did however hold that the Agreement reached between Denmark and the Netherlands on 31 March 1966, which was claimed to be valid *erga omnes*, could not be based on Article 6, since Denmark and the Netherlands were neither adjacent States nor States with opposite coasts, and that the validity of this delimitation must be sought in some other source of law.[6]

The Court then examined at length the second part of the main question mentioned above, namely, whether the equidistance – special circumstances principle embodied in Article 6 of the 1985 Convention was a part of customary international law, which would be applicable to all States whether or not they were Parties to the Convention. It examined the question from two angles, namely first, whether equidistance was inherent in the concept of the continental shelf itself which was the natural prolongation of the land territory of a coastal State under the sea and therefore had the qualities of adjacency and proximity to the landmass, and secondly, whether equidistance had attained the status of a customary rule on a positive law basis or by way of State practice.

As to the inherency argument, the Court recognised that the argument of Denmark and the Netherlands about closer proximity, namely that all those parts of the shelf should be considered as appurtenant to a particular coastal State which are closer to it than to any other State, had much force since as a matter of normal topography, the greater part of a State's continental shelf areas will in fact be nearer to its coast than to any other, but added that '*post hoc* is not *propter hoc*, and this situation may only serve to obscure the real issue'.[7] It held that there was no necessary or complete identity between the notions of adjacency and proximity, and said that 'by no stretch of imagination can a point on the continental shelf situated say a hundred miles, or even much less, from a given coast, be regarded as "adjacent" to it, or to any coast at all, in the normal sense of adjacency, even if the point concerned is nearer to some one coast than to any other'.[8] As to equidistance inherently resulting from the concept of the natural prolongation or extension of land territory, the Court said that this method would 'frequently cause areas which are the natural prolongation or extension of the territory of one State to be attributed to another, when the configuration of the latter's coast makes the equidistance line swing out laterally across the former's coastal front, cutting it off from areas situated directly before that front'.[9]

131

The Court said that the fluidity of these notions is well illustrated by the case of the Norwegian Trough, and added:

> Without attempting to pronounce on the status of that feature, the Court notes that the shelf areas in the North Sea separated from the Norwegian coast by the 80-100 kilometres of Trough cannot in any physical sense be said to be adjacent to it, nor to be its natural prolongation. They are nevertheless considered by the States parties to the relevant delimitations . . . to appertain to Norway up to the median lines . . . True these median lines are themselves drawn on equidistance principles; but it was only by first ignoring the existence of the Trough that these median lines fell to be drawn at all'.[10]

The Court concluded that 'the notion of equidistance as being logically necessary, in the sense of being an inescapable *a priori* accompaniment of basic continental shelf doctrine, is incorrect'.[11]

Nor was the inherency argument noticeable in the history of the development of the equidistance method of delimitation. The Truman Proclamation of 28 September 1945, which was the 'starting point of the positive law on the subject, and the chief doctrine it enunciated, namely, that of the coastal State as having an original, natural and exclusive (in short a vested) right to the continental shelf off its shores', provided that delimitation between the States shall be by agreement and in accordance with equitable principles. These two concepts 'have underlain all the subsequent history of the subject'.[12]

Reviewing the work of the International Law Commission from 1950 to 1956, the Court held that equidistance as a mandatory rule or as having *a priori* character of inherent necessity 'was never given any special prominence at all, and certainly no priority'. Apart from equidistance, the Commission discussed various other possibilities, for example, the continuation in the seaward direction of the land frontier between the two adjacent States concerned, the drawing of a perpendicular to the coast at the point of its intersection with the land frontier, and the drawing of a line perpendicular to the line of the 'general direction' of the coast. All these were referred by the Commission to a Committee of Experts in 1953, which examined the question of lateral boundary between adjacent territorial waters, and only incidentally the lateral continental shelf boundary.

The Committee of Experts decided that 'the (lateral) boundary through the territorial sea — if not already fixed otherwise — should be drawn according to the principle of equidistance from the respective coastlines'. They recognised that in 'a number of cases this may not lead to an equitable solution, which should be then arrived at by negotiation'. As a rider to this conclusion, the Committee said that the same 'could also be used for the delimitation of the respective continental shelves of two States bordering the same continental shelf'.[13]

132

The Commission accepted this recommendation in 1953 and drafted Article 6 accordingly by adding reference to 'special circumstances'.

The Court thought 'it to be a legitimate supposition that the experts were actuated by considerations not of legal theory but of practical convenience and cartography'.[14] There was no end to the Commission's hesitations and doubts continued to be expressed in 1956 that its rigid application would be open to the objection that 'the geographical configuration of the coast would render a boundary drawn on this basis inequitable'.[15]

Nor did the Commission or the 1958 Conference consider the case of 'two or more' adjacent States for the purpose of delimitation in Article 6, which was the situation in the present case.

The history showed, the Court concluded, that 'at no time was the notion of equidistance as an inherent necessity of continental shelf entertained', that current legal thinking was that 'no one single method of delimitation was likely to prove satisfactory in all circumstances', and that delimitation should therefore be carried out by agreement (or by reference to arbitration) and that it should be effected on equitable principles. Accordingly, in drafting Article 6, the Commission gave priority to agreement and introduced the exception in favour of 'special circumstances'. However, 'even with these mitigations, doubts persisted, particularly as to whether the equidistance principle would in all cases prove equitable'.[16]

The Court did however recognise that for good reason the same difficulty may not apply for a median line boundary between opposite States, and said:

> The continental shelf area off, and dividing, opposite States, can be claimed by each of them to be a natural prolongation of its territory. These prolongations meet and overlap, and can therefore only be delimited by means of a median line; and, ignoring the presence of islets, rocks and minor coastal projections, the disproportionally distorting effect of which can be eliminated by other means, such a line must effect an equal division of the particular area involved.[17]

The Court distinguished the two situations as follows:

> . . . whereas a median line divides equally between the two opposite countries areas that can be regarded as being the natural prolongation of the territory of each of them, a lateral equidistance line often leaves to one of the States concerned areas that are a natural prolongation of the territory of the other.[18]

The justification for a lateral boundary between adjacent *territorial waters* drawn on an equidistance basis was given by the Court on the ground that the distorting effect of coastal configurations are comparatively small and on the ground of the nature of rights therein. As to the latter, the Court said:

> There is also a direct correlation between the notion of closest proximity to the coast and the sovereign jurisdiction which the coastal State is entitled

133

to exercise and must exercise, not only over the seabed underneath the the territorial waters but over the waters themselves, which does not exist in respect of continental shelf areas where there is no jurisdiction over the superjacent waters, and over the seabed only for purposes of exploration and exploitation.[19]

Turning now to the positive law basis of equidistance being a mandatory rule of customary international law, the Court said that for this purpose 'it is necessary to examine the status of the principle as it stood when the Convention was drawn up, as it resulted from the effect of the Convention, and in the light of State practice subsequent to the Convention'.[20] It held that Article 6 of the 1958 Convention was not declaratory of a customary rule. Reviewing the history of equidistance, it added that the 1958 Convention did not crystallise equidistance as an emergent rule of customary law by including it in Article 6. Moreover, reservations were also allowed to that Article, even though only a few were actually made. The position was summed up by the Court as follows:

> . . . the Court reaches the conclusion that the Geneva Convention did not embody or crystallize any pre-existing or emergent rule of customary law, according to which the delimitation of continental shelf areas between adjacent States must, unless the Parties otherwise agree, be carried out on an equidistance – special circumstances basis. A rule was of course embodied in Article 6 of the Convention, but as a purely conventional rule'.[21]

The Court then dwelt at length on the question whether equidistance had since 1958 developed as a customary rule through the requisite quality of State practice. It held that to develop such quality, a provision in a Convention should be of a 'norm-creating character' and added that within the period in question, although short, 'State practice, including that of States whose interests are specially affected, should have been both extensive and virtually uniform in the sense of the provision invoked; – and should moreover have occurred in such a way as to show a general recognition that a rule of law or legal obligation is involved'.[22] As to the norm-creating character, the Court held that Article 6 did not have such a quality, since under this Article, equidistance will apply only in the absence of agreement, it was qualified by 'special circumstances', and reservations could be made to the Article. Nor was there a widespread and representative participation in the Convention since 1958 (46 signatures and 39 ratifications or accessions by 1969) – 'the reasons may be speculative, but the facts remain'.[23]

As to State practice, leaving out the Agreements concluded between the Parties to the case before the Court, and those which did not establish international boundaries, only 15 cases were cited before the Court as having been concluded since 1958. Four of these related to the North Sea. Over half of the total were among States which were parties to the 1958 Convention and therefore they applied the conventional rule embodied in Article 6. In the remaining cases, their action in applying equidistance 'can only be problematical and must remain entirely speculative . . . there is no lack of other reasons for using the equidistance method'.[24] For assessment of the evidence of State practice, the Court said the following:

> The essential point in this connection − and it seems necessary to stress it − is that even if these instances of action by non-parties to the Convention were much more numerous than they in fact are, they would not, even in the aggregate, suffice in themselves to constitute the *opinio juris*: − for, in order to achieve this result, two conditions must be fulfilled. Not only must the acts concerned amount to a settled practice, but they must also be such, or be carried out in such a way, as to be evidence of a belief that this practice is rendered obligatory by the existence of a rule of law requiring it. The need for such a belief, i.e., the existence of a subjective element, is implicit in the very notion of the *opinio juris sive necessitatis*.[25]

These conditions were not fulfilled in the present case, the Court held.

Most of the Agreements cited were also among opposite States, which should not constitute a precedent for the delimitation of lateral boundaries, the Court said. Only one case was comparable to the situation in the cases before the Court, but here the delimitation had not yet been completed.

Against this background, on the question of a positive law basis for the customary rule of equidistance, the Judgment concluded as follows:

> The Court accordingly concludes that if the Geneva Convention was not in its origins or inception declaratory of a mandatory rule of customary international law enjoining the use of the equidistance principle for the delimitation of continental shelf areas between adjacent Staes, neither has its subsequent effect been constitutive of such a rule; and that State practice up-to-date has equally been insufficient for the purpose.[26]

In view of these conclusions, the Court did not consider it necessary to determine whether or not the configuration of the German North Sea coast constitutes a 'special circumstance' under Article 6 of the 1958 Convention or any rule of customary international law.

Having rejected the contention of Denmark and the Netherlands that equidistance was a mandatory rule of customary international law on delimitation, either in its fundamental aspects or on the basis of positive law, the Court said that the basic principles, which have from the beginning reflected the *opinio juris*, are that 'delimitation must be the object of agreement between the States concerned, and that such agreement must be arrived at in accordance with equitable principles'.[27]

The Court then elaborated the principles which govern the delimitation of adjacent continental shelves, emphasising that 'it is not a question of applying equity simply as a matter of abstract justice, but of applying a rule of law which itself requires the application of equitable principles'. The elaborated rules

135

were: (1) that negotiations between the parties with a view to arriving at an agreement must be meaningful, (2) that taking all the circumstances into account equitable principles are applied — 'for this purpose the equidistance method can be used, but other methods exist and may be employed, alone or in combination, according to the areas involved', and (3) that the continental shelf of any State must be the natural prolongation of its land territory and must not encroach upon what is the natural prolongation of the territory of another State.[28]

The Court again stressed how in the present case, because of the geographical circumstances, the application of the equidistance method would be inequitable,[29] and explained the relations between equality and equity in the context of the present case as follows:

> Equity does not necessarily imply equality. There can never be any question of completely refashioning nature, and equity does not require that a State without access to the sea should be allotted an area of continental shelf, any more than there could be a question of rendering the situation of a State with an extensive coastline similar to that of a State with a restricted coastline. Equality is to be reckoned within the same plane, and it is not such natural natural inequalities as these that equity could remedy. But in the present case there are three States whose North Sea coastlines are in fact comparable in length and which, therefore, have been given broadly equal treatment by nature except that the configuration of one of the coastlines would, if the equidistance method is used, deny to one of these States treatment equal or comparable to that given the other two. Here indeed is a case where, in a theoretical situation of equality within the same order, an inequity is created. What is unacceptable in this instance is that a State should enjoy continental shelf rights considerably different from those of its neighbours merely because in the one case the coastline is roughly convex in form and in the other it is markedly concave, although those coastlines are comparable in length. It is therefore not a question of totally refashioning geography whatever the facts of the situation but, given a geographical situation of quasi-equality as between a number of States, of abating the effects of an incidental special feature from which an unjustifiable difference of treatment could result.[30]

Elaborating methods for ensuring equity, the Court emphasised that 'it is necessary to seek not one method of delimitation but one goal',[31] that 'there is no legal limit to the considerations which States may take account of for the purpose of making sure that they apply equitable procedures, and more often than not it is the balancing up of all such considerations that will produce this result rather than reliance on one to the exclusion of all others. The problem of the relative weight to be accorded to different considerations naturally varies with the circumstances of the case'.[32]

136

The Court specified the factors which have to be balanced and taken into account in delimitation as follows:

(1) the geographical aspects of the coastline and the area:

. . . the land dominates the sea; it is consequently necessary to examine closely the geographical configuration of the coastline of the countries whose continental shelves are to be delimited. . . . since the land is the legal source of the power which a State may exercise over territorial extensions to seaward, it must first be clearly established what features do in fact constitute such extensions. . . . the legal regime of the continental shelf is that of a soil and a subsoil, two words evocative of the land and not the sea;[33]

(2) the geology of the shelf in order to find out whether the direction taken by certain configurational features should influence delimitation;

(3) the unity of any deposits;

(4) a reasonable degree of proportionality between the extent of the continental shelf appertaining to the States concerned and the length of their respective coastlines, measured according to their general direction in order to reduce the effect of concavity, convexity or irregularity of their coastlines:

One method discussed in the course of the proceedings, under the name of the principle of the coastal front, consists in drawing a straight baseline between the extreme points at either end of the coast concerned, or in some cases a series of such lines. Where the parties wish to employ in particular the equidistance method of delimitation, the establishment of one or more baselines of this kind can play a useful part in eliminating or diminishing the distortions that might result from the use of that method;[34]

(5) if any overlap of areas arose from the application of these principles, the parties should resolve it by agreement, failing which it should be divided equally or the parties may agree to joint exploitation in order to preserve the unity of the deposit.[35]

The Court concluded the case by reaching the following decision by eleven votes to six:

The Court . . . finds that, in each case,

(A) the use of the equidistance method of delimitation not being obligatory as between the Parties; and

(B) there being no other single method of delimitation the use of which is in all circumstances obligatory;

(C) the principles and rules of international law applicable to the delimitation as between the Parties of the areas of the continental shelf in the North Sea which appertain to each of them beyond the partial boundary determined by the agreements of 1 December 1964 and 9 June 1965, respectively, are as follows:

(1) delimitation is to be effected by agreement in accordance with

equitable principles, and taking account of all the relevant circumstances, in such a way as to leave as much as possible to each Party all those parts of the continental shelf that constitute a natural prolongation of its land territory into and under the sea, without encroachment on the natural prolongation of the land territory of the other;

(2)   if, in the application of the preceding subparagraph, the delimitation leaves to the Parties areas that overlap, these are to be divided between them in agreed proportions or, failing agreement, equally, unless they decide on a regime of joint jurisdiction, user, or exploitation for the zones of overlap or any part of them;

(D)   in the course of negotiations, the factors to be taken into account are to include:

(1)   the general configuration of the coasts of the Parties, as well as the presence of any special or unusual features;

(2)   so far as known or readily ascertainable, the physical and geological structure, and natural resources, of the continental shelf areas involved;

(3)   the element of a reasonable degree of proportionality, which a delimitation carried out in accordance with equitable principles ought to bring about between the extent of the continental shelf areas appertaining to the coastal State and the length of its coast measured in the general direction of the coastline, account being taken for this purpose of the effects, actual or prospective, of any other continental shelf delimitations between adjacent States in the same region.[36]

The Judgment in the case was contained in 54 pages of the Report, which altogether consists of 257 pages. The remaining 203 pages contain the declarations and separate but concurring opinions by six Judges and dissenting opinions by five Judges. Among the separate opinions, President Bustamente y Rivero supported the convergence theory, which appears to have in fact affected the FRG's approach in subsequent negotiations which led to the conclusion of an Agreement between the FRG and the UK of a common boundary along the median line of the seabed of the North Sea.[37] Judge Ammoun in a detailed separate opinion supported the rule of equidistance-cum-special circumstances, and proposed an equitable delimitation where the two boundary lines between the FRG and Denmark on the one hand and the FRG and the Netherlands on the other would meet further than the true equidistance points but short of the median line in the seabed of the North Sea.[38]

The dissenting Judges emphasised that the equidistance principle was a rule of customary international law. Judge Manfred Lachs supported it on the basis of State practice and held that there were no special circumstances operating in the area which would warrant a modification of the equidistance line. He said 'that a special situation, created by "special circumstances" calls for a special, *ad hoc* arrangement'. In the present case he found 'no adequate basis for exemption from the equidistance rule'.[39]

Pursuant to this Judgment, the Parties undertook further negotiations and reached several decisions and Agreements in 1971, by which

(i)   the Agreement reached between the Netherlands and Denmark of 31 March 1966 settling the boundary between the true equidistant point between them and the median line of the seabed of the North Sea was cancelled;

(ii)   new Agreements were concluded between the FRG and Denmark on the one hand and the FRG and the Netherlands on the other, whereby the two boundary lines did not join together but joined the median line of the seabed of the North Sea at separate places (see Chart 4 above);

(iii)   accordingly, an Agreement was reached between the FRG and the UK in September 1971 settling the boundary between the two countries along the median line of the seabed of the North Sea;

(iv)   the Agreements between Denmark and the UK on the one hand and the Netherlands and the UK on the other were revised or amended in conformity with the above decisions.

The new Agreements referred to in the preceding paragraph have been dealt with in Chapter 9, and the result of the new boundary delimitation on the additional area received by the FRG has been indicated therein, as well as the factors which appear to have been taken into account during the negotiations in settling the new boundary lines (see pages 110-113 above).

As far as the *North Sea Continental Shelf* cases 1969 are concerned, although they were confined to lateral continental shelf boundary delimitation, they had a tremendous impact on further refinement and development of international law on delimitation. However, in comments made on the Judgment, and at the Third United Nations Conference on the Law of the Sea, as well as in State practice, its practical impact or effect has been varied. It has been hailed by countries which have insisted upon equity as the governing principle of delimitation. It has been criticised by others who have insisted on equidistance, supplemented by special circumstances, as the reliable guide for delimitation and they have cited State practice in support. The polarisation of views between the equity and equidistance groups continued at the Third United Nations Conference on the Law of the Sea between 1978 and 1981, which ultimately led to a compromise which did not make an express reference either to equitable principles or to equidistance. This aspect will be dealt with in Chapter 13 below.

In the meantime, the applicable principles and rules of delimitation have also been reviewed by a Court of Arbitration in the case between the United Kingdom and France, which gave its decision in 1977. In this decision, the Court of Arbitration appeared to have reviewed the Judgment in the *North Sea Continental Shelf* cases 1969 and established a single rule, namely the 'equidistance-cum-special curcumstances' rule, as the conventional and customary rule of law on delimitation. To this decision, let us now turn.

B. Arbitration between the United Kingdom and France on delimitation of the continental shelf

There were two decisions of the Court of Arbitration in this case, the first given on 30 June 1977 and the second on 14 March 1978.[40]

1. The decision of 30 June 1977

The first decision related to a dispute which had arisen between the United Kingdom and France regarding the alignment of the maritime boundary in the English Channel and the Atlantic region. The parties had agreed on 10 July 1975 that the Court would be requested to decide, in accordance with the rules of international law applicable in the matter as between the Parties, the following question:

What is the course of the boundary (or boundaries) between the portions of the continental shelf appertaining to the United Kingdom and the Channel Islands and to the French Republic, respectively, westward of 30 minutes west of the Greenwich Meridian as far as the 1,000 metre isobath?[41]

It was also agreed between them that the Court's decision 'shall include the drawing of the course of the boundary (or boundaries) on a chart'.[42]

Unlike the *North Sea Continental Shelf* cases 1969, therefore, the Tribunal was asked to determine the boundary.

The choice of the starting point, namely 30 minutes west of the Greenwich Meridian, was a matter of convenience to the Parties. The boundary east of the starting point was to be determined between the United Kingdom and France separately. The choice of the 1,000 metre isobath was due to the developments in the Third United Nations Conference on the Law of the Sea wherein the continental shelf had been defined to extend beyond the territorial sea of a coastal State throughout the natural prolongation of its land territory to the outer edge of the continental margin, which has since 1975 been given precise limits. France would have initially liked the continental shelf to be restricted to the 200-metre isobath and mentioned this indirectly in its reservation to the Convention on the Continental Shelf, 1958. Later it was agreeable to the continental shelf extending up to 200 nautical miles. In the Agreement of 10 July 1975, both parties agreed to the 1,000-metre isobath limit which is between 160 and 180 nautical miles from their respective coasts 'without prejudice to the position of either Government concerning the outer limit of the continental shelf'.[43]

Both parties agreed that their coasts were opposite in the Channel. During the course of negotiations between 1970 and 1974, they had also agreed on portions of the boundary line in the Channel to follow a 'simplified' median line. Differences had arisen about the alignment of the boundary line in relation to

140

the Channel Islands which were located close to the French mainland, that is, across the median line drawn with reference to the mainland of the two countries. The United Kingdom wanted the median line to be drawn between these islands and the French mainland whereas France wanted the main boundary line to be drawn between the mainland of the two countries by ignoring these islands as special circumstances. Differences had also arisen regarding the effect to be given to the Eddystone Rocks as a base point for determining the median line. Finally, differences had arisen regarding the extension of the median line in the Atlantic region up to the 1,000-metre isobath.

The Court of Arbitration, consisting of five members with Mr. Eric Castren of Finland as President, gave the unanimous decision on 30 June 1977 which was delivered to the representatives of the two Governments on 18 July 1977. The outline map indicating the boundary as determined by the Court is given in Chart 6. The lines joining (i) points A, B, C, D, (ii) points E, F and (iii) points G, H, I, J, were simplified median lines agreed to between the parties and reported to the Court. The Court adopted these lines and stated as follows:

> In these circumstances, and since a median line delimitation is indicated by the applicable law, the Court considers it appropriate under Article 2(1) of the Arbitration Agreement, to adopt as the continental shelf boundary in three segments of the English Channel the simplified median line traced between the agreed points A – D, E – F, and G – J.[44]

The gap between points D – E has been filled by adding new turning points, namely, D1, D2, D3 and D4 on the basis of the median line drawn with reference to the mainland of the two countries by ignoring the Channel Islands which will be the primary boundary between the United Kingdom and France in this area. Similarly, points F – G have been joined through F1 as the median line, by giving full effect to the Eddystone Rocks.

From point J, the boundary has been extended to points K, L and M on the basis of equidistance. From point M, the boundary goes up to point N on the 1,000-metre isobath by giving half effect to the Isles of Scilly which lie near the Cornish coast and between 21 miles and 31 miles from Land's End.

The UK Channel Islands will be enclaved and surrounded by the French continental shelf. Their boundary is shown by joining points X, X1, X2, X3, X4 and Y, all of which are at a distance of 12 miles from the established baselines of these islands.

The territorial sea boundary between the Channel Islands and the French coast will be settled between the United Kingdom and France separately by bilateral negotiations. The Court held that it had no competence in the matter since the present reference to the Court was only relating to the continental shelf boundary.

The important aspects of this arbitration relate to (1) separate treatment given to the UK Channel Islands by making them enclaves, (2) recognition of the

141

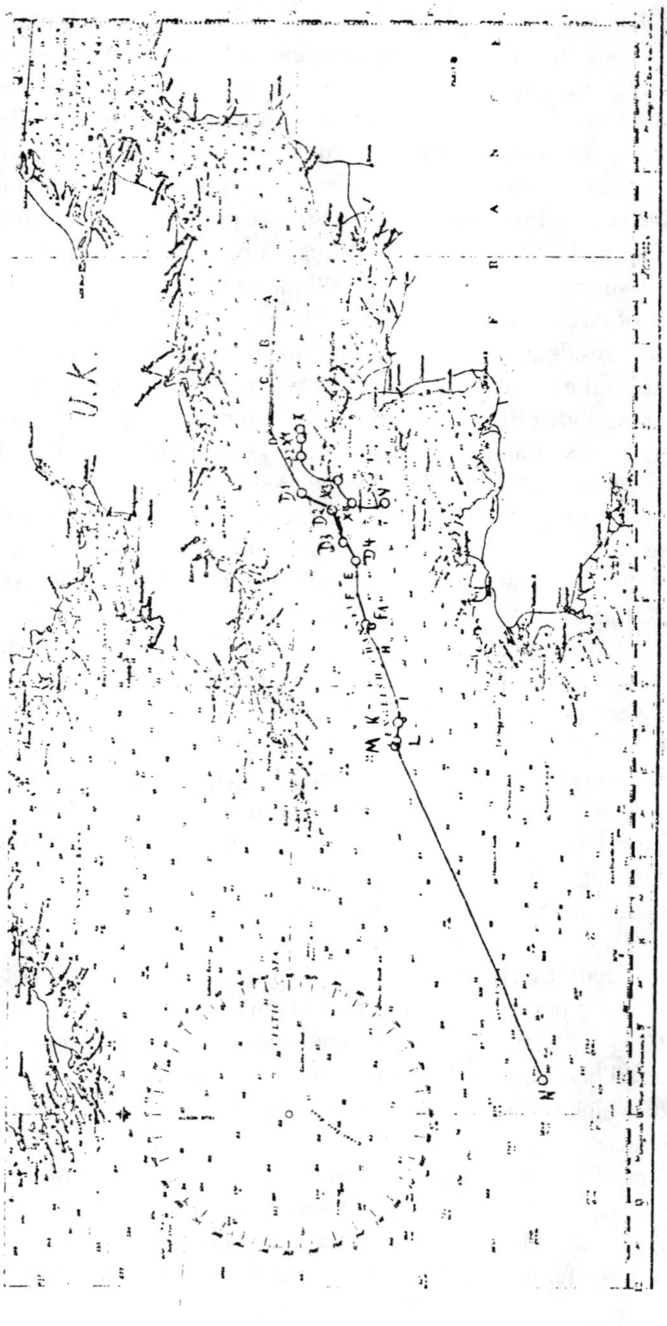

Chart 6. Boundary determined by the UK – France Court of Arbitration, 1977.

Eddystone Rocks as an island for the purpose of delimitation, and (3) giving half effect to the Isles of Scilly in the boundary delimitation between the United Kingdom and France in the Atlantic region as a measure of equity.

The decision of the Court on these three points and the alignment of the boundary in the relative sectors was preceded by an exhaustive discussion of the rules of international law applicble to the matter as between the parties. In this respect also the Court decision has had a substantial impact on the development of international law at the Third United Nations Conference on the Law of the Sea and will have a similar impact on State practice. Although the Court was consciously attempting to indicate that its own Judgment was in conformity with the Judgment of the International Court of Justice in the North Sea Continental Shelf cases 1969, in fact the Court of Arbitration did develop a new concept of a rule of international law regarding maritime delimitation.

There were two major differences between the references to the International Court of Justice and to this Court of Arbitration: In the 1969 cases, the Court was only to indicate the applicable principles or rules of international law but not to determine the boundary, whereas in the present case the Court of Arbitration was asked to determine the course of the boundary (or boundaries) between the two countries in the specified area. Secondly, in the 1969 cases, the boundary related to States with adjacent coasts, whereas in the present case the boundary related mainly to States with opposite coasts. Even in the 1969 cases, the International Court of Justice had recognised that a median line should be equitable in determining the maritime boundary among States with opposite coasts. In the present case also, the two countries had themselves recognised that in some sectors the boundary will be the median line, which had in fact been drawn by them and adopted by the Court.

Even in the present case, the extension of the boundary in the Atlantic region up to the 1,000-metre isobath had aspects of adjacent States because the coasts were not physically opposite to each other in this area and there was an expanse of water separating them. The Court, however, continued to regard this situation as covered by the concept of States with opposite coasts.

Because of these differences in the two situations, the Court of Arbitration took a more practical view of finding a workable principle or rule of international law which could be applied to concrete situations in a manner which was fair and equitable to both sides. The fact that their decision was unanimous, and that the members of the Court were eminent jurists as Judges of the International Court of Justice or members of the International Law Commission, also contributed to the value of their decision.

Rules of international law

Turning now to the rules or principles of international law relating to delimitation, both the United Kingdom and France made elaborate submissions in their written and oral pleadings before the Court of Arbitration. The United Kingdom submitted that since the coasts between the two States were opposite in the arbitration area, Article 6(1) of the 1958 Convention on the Continental Shelf should apply and since the parties had not reached an agreement, and unless France could discharge the burden of proving the existence of special circumstances, the median line should be the boundary in the arbitration area, including in the western approaches to the Channel. Alternatively, if a continuous median line could not be adopted as a boundary throughout the arbitration area, the axis of the Hurd Deep and Hurd Deep Fracture Zone provided the only appropriate dividing line between the natural prolongation of their respective continental shelves.

France on the other hand emphasised that in view of their reservations to the 1958 Convention, Article 6 thereof could not apply between them, and the boundary should be drawn on the basis of customary international law and the equitable principles as elaborated by the International Court of Justice in the *North Sea Continental Shelf* cases, 1969. France added that the application of the median line in relation to the Channel Islands which were located close to the French coast would be inequitable, and that in the Atlantic region up to the 1,000 metre isobath, where the situation between France and the UK was neither of opposite coasts nor of adjacent coasts, but was *sui generis*, the boundary line should be drawn by a bisector of the angle made by the general directions of the coasts of France and the UK.

On the question of the possible impact of the present decision on the maritime boundary between the UK and Ireland, the Court, having regard to the views expressed by the parties, stated it formally at the outset that 'no inferences may be drawn from this Decision as to view of the Court concerning the prospective course of the continental shelf boundary still to be delimited between the United Kingdom and the Republic of Ireland nor concerning the legal and factual considerations relevant to the delimitation of that boundary'.[45]

The reservations made by France to Article 6[46] of the 1958 Convention on the Continental Shelf, while acceding to the Convention on 14 June 1965, were as follows:

Article 6 (paragraphs 1 and 2)

In the absence of a specific agreement the Government of the French Republic will not accept that any boundary of the continental shelf determined by application of the principle of equidistance shall be invoked against it:

144

    – if such boundary is calculated from baselines established after 29 April 1958;

    – if it extends beyond the 200-metre isobath;

    – if it lies in areas where, in the Government's opinion, there are 'special circumstances' within the meaning of Article 6, paragraphs 1 and 2, that is to say: the Bay of Biscay, the Bay of Granville, and the sea areas of the Straits of Dover and of the North Sea off the French coast.[47]

The United Kingdom had, on 14 January 1966, objected to these reservations to Article 6 by stating that they 'are unable to accept the reservations made by the Government of the French Republic'.[48]

The Court held that 'the three (French) reservations to Article 6 are true reservations and admissible',[49] and in view of the objections made by the United Kingdom thereto, without intending to treat the Convention as non-applicable between them, their combined effect is 'to render the Article (Article 6) inapplicable as between the two countries to the extent, but only to the extent, of the reservations',[50] where customary law will apply.

The Court, however, interpreted Article 6 of the 1958 Convention, as well as the customary rules of international law, to have no practical difference in the present case, since in either case the appropriateness of the equidistance method or any other method for delimitation would depend upon the geographical and other relevant circumstances.

Some of the relevant excerpts from the Decision of the Court are as follows:

Article 6, as both the United Kingdom and the French Republic stress in the pleadings, does not formulate the equidistance principle and 'special circumstances' as two separate rules. The rule there stated in each of the two cases is a single one, a combined equidistnce – special circumstances rule. This being so, it may be doubted whether, strictly speaking, there is any legal burden of proof in regard to the existence of special circumstances. The fact that the rule is a single rule means that the question whether 'another boundary is justified by special circumstances' is an integral part of the rule providing for application of the equidistance principle. As such, although involving matters of fact, that question is always one of law of which, in case of submission to arbitration, the tribunal must itself, *proprio motu*, take cognisance when applying Article 6.[51]

. . . As already pointed out, the provisions of Article 6 do not define the condition for the application of the equidistance – special circumstances rule; moreover, the equidistance – special circumstances rule and the rules of customary law have the same object — the delimitation of the boundary in accordance with equitable principles. In the view of this Court, therefore, the rules of customary law are a relevant and even essential means both for interpreting and completing the provisions of Article 6. Indeed, the Court observes that in the present case, whether discussing the application of Article 6 or the position under the customary law, both parties have had free recourse to pronouncements of the International Court of Justice regarding the rules of customary law applicable in the matter.[52]

In this context, the Court of Arbitration also reviewed the provisions (Articles 62 and 71) in the Revised Single Negotiating Text prepared at the Third United Nations Conference on the Law of the Sea in 1976,[53] and came to the following conclusion:

> . . . this Court has examined their provisions and it finds no reason to suppose that, if they were applicable, they would make any difference to the determination of the course of the boundary in the present case. Those texts speak of delimitation between 'adjacent' or 'opposite' States in accordance with equitable principles as distinct cases; and they envisage that, where appropriate, the equidistance or median line shall be employed, taking account of all the relevant circumstances. Since it is the geographical circumstances which primarily determine the appropriateness of the equidistance or any other method of delimitation in any given case, the Revised Single Negotiating Text would not appear to visualise the solution of cases like the present one on principles materially different from those applicable under the 1958 Convention or under general international law.[54]

The Court then reached the following conclusion:

> In short, this Court considers that the appropriateness of the equidistance method or any other method for the purpose of effecting an equitable delimitation is a function or reflection of the geographical and other relevant circumstances of each particular case. The choice of the method or methods of delimitation in any given case, whether under the 1958 Convention or customary law, has therefore to be determined in the light of those circumstances, and of the fundamental norm that the delimitation must be in accordance equitable principles. Furthermore, in appreciating the appropriateness of the equidistance method as a means of achieving an equitable solution, regard must be had to the difference between a 'lateral' boundary between 'adjacent' States and a 'median' boundary between 'opposite' States.[55]

The Court also gave a restrictive interpretation and application to the principles of 'proportionality' and the 'reasonable evaluation of the effects of natural features'. It did not regard proportionality as a general feature providing an independent source of rights to areas of a continental shelf, but as an element in the appreciation of a particular method of delimitation. 'Proportionality . . . is to be used as a criterion or factor relevant in evaluating the equities of certain geographical situations, not as a general principle providing an independent source of rights to areas of continental shelf', the Court said.[56] Regarding the natural features, the Court gave a restricted interpretation, and while applying it to the case, it refused to regard the Hurd Deep – the Hurd Deep Fault Zone as a feature which would 'interrupt the essential geological continuity of the continental shelf' in the English Channel. This zone, as compared to the Norwegian Trough in the North Sea, was a minor fault, the Court said, and added that attaching critical significance to such a feature 'would run counter to the whole tendency of State practice on the continental shelf in recent years'.[57]

Application of the rules

Applying these rules to the facts of the present case, the Court of Arbitration adopted the simplified median line agreed to between the Parties in the English Channel in the sectors east and west of the Channel Islands, and addressed itself to the three questions referred to above, namely (1) the status of the Eddystone Rocks, (2) the position of the Channel Islands, and (3) the alignment of the boundary in the Atlantic region.

Eddystone Rock. Regarding the Eddystone Rock, the question was raised in the extensive arguments of the Parties whether it was an island or a low-tide elevation and whether it would generate a territorial sea of its own. Without pronouncing itself on this question, the Court noted that the conduct of the Parties showed that 'it was in the context of a baseline of the territorial sea, as well as in the context of fisheries, that the French Republic in 1964 – 65 acknowledged the relevance of the Eddystone Rock as a base-point'.[58] The Eddystone Rock was also treated as relevant by the experts of the Parties for drawing up a 'simplified' median line in the English Channel in 1971, and this was also confirmed by the Court's own expert. The Court accordingly concluded that 'it should treat the Rock as a relevant base-point for delimiting the continental shelf boundary in the Channel',[59] and accordingly in the portion of the boundary line between points F and G, a point F1 which was equidistant between Eddystone Rock and the French coast was designated by the Court and shown in the chart prepared by its expert, and forms part of the Court's Decision.

Channel Islands. Regarding the position of the Channel Islands comprising the two Bailiwicks of Jersey and Guernsey, which the Court treated as islands of the United Kingdom despite the autonomy enjoyed by them, and which are located near the Frech coast of Normandy and Brittany, the Court dealt with the elaborate arguments of the Parties at length. France had contended that having regard to the geography, geology and the equitable principles, as well as the security, economic and navigational interests of France, the equality of States, and the principle of proportionality, there should be two boundaries between France and the UK in this region, one between the mainlands of France and the UK taking no account of islands, and the second relating directly to the

147

Channel Islands. As to the latter, the boundary between the Islands and the French coast of Normandy and Brittany should be the median line, but to the north and the west of the Channel Islands, where they face the open sea, the Islands should have a continuous six-mile zone around them, comprising three miles of territorial sea and three miles of continental shelf. Beyond this six-mile zone, the French continental shelf will extend up to the median line between the mainlands of France and the UK.

The United Kingdom contended that since islands were entitled to their own continental shelf irrespective of their location, and since the Channel Islands were not mere 'islets, rocks and minor coastal projections', but populated islands enjoying autonomy in many spheres, the boundary between the UK and France in the region should be the median line which forms a loop around the Channel Islands close to Normandy and Brittany. Such line will be supported by the basic concept of the continental shelf being the natural prolongation of the land mass of a State and its islands, as well as by State practice supporting the concept of semi-enclaves. In response to a question from the Court, the United Kingdom stated that 'there is a portion of continental shelf appertaining to the south coast of England and a portion of continental shelf appertaining to the Channel Islands. These separate portions merge together in mid-Channel'[60]. Finally, the UK contended that 'if there were to be considered any justification for an enclave around the Channel Islands, there could in any event be no justification for an enclaved zone of six miles', since the Channel Islands already possessed an existing fishing zone of 12 miles delineated from the baselines of their coasts, and international law also accepted the 12-mile territorial sea as a right of coastal States.[61]

In their Decision, the Court held that in view of the French reservations, and the UK objections thereto, the legal rules for delimitation in the Channel Islands region will be those of customary international law, rather than Article 6 of the 1958 Convention on the Continental Shelf, even though the practical results in either case may be the same. Examining the geographical facts of the area, the Court said:

> It follows that where the coastlines of two opposite States are themselves approximately equal in their relation to the continental shelf not only should the boundary in normal circumstances be the median line but the areas of the shelf left to each Party on either side of the median line should be broadly equal or at least broadly comparable. Clearly, if the Channel Islands did not exist, this is precisely how the delimitation of the boundary of the continental shelf in the English Channel would present itself.[62]

But the Channel Islands do exist, and are situated 'on the wrong side of the median line', which 'disturbs the balance of the geographical circumstances which would otherwise exist between the Parties in this region as a result of the broad equality of the coastlines of their mainlands'.[63] These islands could not be regarded as the projection of the UK mainland in this region, justifying the median line to extend southwards in a long loop around the Channel Islands. Such an interpretation, the Court said, 'would be as extravagant legally as it manifestly is geographically'.[64] The question for it to decide, the Court said, is 'what areas of continental shelf are to be considered as *legally* the natural prolongation of the Channel Islands rather than of the mainland of France'.[65] The true position, the Court added, is that 'the principle of natural prolongation of territoriy is neither to be set aside nor treated as absolute in a case where islands belonging to one State are situated on continental shelf which would otherwise constitute a natural prolongation of the territory of another State'.[66] The situation has to be appreciated in the light of all the relevant geographical and other circumstances. The Court concluded as follows:

> The presence of these British islands close to the French coast, if they are given full effect in delimiting the continental shelf, will manifestly result in a substantial diminution of the area of continental shelf which would otherwise accrue to the French Republic. This fact by itself appears to the Court to be, *prima facie*, a circumstance creative of inequity and calling for a method of delimitation that in some measure redresses the inequity.[67]

It further added:

> The case is quite different from that of small islands on the right side of or close to the median line, and it is also quite different from the case where numerous islands stretch out one after another long distances from the mainland. The precedents of semi-enclaves, arising out of such cases, which are invoked by the United Kingdom, do not, therefore, seem to the Court to be in point. The Channel Islands are not only 'on the wrong side' of the mid-Channel median line but wholly detached geographically from the United Kingdom.[68]

In view of the above, and ignoring the arguments of security, economy or navigation as not relevant, the Court held that 'the situation demands a twofold solution', namely, *first,* a primary boundary between the UK and France as a median line, linking point D of the agreed eastern segment to point E of the western agreed segment, or, in other words, a mid-Channel median line, and *secondly,* a 12-mile boundary for the Channel Islands drawn to the north and west from their established baselines.

'The effect will be', the Court said, 'to accord to the French Republic a substantial band of continental shelf in mid-Channel which is continuous with its continental shelf to the east and west of the Channel Islands region; and at the same time to leave to the Channel Islands, to their north and to their west, a zone of seabed and subsoil extending 12 nautical miles from the baselines of the two Bailiwicks'.[69] The Channel Islands will thus be enclosed in an enclave surrounded by the French territorial sea and the continental shelf. The boundary between the Channel Islands and the coasts of Normandy and Brittany will be determined between the UK and France separately, this being not within the competence of the Court in the present case.

The Court then indicated the geographical coordinates of these two boundary lines in the region of the Channel Islands, namely points D1, D2, D3 and D4 joining points D and E in the mid-Channel, and points X, X1, X2, X3, X4 and Y around the Channel Islands. In the latter case, the terminal points X and Y were the points of intersection of a 12-mile arc drawn from the basepoints on these Islands and the French coasts of Normandy and Brittany, respectively. These points were drawn by the Court's expert on the Boundary-Line Chart and approved by the Court (see Chart 6). The coordinates of these points are given in the *dispositif*.

Atlantic region. Regarding the course of the boundary in the *Atlantic region*, that is west of point J on the map up to the 1,000 metre isobath, France submitted that since the coasts of the Parties were neither opposite nor adjacent in this region, the boundary should be drawn not with reference to Article 6 of the 1958 Convention but with reference to customary international law, which required that the boundary line should delimit the natural prolongation of the land territory of the Parties and be based on the equitable principles. France argued that the United Kingdom had no coastal or maritime facade in the Atlantic, that its Scilly Isles protruded much further from Cornwall than the French Ushant Island, and that any equidistance line measured with reference to the base-points on these islands alone to long distances seawards in the Atlantic region would be inequitable to France. On the positive side, France proposed that the boundary line should be drawn as a bisector of the angle formed by the lines along the general direction of the coasts of the UK and France in the Channel. In drawing such lines, the French island of Ushant and the British Scilly Isles were not to be taken into account. Such a bisector line will also ensure the application of the principle of proportionality.

The United Kingdom submitted that the continental shelf in the Atlantic region was the natural prolongation of the land territories of the UK and France and was a continuation of the shelf in the English Channel, that Article 6 of the 1958 Convention should apply as the coasts between the two States were opposite and not adjacent, that the median line drawn in the Channel should be extended into the Atlantic region, that the Scilly Islands and Ushant, both of which were populated, should be used as the base-points for drawing such median line, that these islands did not constitute any 'special circumstances' having distorting effect on the boundary and justifying a boundary other than the median line, that full treatment of islands close to their coassts was supported by State practice, and that there was no basis in law nor any objective validity for adopting a new method or basis for drawing a boundary line by taking into

150

account the general direction of the coasts, as proposed by France, which had not been used for drawing the boundary in the English Channel.

In its Decision, the Court said that since the French reservations to the 1958 Convention on the Continental Shelf did not relate to the Atlantic region, Article 6 thereof will apply for the delimitation of the boundary in this region. The distinction made in paragraphs 1 and 2 of Article 6 between States with opposite coasts and States with adjacent coasts 'reflects not a difference in the *legal* regime applicable to the two situations but a difference in the *geographical* conditions in which the applicable legal regime operates'.[70] In either case, in the absence of agreement, and unless another boundary is justified by special circumstances, 'the boundary is to be the line which is equidistant from the nearest points of the baselines from which the breadth of the territorial sea of each State is measured'.[71]

Reviewing the geography and other features of the Channel and the Atlantic region, the Court said that 'the Atlantic region falls within the terms of paragraph 1 rather than paragraph 2 of Article 6',[72] in other words, as having features of States with opposite coasts. It recognised that the United Kingdom had a coastal frontage 'which is comparable broadly in its extent with that of the French Republic, as well as having the same relation to the continental shelf to be delimited'.[73] However, it noted that 'its coastal frontage projects further into the Atlantic than that of the French Republic',[74] due also to 'the greater extension westwards of the Scilly Isles beyond the United Kingdom mainland than that of Ushant beyond the French mainland'.[75] The Court elaborated it as follows:

> . . . The effect of the presence of the Scilly Isles west-south-west of Cornwall is to deflect the equidistance line on a considerably more southwesterly course than would be the case if it were to be delimited from the baseline of the English mainland. The difference in the angle is 16°36′14′′; and the extent of the additional area of shelf accruing to the United Kingdom, and correspondingly not accruing to the French Republic, in the Atlantic region eastwards of the 1,000 metre isobath is approximately 4,000 square miles.[76]

The situation of the Scilly Isles was 'a geographical fact, a fact of nature'. Together with Ushant, they constituted the natural geographical facts of the Atlantic region which could not be disregarded in delimiting the continental shelf without 'refashioning geography'. But the situation created by the Scilly Isles was a 'special circumstance justifying a boundary other than the strict median line', the Court said.[77]

In delimiting the boundary in this region, however, the Court did not consider it proper to change the method of delimitation, such as the one proposed by France by bisecting the angle formed by the lines along the general direction of the two coasts. Nor did it accept the relevance of proportionality. It said:

Equity does not . . . call for coasts, the relation of which to the continental shelf is not equal, to be treated as having completely equal effects. What equity calls for is to an appropriate abatement of the disproportionate effects of a considerable projection on to the Atlantic continental shelf of a somewhat attenuated portion of the coast of the United Kingdom.[78]

Relying on State practice on giving partial effect to offshore islands situated outside the territorial sea of the mainland of a coastal State and a precedent, and the fact that the Scilly Isles and Ushant extended the coastline of their respective mainland in the ratio of two to one, the Court decided to give half-effect to the Scilly Isles as a means of arriving at an equitable delimitation in the present case.

The boundary line was accordingly extended from point J to points K and L as the true median line in the Channel, since the Court regarded the coasts as still opposite here. Thereafter, the coasts face the continental shelf side by side. The boundary line was extended from point L to point M briefly, and from point M it was extended to point N at the 1,000 metre isobath by giving half-effect to the Scilly Isles, that is, the boundary between points M and N 'follows the line which bisects the area formed by, on its south side, the equidistance line delimited from Ushant and the Scilly Isles and, on its north side, the equidistance line delimited from Ushant and Land's End, that is, without the Scilly Isles'.[79]

To sum up, in determining the boundary in the arbitration area, the Court thus adopted the simplified median line agreed to between the Parties in the English Channel between 1970 and 1974, covered the gaps therein by giving full value to Eddystone Rock as a basepoint and by establishing the primary boundary in the region of the Channel Islands as the median line measured from the respective mainlands, and extended the median line of the English Channel into the Atlantic region for a distance of 170 nautical miles between points M and N up to the 1,000 metre isobath by giving half-effect to the Scilly Isles.

To the north and west of the Channel Islands, the Court established an enclosed continental shelf boundary extending up to 12 nautical miles from these islands.

The boundary was drawn on the Boundary-Line Chart included with the Decision (see Chart 6). The coordinates of the points were given in the *dispositif* which read as follows:

For these reasons,

The Court, unanimously, decides, in accordance with the rules of international law applicable in the matter as between the Parties, that:

(1) Except as provided in paragraph (2) below, the course of the boundary between the portions of the continental shelf appertaining to the United Kingdom and to the French Republic respectively, westward of 30

152

minutes west of the Greenwich Meridian as far as the 1,000-metre isobath shall be the line traced in black on the Boundary-Line Chart included with this Decision between Points A, B, C, D, D1, D2, D3, D4, E, F, F1, G, H, I, J, K, L, M and N, the coordiantes of which Points are as follows:

Point A : 50°07′29′′N 00°30′00′′W
Point B : 50°08′27′′N 01°00′00′′W
Point C : 50°09′15′′N 01°30′00′′W
Point D : 50°09′14′′N 02°03′26′′W
Point D1 : 49°57′50′′N 02°48′24′′W
Point D2 : 49°46′30′′N 02°56′30′′W
Point D3 : 49°38′30′′N 03°21′00′′W
Point D4 : 49°33′12′′N 03°34′50′′W
Point E : 49°32′42′′N 03°42′44′′W
Point F : 49°32′08′′N 03°55′47′′W
Point F1 : 49°27′40′′N 04°17′54′′W
Point G : 49°27′23′′N 04°21′46′′W
Point H : 49°23′14′′N 04°32′39′′W
Point I : 49°14′28′′N 05°11′00′′W
Point J : 49°13′22′′N 05°18′00′′W
Point K : 49°13′00′′N 05°20′40′′W
Point L : 49°12′10′′N 05°40′30′′W
Point M : 49°12′00′′N 05°41′30′′W
Point N : 48°06′00′′N 09°36′30′′W

(2) To the north and west of the Channel Islands, the boundary between the portions of the continental shelf appertaining to the United Kingdom (Channel Islands) and to the French Republic respectively shall be the line composed of segments of arcs of circles of a 12-mile radius drawn from the baselines of the Bailiwick of Guernsey and traced in black on the Boundary-Line Chart included with this Decision between Points X, X1, X2, X3, X4 and Y, the coordinates of which Points are as follows:

Point X : 49°55′05′′N 02°03′26′′W
Point X1 : 49°55′40′′N 02°08′45′′W
Point X2 : 49°55′15′′N 02°22′00′′W
Point X3 : 49°39′40′′N 02°40′30′′W
Point X4 : 49°34′30′′N 02°55′30′′W
Point Y : 49°18′22′′N 02°56′10′′W

Mr. Herbert W. Briggs, while agreeing with the unanimous Decision, appended a declaration to the effect that since the intent of the French reservations to Article 6 of the 1958 Convention was to prevent unilateral delimitation by another State based upon equidistance, and 'there can be no unilateral aspect in the Court's decision', and having regard to the facts and the other aspects of these reservations, he would conclude that 'in the particular circumstances of this Arbitration, the French reservations have no object or relevance'. The applicable law in the present case is therefore 'to be found in the 1958 Convention on the Continental Shelf, including Article 6, supplemented, where required, by customary international law'. However, he agreed with the Court that 'little practical effect on the delimitation which the Court is required to make would result from applying one or the other in the circumstances of this case'. He further added:

> My principal concern in this respect is that the Court's interpretation of Article 6 seems, in effect, to shift 'the burden of proof' of 'special circumstances' from the State which invokes them to the Court itself, and constitutes some threat that the rule of positive law expressed in Article 6 will be eroded by its identification with subjective equitable principles, permitting attempts by the Court to redress the inequities of geography.[80]

2. The decision of 14 March 1978

In the second Decision of 14 March 1978 concerning the dispute as to the meaning and scope of the Award of 30 June 1977, pursuant to an Application made by the United Kingdom, the Court of Arbitration dealt with two matters: the first related to the correction of the boundary line to the north and west of the Channel Islands; the second related to the correction of an alleged error in the delineation of the boundary between points M and N where the Isles of Scilly had been given half-effect.

As to the *first* matter, the United Kingdom submitted that the Court had decided in paragraph 202 of its Decision of 30 June 1977 that the 12-mile boundary to the north and west of the Channel Islands should be delimited 'from the established baselines of the territorial sea of the Channel Islands', but that in the *dispositif* and the Boundary-Line Chart, the boundary had been delimited by ignoring the five low-tide elevations and the two dry-land low-water features as base-points which had been the basis of the established baselines of the territorial sea of the Channel Islands. There was thus a discrepancy which the Court was requested to rectify.

The Court of Arbitration, noting that the French Government did not contest the identification of the relevant base-points, found that 'there is no dispute between the Parties as to the base-points relevant for the delimitation of a 12-mile boundary from the baselines of the Bailiwick of Guernsey', that there was accordingly indeed a 'discrepancy' between the boundary indicated in the Decision and defined in the *dispositif* and traced on the Boundary-Line Chart, that the 'discrepancy' was a 'material error' that appears on the face of its decision, 'analogous to one resulting from a "slip of the pen" or from miscalculation or miscasting of arithmetical figures', and that the Court had inherent

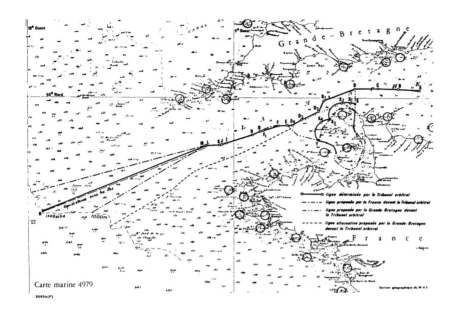

Chart 7. Map indicating claims by the UK and France in 1978.
Source: Reports of International Arbitral Awards, Vol. XVIII, United Nations, p. 270.

power to rectify the resulting error. The boundary defined in paragraph 2 of the *dispositif* (joining points X, X1, X2, X3, X4 and Y) was accordingly corrected by the Court. The new line will be the line composed of segments of arcs of circles of a 12-mile radius drawn from the base-points A to M on the baselines of the Bailiwick of Guernsey, and joining the 12 points of intersection of these arcs of circles, as proposed by the UK, agreed to by France and verified by the Court's expert. The corresponding correction of the boundary traced in the Boundary-Line Chart was left to the Parties by the Court.[81]

The major controversy between the Parties related to the second matter, namely the course of the boundary between points M and N in the Atlantic region.

In summary, the main points made by the United Kingdom in its submissions and oral arguments were as follows:

The Court had in paragraphs 251, 253 and 254 of its Decision of 30 June 1977 given its reasoning for delimiting the course of the boundary from point M westward to the 1,000-metre isobath and indicated the principle and the method to be applied in this sector, which was that 'in principle . . . the boundary in the remainder of the Atlantic region (i.e. between points M and N) is to be determined by the equidistance method by giving only half-effect to the Scillies'.[82] The line traced on the chart by the Court's Expert and embodied by the Court in its *dispositif* was in contradiction with its reasoning since the line M-N was a 'loxodrome' or a straight line drawn on the Mercator Projection Chart used for the Boundary-Line Chart. The Mercator navigational map projection depicts the geographical facts in terms of 'plane geometry' which does not make any allowance for the curvature of the earth. The horizontal distance scales of such charts are not constant but vary with the latitude. The UK had illustrated this in the five maps submitted with its Memorial, and explained it further in its Counter-Memorial. The line M-N drawn by the Court's Expert and adopted by the Court was thus not a line bisecting the area between the true equidistance lines based on Ushant and the Scilly Isles, and on Ushant and Land's End, respectively. Since the length of the line M-N was 170 nautical miles, measured from a limited number of base-points, and point N was not a primary point but a 'derived' point, the scale distortion of the chart used affected the location of point N to the disadvantage of the UK. The true equidistance lines would have pushed the terminal point N of the bisector line four nautical miles southward on its longitude, and if the boundary line were extended up to 200 nautical miles, the discrepancy would increase to six miles, and the difference would have been larger if the the boundary line extended to the outer edge of the continental margin. It was therefore essentially the position of point N itself that was in issue.

This discrepancy between the reasoning of the Court and its Decision embodied in the *dispositif* and included in the Chart should therefore be rectified by using geodetic lines on Transverse Mercator Projection which would take into account the curvature of the earth. The United Kingdom also submitted a chart indicating the alignment of the corrected boundary line, which would extend the line from point M as a geodetic line following the same bearing westwards as that stated in the Court's Decision, namely 247°09′37′′, but displacing point N to a new point R eastward.

In summary, the main points made by France in its submissions and oral arguments before the Court of Arbitration (apart from the preliminary objections to the Court's jurisdiction which were not accepted by the Court), were as follows:

There was no contradiction between the reasoning of the Court and its Decision embodied in the *dispositif* and traced on the Boundary-Line Chart. The coasts of France and the UK in the Atlantic region were not opposite. The effect of the protruding Scilly Isles on the alignment of the boundary in this sector was inequitable. Accordingly, the Court decided to give half-effect to the Scilly Isles and indicated the method by which the boundary line would be drawn from simplified base-points. The half-effect method was a variation and approximation of the equidistance line and therefore no absolute mathematical equality was involved. The method had been scrupulously followed by the Court's Expert in drawing the boundary line on the Boundary-Line Chart which was adopted by the Court. The line had been drawn on a Mercator Projection Chart, but the use of such charts and the method of drawing such equidistance lines was common practice in delimiting a maritime boundary and had been used even for boundaries extending to long distances. If the technical aspects of the construction of a true median line as a geodetic line rather than as a loxodrome were now to be discussed, it would also involve a discussion of the use of all the relevant base-points in drawing such geodetic lines. Such consideration would not be a part of the 'interpretation' of the Decision. With its observations, France submitted a chart using new basepoints and drawing true median lines as geodetic lines from which the boundary line would be drawn to join points O and Q with 11 turning points in between, in place of points M and N of the Boundary-Line Chart. Point O in the French line would be located a little to the north of point M in the Boundary-Line Chart, the major course of the French line would be to the north of the line M-N, but the terminal point Q would be slightly south of point N in the Boundary-Line Chart. This demonstrated, according to France, that the Court's line M-N was an excellent 'simplification' of the 'strict' mathematical line O-Q as drawn by them.

Apart from some other questions, the Court put the following two questions to the Agents of the Parties:

(1) What is the general practice in regard to the nature of the charts used for the delimitation of continental shelf and other maritime boundaries? Are charts based on Transverse Mercator Projection in general use in Hydrographic Departments?

(2) During the negotiations which took place in the years 1964 and 1970 – 1974 was there any understanding or discussion between the Parties regarding the use of the Mercator or Transverse Mercator Projection in determining the boundary in the Arbitration Area?[83]

The responses of the Parties to the second question were conflicting particularly as to whether there was any understanding that the lines joining the terminal points would be geodesics or loxodromes or whether the discussions related only to the precise location of the terminal points as strict equidistance points, and as to whether any such understanding related to the delimitation of the boundary in the Atlantic region.

On the first question, although both Parties differed as to whether a geodetic or a loxodrome was more suitable for delimitation of a maritime boundary or for concessionaires of blocks on the continental shelf and as to the general practice in the matter, there appeared to be a small area of agreement between them on the point that the hydrographic departments of several maritime States were conscious of the technical differences between a loxodrome and a geodetic line, particularly in higher latitudes, that in some agreements on maritime boundaries the geodetic lines had been specifically used or mentioned but that in other cases, straight lines or loxodromes had been used to join the turning points of the boundary line on Mercator Projection Charts, and examples of both were given by the Parties.

After a detailed discussion of the submissions and the oral arguments of the Parties and of their responses to the Court's questions, the Court recognised that the main points made by the United Kingdom in its Application related to the technical aspects of the construction of an equidistance line. The issue before the Court related to the interpretation of its earlier Decision and not 'what in the light of fresh facts and fresh arguments ought to have been the Court's Decision regarding the boundary in that (Atlantic) region'.[84] The Court said that they had arrived at their conclusion to give half-effect to the Scilly Isles to mitigate its inequitable effect on the boundary line in the Atlantic region where the coasts were not opposite, and that this solution was therefore an approximation of the strict application of the use of the equidistance lines for drawing the boundary. The Court had discussed the method of giving such half-effect with their Expert in the light of the precedents available and had selected the solution embodied in its Decision in the *dispositif* and traced on the Boundary-Line Chart. It had not given any directions to its Expert as to whether the equidistance lines with reference to which the line joining points M and N was to be drawn should be loxodromes or geodetic lines, but taking into account the nature of its decision to give half-effect to the Scilly Isles, there was no contradiction between its reasoning and the method adopted by its Expert and accepted by the Court. This method was not against the current practice in maritime delimitation. The Court said that 'in maritime delimitations the equidistance

158

principle is generally applied in a somewhat qualified manner', and recalled their interpretation of Article 6 of the 1958 Convention on the Continental Shelf as embodying a combined equidistance – special circumstances rule in this regard.[85] If technical aspects were to be reviewed again, which could not be done in the present case which was confined to the interpretation of the award, many other aspects and factors might have to be considered, including the selection of the relevant base-points and the course of the resulting boundary.

Some relevant excerpts from the Court's Decision in this case are given below:

> In the present instance, the Court found as a fact that, in the light of the particular geographical circumstances of the Atlantic region the projection seawards of the Scilly Isles and their tendency to obtrude upon the continental shelf lying off the more westerly facing French coasts constituted a 'special circumstance' having a distorting effect on the delimitation of an equidistance boundary. From this it concluded that it must adopt a method of delimitation that would abate the effects of the distortion and remedy the inequity resulting from the particular location of those islands. Having made its appreciation of the various elements of the geographical situation, it further concluded that, in principle, it shouls adopt a method of delimitation based upon the use of the equidistance principle but giving only half-effect to the Scilly Isles. The Court then consulted its Expert, as appears from the Decision and the Technical Report, regarding the possible techniques for applying the concept of giving half-effect to the Scillies and at the same time taking account of the change in the problem of delimitation from that of median line between 'opposite' States in the Channel to that of a delimitation between laterally related States in the Atlantic region giving half-effect to those islands. After considering illustrations of the possible techniques and their results presented to it on standard navigational charts, the Court adopted the technique, including the specific base-points to be used, which is defined in paragraph 254 of the Decision and in paragraphs 7 to 10 of the Expert's Technical Report.[86]

> Paragraphs 251, 253 and 254 do not specify either the projection used in constructing the boundary or whether the course of the bisector line forming it should be calculated by reference to 'equidistance' lines delimited as loxodromes or as geodesics; nor did the Court give any directions to the Expert on these technical aspects of the problem. However, as the United Kingdom stresses, the three lines in question were, in fact, calculated by the Expert on standard navigational charts and as loxodromes, without correction for scale error. The bisector line resulting from the Expert's calculations and drawn as a loxodrome on a standard navigational chart – British Admiralty Chart No. 1598 – on Mercator Projection was then examined and adopted by the Court. This line, together with the position and

coordinates of its point of intersection with the 1,000-metre isobath (Point N), was accordingly endorsed and defined in paragraph 254 of the Decision and paragraph 1 of the *dispositif*, and finally reproduced on the Boundary-Line Chart.[87]

The question before the Court is not, however, whether the two loxodromes employed in the Expert's calculations may be considered as a simplified form of 'strict' or 'true' equidistance lines. It is whether they can and ought to be considered as 'equidistance lines' within the meaning, and for the purpose, of the half-effect method of delimitation adopted and defined in paragraphs 251, 253 and 254 of the Decision. In answering this question the Court has necessarily to take as its starting point the fact, which is undisputed, that the calculation by the Expert, on the standard navigational charts employed by him, of the two loxodromes as lines equidistant from the specified base-points is meticulously exact. It has also necessarily to take as another starting point the fact that the half-effect solution was adopted by the Court as an equitable variant of the equidistance principle expressing a necessarily approximate appreciation of diverse considerations; and that the method for implementing it was devised as a modified rather than as a strict application of the equidistance method. This method, the Court has in addition to recall, was selected *ad hoc*, after a study of various possibilities and of several factors considered by it to be pertinent. The *ad hoc* character of the devise and the fact that it is a special application of the equidistance method is, indeed evidenced by the Court's selection of two particular pairs of base-points for the calculation of the lines determining the half-effect boundary rather than all the potentially relevant points on the respective coastlines. The question for decision, therefore, is whether the Expert's construction of the course of the boundary by reference to the two loxodromes, correctly calculated on Mercator projection from the specified base-points, is compatible with the simplified frame for applying the half-effect solution which has just been described; or whether his omission to allow for the scale of error inherent in that projection renders it incompatible with this frame.[88]

The information available to the Court, as already indicated, does not appear to it to establish that the delimitation of maritime boundaries by a loxodrome line on a standard navigational chart based on Mercator projection without correction for scale error is either inadmissible in law or as yet so outmoded in practice as to make its use open, in general, to challenge. The Court, therefore, finds itself bound to conclude that the techniques used in the calculation of the half-effect boundary may not be considered as incompatible with the method for its delimitation laid down in paragraphs 251, 253 and 254 of its Decision of 30 June 1977.[89]

In view of the above, the Court held that there was no contradiction between the reasoning of the Court and the relevant provision in the decision in the *dispositif*. 'It follows', the Court concluded, 'that the principle of *res judicata* applies and that it is not open to the Court to entertain the request of the United Kingdom for the rectification of this segment of the boundary'.[90] The Court decided, by four votes to one, that the course of the line M-N defined in the *dispositif* and traced on the Boundary-Line Chart was not incompatible with the method of delimitation mentioned in the Decision and that the United Kingdom's request for the rectification of this segment of the boundary was 'not well-founded and must be rejected'.[91]

Mr. Herbert W. Briggs of the United States gave a dissenting opinion. He concluded that 'the technical misapplication of what the Court decided should be corrected as a part of the process of interpretation by the Court of the obscurities resulting from the contradictory passages of its Decision'.[92]

Sir Humphrey Waldock gave a separate opinion. He said that 'the delimitation of the half-effect boundary in the Atlantic region by loxodrome without correction for scale error at least has the appearance of disregarding an equitable consideration that the Court made one of the foundations of its decision with respect to this region'.[93] He added that 'if the matter were now to be open to reconsideration, I am of the opinion that the Court ought certainly to take account of the effect of the curvature of the eart on the operation of the equidistance principle over great distances such as those in the Atlantic region'.[94] But in the light of the information before the Court regarding State practice in the matter, he said that 'it might be going too far to say that the "equidistance" lines calculated by the Expert fall wholly outside the concept of what may pass for equidistance lines in maritime boundary delimitations'.[95] He did entertain some doubts as to whether the substitution of geodesic for loxodrome lines would have affected the Court's appreciation either of the problem or of the base-points to be selected. But it was difficult to discount altogether such a possibility. He therefore decided not to press his doubts to the point of dissenting from the Court's Decision, although he did so with reluctance.

The revised boundary line following the second Decision of te Court of Arbitration is shown in Chart 8.

The importance of the Decision in the United Kingdom – France case arises from the fact that it enunciated the applicable rule as the single rule of equidistance – special circumstances, particularly for delimitation among States with opposite coasts. This rule will apply without any onus of proof on the party invoking special circumstances. To this extent, the conventional rule in Article 6 of the Convention on the Continental Shelf 1958 and the customary international law were identical. In their application, both should lead to an equitable result. In this case, the Court of Arbitration recognised the special circumstances created by the Channel Islands and the Isles of Scilly. The former were given restricted marine spaces and enclaved within the French continental shelf

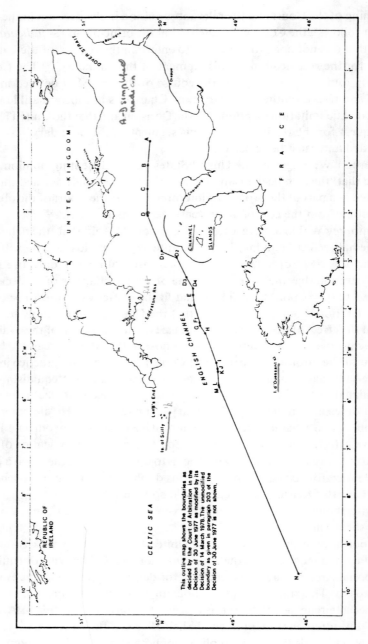

Chart 8. Boundary determined by the UK – France Court of Arbitration, 1977, as modified in 1978.

surrounding them. The latter were given half-effect in determining the boundary line in the Atlantic Ocean region. The technical aspects of the construction of a boundary line in higher latitudes, which led to the second case and was settled in 1978, will also have a cautionary effect. In fact, Robert D. Hodgson, the late US geographer, and E. John Cooper, the Canadian hydrographer, had in an article published in 1976 invited specific attention to the technical aspects of using Mercator projection charts in higher latitutdes, and shown by way of an example that the 200 nautical mile equidistant boundary line drawn at around 5° North between two adjacent States on the two types of charts could make a difference of more than 700 square nautical miles in the area.[96]

Thus, in some respects this Decision modified the Judgment in the *North Sea Continental Shelf* cases, 1969. Both these cases had an important impact on the deliberations at the Third United Nations Conference on the Law of the Sea and on State practice.

C. Controversy concerning the Beagle Channel Region (Chile/Argentina), 1977

The case related primarily to title to territory, namely the islands of Picton, Nueva and Lennox, and the question whether these were located 'south of the Beagle Channel' in terms of Article III of the Boundary Treaty of 1881 between Argentina and Chile. The Court of Arbitration held that this was so and accordingly decided that the islands belonged to Chile. It also dealt with the maritime boundary between the two countries in the Beagle Channel and traced the boundary line on a chart. The boundary line followed 'in princple a median line adjusted in certain relatively unimportant respects for reasons of local configuration or of better navigability for the Parties'.[97] Title to the islands, islets, reefs, banks and shoals, if situated on the northern side of the boundary line, was vested in Argentina and, if situated on the southern side of the boundary line, was vested in Chile.

The decision was given by the Court of Arbitration on 18 February 1977 and was affirmed as the Award by the British Queen on 18 April 1977. On 25 January 1978, the Argentine Government denounced the Award by issuing a declaration of nullity. This was rejected by the Government of Chile on 26 January 1978. The controversy has continued. Talks have been held between the two Governments through the intermediary of the representative of the Pope, but have not yet led to a mutually acceptable solution.

163

D. Aegean Sea Continental Shelf Case (Greece v. Turkey), Judgment of 19 December 1978

This Judgment related to the jurisdiction of the International Court of Justice to deal with a dispute concerning the Aegean Sea continental shelf. The proceedings were instituted by Greece on 10 August 1976. Turkey did not enter appearance, although it did send observations to the Registry both on the question of interim measures and on the question of jurisdiction of the Court to entertain the Greek application. The main point related to the interpretation of reservation (b) made by Greece to its accession to the General Act of 1928, under which it claimed to found the jurisdiction of the Court. The reservation excluded 'disputes relating to the territorial status of Greece' from compulsory jurisdiction. The Court interpreted this reservation to include the present dispute before it.

Some excerpts from the Judgment are as follows:

The basic question in dispute is whether or not certain islands under Greek sovereignty are entitled to a continental shelf of their own and entitle Greece to call for the boundary to be drawn between those islands and the Greek coast. The very essence of the dispute, as formulated in the Application, is thus the entitlement of those Greek islands to a continental shelf, and the delimitation of the boundary is a secondary question to be decided after, and in the light of, the decision upon the first basic question . . .[98]

Quite apart from the fact that the present dispute cannot, therefore, be viewed as one simply relating to delimitation, it would be difficult to accept the broad proposition that delimitation is entirely extraneous to the notion of territorial status. Any disputed delimitation of a boundary entails some determination of entitlement to the areas to be delimited . . .[99]

The question for decision is whether the present dispute is one 'relating to the territorial status of Greece', not whether the rights in dispute are legally to be considered as 'territorial' rights; and a dispute regarding entitlement to and delimitation of areas of continental shelf tends by its very nature to be one relating to territorial status. The reason is that legally a coastal State's rights over the continental shelf are both appurtenant to and directly derived from the State's sovereignty over the territory abutting on that continental shelf. This emerges clearly from the emphasis placed by the Court in the *North Sea Continental Shelf* cases on 'natural prolongation' of the land as a criterion for determining the extent of a coastal State's entitlement to continental shelf as against other States abutting on the same continental shelf (*ICJ Reports 1969*, pp. 31 *et seq.*); and this criterion, the Court notes, has been invoked by both Greece and Turkey during their negotiations concerning the substance of the present dispute. As the Court explained in the above-mentioned cases, the continental shelf is a legal concept in which 'the principle is applied that the land dominates the sea' (*ICJ Reports 1969*, p. 51, para. 96); and it is solely by virtue of the coastal State's sovereignty over the land that rights of exploration and exploitation in the continental shelf can attach to it, *ipso jure*, under international law. . . . A dispute regarding those rights would, therefore, appear to be one which may be said to 'relate' to the territorial status of the coastal State.[100]

The Court also held that the Joint Communique issued by the Greek and Turkish Prime Ministers at Brussels on 31 May 1978 did not contain a decision 'to accept unconditionally the unilateral submission of the present dispute to the Court'.[101] Accordingly, the Court held on 19 December 1978, by 12 votes to 2, that it was without jurisdiction to entertain the Greek Application.

E. Report of the Conciliation Commission on the continental shelf area between Iceland and Jan Mayen (Norway), 1981

The island of Jan Mayen (Norway) is located at about 290 nautical miles north east of Iceland. Iceland had in 1979 established a 200-mile exclusive economic zone around its country. Between Iceland and Jan Mayen lies the Jan Mayen Ridge, the northern portion of which may contain hydrocarbon resources. Iceland was accordingly asserting that it was entitled to a continental shelf area extending beyond its 200-mile economic zone line. Since no agreement was reached on this question between Iceland and Norway, they agreed to refer it to a Conciliation Commission which was established under the Agreement of 28 May 1980. The Conciliation Commission consisted of three members, one nominated by Iceland, another by Norway, and the third, who was to be Chairman, to be agreed upon between the parties. Elliot L. Richardson, (then) leader of the United States Delegation to the Third United Nations Conference on the Law of th Sea, was appointed as Chairman. The other two members were Hans Anderson (Iceland) and Jens Evensen (Norway), both of whom were also leaders of their respective Delegations to the aforesaid Conference. The Commission was established on 16 August 1980. It was asked to make its unanimous recommendations to the two Governments for their consideration. These recommendations were not to be legally binding on the parties.

The Conciliation Commission submitted its recommendations in May 1981.[102]

The Commission consulted a group of experts concerning morphology and geology of Jan Mayen Ridge as well as the possibility of prospective areas for hydrocarbons in that area. The Commission also reviewed the stages of petroleum exploration and exploitation and forms of joint cooperation agreements. They also surveyed the legal aspects of maritime delimitation, including State practice, judicial decisions and provisions of the Draft Convention on the Law of the Sea on the entitlement of islands to marine spaces and on maritime delimitation.

The Commission referred to the report of the technical experts to the effect that historically Jan Mayen Ridge is a thin, long sliver which was previously a part of Greenland, and that 'geologically Jan Mayen Ridge is a microcontinent that predates both Jan Mayen and Iceland which are composed of younger volcanics; therefore the Ridge is not a natural geological prolongation of either Jan Mayen or Iceland'.[103] However, the northern part of Jan Mayen Ridge could morphologically be considered a southward extension from the shelf of Jan Mayen.[103]

In the light of these findings, the Commission concluded that Iceland could not claim any area of Jan Mayen Ridge beyond the 200-mile line on the basis of the natural prolongation of its landmass. Bearing in mind Iceland's strong economic interests in these sea areas, and the fact that Iceland was totally dependent on imports of hydrocarbon products, the Commission recommended that although no new boundary line might be established between Iceland and Jan Mayen (Norway) as the continental shelf boundary beyond the 200-mile economic zone limit of Iceland in the area, a specified area for joint development should be established. The area proposed by the Commission comprises some 45,475 square kilometres, out of which the part north of the 200-mile economic zone line comprises 32,750 sq.km and the area south of the line comprises 12,725 sq. km.

In this joint development area, the interests of both Iceland and Norway were recognised, with some preferential treatment for Iceland.

Thus Iceland could be entitled to acquire a 25 per cent interest in joint venture arrangements or other forms of exploitation in the area north of the 200-mile economic zone line. Its interest will be protected and carried even if it does not participate in such arrangements at the survey and exploration stage. If a commercial find is made, Iceland could still acquire its share of participation in the development phase, after paying its share of exploration and drilling costs incurred before that phase. This facility is not allowed to Norway in that portion of the joint development area which falls south of the 200-mile economic zone line of Iceland, although Norway could also acquire a 25 per cent interest in such joint-venture arrangements in this area.

Similarly, detailed recommendations have been made concerning the resource which may extend on both sides of the demarcation line of the joint development area. If such straddling takes place in the area north of the Icelandic 200-mile economic zone line, the whole deposit should be considered as lying inside the specified area where Norway and Iceland have joint interests. If such straddling takes place in other areas, such as across the 200-mile economic zone line, or south of such line, the deposit should be divided in accordance with a fair assessment and unitised exploitation procedures.

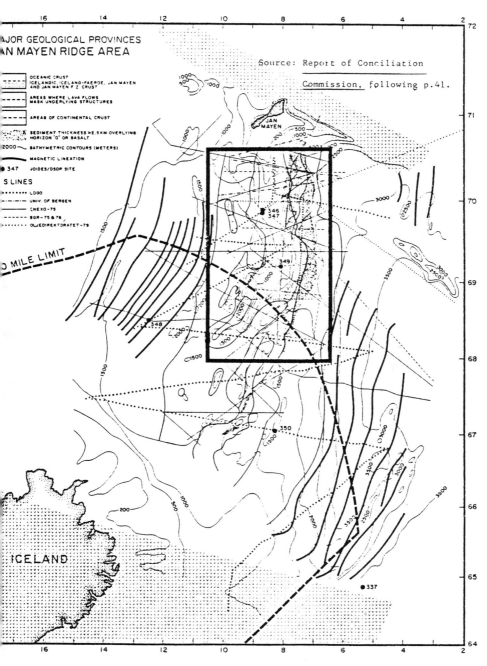

Chart 9. Map indicating joint development area between Iceland and Jan Mayen (Norway), as proposed by the Conciliation Commission in 1981.
Source: Report of Conciliation Commission, following p. 41.

167

In the zones of the joint development area, north or south of the 200-mile economic zone line of Iceland, the laws, oil policy and control, and safety and environmental regulations and administration of Norway and Iceland will apply, respectively.

The joint development area as recommended by the Conciliation Commission is shown in Chart 9.

The recommendations of the Conciliation Commission were made in May 1981. These were accepted by the two Governments. An Agreement between Norway and Iceland was signed on 22 October 1981, which entered into force on 2 June 1982.[104]

F. Case concerning the continental shelf (Tunisia/Libyan Arab Jamahiriya), Judgment of 24 February 1982

The case decided by the International Court of Justice on 24 February 1982 related to the delimitation of the continental shelf boundary between Tunisia and the Libyan Arab Jamahiriya in the Mediterranean Sea. The two States are adjacent. By a Special Agreement of 10 June 1977, the two States agreed to refer their dispute to the International Court of Justice. The Court was requested to indicate the applicable principles and rules of international law relating to maritime delimitation and, in rendering its decision, to take account of equitable principles, the relevant circumstances which characterise the area, and the new accepted trends in the Third United Nations Conference on the Law of the Sea. The Court was also requested to 'specify precisely the practical way' or to 'clarify the practical method' for the application of these principles and rules in the present case, so as to enable the experts of the two countries to delimit these areas without any difficulties.

The Agreement of 10 June 1977 provided that following the delivery of the Judgment of the Court, the Parties shall meet to apply these principles and rules in order to determine the line of delimitation of the area of the continental shelf appertaining to each of the two countries with a view to the conclusion of a treaty in this respect. If within three months of the date of delivery of the Judgment, renewable by mutual agreement, no such treaty was concluded, the two Parties shall together go back to the Court for any explanations and clarifications. It was agreed that 'the two Parties shall comply with the Judgment of the Court and with its explanations and clarifications'.[105]

The 1977 Agreement was filed in the Court by Tunisia at the end of November 1978. The written pleadings were submitted by the Parties within the specified time limits by the middle of 1981. The oral pleadings were held in September and October 1981, and the Judgment was delivered on 24 February 1982.

Earlier, the Court decided on 14 April 1981 that the request of Malta for permission to intervene in the case could not be granted.[106]

168

At the moment of writing (end of 1983), it was not known whether Tunisia and Libya had concluded the delimitation treaty pursuant to the Judgment.

The role of the Court in this case was thus in between that of the International Court of Justice in the *North Sea Continental Shelf* cases, 1969, where the Court indicated the applicable principles and rules, leaving the actual delimitation of the boundaries to the parties, and that of the Court of Arbitration in the *Arbitration between the United Kingdom and France on Delimitation of the Continental Shelf*, 1977 – 78, where the Court decided, in accordance with the applicable rules of international law, the course of the boundary/boundaries in the arbitration area and traced them on the Boundary-Line Chart.[107]

Maps

In order to appreciate the pleadings of the Parties and the decision of the Court, it may be useful to look at the three maps reproduced from the Judgment: Chart No. 10A indicates the coastal configuration of the Parties, the location of the neighbouring States of Italy and Malta, the delimitation line between Tunisia and Italy following the Agreement of 20 August 1971, and the setting for determining the delimitation area by the Court; Chart 10B indicates the limits of the territorial waters claimed by each Party, the delimitation line proposed by Libya, and the 'sheaf of lines' resulting from the Tunisian methods of delimitation; and Chart 10C indicates the delimitation line decided by the Court 'for illustrative purposes, and without prejudice to the role of the experts in determining the delimitation line with exactness'.[108]

Facts and the Judgment in outline

It may also be useful to bear in mind the facts of the case and, in order not to get lost in the contentions of the Parties and the reasoning of the Court, to bear in mind the outcome of the Court's Judgment. These may be summarised as follows:

Tunisia and Libya are adjacent neighbouring States in North Africa adjoining the Mediterranean Sea. Their land boundary is settled and the terminal point at the coast is Ras Ajdir. The Libyan coastline from Ras Ajdir is in east-south-east direction. The Tunisian coastline is in west-north-west direction for some 97 miles when it turns suddenly to north-east direction in the Gulf of Gabes. Tunisia has two main islands or island groups in this area: the island of Jerba is some 45 miles west of Ras Ajdir and the Kerkennah Islands are located 11 miles east of the Tunisian coast. The water between the Kerkennah Islands and the Tunisian mainland is shallow. These Islands cover an area of some 180

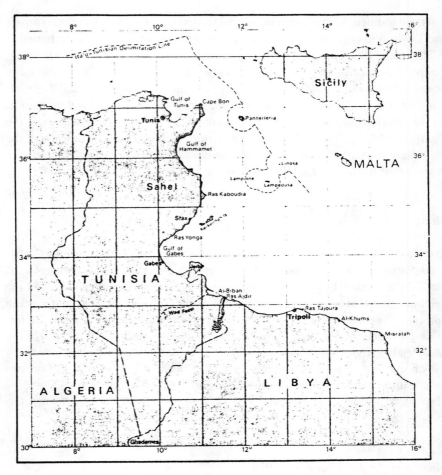

MAP NO. 1

Chart 10A. Case concerning the continental shelf Tunisia – Libyan Arab Jamahiriya, 1982
Coastal configuration of the Parties and neighbouring States
Source: ICJ Reports 1982, at p. 36.

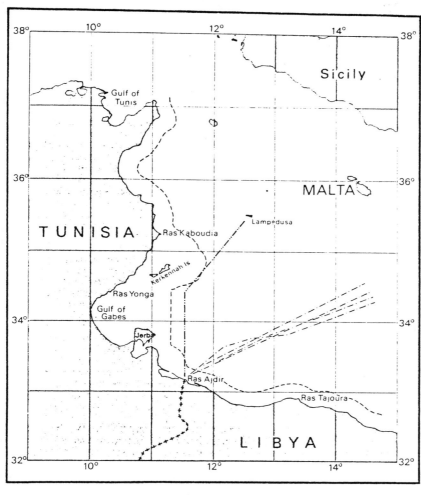

MAP No. 2

- - - - - - - Limit of territorial waters claimed by each Party.
- .. - .. - .. - .. Line resulting from Libyan method of delimitation.
- . - . - . - . - . Sheaf of lines resulting from Tunisian methods of delimitation.

Chart 10B. Case concerning the continental shelf Tunisia – Libyan Arab Jamahiriya, 1982
        Lines claimed by Parties
Source: ICJ Reports 1982, at p. 81.

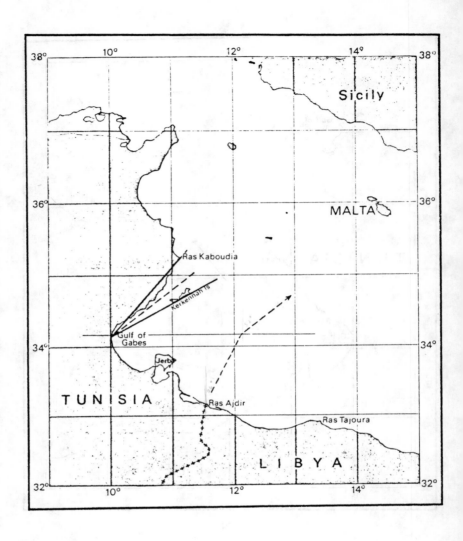

Chart 10C. Case concerning the continental shelf Tunisia – Libyan Arab Jamahiriya, 1982
         Line decided by the Court
Source: ICJ Reports 1982, at p. 90.

square kilometres and have a number of shoals and low-tide elevations to their east between 9 and 27 kilometres therefrom. Tunisa has enclosed the waters around the Kerkennah Isalnds and in the Gulf of Gabes by straight baselines, and also claims historical fishing rights up to the 50-meter isobath. Tunisia has settled its maritime boundary with Italy, and the boundary lines are indicated on Chart 10A.

In its Judgment, the Court defined the delimitation area relevant to the present case as the area enclosed by the parallel passing through Ras Kaboudia (Tunisia) and the meridian passing through Ras Tajoura (Libya), ignored the arguments of geology and the physical features of the seabed, gave primacy to the equitable principles, assessed the relevant circumstances which characterise the area, including the past conduct of the Parties, and for the purpose of indicating the practical method of delimitation, divided the delimitation line into two sectors, the first being closer to the coasts of the Parties, the second being further away.

The line in the first sector started from the outer limit of the territorial sea of the Parties off Ras Ajdir, the terminal point of the land boundary. It continued up to the point of intersection with the parallel passing through the most westerly point in the Gulf of Gabes. The line, which was a straight line, had a bearing of approximately 26° east of north at Ras Ajdir, and corresponded to a line perpendicular to the coast at that point. It was based on the conduct of the Parties concerning the limits of off-shore petroleum concessions.

The line in the second sector, which was also a straight line, extended the first sector line further northeastwards and made an angle of 52° to the meridian. It was drawn by giving a half-effect to the Kerkennah Islands of Tunisia. The terminal point seaward of the second sector line was left undetermined and shown as an arrow, since it would depend upon the delimitation to be agreed upon with third States.

We may now turn to the details of the case.

Submissions of Parties

The *submissions and oral arguments of Tunisia* may be summarised as follows:

As to the applicable principles and rules, Tunisia submitted that the delimitation should be effected in such a way, taking into account the physical and natural characteristics of the area, as to leave to each Party all those parts of the continental shelf that constitute a natural prolongation of its land territory into and under the sea, without encroachment on the natural prolongation of the land territory of the other. 'The delimitation must also be effected in conformity with equitable principles and taking account of all the relevant circumstances which characterize the case, it being understood that a balance must be established between the various circumstances, in order to arrive at an equitable result, without refashioning nature'.[109]

As to the physical and natural characteristics of the area, the geomorphology and bathymetry of the region clearly establish that the natural prolongation of Tunisia extends eastwards as far as the zone constituted by the Zira and Zuwarah Ridges which run parallel to the Libyan coast, and thus 'the natural prolongation of Tunisia is oriented west-east, and that of Libya southwest-northeast'.[110] Within this area, Tunisia exercised well-established historic rights extending up to the 50-metre isobath in the open sea and the line ZV-45° (Zenith Vertical) towards Libya, and delimitation should not at any point encroach upon this area and should exclude it.

The relevant circumstances of the area which should be taken into account included (a) the existence of islands, islets and low-tide elevations which form a constituent part of the Tunisian littoral, (b) the cut-off effect for Tunisia arising from its coastal configuration in relation to the terminal point of the land boundary on the coast between the two States, (c) the concavities and convexities of the Tunisian coast in relation to the regularity of the Libyan coast, and (d) the contiguity between Tunisia and other opposite States and the effects of actual or prospective delimitation carried out with these States.

As to the precise and practical way for delimitation, Tunisia suggested that the delimitation line should take into account the geomorphological features of the region, the existence of the ridges, and the general orientation of the natural prolongation of their territories towards the abyssal plain of the Ionian Sea. The delimitation line from the terminal land boundary point could either (a) run parallel to the bisector of the angle formed by the Tunisian-Libyan littoral in the Gulf of Gabes, or (b) follow the angle of aperture of the coastline at Ras Ajdir in proportion to the length of the relevant coasts of the two States.

The *submissions and oral arguments of Libya* may be summarised as follows:

As to the applicable principles and rules, any delimitation of the continental shelf should be based on the recognition of the fundamental principle that the continental shelf of a State is the natural prolongation of its land territory into and under the sea, and should leave as much as possible to each Party all those parts of the continental shelf that constitute such a prolongation. Such a delimitation respected the inherent *ipso jure* rights of each State, and the assertion of such rights was therefore in accordance with equitable principles.

The direction of the natural prolongation was determined by the whole physical structure of the landmass as indicated primarily by geology, and not by the incidental or accidental direction of any particular part of the coast, or by surface features like submarine ridges which did not disrupt the essential unity of the continental shelf, or by bathymetry and geomorphology.

'In the present case, the continental shelf off the coast of North Africa is a prolongation to the North of the continental landmass, and therefore the ap-

174

propriate method of delimitation of the areas of continental shelf appertaining to each Party in this specific situation is to reflect the direction of this prolongation northward of the terminal point of the land boundary', Libya submitted.[111]

Whether the application of a particular method of delimitation was in accordance with equitable principles was to be tested by its results.

The equidistance method was neither a 'rule' nor a 'principle' and its application in the present case, given the particular geographical configuration, would be inequitable, inappropriate and not in conformity with international law.

The baselines promulgated by Tunisia in 1973 were not opposable to Libya. For the purpose of achieving an equitable delimitation, the whole of the seabed and subsoil beyond the low-water mark along the coast of each Party was to be taken into account. The 'fishing rights' claimed by Tunisia as 'historic rights', even if and where ascertained, were irrelevant to continental shelf delimitation in the present case.

The concept of proportionality, while not applicable to geological and juridical appurtenance of the continental shelf, may properly be used as a criterion to evaluate the effect of geographical features on a delimitation in marginal areas.

The practical method of delimitation in the present case, Libya suggested, was 'to continue the reflection of the natural northward prolongation from the outer limit of the continental shelf, at least as far as the parallel where there occurs a significant change in the general direction of the Tunisian coast which might reasonably be required to be taken into account in order to achieve a delimitation respecting the relevant circumstances in accordance with equitable principles, without affecting the rights of States not Parties to these proceedings'.[112]

It will thus be observed that there was no material difference between the Parties about the applicable principles and rules of delimitation. Both emphasised the equitable principles,[113] taking account of all the relevant circumstances which characterise the area, balancing them, testing them by the results, and effecting a delimitation which would leave to each Party all those parts of the continental shelf that constitute the natural prolongation of its land territory into and under the sea.

The differences between the Parties related to the *inter se* emphasis of these elements and their application to the relevant circumstances operating in the delimitation area. Libya asserted that geology clearly indicated that the continental shelf off the coast of North Africa had a natural prolongation northward, and that the boundary drawn in that direction, later deflected northeastward to take care of the change in the direction of the Tunisian coast, would be in accordance with the equitable principles, respecting the relevant circumstances.

Tunisia insisted that the natural prolongation of its continental shelf beyond its territorial sea was eastward and south-eastward, sought protection for its historic rights, and highlighted the circumstances of the area relevant to equitable delimitation, including the configuration of its coast, the cut-off effect, the presence of islands, and regular bathymetry.

In its Judgment, the Court defined the delimitation area, assessed the relevance of the principle and scope of the natural prolongation in relation to equitable principles, elaborated the applicable principles and rules of delimitation, assessed the relevant circumstances, and determined the practical method of application of the rules to the specific area, illustrating it on Chart 10C (see p. 172 above).

These aspects of the Court's Judgment may now be summarised as follows:

The delimitation area

Taking into account the geographical configuration of the coasts of Tunisia and Libya and the location of their neighbouring States, the Court decided to define the area of delimitation as that part of the area of the Pelagian Sea which falls between Ras Kaboudia on the Tunisian coast and Ras Tajoura on the Libyan coast and is enclosed by the parallel of latitude from Ras Kaboudia and the meridian from Ras Tajoura. The starting point was thus the coastline of the two Parties, and only those parts of the coasts in question were taken into account which had a relationship with each other for the purposes of submarine delimitation.[114]

Natural prolongation and equitable principles

The bulk of the written and oral pleadings before the Court and a significant part of the Court's Judgment dealt with the principle of natural prolongation of land territory as the basis of delimitation and its practical application to the area. Both Parties had relied on the decision of the International Court of Justice in the *North Sea Continental Shelf* cases, 1969, where the Court had said the following:

> delimitation is to be effected by agreement in accordance with equitable principles, and taking account of all the relevant circumstances, in such a way as to leave as much as possible to each Party all those parts of the continental shelf that constitute a natural prolongation of its land territory into and under the sea, without encroachment on the natural prolongation of the land territory of the other.[115]

The Court in that case had also emphasised 'the element of a reasonable degree of proportionality . . . between the extent of the continental shelf areas apper-

176

taining to the coastal State and the length of its coast measured in the general direction of the coastline'.[116]

The differences between the Parties in the present case related to the terrestrial reference unit for determining the natural prolongation: Libya relied on the continental landmass of North Africa and its fundamental geological history; Tunisia relied on the extension of the territory of the States in question and the geographical, bathymetric and geomorphological features of the seabed. Libya also emphasised that equitable delimitation should run along the direction of the natural prolongation, and that equitable principles have no further role. Tunisia emphasised that 'the satisfying of equitable principles in a particular geographical situation is just as much a part of the process of the identification of the natural prolongation as the identification of the natural prolongation is necessary to satisfy equitable principles'.[117]

The Court did not accept either argument and concluded as follows:

> The Court is . . . unable to accept the contention of Libya that 'once the natural prolongation of a State is determined, determination becomes a simple matter of complying with the dictates of nature'. It would be a mistake to suppose that it will in all cases, or even in the majority of them, be possible or appropriate to establish that the natural prolongation of one State extends, in relation to the natural prolongation of another State, just so far and no farther, so that the two prolongations meet along an easily defined line.[117]

Referring to the Tunisian argument, the Court said:

> The satisfaction of the equitable principles is, in the delimitation process, of cardinal importance . . . and identification of natural prolongation may, where the geographical circumstances are appropriate, have an important role to play in defining an equitable delimitation, in view of its significance as the justification of continental shelf rights in some cases; but the two considerations − the satisfying of equitable principles and the identification of the natural prolongation − are not to be placed on a plane of equality.[117]

The Court elaborated the concept of the natural prolongation in relation to the continental shelf and its delimitation both with reference to its earlier decision in the *North Sea Continental Shelf* cases, 1969, and in relation to the 'new accepted trends' at the Third United Nations Conference on the Law of the Sea. The Court said that in 1969, it did not regard an equitable delimitation and a determination of the limits of the 'natural prolongation' as synonymous, and the operative part of its decision of 1969 had referred only to the delimitation being effeted in such a way as to leave 'as much as possible' to each Party the shelf areas constituting its natural prolongation.[118] The facts of the North Sea cases were also different, since the depth of water in the area at no place exceeded 200 metres. The concept of natural prolongation was and remains a concept to be examined within the context of customary law and State practice. The concept of natural prolongation was not an exclusive part of the legal definition of the continental shelf. The Geneva Convention on the Continental Shelf, 1958, had in Article 1 not referred to natural prolongation in its definition of the continental shelf. That Article included a reference to the exploitability criterion for determining the outer limits of the continental shelf and the coastal State's sovereign rights therein. The Court noted that following its Judgment of 1969, the Third United Nations Conference on the Law of the Sea had in Article 76(1) of the Draft Convention on the Law of the Sea defined the continental shelf of a State to 'extend beyond its territorial sea throughout the natural prolongation of its land territory to the outer edge of the continental margin, or to a distance of 200 nautical miles from the baselines from which the breadth of the territorial sea is measured where the outer edge of the continental margin does not extend up to that distance'. Paragraph 10 of Article 76 had provided that these provisions are 'without prejudice to the question of delimitation of the continental shelf between States with opposite or adjacent coasts'. Referring to the second part of paragraph 1 of Article 76, which mentions the distance of 200 nautical miles, the Court said:

> The legal concept of the continental shelf as based on the 'species of platform' had thus been modified by this criterion. The definition in Article 76, paragraph 1, also discards the exploitability test which is an element in the definition of the Geneva Convention of 1958.[119]

The Court further said that the new definition in Article 76(1) 'departs from the principle that the natural prolongation is the sole basis of the title' to the continental shelf or of the rights therein, and added that since both Parties had relied on the principle of natural prolongation, but not advanced any argument based on the 'trend' towards the distance principle, the new definition 'affords no criterion for delimitation in the present case'.[120]

The Court also referred to Article 83(1) of the Draft Convention on the Law of the Sea concerning the delimitation of the continental shelf between States with opposite or adjacent coasts, including the proposal made by the President of the Conference on 28 August 1981, but concluded that 'the new text does not affect the role of the concept of natural prolongation in this domain'.[121]

Natural prolongation and the delimitation area

In a nutshell, therefore, the Court gave primary or cardinal importance to equitable principles for delimitation, but recognised the important role of the identification of natural prolongation where the geographical circumstances were appropriate. This was described by the Court as its 'proper perspective'. The Court then proceeded to examine the contentions of the Parties as to the application of the natural prolongation principle to the present case. It summarised the Libyan arguments based on the theory of 'plate tectonics', according to which the crustal and sub-crustal formations of the earth were divisible into plates which rifted or collided, or converged and diverged, in relation to one another and to the molten asthenosphere below. These movements of the plates in geologic time had caused valleys, oceans and mountains. Their application to the area of controversy between the Parties showed that the submarine area to the north of Libya was a part of the stable African plate or Saharan platform which had rifted from the Eurasian plate, but that what is presently northern Tunisia had later emerged from the sea due to the collision between that part of the African plate and the Eurasian plate. The specific features of the area, namely the 'fall line', the 'hinge line', the valleys, the ridges and the faults were referred to by Libya to support the 'northwest thrust' of the African landmass, and to prove that the area in front of the coast of Libya constituting the Pelagian Block was the 'natural prolongation' northward of the North African landmass, including Libya and Tunisia.

Tunisia, on the other hand, argued that the Pelagian Block was geologically an extension of the Tunisian landmass to the East and that this was supported, among others, by the lines of equal sedimentary thickness (isopachs), the existence of a series of 'moles' following a west – east orientation, the presence of homogeneous stratigraphic facies in a west – east direction, subject to some local disturbance by the 'north – south axis', and by the location of the hinge line which separated the Saharan platform from the Pelagian Block.[122]

Rejecting these contentions, the Court concluded as follows:

> . . . despite the confident assertions of the geologists on both sides that a given area is 'an evident prolongation' or 'the real prolongation' of the one or the other State, for legal purposes it is not possible to define the areas of continental shelf appertaining to Tunisia and to Libya by reference solely or mainly to geological considerations. . . . It is of the view that what must be taken into account in the delimitation of shelf area are the physical circumstances as they exist today; that just as it is the geographical configuration of the present day coasts, so also it is the present day sea-bed, which must be considered. It is the outcome, not the evolution in the long distance past, which is of importance.[123]

The Court also examined the arguments of the Parties based on geomorphology and bathymetry, which had been relied on more by Tunisia. Tunisia had relied on the fidelity of the bathymetric curves, and on the location of low areas or valleys, running eastward, 'one on the North prolonging the Gulf of Hammamet and the other on the South prolonging the Gulf of Gabes', to contend that physically and geologically the Pelagian Block was the natural prolongation of the Tunisian coast to the East, and that the orientation of the Libyan submarine areas was southwest – northeast.[124]

To Libya, the superficial or topographic features of the shelf were not true indicators of natural prolongation, which was determined by fundamental geology. The natural prolongation of Libya and Tunisia in the area was therefore northward, although Libya was ready to deflect the boundary line eastward later on to take account of 'a relevant geographical circumstance which characterizes the area', but the veering would not be dictated by a change in direction of the natural prolongation.[125]

The Court rejected the Tunisian argument and concluded that it was unable to find that any of the features relied on by Tunisia 'involve such a marked disruption or discontinuance of the sea-bed as to contribute an indisputable indication of the limits of two separate continental shelves, or two separate natural prolongations',[126] and mentioned how so substantial a feature as the Hurd Deep had been ignored in the Franco-British Arbitration of 1977.

The Court summed up its position on the relevance of natural prolongation to delimitation as follows:

> The submarine area of the Pelagian Block which constitutes the natural prolongation of Libya substantially coincides with an area which constitutes the natural submarine extension of Tunisia. Which parts of the submarine area appertain to Libya and which to Tunisia can, therefore, not be determined by criteria provided by a determination of how far the natural prolongation of one of the Parties extends in relation to the natural prolongation of the other. In the present case . . . the ascertainment of the extent of the areas of shelf appertaining to each State must be determined by criteria of international law other than those taken from physical features.[127]

> Since the Court considers that it is bound to decide the case on the basis of equitable principles, it must first examine what such principles entail, divorced from the concept of natural prolongation which has been found not to be applied for purposes of delimitation in this case. The result of the application of the equitable principles must be equitable.[128]

> . . . what is reasonable and equitable in any given case must depend on its particular circumstances.[129]

It is against this background that the Court then examined the 'relevant circumstances which characterize the area' and defined the delimitation area as indicated above.

Relevant circumstances

Having decided that the reliance on natural prolongation in the present case was not conclusive for maritime delimitation, which must be determined in accordance with equitable princples, the Court examined at length the 'relevant cir-

180

cumstances which characterize the area'. Tunisia had referred to the presence of islands, islets and low-tide elevations, the potential cut-off effect arising from the configuration of its coastline in relation to the land boundary terminal point, the geomorphological and bathymetric features which indicated the physical and geological structure of the region, the position of other neighbouring States, and its claimed historic rights in relation to fisheries. Libya had in its case concentrated on the geological structure of the shelf and the geographical configuration of the coasts, although in the oral proceedings the counsel for Libya had also mentioned other relevant circumstances or factors, including the existence of a number of legislative acts by both parties relating to fishing, the territorial sea and petroleum concessions, and the existence of petroleum fields or wells within the relevant area.

With respect to the relevant circumstances having a bearing on equitable delimitation, the Court reached the following conclusions:

(1) The marked change in the direction of the Tunisian coast west of the land terminal point is 'legally significant' since it may be said to 'modify the situation of lateral adjacency of the two States'. This is therefore 'one of the relevant circumstances which characterize the area'.[130]

(2) The presence of the islands, islets and low-tide elevations close to the Tunisian coast were related closely to Tunisia's claim of historic fishing rights. However, the island of Jerba and the Kerkennah Islands constituted relevant circumstances and could not be excluded from consideration. The Court then added the following:

> The practical method for the delimitation to be expounded by the Court hereafter is in fact such that, in part of the area to be delimited in which the island of Jerba would be relevant, there are other considerations which prevail over the effect of its presence; the existence and position of the Kerkennah Islands and surrounding low-tide elevations, on the other hand, are material.[131]

(3) The 'cut-off' effect contended by Tunisia could have arisen from the application of the equidistance method of delimitation, or in relation to a line drawn from the frontier point on the basis of a predetermined direction, such as the northward line contended for by Libya. Since neither of these were upheld by the Court, it concluded that the 'cut-off effect' was not here a relevant circumstance.[132]

(4) As to the geomorphological features of the seabed, the Court referred in particular to the Tripolitanian Furrow, which had been interpreted by Tunisia 'as a continuation under the sea of the Gulf of Gabes', and said that since the greater part of this feature lies beyond Ras Tajoura, that is beyond the limits of the delimitation area, and did not disrupt the essential unity of the continental shelf, it was 'inappropriate for inclusion among the factors to be balanced up with a view to equitable delimitation'.[133]

(5) Apart from the facts of geography and geomorphology, the Court also considered *the conduct of the Parties* concerning the possible maritime limits. It noted that the terminal point of the land frontier between Tunisia and Libya, although controversial in history, was now undisputed, namely Ras Ajdir. It noted *four claimed maritime lines*, two unilateral and two establishing a *modus vivendi*, using Ras Ajdir as the starting point, and mentioned them as follows:

> Indeed Ras Ajdir is the starting point of two such [i.e.unilateral] attempts relating to lines projecting seawards: the ZV (Zenith vertical) 45° line north-east claimed by Tunisia; and the northward line claimed by Libya to be a continuation seaward of the last segment of the land frontier, under Petroleum Law No. 25 of 1955, and Regulation No. 1 thereof. Ras Ajdir is also the point of departure of the line perpendicular to the coast proposed by Italy in 1914, and of the line of 26° north-east which had been followed by the two Parties in the granting of concessions for the exploration and exploitation of mineral resources during the period 1964 – 1972.[134]

The Court dealt with these *four claim lines* as follows:

At the outset, it observed that 'an attempt by a unilateral act to establish international boundary lines regardless of the legal position of the other States is contrary to recognised principles of international law'.[135] This observation applied to the first two claims, namely the ZV 45° line and the Libyan claim line of 1955.

The Tunisian claim line of ZV 45°, though implied in 1904, was expressly stated only in the Decree of 26 July 1951. It related to the fishing rights and defined the area of control as the 50-metre isobath on the parallel of Ras Kaboudia 'as far as its intersection with a line drawn north-east from Ras Ajdir, ZV 45°'. The Court regarded it as a unilateral claim line for fisheries, which 'was never a line plotted for the purpose of lateral maritime delimitation, either in the seas or on the continental shelf below them'. The ZV 45° line was thus not opposable to Libya.[136]

Similarly the line referred to in the Libyan Petroleum Regulation of 15 June 1955, issued pursuant to the Petroleum Law of 1955, which showed the boundary line running from Ras Ajdir due north up to a distance of some 62.9 nautical miles, was also not opposable to Tunisia, since it was a unilateral claim and not acquiesced in by Tunisia.[137]

The third line of delimitation, namely the perpendicular to the coast at the border point, the approximate bearing of which was north-north-east from Ras Ajdir, was developed by Italy, the successor of Turkey in the exercise of sovereignty over Tripolitania, in 1913, 1919 and 1931, in modification of the Tunisian ZV 45° line. The Court regarded it as a 'tacit *modus vivendi'* and added that 'such a *modus vivendi*, resting only on the silence and lack of protest on the side of the French authorities responsible for the external relations of Tunisia, falls short of proving the existence of a recognised maritime boundary between the two Parties'.[138] It could in any event imply that the Tunisian claimed historic rights extending to ZV 45° could not be opposable to Libya east of the *modus vivendi* line. It could also warrant its acceptance as a historical justification for the choice of the method of delimitation of the continental shelf between the two States, the Court said.

The fourth line of delimitation, namely a *de facto* line from Ras Ajdir at an angle of some 26° east of north, 'which was the result of the manner in which both Parties initially granted concessions for offshore exploration and exploitation of oil and gas', and was tacitly respected for a number of years, and which approximately corresponded to the line perpendicular to the coast (the third line in the preceding paragraph) was regarded by the Court as a 'circumstance of great relevance for the delimitation', and was in fact used by it in the Judgment in developing the practical method of delimitation.[139]

(6)   The Court also dealt at length with (a) the question of historic fishing rights claimed by Tunisia as dating from the time 'whereof the memory of man runneth not to the contrary', (b) the Tunisian baselines established by a series of legislations culminating in the law of 2 August 1973 and a decree of 3 November 1973 which enclosed the Kerkennah Islands where sedentary fisheries are to be found and declared the waters of the Gulf of Tunis and the Gulf of Gabes as 'internal waters', and from which baselines the outer limits of the Tunisian territorial sea were to be measured, and (c) the question of the relevance of the internal waters and the territorial waters for applying the test of proportionality in determining an equitable continental shelf delimitation.

On historic rights, in relation to the continental shelf delimitation, the Court emphasised that 'the notion of historic rights or waters and that of the continental shelf are governed by distinct legal regimes in customary international law. The first regime is based on acquisition and occupation, while the second is based on the existence of rights "*ipso facto* and *ab initio*"'.[140]

The Court examined the claimed historic rights both in relation to the baselines and the test of proportionality. It made no ruling 'as to the validity or opposability to Libya of the straight baselines', from which the outer limits of the territorial sea of Tunisia are to be measured. Nor did it pass on the question of historic rights as justification for the Tunisian baselines.

As to proportionality, the Court did not agree with Tunisia that the areas of internal waters and territorial waters must be excluded, and elaborated its reasoning as follows:

> It should be reaffirmed that the continental shelf, in the legal sense, does not include the sea-bed areas below territorial and internal waters; but the question is not one of definition, but of proportionality as a function of equity. The fact that a given area is territorial sea or internal waters does not mean that the coastal State does not enjoy 'sovereign rights for the pur-

183

pose of exploring it and exploiting its natural resources'; it enjoys those rights and more, by virtue of its full sovereignty over that area. Furthermore, the element of proportionality is related to the lengths of the coasts of the States concerned, not to straight baselines drawn round those coasts. The question raised by Tunisia: 'how could the equitable character of a delimitation of the continental shelf be determined by reference to the degree of proportionality between areas which are not the subject of that delimitation?' is beside the point; since it is a question of proportionality, the only absolute requirement of equity is that one should compare like with like. If the shelf areas below the low water mark of the relevant coasts of Libya are compared with those around the relevant coasts of Tunisia, the resultant comparison will, in the view of the Court, make it possible to determine the equitable character of a line of delimitation.[141]

On the validity and scope of historic rights claimed by Tunisia and their opposability to Libya, the Court said that this question will be unnecessary if the matter of continental shelf delimitation arrived at by the Court, 'independently of the existence of these rights, is such that the delimitation line will undoubtedly leave Tunisia in the full and undisturbed exercise of these rights – whatever they may be – over the area claimed to be subject to them, so far as opposable to Libya'.[142] Since this was indeed to be the case, the Court did not examine the question of historic rights further.

(7)   As to economic considerations concerning the resources position of the Parties, the Court did not consider them as relevant circumstances to be taken into account for continental shelf delimitation. These are extraneous and variable factors. 'A country might be poor today and become rich tomorrow as a result of an event such as the discovery of a valuable economic resource', the Court said. The presence of oil wells in the delimitation area would however be taken into account in the process of weighing all relevant factors to achieve an equitable result.[143]

To sum up, it would thus appear that the relevant circumstances recognised by the Court for an equitable delimitation of the continental shelf between Tunisia and Libya related to the configuration of the relevant coastlines, the position of the Kerkennah Islands, the positive conduct of the Parties in relation to a delimitation line as *modus vivendi*, and the inclusion of the sea-bed of the internal and territorial waters below the low-water mark of the relevant coasts for applying the test of proportionality.

The practical method for delimitation

The Court then turned to indicating the practical method for delimitation. Although not called upon by the Parties to draw the boundary line precisely on

184

a chart, the Court thought that in order to ensure equitable delimitation, tested by proportionality as indicated above, it should 'define approximately the course of the line which it will be the task of the experts to plot with accuracy'.[144]

As to the method of delimitation, the Court reviewed the developments since the 1969 *North Sea Continental Shelf* cases involving adjacent States and noted that 'Treaty practice, as well as the history of Article 83 of the draft convention on the Law of the Sea, leads to the conclusion that equidistance may be applied if it leads to an equitable solution; if not, other methods should be employed'.[145] Since equidistance was not 'either a mandatory legal principle, or a method having some privileged status in relation to other methods', its use in the present case could only be based on the evaluation and balancing up of all relevant circumstances. It noted that both Tunisia and Libya had regarded the results of the application of the equidistance method as inequitable, but said that this would not prevent the Court from adopting an equidistance line if that would 'bring about an equitable solution of the dispute'.[146]

This is indeed how the Court decided to proceed generally in the second sector of the boundary line, where the situation of adjacency between the coasts of Libya and Tunisia had been modified by the geographical configuration of the Tunisian coast, and where the Court decided to give a half-effect to the Kerkennah Islands of Tunisia.[147]

The Court noted the submissions of the Parties concerning the practical method of delimitation. Libya had submitted that the boundary line in the delimitation area should move northward from Ras Ajdir in conformity with the natural prolongation of the African continental landmass; the line could later be moved eastward to take account of the geographical circumstances of the Tunisian coast for achieving an equitable result. The Tunisian 'sheaf of lines', drawn beyond the area of the claimed 'historic rights', which made an angle between 52° and 65° to the meridian at Ras Ajdir, were based either on the geological, geophysical or bathymetric data, or were drawn on a geometrical basis, taking account of the coastal front and proportionality and other relevant criteria for equitable delimitation. The resulting lines proposed by Tunisia in either case were more or less similar.[148] The Libyan and Tunisian lines were noted by the Court in Chart 10B, which has been reproduced on page 171 above.

The Court did not agree with either method.

As to its own method of delimitation, having defined the delimitation area, the Court noted that the delimitation line therein would extend to a long distance from the land terminal point Ras Ajdir. It therefore decided to adopt a method of delimitation which would divide the delimitation line into two sectors, the first sector being closer to the coastline of the Parties, the second being farther. This distinction was justified not only on grounds of the changes in

185

coastal configuration, namely the northeastward extension of the Tunisian coast from the Gulf of Gabes, but also to avoid the unreasonable practical effects of extending the first sector line to long distances.

The first sector

As to the delimitation line in the first sector closer to the coasts, the Court was conscious that the continental shelf delimitation should start from the outer limits of the territorial sea, and that it had not been requested to indicate the method for territorial sea delimitation starting from Ras Ajdir. The Court however said that 'it is nevertheless the area immediately surrounding the starting point of the land frontier on which the Court must concentrate its attention with a view to the determination and appreciation of the relevant circumstances characterising that area'.[149]

The circumstances relevant to the first sector were the conduct of the Parties concerning the enactment of petroleum licensing legislation and the granting of successive petroleum concessions between 1955 and the signing of the Special Agreement for referring the dispute to the Court in 1977. The Court noted that the phenomenon of actual overlapping of claims did not occur until 1974, and then only in respect of areas some 50 miles from the coast. The eastern limits of the block in a Tunisian concession of 21 October 1966 lay on a straight line which made an angle of 26° to the meridian. Similarly, the Libyan concession (No. 137) granted in 1968 was eastward of a line joining the point 33°55′N and 12°E to a point about one nautical mile offshore, the angle of which from Ras Ajdir being 26°. The same western limits were followed by the subsequent Libyan concessions.

The Court noted that the Parties had in fact made more extensive claims. While referring to the conduct of the Parties, the Court said that they were not 'making a finding of tacit agreement between the Parties', or applying the doctrine of estoppel.[150] The Court referred to the aforementioned conduct of the Parties as indicating a method of delimitation which would ensure equitable delimitation, which the Parties themselves may have considered equitable or acted upon as such 'if only as an interim solution affecting part of the area to be delimited'.[150]

The 26° line, established by conduct of the Parties, was neither arbitrary nor without precedent, the Court said. It was roughly perpendicular to the coast, which is a relevant criterion for equitable delimitation, and had also been considered by the Committee of Experts for the International Law Commission in 1953. It was also the basis of a *modus vivendi* concerning the lateral delimitation of fisheries jurisdiction established between France and Italy between 1919 and 1931, who were the territorial predecessors of Tunisia and Libya.

186

In assessing the direction of the coastline, the Court also considered it legitimate to disregard the island of Jerba which is 'more than a comparatively short distance' from the land terminal Ras Ajdir (some 45 miles west of it), since the Court, in the first sector, was confining its attention to the delimitation of the seabed area which is closer to the coast at Ras Ajdir.

In the first sector, the Court thus held that the delimitation line should run as follows:

> There should first be determined what point on the outer limit of the territorial sea corresponds to the intersection of that limit with a line drawn from the terminal point of the land frontier through the point 33°55′N, 12°E, thus at an angle to the meridian corresponding to the angle of the western boundary of Libyan Petroleum Concessions Nos. NC 76, 137, NC 41 and NC 53, which was aligned with the eastern points of the zig-zag south-eastern boundary of the Tunisian concession 'Permis complémentaire offshore du Golfe de Gabes' (21 October 1966). On the information available to the Court, that angle appears to be 26°; it will, however, be for the experts of the Parties to determine it with exactness. From the intersection point so determined, the line of delimitation of continental shelf areas between the Parties should initially run at that same angle to the meridian.[151]

Since the Court had held that the Tunisian claimed historic fishing rights would have extended up to the perpendicular to the coast, rather than ZV 45° as claimed by Tunisia, and the 26° line now proposed by the Court was approximately along the perpendicular to the coast, the Court said that it was not necessary for it 'to decide on the validity or opposability to Libya of the historic rights claimed'.[151]

The Court also decided to extend the 26° line joining the point on the outer limits of the territorial sea to 33°55′N 12°E in the same direction further up to the point of intersection with the parallel of latitude 34°10′30′′N. This extension was made to take account of the change in direction of the Tunisian coast in the Gulf of Gabes and latitude 34°10′30′′N touched the most westerly point of the Tunisian coastline between Ras Kaboudia and Ras Ajdir, that is to say, the most westerly point on the shoreline (low-water mark) of the Gulf of Gabes. The Court however recognised that 'the precise coordinates of this point will be for the experts to determine', although the Court also indicated them as approximately 34°10′30′′ north.[152]

The Court earlier referred to the contentions of the Parties as to the precise point or angle at which the Tunisian coast changed its direction, and said that it was not called upon to decide that question. Since, however, it was a fact which must be taken into account, and in order to remove difficulties for the Parties, the Court selected the most westerly point in the Gulf of Gabes as indicated in the preceding paragraph.

Thus the method of delimitation for the first sector indicated by the Court was to draw a line from the point on the outer limits of the territorial sea up to 34°10′30′′N, which line has a bearing of 26° to the meridian at the land terminal point Ras Ajdir.

The second sector

In the second sector, namely the extension of the delimitation line beyond the point where the 26° line in the first sector intersected the parallel of latitude 34°10′30′′N, the Court was of the view that the continuation of the same angle to the meridian, namely 26° east of north, would be inequitable. It referred to the Tunisian claims to delimitation on an equidistance line basis in 1974 and in 1976. It also noted that, although the Tunisian equidistance line was drawn with reference to their unilaterally declared baselines, its alignment would be similar in effect if the island of Jerba and the Kerkennah Islands were used for locating basepoints without reference to the baselines. In the second sector, the Court said that two special circumstances must be taken into account, namely (a) the general change in the direction of the Tunisian coast in the Gulf of Gabes, and (b) the existence and position of the Kerkennah Islands which are located about 11 miles east of the town of Sfax, and are surrounded by a belt of low-tide elevations and shoals varying from 9 to 27 kilometers in width. The Court said that the major change in the coastal direction of Tunisia goes in some way to transform 'the relationship of Libya and Tunisia from that of adjacent States to that of opposite States, and thus to produce a situation in which the position of the equidistance line becomes a factor to be given more weight in the balancing of equitable considerations than would otherwise be the case'.[153] Secondly, the Court held that, although the Kerkennah Islands and the low-tide elevations should be taken into account, equity demanded that these Islands should not be given a full value. They should be given a 'half-effect' in the extension of the delimitation line in the second sector. The 'half-effect' was applied by the Court by bisecting the angle formed by joining the most westerly shore point in the Gulf of Gabes with Ras Kaboudia, which had a bearing of 42° to the meridian, and by joining the same most westerly point with the line along the seaward coast of the Kerkennah Islands, which had a bearing of 62° to the meridian. The bisector will thus have a bearing of 52° to the meridian. The delimitation line in the second sector should thus extend the turning point of the delimitation line in the first sector in the north-east direction at an angle of 52° to the meridian, namely parallel to the bisector of the angle referred to above. This was 'without prejudice to the role of the experts in determining the line with exactness'.[154]

As in the first sector, the delimitation line in the second sector was also to be a straight line. The terminal point of the delimitation line in the second sector was left undetermined. The map prepared by the Court (Chart 10C at p. 172 above) indicated it with an arrow mark thereby implying that the preciseness of the terminal point would depend on the delimitations agreed with the neighbouring States on the other side of the Pelagian Sea.

The Court tested the equitableness of its proposed lines in the first and the second sectors by the criterion of proportionality, that is, by the respective shares of Libya and Tunisia in the seabed within the delimitation area. The total area was computed from the shorelines of the two States and the ratio was determined with reference to the length of the respective coasts or their coastal fronts. The Court computed that the length of the coast of Libya from Ras Tajoura to Ras Ajdir was approximately 185 kilometres. The length of the coast of Tunisia from Ras Ajdir to Ras Kaboudia was approximately 420 kilometers. Their proportion was therefore approximately 31:69. With reference to the coastal fronts, their proportion was approximately 34:66. In respect of proportionality, the Court concluded as follows:

> With regard to sea-bed areas, it notes that the areas of shelf below low-water mark within the area relevant for delimitation appertaining to each State following the method indicated by the Court stand to each other in approximately the proportion: Libya 40; Tunisia 60. This result, taking into account all the relevant circumstances, seems to the Court to meet the requirements of the test of proportionality as an aspect of equity.[155]

In conclusion, the Court said that although it had reviewed the entire historical evolution of the concept of continental shelf up to the Draft Convention of the Third UN Conference on the Law of the Sea, as well as its evolution in State practice, and had endorsed and developed those general principles and rules which have thus been established, it was conscious that 'each continental shelf case in dispute should be considered and judged on its own merits, having regard to its peculiar circumstances', and added that, 'therefore, no attempt should be made here to overconceptualise the application of the principles and rules relating to the continental shelf'.[156]

The operative part of the Court's Judgment read as follows:

The Court

by ten votes to four,

finds that:

A.   The principles and rules of international law applicable for the delimitation, to be effected by agreement in implementation of the present Judgment, of the areas of continental shelf appertaining to the Republic of Tunisia and the Socialist People's Libyan Arab Jamahiriya respectively, in the area of the Pelagian Block in dispute between them as defined in paragraph B, subparagraph (1), are as follows:

(1)   the delimitation is to be effected in accordance with equitable principles, and taking account of all relevant circumstances;

(2)   the area relevant for the delimitation constitutes a single continental shelf as the natural prolongation of the land territory of both Parties, so that in the present case, no criterion for delimitation of shelf areas can be derived from the principle of natural prolongation as such;

(3)   in the particular geographical circumstances of the present case, the physical structure of the continental shelf areas is not such as to determine an equitable line of delimitation.

B.   The relevant circumstances referred to in paragraph (1) above, to be taken into account in achieving an equitable delimitation include the following:

(1)   the fact that the area relevant to the delimitation in the present case is bounded by the Tunisian coast from Ras Ajdir to Ras Kaboudia and the Libyan coast from Ras Ajdir to Ras Tajoura and by the parallel of latitude passing through Ras Kaboudia and the meridian passing through Ras Tajoura, the rights of third States being reserved;

(2)   the general configuration of the coasts of the Parties, and in particular the marked change in direction of the Tunisian coastline between Ras Ajdir and Ras Kaboudia;

(3)   the existence and position of the Kerkennah Islands;

(4)   the land frontier between the Parties, and their conduct prior to 1974 in the grant of petroleum concessions, resulting in the employment of a line seawards from Ras Ajdir at an angle of approximately 26° east of the meridian, which line corresponds to the line perpendicular to the coast at the frontier point which had in the past been observed as a de facto maritime limit;

(5)   the element of a reasonable degree of proportionality, which a delimitation carried out in accordance with equitable principles ought to bring about between the extent of the continental shelf areas appertaining to the coastal State and the length of the relevant part of its coast, measured in the general direction of the coastlines, account being taken for this purpose of the effects, actual or prospective, of any other continental shelf delimitation between States in the same region.

C.   The practical method for the application of the aforesaid principles and rules of international law in the particular situation of the present case is the following:

(1)   the taking into account of the relevant circumstances which characterize the area defined in paragraph B, subparagraph (1), above, including its extent, calls for it to be treated, for the purpose of its delimitation between the Parties to the present case, as made up of two

sectors, each requiring the application of a specific method of delimitation in order to achieve an overall equitable solution;

(2) in the first sector, namely in the sector closer to the coast of the Parties, the starting point for the line of delimitation is the point where the outer limit of the territorial sea of the Parties is intersected by a straight line drawn from the land frontier point of Ras Ajdir through the point 33°55'N, 12°E, which line runs at a bearing of approximately 26° east of north, corresponding to the angle followed by the north-western boundary of Libyan petroleum concessions numbers NC 76, 137, NC 41 and NC 53, which was aligned on the south-eastern boundary of Tunisian petroleum concession 'Permis complémentaire offshore du Golfe de Gabes' (21 October 1966); from the intersection point so determined, the line of delimitation between the two continental shelves is to run north-east through the point 33°55'N, 12°E, thus on that same bearing, to the point of intersection with the parallel passing through the most westerly point of the Tunisian coastline between Ras Kaboudia and Ras Ajdir, that is to say, the most westerly point of the shoreline (low-water mark) of the Gulf of Gabes;

(3) in the second sector, namely in the area which extends seawards beyond the parallel of the most westerly point of the Gulf of Gabes, the line of delimitation of the two continental shelves is to veer to the east in such a way as to take account of the Kerkennah Islands; that is to say, the delimitation line is to run parallel to a line drawn from the most westerly point of the Gulf of Gabes bisecting the angle formed by a line from that point to Ras Kaboudia and a line drawn from that same point along the seaward coast of the Kerkennah Islands, the bearing of the delimitation line parallel to such bisector being 52° to the meridian; the extension of this line northeastwards is a matter falling outside the jurisdiction of the Court in the present case, as it will depend on the delimitation to be agreed with third States.

Judges Ago and Schwebel and Judge *ad hoc* Jimenez de Arechaga appended separate opinions to the Judgment of the Court. Judges Gros and Oda and Judge *ad hoc* Evensen appended dissenting opinions.

Summing up

Before summarising the separate and dissenting opinions, it may be useful to note the substance of the Judgment. In a nutshell, the Court ignored the basic arguments of natural prolongation, geology, geomorphology, bathymetry, historic rights, fishing zones, and baselines, which were elaborated in the written pleadings of the Parties in documents 'reaching the height of almost a metre' (as Judge Oda once remarked) as deposited with the Court, as well as in oral proceedings. The Court regarded the seabed of the Pelagian Sea off the coasts of Libya and Tunisia as comprising the common continental shelf which had to be delimited in accordance with equitable principles, and taking into account the relevant circumstances, which were also invoked by both Parties in their submissions. Applying these principles, the Court relied on the conduct of the Parties in indicating the delimitation line in the first sector closer to the coast. In the second sector, it gave half-effect to the Kerkennah Islands by bisecting the angle of aperture at the most westerly point in the Gulf of Gabes and veering the delimitation line by that half angle. Thus the half-effect was not computed in the manner the Court of Arbitration had done in the UK – France Arbitration Case, 1977, with reference to the equidistance line between the two coasts. It was computed with reference to the coastline of Tunisia due to the change in the coastal configuration of Tunisia which was recognised by the Court as a special circumstance prevailing in the area.

In both sectors, the delimitation lines were straight lines, having a bearing of a specified angle to the meridian, namely 26° in the first sector and 52° in the second sector. The prior conduct of the Parties was relied on as evidence of equity rather than as evidence of tacit agreement or for the application of estoppel. The modified equidistance line in the second sector, with half-effect to the Kerkennah Islands, was also applied as a measure of equity. Thus, although the Judgment might appear to be *ex aequo et bono*, the Court consciously adopted the aforementioned criteria for equitable delimitation, although it cautioned against over-conceptualisation of the principles towards the close of the Judgment.

Differences may arise on the point whether the reliance by the Court on the conduct of the Parties, which reflected interim or provisional measures adopted by the Parties by way of caution and restraint without affecting their separate legal claims, would not dissuade the other States from developing a *modus vivendi* pending resolution of their disputes. A number of Agreements have established such provisional demarcation lines, such as the Agreement between Malaysia and Thailand, 1979.

Mark B. Feldman, reflecting on this aspect of the Judgment, comments as follows:

> It would be contrary to the public interest in the peaceful resolution of international disputes if a state that exercised restraint in its activities in an area claimed by another state were punished by implying it had consented to that claim. Nothing could be more inflammatory than drilling on the continental shelf claimed by another state.[157]

As has been mentioned earlier, the Court relied on the conduct of the Parties cautiously. It did not refer to the conduct as implying a tacit agreement or as

192

attracting estoppel. Under these circumstances, in the view of the present author, the Judgment of the Court may not necessarily have adverse effect on other transitional arrangements, although the Judgment would certainly make parties to a potential delimitation dispute more cautious.

Secondly, the question of giving half-effect to the Kerkennah Islands, and the method of its application, namely the bisector of an angle formed by a straight line drawn from the most westerly point in the Gulf of Gabes to Ras Kaboudia passing through the landmass of Tunisia to indicate the general direction of its coast, and the other line from the same point along the seaward points of the Kerkennah, may be a subject of comment. The justification for the half-effect has not been well-reasoned by the Court. As to the technical method applied by the Court, it will be observed from the map included in the Court's Judgment (Chart 10C) that the bisector of the angle in fact touches the eastermost seaward points of the main coast of Tunisia, which could be argued to imply that the extension of the delimitation line in the second sector has in fact ignored the presence of the Kerkennah Islands.

The separate and dissenting opinions to the Judgment, which cover pages 95 to 323 of the *ICJ Reports 1982*, may now be summarised as follows:

Separate opinions

Separate opinions were recorded by Judges Ago, Schwebel and Arechaga, and comprise pages 95 to 142 of the *ICJ Reports 1982*.

Judge Ago, while concurring in the conclusions reached by the Court, and supporting the two-sector delimitation line indicated by the Court as 'a good illustration of that "equitable solution" which the final text of Article 83 of the 1981 Draft Convention on the Law of the Sea indicates', expressed the view that a higher value should have been given by the Court to the *modus vivendi* line proposed by Italy to the French protectorate authorities, the predecessor States of Libya and Tunisia, in 1914, which was implemented by Italy through 'Instructions' having an official and public character, and which was acquised in by the Tunisian authorities 'connoting consent evinced by inaction'. This boundary line was 'no mere embryonic maritime boundary'. It was restricted in its application to the territorial waters and the zones of fishing surveillance. It is on this line, 'already historically and legally established', that the line established by the Parties' conduct concerning the granting of licenses and concessions for the exploration and exploitation of the hydrocarbon resources of the continental shelf up to 1974 was grafted. Thus in Judge Ago's view, 'the order and hierarchy of the arguments put forward by the Court to justify adoption of the practical method . . . as governing the first segment of the line . . . should have been reversed'.[158]

Judge Schwebel stated that 'the Court has not carried the burden of demon-strating why granting full effect to the Kerkennahs would result in giving them "excessive weight".' He noted that 'The Kerkennahs are substantial islands, close to the Tunisian mainland, divided from it by shallow waters in whose banks fisheries are fixed; the considerable population has an ancient and sus-tained fishing and maritime tradition'.[159]

Judge Arechaga (Judge *ad hoc* designated by Libya), while concurring in the Judgment and supporting the Court's interpretation of its role in indicating the practical method of delimitation, expressed the view that 'the operative part of the Judgment should have been framed on the basis, not of degrees of latitude or longitude but of concepts such as the line perpendicular to the coast at Ras Ajdir, going as far as the parallel of the westernmost point in the Gulf of Gabes, and from that point successive veerings parallel to the successive inclinations of the coast of the Tunisian mainland, all of these geographical facts to be de-termined by the experts'.[160]

In concrete, however, he stated that the Court 'should have indicated that the perpendicular line applicable for the first sector is that of 22°, because this is the one resulting from the historical records',[161] which he elaborated in his Opinion with reference to the *modus vivendi* developed between France and Italy, the predecessor States of Tunisia and Libya.[162] He also held that in the *second sector*, there should have been two veerings of the line of delimitation reflecting the change of direction of the Tunisian coast, first in the Gulf of Ga-bes at some 15' north of the 34th parallel, and second at the latitude of Ras Yonga.[163]

In the second sector, however, the Kerkennah Islands would be ignored.

Applying the test of proportionality to his above proposals, he summed up his position as follows:

> . . . a line as the one suggested of 22° with a veering parallel to that of the Tunisian coast, would ahve resulted in assigning to each Party almost 50 per cent of the area in dispute. Such a line of delimitation would thus have complied with the test of a reasonable degree of proportionality, and have achieved an equitable result.[164]

However, he concluded that

> . . . since I concur fully with most of the Court's reasoning, and the above indicated differences do not result in too great a disagreement with respect to the line of delimitation, I consider that I ought not to press these differ-ences and doubts to the point of dissenting from the Court's decision.[165]

Dissenting opinions

Judge Gros, in his dissenting opinion, expressed the view that the Court should have more positively asserted its own jurisdiction under the United Nations Charter, and its own Statute and the Rules, vis-à-vis the Special Agreement between the Parties and the role of the negotiations between them pursuant to the Judgment.

He felt that the Court had not applied the equitable principles of delimitation after proper assessment of the relevant circumstances and the rules and means of their application, as were elaborated and applied by the Court in the *North Sea Continental Shelf* cases, 1969. 'This was not done, and this lack of a systematic search for the equitable has produced a result the equity of which remains to be proved', he said.[166] The Court's first task was to see 'what an equidistance line would produce in order to identify the "extraordinary, unnatural or unreasonable" result to which, it is said, this method might lead'.[166] This also was not done.

The Court proceeded, Judge Gros said, to find an equitable solution by giving a higher value to proportionality:

> . . . the main thrust of the Judgment's approach seems to be that, equity being the goal, proportionality is the method − the Court even says 'principle' − for reaching it; and the Court makes general use of it throughout the present Judgment. This goes much farther than the remark in the 1969 Judgment . . . indicating proportionality as a verifying factor . . . but not as a method for achieving that end.[167]

He added:

> . . . the present Judgment has ruled out the geological argument and effaced the geographical configuration, and has chosen to draw lines of direction which no principle dictates and to adopt angles without justifying their selection in terms of any relevant facts, . . . is it still a conception of equity?[167]

Later, he answered the question with the following comment:

> The Judgment states that there can be no question in the instant case of applying *ex aequo et bono*. Statements are one thing, the effective pronouncement of the Judgment are another. . . . it is not equity which has struck me as presiding over the construction of the Judgment.[168]

As to the practical method of delimitation and the line adopted by the Court in two sectors, Judge Gros felt that, in the first sector, the reliance on the *modus vivendi* between Italy and France, and not on the limits of oil concessions, was not justified. As to the former, he said:

> Well may the Court now regard a 'historical' buffer zone as a *modus vivendi de facto*: legally speaking, it is still nothing more than it was between 1919 and 1940, that is, the unilateral claim of one State to surveillance of its sedentary fisheries.[169]

195

As to the limits of the oil concessions, he said that Tunisia had entered a formal reservation, namely that it was 'pending an agreement between Tunisia and Libya defining the limit of their respective jurisdictions over the continental shelf', and the Libyan concession was not opposable to Tunisia, the other interested party. Judge Gros then asked the question and commented as follows:

> . . . by what coincidence does it become the delimitation line of the continental shelf and, on that account, opposable to Tunisia? The transformation of the unilateral into the equitable remains unexplained. The Judgment has taken on this point a position, which, in my view, is opposed to the applicable rules of law.[170]

As to the second sector, he felt strongly that the Kerkennahs should have been given a full value, and concluded as follows:

> The angle of 52° supposed to represent a 'veering' of the coast shows the persistent effacement of the relevant coasts; at that position it is the Kerkennahs which influence any delimitation, not directions of the coastline. As for the reasoning given in . . . the Judgment in order to justify the angle of 52°, it merely serves to demonstrate that any calculation chosen for the purpose can be substituted for the facts of geography.[171]

Judge Oda, in his comprehensive dissenting opinion,[172] reviewed the elements of the applicable law relating to delimitation in the historical perspective, suggested the application of the qualified equidistance method as a practical method of delimitation in the present case, and, pursuant thereto, suggested a line of delimitation which was delineated on two maps, by way of illustration, one showing the suggested boundary line in the area offering itself for delimitation and the other giving the position of the line in the perspective of the full coastlines of both Parties.

As to the Judgment, Judge Oda felt that it was not based on a proper appreciation of the 'trends' at the Third United Nations Conference on the Law of the Sea and had ignored the changes in the concept of the continental shelf and the impact of the exclusive economic zone thereon. The Court had applied as positive principles 'only equitable principles and the taking into account of all relevant circumstances', which appears simply to suggest 'the principle of non-principle'. He said: 'The Judgment does not even attempt to prove how the equidistance method, which has often been maintained to embody a rule of law for delimitation of the continental shelf, would lead to an inequitable result'.[173] The practical method of delimitation is also 'not grounded on any persuasive considerations'. 'The Judgment appears, to my eyes', said Judge Oda, 'simply as one appropriate to a case *ex aequo et bono* such as might have been decided, if the Parties so agreed. . . . But the present case is certainly not one of that kind'.[174]

Judge Oda did not agree with the line of delimitation specified by the majority of the Court in two segments. As to the *first segment*, where a straight line was drawn from Ras Ajdir corresponding to the western boundary of the Libyan concessions, Judge Oda asked:

> What justification can there be for prescribing a delimitation identified with a line already emplaced by one Party, even if the other Party subsequently granted some concessions in such a way as not to encroach upon it? Is it not a fact that the present case was brought to the Court by the Parties because this line was not mutually satisfactory.[175]

He also questioned the significance, from any objective viewpoint, of the point of intersection of the line in the first sector with the parallel passing through the most westerly point of the Gulf of Gabes. Why that point and why the parallel, he asked, and added:

> . . . the translation of this connection into terms of a parallel of latitude can only result from an optical illusion in which a conventional lattice of cartography is treated as part of the natural configuration. This is the more disconcerting in that the Court has rightly resisted the Parties' efforts to persuade it to view the area as imprinted with a north-south or west-east orientation, as the case may be.[175]

As to the *second segment*, Judge Oda said:

> . . . the Court suggests a bearing of 52°. Is it possible to find any principle or rule of international law which will provide a ground for this inclination? Surely not. . . . Why should this segment of the line be parallel with the coast of Tunisia rather than the coast of Libya? In any case, a line in parallel to the coastline can appropriately be used for the outer limit of maritime zones, but not for the lateral or common boundaries of the zones of adjacent or even opposite States. . . . why should not this idea of bisecting angles have been applied for drawing the first segment of the boundary?[176]

And why were the low-tide elevations ignored 'in recommending an angle of 52° to the meridian',[177] he asked.

Judge Oda said that the bisector appears to have been employed by the Court 'simply to justify the somewhat arbitrarily determined angle of the second segment. In fact, the angle of 52° seems to depend on the happy coincidence that the seaward coast of the Kerkennahs happens to lie in the path of the line extended from the most westerly point of the Gulf of Gabes. That being so, I am personally at a loss to see any reason why this particular parallelism adds to the persuasiveness of the inclination of 52° preferred for the second segment'.[177]

In relation to the delimitation line in the Judgment as a whole, Judge Oda concluded as follows:

> I feel bound to point out the inconsistencies in the Court's preference for bisected angles, compromise boundaries, half-effects, etc. Not only do these attempts to 'split the difference' derive from an implicit purpose of

197

apportionment, but they are all simply approximations to the consistent geometrical approach, based on a distance criterion, which the Court has rejected for no stated reason. And a distance criterion is precisely the one established feature of the exclusive economic zone regime which is destined to replace natural prolongation as a test in delimitation of the continental shelf.[178]

The conclusions reached by Judge Oda from his detailed survey of the 'trends' at the Third United Nations Conference on the Law of the Sea, the concepts of the continental shelf and the exclusive economic zone, sedentary fisheries and historic rights, and the trends in the delimitation of the continental shelf/exclusive economic zone at the Third United Nations Conference on the Law of the Sea, may be summed up as follows:

(1) The Draft Convention on the Law of the Sea could not in February 1982 be regarded 'as reflecting the principles and rules of international law',[179] and the Court should have examined more thoroughly the progress in these discussions and the trends in the law of the sea during the past few decades in a much wider perspective.[180]

(2) Article 6 of the 1958 Convention on the Continental Shelf may be interpreted to mean that it 'suggested the "equidistance/special circumstances" method as a normal basis of agreement as well as of third-party determination'.[181]

(3) The 1958 Convention on the Continental Shelf, and the Judgment of the Court in 1969 (*North Sea Continental Shelf* cases), did not attempt to define the outer limit of the continental shelf by the use of the concept of 'natural prolongation'. That term was used simply 'to justify the appurtenance to a coastal State of the continental shelf geographically adjacent to it'.[182]

Noting the changing concept of the continental shelf by 1981, Judge Oda said:

> . . . in parallel with the change in the outer limit of the continental shelf, the notion of natural prolongation by which the concept of the continental shelf was embellished in the 1969 Judgment has greatly lost its significance, particularly with the introduction of the criterion of the 200-mile distance under the strong influence of the concept of the exclusive economic zone . . . the geomorphological notion of natural prolongation . . . may be said to have remained in the case where the (geomorphological) continental shelf or slope extends farther than 200 miles . . .'.[183]

(4) The sedentary fisheries might give rise to historic rights to such fishing, 'but not to any submarine areas' or 'for claiming such areas as continental shelf'.[184] '. . . historic title by reason of longstanding practice of sedentary fisheries might justify some deviation in the line of the delimitation of the territorial sea, but otherwise historic title would not have any impact on delimitation of the continental shelf'.[185]

Judge Oda felt that neither the Gulf of Gabes nor the Tunisian claimed ZV 45° line were relevant to the present case, and said:

> ... the question whether or not the Gulf of Gabes may be claimed by Tunisia as historic waters or historic bays because of its longstanding sedentary fisheries is not relevant to the present case. ... The area claimed by Tunisia, extending to offshore areas west of the ZV 45° line not framed by any part of the Tunisian coast, apart from the Gulf of Gabes, does not meet the geographical conditions for internal waters.[186]

(5) The question facing the Court could equally well have concerned the exclusive economic zone as the continental shelf. Judge Oda said:

> ... this trend towards the absorption of the continental shelf regime into that of the exclusive economic zone is too pronounced to be ignored. Hence the Court would have shown realism in paying more serious attention to the question whether a case submitted as one of continental shelf delimitation was not also a case implying the delimitation of the exclusive economic zone.[187]

(6) Referring to Articles 74/83 of the Draft Convention on the Law of the Sea, Judge Oda said:

> It could be pointed out that Articles 74/83 of the draft convention on the Law of the Sea form a catchall provision that ought to satisfy both [i.e. the 'equidistance' and the 'equitable principles' schools of thought], and that is indeed its merit. Given, however, the difficulty of deriving any positive meaning from these provisions, it would seem that the satisfaction must be of a negative kind, i.e., pleasure that the opposing school has not been expressly vindicated.[188]

The effect of the reference to 'agreement' in these Articles 'is merely to confirm that a general rule for the conduct of inter-State relations is applicable to the subject of delimitation'. He continued:

> Secondly, the simple reference to 'the basis of international law as referred to in Article 38 of the Statute of the International Court of Justice' does not furnish any practical assistance towards a solution, in the absence of any more specific designation of which principles and rules from out of the entire panoply of customary, general, positive and conventional law are of particular significance. Thirdly, the idea of an equitable solution, although not specifically mentioned in Article 6 of the 1958 Convention, lay at the basis of that provision, but the draft convention does not supply any answer to the question of what the equitable solution is, and no method for reaching such an equitable solution is specified.[189]

However, despite the resultant vagueness, there is one firm conclusion arising from the identical provisions on delimitation in Articles 74/83, namely that 'the principles and rules of international law applicable to the delimitation of the continental shelf will not be different from those applicble to the delimitation of the exclusive economic zone'.[190] Accordingly, the Court ought to have considered, Judge Oda said, 'whether criteria of *distance*, being intrinsic to the Exclusive Economic Zone and also favoured by the latest concept of the continental shelf (which sounds the knell of both the depth and the exploitability tests), ought not to play a role in the common delimitation of the area'.[191]

As to the applicable principles and rules for the delimitation of the continental shelf/exclusive economic zone, Judge Oda, elaborating the *equitable principles*, said:

> There was . . . insufficient reason for the present Court, in 1982, to be inhibited from realizing that the present delimitation was simply a question of equitably dividing, or apportioning, between the Parties, by means of a justifiable line of demarcation, those submarine areas which either could potentially have claimed'.[192]

He also emphasised the principles of geographical equity, and of *proportionality* as a function of geographical equity, which should apportion the area equitably in proportion to the length of the coastlines of the Parties rather than divide, by a predetermined ratio, an area 'defined in advance in terms of definite parallels and meridians'.[193]

He highlighted the *equidistance method* as a rule of delimitation, and said:

> If this method is one which, in principle, should apply in normal situations, as suggested by the 1958 Convention and the 1969 Judgment of the Court, how can one say that this cannot be a rule of delimitation? This does not of course mean that it is a compulsory rule in abnormal circumstances.[194]

Referring to the 1969 Judgment, he said:

> If the baselines had been adjusted to rectify the irregularity of the coastlines, the Court would surely have hesitated to refuse merit to the equidistance method.[194]

He added that while applying the equidistance method, 'account should always be taken of various elements and factors when determining the baselines from which the equidistance line is to be plotted'.[195]

As to *baselines*, Judge Oda elaborated that 'it should be clear that the normal baseline for measuring the breadth of the territorial sea could not always be used for the equidistance method as applied to the delimitation of the continental shelf, despite the provisions of Article 6 of the 1958 Convention on the Continental Shelf'.[196] The geographical location of an *island* may 'influence the equity of a delimitation', and may require a modification of the baseline for delimitation. Thus the position of an island in relation to the baseline should be considered on its own merits.[196] As to the *low-tide elevations*, Judge Oda said:

> . . . despite the provisions of the Convention on the Continental Shelf, it would be proper to ignore the existence of low-tide elevations in the case

200

of a delimitation of the continental shelf, now that the wider 12-mile limit of the continental shelf has become an established rule of international law.[197]

Summing up, Judge Oda said:

In conclusion, I would suggest that, considering geography as the sole factor to be employed for the division of the sea-bed area, a division of the area concerned in proportion to the length of the relevant coast of each State facing that area will, in principle, satisfy the requirement of equity, and the geometrical method of equidistance will, in principle, serve to achieve this purpose. . . . The geographical circumstances will have to be evaluated in each case in the light of what is regarded as representing equity . . .'.[197]

Applying these principles to the present case, Judge Oda concluded as follows:

(1)   The delimitation of the continental shelf between Tunisia and Libya should be determined by the application of the qualified equidistance method, which is 'the equitable method *par excellence*'.[198]

(2)   The coastlines of Tunisia and Libya from Cap Bon to Ras al-Hamamah do not show any feature 'which calls for any departure from the coastal configuration in determining the baselines from which to plot the equidistance line for the delimitation of the continental shelf'.[198]

(3)   The Island of Jerba, because of its size, configuration, contiguity to the coast and *nearness to the frontier point*, should not be disregarded but given full value in determining the baseline from which the equidistance line is to be plotted.

On the other hand, the Kerkennahs should be excluded from the determination of the applicable baseline. In this connection, Judge Oda said:

Now, although within easy reach of the mainland, the Kerkennahs are separated from it by approximately 11 miles and, being elongated and far from parallel to the coast, project far out to sea; they have thus pushed the baseline for the territorial sea of Tunisia far to the east. While this effect is tolerable and necessary for the territorial sea, it would be so pronounced if applied to a vast and economically important zone like the continental shelf that I feel impelled to recommend the exclusion of the Kerkennahs from consideration in determining the baseline from which the equidistance line is to be plotted, despite their demographic importance.[199]

The rationale of the inclusion of Jerba and the exclusion of the Kerkennahs was further explained by Judge Oda as follows:

. . . the textent to which a geographical feature can be treated as an irregularity and disregarded may depend on its distance from the frontier point. It may be inequitable to disregard a feature near to that point, because to do so would bring the dividing line too close to it, and in any case a feature near to the frontier will not affect the course of the line for a very great

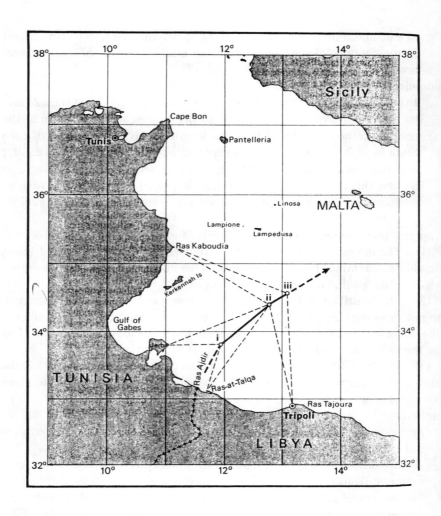

Chart 11A. Case concerning the continental shelf Tunisia – Libyan Arab Jamahiriya, 1982
Dissenting opinion Judge Oda
Source: ICJ Reports 1982, at p. 274.

202

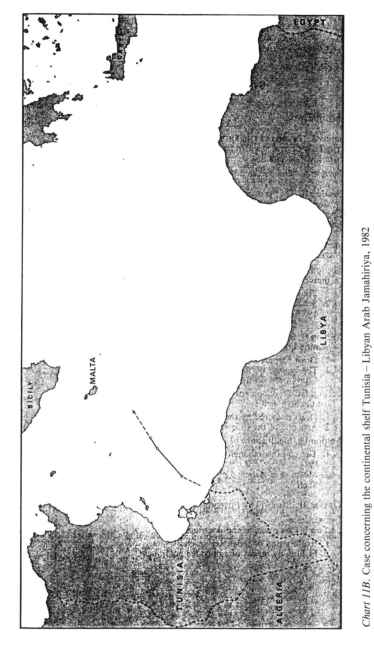

Chart 11B. Case concerning the continental shelf Tunisia – Libyan Arab Jamahiriya, 1982
Dissenting opinion Judge Oda
Source: ICJ Reports 1982, facing p. 274.

distance. A similar feature far from the frontier-point may, on the contrary, have an altogether disproportionate effect, but that feature can be disregarded without bringing the dividing line in any case closer to it. Thus even if, for the sake of argument, the island of Jerba had not been contiguous to the mainland and had had a similar configuration to the Kerkennahs, it would have been very doubtful that it could be disregarded.[199]

(4) The low-tide elevations should be ignored in the delimitation of the continental shelf. Judge Oda said:

> . . . it is only on the coast of Tunisia that a significant number of low-tide elevations exist, and their effect has been to place the baseline for measuring the territorial sea of that country at a far remove from the real coastline of the mainland. This simply reinforces my view that low-tide elevations should be disregarded as an element of the baseline for the delimitation of the continental shelf.[199]

The *delimitation line*, suggested by Judge Oda, consisted of three points, points (i), (ii) and (iii), with specified geographical coordinates. Point (i), which was roughly 40 miles from Ras Ajdir, is equidistant from Ras Ajdir, Jerba (Tunisia) and Ras at-Talqa (Libya). Point (ii) is equidistant from Ras Kaboudia (Tunisia) and Tripoli (Libya), as well as from Jerba and Ras at-Talqa. Point (iii) is equidistant from Ras Kaboudia and Tripoli, as well as from Malta. 'Since Malta is not a party to the present case, this point is marked on the line simply to indicate the direction of the line to be drawn from point (ii)', Judge Oda added.[200]

Judge Oda also suggested that point (i) may be joined with Ras Ajdir (the frontier point) by a straight line, which will be 'a perpendicular to the coasts of both Parties measured over a distance which is relatively short in comparison with that of about 40 miles from Ras Ajdir to point (i)'.[200]

As to the test of proportionality, Judge Oda said that 'the line in question provides a useful yardstick against which to verify the equitable nature of the two-part line prescribed by the Court'.[200] Finally, an important advantage of the equidistance method was 'that its inherent property of equity remains constant whatever the "area relevant to the delimitation"',[200] he said.

The delimitation line suggested by Oda is shown in Charts 11A and 11B.

Judge Evensen, ad hoc Judge designated by Tunisia, in his concluding dissenting opinion,[201] disagreed with the two-sector line of delimitation indicated in the Judgment as well as with the reasons given therefor. He felt that in the application of equitable principles, the Court had blurred the distinction between the principles of equity and considerations *ex aequo et bono*. Nor have the equity considerations involved led to an equitable solution. He felt that the Court should have followed the equidistance line, even though it is not a mandatory principle for delimiting the continental shelf, which should have been adjusted or tempered by considerations of equity, as may be required by the relevant circumstances prevailing in the area. This would have given 'a more

equitable and a more verifiable solution than the line given by the Court'.²⁰²
On the other hand, the line proposed by the Court 'is in its whole length almost twice as close to the coasts of Tunisia as to the coasts of Libya'.²⁰³

The Court should also have taken into account the accepted trends at the Third United Nations Conference on the Law of the Sea relating to the exclusive economic zone and the 200-mile limit for the continental shelf in certain cases, where the concept of the natural prolongation would not be relevant, a well as the position of islands, low-tide elevations, and baselines for the proper application of the law.

Referring to the sheaf of lines for a practical method of delimitation submitted by Tunisia, Judge Evensen said that 'I share the view of the Court that none of these lines is tenable as the equitable line of delimitation'.²⁰⁴

As to the delimitation line specified by the Court for the *first sector*, that is 26° to the meridian from Ras Ajdir up to 34°10'30''N, this was done by relying on the Parties' conduct vis-à-vis the unilateral claim of Libya, or the *modus vivendi* or interim arrangements between the Parties concerning the fisheries jurisdiction or the grid system of the petroleum concessions. A *modus vivendi* arrangement is *'provisional* pending a solution of the disagreement' and the 'arrangement is *non-prejudicial* for the two Parties', Judge Evensen said. Nor had Tunisia ever acquiesced in or accepted that the line of the petroleum grid was equitable, he noted.²⁰⁵

Nor could the 26° angle be justified as a perpendicular to the general direction of the coasts of the Parties, because it would approximate to an equidistance line only if it was limited up to the outer limit of the 12-mile territorial sea. Its extension up to 34°10'30''N that is 50-60 miles seawards 'would be inequitable'.²⁰⁶ A perpendicular to the general direction of the coastline for that distance should have been drawn from 'the easternmost point of the island of Jerba on the Tunisian side to a point at an equal distance from Ras Ajdir on the Libyan side'.²⁰⁶ The 26° angle thus gave no value to the Island of Jerba or the Zarzis promontories, which were totally ignored.

The point of intersection of the 26° line with the parallel 34°10'30''N has been determined by the latter being the 'most westerly point of the Tunisian coastline' in the Gulf of Gabes. Judge Evensen said:

> The Court has not explained why the most westerly bottom point of the Gulf of Gabes should be the relevant point here while at the same time the Court is ignoring the island of Jerba and the promontories of Zarzis. These configurations change completely the direction of the Tunisian coastline northward at a longitude more than 60 miles to the east of the bottom point of the Gulf of Gabes actually used by the Court. . . . this choice of the Court is discretionary and not equitable.²⁰⁷

As to the delimitation line in the *second segment*, he felt that the disregarding of the Island of Jerba and the giving of half-effect to the Kerkennah Archipelago was 'a refashioning of nature which is neither warranted in law nor by the facts'.[208]

Judge Evensen also questioned the validity of the method adopted in giving half-effect to the Kerkennah. The line joining the westernmost point of the Gulf of Gabes to Ras Kaboudia, which has a bearing of 42° to the meridian, he said,

> is a totally imaginary line some 160 kilometres long. As a straight line it is *drawn inland* some 6 miles (11 kilometres) from the actual seacoast, thus disregarding the actual shoreline . . . Actually a straight line drawn to the protruding points of the coast in a direction towards Sfax to Ras Busmada would be at an angle of approximately 51° to the meridian, not 42°.[209]

As to the 62° angle formed by joining the westernmost point of the Gulf of Gabes with the seaward limits of the Kerkennahs, Judge Evensen remarked that the Court had not given any reasons why a 62° line would give 'excessive weight to the Kerkennahs'. Nor has it indicated why the surrounding low-tide elevations have been totally disregarded. If they had been taken into account, the angle would have been 66° to the meridian and not 62°. Judge Evensen added:

> Even according to the Court's ruling of giving half effect to the Kerkennahs − a result which to my mind is unequal and a refashioning of nature − the veering should in no event be a 52° line but a line some 57.5° to the meridian. Even this line would be less equitable than an equidistance line.[210]

He also regarded the test of proportionality applied by the Court as wrong in law as well as in the basis of computations, since the internal waters of Tunisia, its straight baselines established in 1973, and the Islands of Jerba and the Kerkennah, had been ignored.[211]

Judge Evensen refrained from suggesting a concrete alternative of delimitation based on an adjusted equidistance principle, because of its 'futility' and 'inappropriateness'.[212]

In his conclusion, Judge Evensen recognised that 'the Court has endeavoured to effect a delimitation which in its view is responsive to search for an equitable solution', and that 'in its decision the Court has endeavoured to draw a line which divided the disputed areas between the two Parties', and hoped that the Court's decision, which is binding on the two Parties, will promote friendship and good neighbourliness between them. He also proposed a joint exploitation zone for the Parties in the area, specifying the limits of the zone, and the broad terms of joint exploitation.[213]

Summing up

In this Part the major judicial, arbitral and other decisions relating to maritime boundary have been reviewed. All these cases related to the delimitation of the continental shelf. The period of time covered is between 1969 and 1982. This was also the time when the entire law of the sea was being reviewed by the international community through the United Nations Seabed Committee and the Third United Nations Conference on the Law of the Sea. This review led to the establishment of new maritime zones, including the 200-mile exclusive economic zone and the continental shelf with precise outer limits. This review also related to the law concerning maritime boundary.

Thus the application of the law to concrete cases in the third party settlement procedures, and the development of the law in the Third United Nations Conference on the Law of the Sea (UNCLOS) and through State practice, interacted. The Courts and Commissions interpreted and applied the law in the light of the developments in UNCLOS, whereas UNCLOS itself reflected the impact of these decisions on the development of the law. In the Case of Tunisia – Libya, decided by the International Court of Justice in February 1982, the Parties had requested the Court, in rendering its decision, to take account of, *inter alia*, 'the recent trends admitted at the Third United Nations Conference on the Law of the Sea'.

The developments in the law relating to maritime boundary at UNCLOS will be reviewed in Part Four below. State practice, reflected in Agreements on maritime boundary, has been reviewed in Part Two above.

The interpretation of the law as embodied in the United Nations Convention on the Law of the Sea, 1982, and its application to concrete cases by the International Court of Justice or other forums, and its impact on further State practice, will be for the future to reveal, particularly relating to the delimitation of the exclusive economic zone and the continental shelf, on which the delimitation criteria are identical but the relevant circumstances may vary.

The role of the Courts and other forums in the cases reviewed in this Part varied from indicating the applicable principles and rules of international law relating to delimitation (*North Sea Continental Shelf* cases, 1969) to determining the course of the boundary (or boundaries) between the portions of the continental shelf appertaining to the Parties (United Kingdom – France Arbitration, 1977 – 78), and specifying, as an intermediate step, the practical method of delimitation of the continental shelf boundary between the Parties (Tunisia – Libya, 1982).

The Judgments of the International Court of Justice in the *North Sea Continental Shelf* cases, 1969, and in the Tunisia – Libya case, 1982, and the decisions of the Court of Arbitration in the United Kingdom – France case, 1977 – 78, have made the most significant contribution not only to settling the disputes referred to them but also to the development of international law on the subject.

The outcome of the law relating to maritime delimitation, as revealed in the cases covered in this Part, may be summed up as follows:

(1)   The basic principle of delimitation as set out in the 1969 Judgment of the International Court of Justice, is that 'delimitation is to be effected by agreement in accordance with equitable principles, and taking account of all the relevant circumstances'.

In the 1969 Judgment, the application of the principle is to leave to each Party all those parts of the continental shelf that constitute a natural prolongation of its land territory into and under the sea, without encroachment on the natural prolongation of the land territory of the other. This emphasises the principles of natural prolongation and of non-encroachment.

The 1969 Judgment indicated the methods of resolution of areas of overlap emerging from the application of the equitable principles, as well as the factors to be taken into account in the course of negotiations, which included the configuration of the coasts, the physical and geological structure and the resources of the continental shelf areas involved, and the test of proportionality taking into account the delimitations between other States in the same region.

Negatively, the Court held that the use of the equidistance method of delimitation was not an obligatory rule of customary international law. This method may be applied and may lead to an equitable solution for delimitation between States with opposite coasts. But among States with adjacent coasts, the equidistance method may not be equitable. It is necessary to seek not one method of delimitation but one goal, the Court said. The relative weight to be accorded to different considerations will vary with the circumstances of each case.

In the case before the Court in 1969 (*North Sea Continental Shelf* cases), the States were adjacent, the coasts of the Parties were more or less equal, and the concavity of the coast of the Federal Republic of Germany made the application of the equidistance line inequitable.

In the UK – France case, 1977 – 78, the Court of Arbitration, while upholding the 'fundamental norm that the delimitation must be in accordance with equitable principles', also said that 'the equidistance – special circumstances rule and the rules of customary international law have the same object – the delimitation of the boundary in accordance with equitable principles'.[214] The equidistance – special circumstances rule should however be applied without an onus of proof on the Party invoking the special circumstances.

As to proportionality, the Court held that it should be a criterion or factor relevant in evaluating the equities of certain geographical situations, not a source of right to areas of the continental shelf.

Thus the Court of Arbitration gave a higher status to the equidistance – special circumstances rule, without supplanting the equitable principles. Their correlation, which was vertical under the 1969 Judgment of the International Court of Justice, appeared to be shaping up horizontally, although the equitable principles held the position of plume.

In the Tunisia – Libya case, both Parties requested the Court to indicate the principles and rules of international law for the delimitation of the continental shelf appertaining to them, by taking into account the equitable principles and the relevant circumstances which characterise the area, as well as 'the recent trends admitted' or 'the new accepted trends' at the Third United Nations Conference on the Law of the Sea. Neither of them invoked the equidistance method.

The Court took an intermediate position on the question of the equidistance method between its decision of 1969 and the decision of the Court of Arbitration in 1977 – 78, and said that 'Treaty practice, as well as the history of Article 83 of the draft convention on the Law of the Sea, leads to the conclusion that equidistance may be applied if it leads to an equitable solution; if not other methods should be employed'. Equidistance was not 'either a mandatory legal principle, or a method having some privileged status in relation to other methods'. Although both Tunisia and Libya had regarded the results of the application of the equidistance method as inequitable, the Court said that this would not prevent it from adopting an equidistance line if that would 'bring about an equitable solution of the dispute'.[215]

On the question of natural prolongation, the 1982 Judgment emphasised the primacy of equitable principles and gave a restrictive role to geology or geomorphology. It is the geographical configuration of the present-day coasts and the present-day seabed which must be considered, not their evolution in the long distant past.

Thus the principles and rules of international law relating to delimitation, as emerging from the judicial and arbitral decisions reviewed in this Part, give a place of primacy to equitable principles, the application of which requires the assessment of all relevant circumstances prevailing in the area, with a view to finding an equitable solution. The equidistance method may be used for this purpose, either by the Parties, or even by the Court, if it leads to an equitable solution. Among States with opposite coasts, the application of the equidistance method may generally lead to an equitable solution. The single rule of equidistance – special circumstances, applied by the Court of Arbitration in 1977 – 78, leading to an equitable solution, may also obtain greater acceptance and application as an accompaniment of the rule of equitable principles. This development, along with the developments in the law of maritime delimitation at UNCLOS which emphasise the equitable solution of a maritime boundary dispute in accordance with international law, may help to maintain the distinction between a decision in accordance with international law and a decision *et aequo et bono*. The applicable rules should neither lead to an automatic or geometric application of a method nor to the discretionary assessment of the relevant circumstances.

The law will continue to develop in its application to new cases involving delimitation of the exclusive economic zone and the continental shelf.

(2)   As to the special circumstances, the 1969 Judgment was affected by the concavity of the coast of the Federal Republic of Germany. The 1977 – 78 case took into account the position of islands 'on the wrong side of the median line', the position of low-tide elevations, and the distorting effect of the Scillies. In the 1982 case, the International Court of Justice relied on the conduct of the Parties to determine an equitable line, and gave half-effect to the Kerkennahs, the computation of which was related to the change in the coastal configuration of Tunisia. In determining the limits of the delimitation area, the Court took into account the interests of third States. The Court, however, did not take into account the arguments relating to geology, geomorphology, bathymetry, historic rights, baselines, and low-tide elevations.

Thus the special circumstances in the area for delimitation may vary and their assessment, with a view to an equitable delimitation, may also vary from case to case.

(3)   The Conciliation Commission in the Iceland – Jan Mayen (Norway) case, 1981, recommended, as a practical measure, the establishment of a joint development area, without establishing two separate boundaries, one for the continental shelf and another for the exclusive economic zone. This may influence State practice and indicate an equitable solution in appropriate and difficult cases.

Notes

1. Arbitral decisions of the period prior to 1939 have been covered by Sang-Myon Rhee in an exhaustive article entitled 'Sea Boundary Delimitation between States before World War II', in *American Journal of International Law (AJIL)*, Vol. 76, No. 3 (July 1982), pp. 555-588. These include (1) the dispute between the UK and the USA about the precise boundary in the Portland Channel area between Alaska and British Columbia (1903) – *ibid.*, pp. 561-562; and (2) the dispute between Norway and Sweden on the lateral territorial waters boundary between them, namely the *Grisbadarna Case* (1909). This case was decided by the Permanent Court of Arbitration on 23 October 1909, which made the distinction between the 'inner area' and the 'outer area', and for the latter decided that delimitation should be made by 'tracing a line perpendicularly to the general direction of the coast', which was further modified to leave the *Grisbadarna* banks on the Swedish side since 'the Swedish utilised the banks in question much earlier and much more effectively than the Norwegians'. – *ibid.*, pp. 566-571.
2. *ICJ Reports 1969*, para. 18.
3. *Ibid.*, para. 21.
4. *Ibid.*, para. 23.
5. *Ibid.*, para. 24.
6. *Ibid.*, para. 36.
7. *Ibid.*, para. 40.
8. *Ibid.*, para. 41.
9. *Ibid.*, para. 44.
10. *Ibid.*, para. 45.

11. *Ibid.*, para. 46.
12. *Ibid.*, para. 47.
13. *Ibid.*, para. 52.
14. *Ibid.*, para. 53.
15. *Ibid.*, para. 53.
16. *Ibid.*, para. 55.
17. *Ibid.*, para. 57.
18. *Ibid.*, para. 58.
19. *Ibid.*, para. 59.
20. *Ibid.*, para. 60.
21. *Ibid.*, para. 69.
22. *Ibid.*, para. 74.
23. *Ibid.*, para. 73.
24. *Ibid.*, para. 75.
25. *Ibid.*, para. 77.
26. *Ibid.*, para. 81.
27. *Ibid.*, para. 85.
28. *Ibid.*, para. 85.
29. *Ibid.*, paras. 88, 92.
30. *Ibid.*, para. 91.
31. *Ibid.*, para. 92.
32. *Ibid.*, para. 93.
33. *Ibid.*, para. 96.
34. *Ibid.*, para. 98.
35. *Ibid.*, paras. 94-99.
36. *Ibid.*, para. 101.
37. *Ibid.*, paras. 61-66.
38. *Ibid.*, pp. 148-149. For map, see p. 153.
39. *Ibid.*, pp. 239-240.
40. The text of the Arbitration Award has been published by Her Majesty's Stationery Office, London, in 1979 in Cmnd. 7438.
41. *Ibid.*, p. 6, Article 2.
42. *Ibid.*, p. 8, Article 9(1).
43. *Ibid.*, Article 2.
44. *Ibid.*, para. 120.
45. *Ibid.*, para. 28.
46. For text of Article 6, see pp. 128, 130 above.
47. *Arbitration Award*, Cmnd. 7438, para. 33.
48. *Ibid.*, para. 34.
49. *Ibid.*, para. 56.
50. *Ibid.*, para. 61.
51. *Ibid.*, para. 68; see also para. 70.
52. *Ibid.*, para. 75.
53. These Articles were the same as Articles 61 and 70 of the Informal Single Negotiating Text. For text, see Part IV, pages 228-229 below.
54. Cmnd. 7438, n. 44, para. 96.
    Referring to the Atlantic region, the Court said that 'in determining whether two States are to be considered as "opposite" or "adjacent", for the purpose of delimiting a continental shelf on which each of them abuts, the Court must have regard to their actual geographical relation to each other and to the continental shelf at any given place along the boundary'. *Ibid.*, para. 94.

'. . . In short, it is the combined effect of the side-by-side relationship of the two States and the prolongation of the lateral boundary for great distances to seawards which may be productive of inequity and is the essence of the distinction between "adjacent" and "opposite" coasts situations'. *Ibid.*, para. 95.

55. *Ibid.*, para. 97.
56. *Ibid.*, para. 101.
57. *Ibid.*, para. 107.
58. *Ibid.*, para. 140.
59. *Ibid.*, para. 144.
60. *Ibid.*, para. 169.
61. *Ibid.*, para. 179.
62. *Ibid.*, para. 182.
63. *Ibid.*, para. 183.
64. *Ibid.*, para. 190.
65. *Ibid.*, para. 191.
66. *Ibid.*, para. 194.
67. *Ibid.*, para. 196.
68. *Ibid.*, para. 199.
69. *Ibid.*, para. 202.
70. *Ibid.*, para. 238.
71. *Ibid.*
72. *Ibid.*, para. 242.
73. *Ibid.*, para. 234.
74. *Ibid.*, para. 235.
75. *Ibid.*
76. *Ibid.*, para. 243.
77. *Ibid.*, paras. 244 and 245.
78. *Ibid.*, para. 249.
79. *Ibid.*, para. 254.
80. *Ibid.*, p. 126. For his declaration, see pp. 120-126.
81. *Ibid.*, paras. 31-37 (pp. 162-166).
82. *Ibid.*, para. 251.
83. *Ibid.*, p. 146.
84. *Ibid.*, para. 86 at p. 183.
85. *Ibid.*, para. 104 at p. 190.
86. *Ibid.*, para. 106 at p. 191.
87. *Ibid.*, para. 107 at pp. 191-192.
88. *Ibid.*, para. 110 at pp. 192-193.
89. *Ibid.*, para. 111 at p. 193.
90. *Ibid.*, para. 113 at p. 194.
91. *Ibid.*, para. 114 at p. 195.
92. *Ibid.*, p. 202.
93. *Ibid.*, p. 199.
94. *Ibid.*, p. 200.
95. *Ibid.*, p. 201.
96. Robert D. Hodgson and E. John Cooper, 'The Technical Delimitation of a Modern Equidistant Boundary', *Ocean Development and International Law*, Vol. 3, No. 4 (1976), pp. 361-388, at pp. 374-376. See also p. 62 above.
97. *Controversy concerning the Beagle Channel Region (Chile/Argentina), Decision of the Court of Arbitration dated 18 February 1977* — Award dated 2 May 1977, Annex IV, para. 4.

98. *Aegean Sea Continental Shelf, Judgment, ICJ Reports 1978*, p. 35, para. 83.

99. *Ibid.*, para. 84.

100. *Ibid.*, para. 86.

101. *Ibid.*, para. 107.

102. *Report and Recommendations to the Governments of Iceland and Norway of the Conciliation Commission on the Continental Shelf area between Iceland and Jan Mayen*, June 1981, pp. 1-60.

103. *Ibid.*, p. 35.

104. For text of the Agreement, see *International Legal Materials*, Vol. 21 (1982), pp. 12-22.

105. For text of the Agreement of 10 June 1977, see *Case Concerning the Continental Shelf* (Tunisia/Libya), *Judgment, ICJ Reports 1982*, p. 18, paras. 2 and 4.

106. *Ibid.*, para. 8.

107. *Ibid.*, p. 25.

108. Chart 10A taken from *ibid.*, p. 36; Chart 10B taken from *ibid.*, p. 81; Chart 10C taken from *ibid.*, p. 90.

109. *Ibid.*, p. 27.

110. *Ibid.*, p. 26.

111. *Ibid.*, pp. 29 and 31.

112. *Ibid.*, p. 31.

113. Both of them regarded the application of the equidistance method as inequitable, although Tunisia mentioned that Libya had in 1972 suggested equidistance (Tunisian *Memorial*, 30 May 1980, p. 6), whereas Libya cited the Tunisian Memorandum of 18 May 1976 to diplomatic missions in which Tunisia had stated that 'the delimitation of the continental shelf between Tunisia and Libya beyond the 50 metre isobath should be in conformity with an equidistance line drawn in accordance with international law, taking into account the geographical facts and zones of economic interests, the long-standing exercise of which stands proof of their reality and importance' (Libyan *Memorial*, 30 May 1980, p. 19).

114. *ICJ Reports 1982*, n. 105, paras. 74-75.

115. For full text of the operative part of the Judgment, see pp. 137-138 above.

116. *Ibid.*

117. *ICJ Reports 1982*, n. 105, para. 44.

118. *Ibid.*

119. *Ibid.*, para. 47.

120. *Ibid.*, para. 48.

121. *Ibid.*, para. 50.

122. *Ibid.*, paras. 58, 59.

123. *Ibid.*, para. 61.

124. *Ibid.*, para. 63.

125. *Ibid.*, para. 62.

126. *Ibid.*, para. 66.

127. *Ibid.*, para. 67.

128. *Ibid.*, para. 70.

129. *Ibid.*, para. 72.

130. *Ibid.*, para. 78.

131. *Ibid.*, para. 79.

132. *Ibid.*, para. 76.

133. *Ibid.*, paras. 80 and 32.

134. *Ibid.*, para. 86.

135. *Ibid.*, para. 87.

136. *Ibid.*, para. 90.

137. *Ibid.*, para. 92.
138. *Ibid.*, para. 95.
139. *Ibid.*, para. 96.
140. *Ibid.*, para. 100.
141. *Ibid.*, para. 104.
142. *Ibid.*, para. 105.
143. *Ibid.*, para. 107.
144. *Ibid.*, para. 108.
145. *Ibid.*, para. 109.
146. *Ibid.*, para. 110.
147. *Ibid.*, para. 126.
148. For details, see Tunisian *Memorial*, 30 May 1980, Vol. I, pp. 197-209 and the charts in Vol. II, and figure 9.14.
149. *ICJ Reports 1982*, n. 105, para. 116.
150. *Ibid.*, para. 118.
151. *Ibid.*, para. 121.
152. *Ibid.*, para. 124.
153. *Ibid.*, para. 126.
154. *Ibid.*, para. 129.
155. *Ibid.*, para. 131.
156. *Ibid.*, para. 132.
157. Mark B. Feldman, 'The Tunisia – Libya Continental Shelf Case: Geographic Justice or Judicial Compromise?', *AJIL*, Vol. 77, No. 2 (April 1983), pp. 219-238 at p. 234.
158. *ICJ Reports 1982*, n. 105, pp. 95-98.
159. *Ibid.*, p. 99.
160. *Ibid.*, p. 102.
161. *Ibid.*, pp. 102-103.
162. *Ibid.*, pp. 122-132.
163. *Ibid.*, p. 136.
164. *Ibid.*, p. 139.
165. *Ibid.*, p. 140.
166. *Ibid.*, p. 149.
167. *Ibid.*, p. 152.
168. *Ibid.*, p. 153.
169. *Ibid.*, p. 154.
170. *Ibid.*, p. 155.
171. *Ibid.*, p. 156.
172. *Ibid.*, pp. 157-277.
173. *Ibid.*, p. 157; see also p. 270.
174. *Ibid.*, p. 157.
175. *Ibid.*, p. 268.
176. *Ibid.*, pp. 268-269.
177. *Ibid.*, p. 269.
178. *Ibid.*, p. 270.
179. *Ibid.*, pp. 170-171; see also p. 172.
180. *Ibid.*, p. 247.
181. *Ibid.*, p. 190 (For text of Article 6, see pp. 128, 130 above).
182. *Ibid.*, p. 192; see also p. 195.
183. *Ibid.*, p. 222; see also p. 248.
184. *Ibid.*, pp. 202 and 209; see also p. 248.

185. *Ibid.*, p. 211; see also p. 248. Judge Oda noted that the term 'historic title' had been included in Article 12 of the 1958 Convention on the Territorial Sea and the Contiguous Zone, and also in Article 15 of the Draft Convention on the Law of the Sea, but not in the relevant Articles on the delimitation of the continental shelf.
186. *Ibid.*, p. 210.
187. *Ibid.*, p. 249.
188. *Ibid.*, p. 246. For text of Articles 74/83, see Annex III to this study below.
189. *Ibid.*, pp. 246-247.
190. *Ibid.*, p. 247.
191. *Ibid.*, p. 249.
192. *Ibid.*, p. 255.
193. *Ibid.*, p. 260.
194. *Ibid.*, p. 261.
195. *Ibid.*, p. 262.
196. *Ibid.*, p. 266.
197. *Ibid.*, p. 267.
198. *Ibid.*, p. 270.
199. *Ibid.*, p. 271.
200. *Ibid.*, p. 273.
201. *Ibid.*, p. 278-323.
202. *Ibid.*, p. 319.
203. *Ibid.*, p. 317.
204. *Ibid.*, p. 289.
205. *Ibid.*, p. 306.
206. *Ibid.*, p. 310.
207. *Ibid.*, p. 304.
208. *Ibid.*, p. 300.
209. *Ibid.*, p. 303.
210. *Ibid.*, p. 304.
211. *Ibid.*, pp. 311-319.
212. *Ibid.*, p. 319.
213. *Ibid.*, pp. 321-323.
214. See pp. 145-146 above.
215. See p. 185 above.

Maritime boundary at the Third United Nations Conference on the Law of the Sea, 1973 – 1982

Maritime boundary at the Third United Nations Conference on the Law of the Sea: 1973 – 1981

A brief reference was made in Part One to the developments at the Third United Nations Conference on the Law of the Sea (abbreviated as UNCLOS) which had worked from December 1973 to December 1982, and had held eleven sessions. On December 10, 1982, the United Nations Convention on the Law of the Sea, which had earlier been adopted by UNCLOS on April 30, 1982, was opened for signature at Montego Bay, Jamaica, and was signed by 117 States, apart from the Cook Islands and the Council for Namibia. By the end of 1983 the Convention had been signed by 131 States, including Japan and the Republic of Korea, and ratified by 9 States, including Fiji, Mexico and Jamaica. The provisions of the Convention on the outer limits of the maritime zones and the delimitation between States with opposite or adjacent coasts were also cited briefly in that Part.

In this Part (Chapters 13 and 14), the consideration of delimitation of maritime zones between States with opposite or adjacent coasts at UNCLOS between December 1973 and December 1982 will be reviewed.

The principal aim of UNCLOS was to review and develop the law of the sea concerning the outer limits of national jurisdiction and to establish an international regime and machinery for the exploitation of the resources of the international seabed area. The question of maritime boundary was considered mainly in relation to the question of the limits of national jurisdiction between States with opposite or adjacent coasts. With the emergence of the concept of a 200-mile exclusive economic zone, and the continental shelf extending to long distances from the applicable baseline, the questions arose as to whether the delimitation criteria should be the same for them as for the territorial sea, as to whether a distinction should be made between delimitation of the exclusive economic zone and delimitation of the continental shelf, and as to whether a distinction should be made between States with opposite coasts and States with adjacent coasts or States having features of both. Concrete proposals were made by delegations to protect their national interests. Soon interest groups were formed, which became particularly prominent between 1978 and 1981. Deliberations at UNCLOS on the maritime boundary were concentrated around three main elements or aspects, namely (1) delimitation criteria, (2) interim arrangements pending agreement between the parties, and (3) settlement of delimitation disputes..The provisions finally adopted for inclusion in the Convention on the Law of the Sea would not only establish the new conventional rules but might also embody the customary rules of international law on the subject. There was, therefore, eagerness to ensure that the provisions on the maritime boundary received widespread support and, if possible, consensus.

As was observed in Parts Two and Three, discussions at UNCLOS were influenced by State practice and judicial, arbitral and other decisions, and these in turn had their impact on the developments at UNCLOS. Thus the Judgment in the *North Sea Continental Shelf* cases, 1969, triggered the assertion at UNCLOS that equitable principles should be the basic delimitation criteria; the United Kingdom – France Arbitration, 1977, developed the concept of a single equidistance-cum-special circumstances rule which promoted a compromise mood; and the United Kingdom – France Arbitration, 1977, interpreted the delimitation provisions developed at UNCLOS in 1976 as being in conformity with the aforementioned single rule. The Iceland – Jan Mayen (Norway) Conciliation Commission, 1981, also relied on the delimitation provisions of the Draft Convention on the Law of the Sea prepared at UNCLOS in August 1980. Finally, State practice showed resilience as States with divergent views on delimitation criteria settled their maritime boundaries *inter se* while maintaining their reserve on criteria (Agreements between France and Spain, 1974, Spain and Italy, 1974, Colombia and the Dominican Republic, 1978, Venezuela and the Dominican Republic, 1979).

The consideration of the maritime boundary at UNCLOS passed through the following phases:
(1) Pre-1973.
(2) 1974 – 1975: Caracas (1974) and Geneva (1975) Sessions of UNCLOS. Preparation of Informal Single Negotiating Text – SNT (May 1975).
(3) 1976 – 1977: Revised Single Negotiating Text – RSNT (May 1976); Informal Composite Negotiating Text – ICNT (July 1977).
(4) 1978 – 1980: Negotiating Group 7 on Maritime Boundary; Revisions to Informal Composite Negotiating Text – ICNT/Rev. 1 (April 1979) and ICNT/Rev.2 (April 1980).
(5) 1980 – 1981: Draft Convention on the Law of the Sea – ICNT/Rev. 3 (August 1980); President's proposal (August 1981); Formalisation of the Draft Convention (A/CONF.62/L.78 of August 28, 1981).
(6) 1982: United Nations Convention on the Law of the Sea adopted by UNCLOS on April 30, 1982, and opened for signature on December 10, 1982.

The main features of the developments at UNCLOS between 1973 and 1981 will

220

be reviewed in this Chapter. The next Chapter will review the developments in 1982.

A. Pre-1973

Prior to the convening of UNCLOS in December 1973, the rules on delimitation had been embodied in the 1958 Conventions and in customary international law. The relevant provisions of the 1958 Conventions have been cited in Part One. It was also mentioned that the move for a review of the law of the sea started in 1967 and a United Nations Seabed Committee was established, but its activity was concentrated until 1970 on evolving an international regime for the exploitation of the resources of the international seabed area. Pursuant to Resolution 2750 (XXV) adopted by the United Nations General Assembly on 17 December 1970, the review process became comprehensive. The United Nations Seabed Committee, whose membership was enlarged to 91, was to act as the preparatory committee for UNCLOS which was to be convened in 1973. Between 1971 and 1973, the Seabed Committee prepared a list of subjects and issues and organised itself into three Sub-Committees − the first to deal with the international seabed area, the second to deal with the other questions on the law of the sea, and the third to deal with the questions of marine scientific research, marine pollution and transfer of technology.

The question of maritime boundary was considered in Sub-Committee II under the following subject headings:

2.3.1   Questions of the delimitation of the territorial sea; various aspects involved.

5.3   Continental Shelf: Question of the delimitation between States; various aspects involved.

6.7.2   Exclusive economic zone: Delineation between adjacent and opposite States.[1]

Since 1971 − 1973 was the formative period of the review of the law of the sea, attention was concentrated more on the substantive questions of the establishment of an exclusive economic zone and an international regime and machinery for the exploitation of the resources of the international seabed area, than on the question of maritime boundary. Nevertheless, during this period, ten proposals were made on delimitation of maritime zones in Sub-Committee II, namely by Greece (A/AC.138/SC.II/L.17), Cyprus (L.19), Turkey (L.22/Rev. 1), Uruguay (L.24), Malta (L.28), China (L.34), Australia and Norway (L.36), Algeria, Cameroon, Ghana, Ivory Coast, Kenya, Liberia, Madagascar, Mauritius, Senegal, Sierra Leone, Somalia, Sudan, Tunisia and Tanzania (L.40), Uganda and Zambia (L.41), and Japan (L.56).[2] Five of these proposals emphasised the principles embodied in the 1958 Conventions, namely by Greece,

Cyprus, Uruguay, Malta, Uganda and Zambia; one proposal emphasised equidistance (Japan); one proposal provided that delimitation should be by agreement (China). Of the three remaining proposals, the proposal by Turkey emphasised the equitable principles as indicated by the International Court of Justice in the *North Sea Continental Shelf* cases, 1969, and made the following additional provision:

> In the absence of special circumstances, due regard should be given to the principles of median line or equidistance in delimitation of respective boundaries.[3]

Similarly, the proposal by Australia and Norway provided that delimitation should be effected by agreement 'in accordance with equitable principles', and added that, subject to this, 'and unless the drawing up of another boundary is justified by special circumstances, the boundary shall be an equidistance line in the case of adjacent coasts and a median line in the case of opposite coasts'.[4] Finally, the proposal of Algeria and 13 other African States provided as follows:

> The delineation of the economic zone between adjacent and opposite States shall be carried out in accordance with international law. Disputes arising therefrom shall be settled in conformity with the Charter of the United Nations and any other relevant regional arrangements.[5]

During the course of discussions, the Working Group of the Whole of Sub-Committee II of the United Nations Seabed Committee tried to consolidate these proposals in the form of variants submitted by delegations, a comparative table of proposals and a consolidated text arranged item-wise.[6] Later, using the comparative table and the consolidated texts as a tool, it attempted to present variants which might, where appropriate, have formed the basis of draft Articles. The Working Group was, however, not able to consider all the variants and the Sub-Committee decided to adopt the Report in its present form and to transmit it to the Committee towards the end of August 1973. The Committee could also not complete its work and accordingly these ten proposals, along with the variants, were carried over to UNCLOS and were considered along with the new proposals moved at the Caracas Session of UNCLOS in 1974. The ideas contained in the last three proposals referred to in the preceding paragraphs had a significant impact on the formulation of compromise proposals both in 1974 and in later years.

Besides these, delimitation provisions were also contained in the Santo Domingo Declaration of 7 June 1972[7] which provided that delimitation of the patrimonial sea should be carried out in accordance with the peaceful procedures stipulated in the Charter of the United Nations. Similarly, the Yaounde Seminar on the Law of the Sea, held from 20 to 30 June 1972[8] provided that the limits between maritime zones 'shall be fixed in conformity with the United Nations Charter and that of the Organisation of African Unity'.

B. 1974 – 1975: Caracas (1974) and Geneva (1975) Sessions of UNCLOS. Preparation of Informal Single Negotiating Text – SNT (May 1975)

Although the United Nations Seabed Committee could not complete its preparatory work, UNCLOS was convened in December 1973. The first session, which was an organisational one, was held in New York from 3 to 15 December 1973. UNCLOS was organised into three main Committees with functions similar to those of the three Sub-Committees of the United Nations Seabed Committee. Since there was no basic proposal prepared either by the International Law Commission or by the United Seabed Committee, UNCLOS had to proceed on the basis of the proposals made in the United Nations Seabed Committee or the new proposals made in UNCLOS. Under a gentleman's agreement, all efforts had to be made to reach decisions by consensus. This turned out to be a laborious and time-consuming process, but one which contributed to the progressive development of the law of the sea in a manner which would be widely acceptable to the world community of States.

The second session of UNCLOS, held in Caracas (Venezuela) from 20 June to 29 August 1974, was a productive substantive session and led to a breakthrough on the question of the establishment of the exclusive economic zone. The question of the maritime boundary was discussed in the Second Committee in connection with the items on the territorial sea, the contiguous zone, the exclusive economic zone, the continental shelf and the regime of islands. Sixteen proposals were made[9] which were elaborated in statements. Towards the end of the session, the Chairman of the Second Committee analysed the main trends reflected in these proposals, as well as in the proposals made in the United Nations Seabed Committee between 1971 and 1973, in 13 informal working papers which were considered by the Second Committee and consolidated into a comprehensive document as 'Main Trends'.

The main features of the 16 proposals on the maritime boundary moved at the Caracas Session of UNCLOS in 1974 may be anlysed broadly as follows:

(i)   The main dividing line was formed by the delimitation criteria: 10 proposals (Turkey 3 proposals, the Netherlands, Romania, Kenya and Tunisia, Ireland, Algeria and 14 other African States, France, Ghana and 16 other African States) supported equitable principles[11], whereas 6 proposals (Greece 3 proposals, Bulgaria and others, and Japan) supported equidistance.[12]

(ii)   In either group, there was variation. In some proposals emphasising equitable principles as the basic delimitation criteria, reference was made to the application of the median line 'in the absence of special circumstances and in so far as it is not inconsistent with equitable principles',[13] or in a negative manner, namely 'the median or equidistance line not being necessarily the only method of delimitation'.[14]

In some proposals emphasising equidistance, reference to special circumstances was omitted,[15] and reference to the median line was made in a negative or residual manner, namely: 'Failing such agreement, no State is entitled to extend its sovereignty over the continental shelf beyond the median line . . .'.[16] Bulgaria and others proposed the inclusion of the relevant provisions of the 1958 Conventions, including those for the contiguous zone.[17]

(iii)   The Netherlands made a comprehensive proposal,[18] which had an impact on the further course of discussion of the subject in UNCLOS. Although it had invoked the equidistance rule in its pleadings in the *North Sea Continental Shelf* cases, 1969, the Netherlands' proposal adopted the law as laid down in the Judgment of the International Court of Justice in that case and added a rule on interim arrangements which emphasised equidistance.

The first two paragraphs of that proposal read as follows:

1.   Where the determination of sea areas under articles . . . (territorial sea, continental shelf, economic zone) by adjacent or opposite States up to the maximum limit would result in overlapping areas, the marine boundaries between those States shall be determined, by agreement between them, in accordance with equitable principles, taking into account all relevant circumstances.

2.   Pending such agreement, neither of the States is entitled to establish its maritime boundaries beyond the line, every point of which is equidistant from the nearest points on the baselines from which the breadth of the territorial sea of each State is measured.

The Netherlands' proposal also contained a provision on the settlement of maritime boundary disputes, first by reference to conciliation, failing which by judicial settlement.

(iv)   Apart from the controversy between equitable principles and equidistance as the delimitation criteria, a special feature of the 16 proposals was the emphasis on the question of islands. Two aspects of the question were raised: one related to the entitlement of islands to marine spaces and the other related to the relevance of islands as special circumstances in maritime delimitation. As to the former, the proposal of Algeria and 14 other African States was most comprehensive.[19] It divided the islands between adjacent and non-adjacent islands, and proposed that for the non-adjacent islands, the marine spaces would be delimited on the basis of equitable criteria, which included the size and location of islands and the needs and interests of their population. This was also proposed by Romania.[20] This aspect was concretised further in the Irish proposal, which provided that account should be taken of an island in determining an equitable median line only if it was located within the territorial sea of a State or if 'it contains at least one-tenth of the land area and population of the State concerned'.[21]

The proposals by Greece suggested full marine spaces for the territory of a coastal State, whether continental or insular.[22]

224

As to the second aspect, namely the relevance of islands as special circumstances, the proposals by Kenya and Tunisia,[23] France,[24] and Turkey[25] made special references thereto. Thus the proposal by Kenya and Tunisia provided as follows:

1. The delimitation of the continental shelf or the exclusive economic zone between adjacent and/or opposite States must be done by agreement between them, in accordance with an equitable dividing line, the median or equidistance line not being necessarily the only method of delimitation.

2. For this purpose, special account should be taken of geological and geomorphological criteria, as well as of all the special circumstances, including the existence of islands or islets in the area to be delimited'.[23]

The proposal by France read as follows:

1. The delimitation of the continental shelf or of the economic zone between adjacent and/or opposite States shall be effected by agreement between them in accordance with an equitable dividing line, the median or equidistance line not being the only method of delimitation.

2. For this purpose, account shall be taken, *inter alia*, of the special nature of certain circumstances, including the existence of islands or islets situated in the area to be delimited or of such a kind that they might affect the delimitation to be carried out.[24]

The proposal by Turkey read as follows:

2. In the course of negotiations, the States shall take into account all the relevant factors, including, *inter alia*, the geomorphological and geological structure of the shelf up to the outer limit of the continental margin, and special circumstances such as the general configuration of the respective coasts, the existence of islands, islets or rocks of one State on the continental shelf of the other.

Where the coasts of two or more States are adjacent or opposite to each other, the delimination of the respective economic zones shall be determined by agreement among them in accordance with equitable principles, taking into account all the relevant factors including, *inter alia*, the geomorphological and geological structure of the sea-bed area involved, and special circumstances such as the general configuration of the respective coats, and the extistence of islands, islets or rocks within the area.[25]

On the basis of these 16 proposals, as well as the proposals made in the United Nations Seabed Committee, the Chairman of the Second Committee prepared the document entitled 'Main Trends' towards the end of the Caracas Session of UNCLOS which contained variants for the maritime delimitation of the territorial sea, the contiguous zone, the continental shelf, the exclusive economic zone and the regime of islands. The variants were organised as 'formulas' under the relevant headings, called 'provisions'. An interesting variant for delimitation of the exclusive economic zone, which appeared to be based on the 14-delegation African proposal in the United Nations Seabed Committee[26], and which emerged into prominence in UNCLOS in 1979 – 1981, was Formula A of Provision 116, which read as follows: 'The delineation of the economic zone between adjacent and opposite States shall be carried out in accordance with international law'.[27]

These variants were neither exhaustive, nor did they indicate the degree of support at UNCLOS. As the Chairman of the Second Committee said on 28 August 1974 in that Committee, these variants should serve as a reference text and 'as a basis and point of departure for the future work of this organ (Second Committee) of the Conference.[28]

Geneva Session of UNCLOS (1975) and preparation of
Informal Single Negotiating Text — SNT (1975)

The Third Session of UNCLOS was held in Geneva from 26 March to 10 May 1975. No general statements were made. It was decided to review the variants included in the document 'Main Trends', prepared in August 1974. On 18 April 1975 the Conference adopted the proposal of the President requesting the Chairman of each Main Committee to prepare a Single Negotiating Text covering the subjects entrusted to his Committee. The President had explained that the single negotiating texts should take account of all the formal and informal discussions held so far. 'The texts would not prejudice the position of any delegation, and would not represent any negotiated text or accepted compromise. They would be a basis for negotiation', he said.[29] Accordingly, although informal discussions continued, the rest of the time was spent by the Chairmen of the three Main Committees in preparing the Single Negotiating Text. Three separate texts were prepared which were cumulatively called the 'Informal Single Negotiating Text' (popularly known as the SNT).[30] These texts were circulated among the delegations at the end of the session and accordingly no discussion took place on the SNT at the session in 1975.

The further discussions at UNCLOS revolved around these texts. In July 1975, a similar Single Negotiating Text was prepared by the President on the subject of settlement of disputes.[31] A Revised Single Negotiating Text was prepared in May 1976 (popularly known as RSNT).[32] In July 1977 the four separate Texts were consolidated into a single 'Informal Composite Negotiating Text' (ICNT),[33] the first revision of which was made in April 1979,[34] the second revision in April 1980[35] and the third revision in August 1980.[36] The third revision was entitled 'Draft Convention on the Law of the Sea (Informal Text)'. All these Negotiating Texts were issued under the symbol of a Working Paper of the Conference. In August 1981 the Conference decided to formalise the Draft Convention as an official document of the Conference, which then appeared in a revised form as A/CONF.62/L.78 of 28 August 1981. The Draft Convention was adopted by UNCLOS on April 30, 1982, by a vote of 130 in favour, 4 against and 17 abstentions. In September 1982, the Conference decided to name the Convention as the United Nations Convention on the Law of the Sea, which was opened for signature on December 10, 1982 at Montego Bay, Jamaica, and was signed by 117 States apart from the Cook Islands and the Council for Namibia. By the end of 1983, the Convention was signed by 131 States, and ratified by 9 States.

To revert to the SNT prepared in 1975, the main features of the provisions on maritime boundary contained therein may be summarised as follows:

(1)   A single set of provisions was made on maritime delimitation. The system of variants included in the document 'Main Trends' prepared in 1974 was discarded.

(2)   Separate provisions were made in the SNT on delimitation of the territorial sea (Article 13), the exclusive economic zone (Article 61) and the continental shelf (Article 70). The provision concerning the territorial sea followed the text of Article 12 of the 1958 Convention on the Territorial Sea and the Contiguous Zone. The provisions on the exclusive economic zone and the continental shelf (Articles 61 and 70) were identical; in other words, no distinction was made between the delimitation of the exclusive economic zone and the continental shelf. Nor was any distinction made between States with opposite or adjacent coasts. The provisions in both cases referred to delimitation criteria, settlement of disputes and interim arrangements. The delimitation criteria were a compromise between the contending principles, namely equitable principles, equidistance and special circumstances. The interim arrangements emphasised the median line, as suggested in the Dutch proposal referred to above.[37]

(3)   On the question of islands, Article 132 of the SNT excluded rocks which could not sustain human habitation or economic life of their own from having any exclusive economic zone or continental shelf. Otherwise, it made no specific reference to islands in relation to special circumstances to be taken into account in maritime delimitation.

(4)   On the settlement of maritime boundary disputes, the SNT allowed exception for compulsory settlement procedures provided therein to States making such a declaration, provided that such a State 'shall indicate therein a regional or other third-party procedure, entailing a binding decision, which it accepts for the settlement of these disputes'.[38]

(5)   The SNT made no reference to delimitation of the contiguous zone, presumably because this would be covered by the principles applicable to the delimitation of the exclusive economic zone.

Since these Articles continued to be included in the later negotiating texts, it may be useful to note their contents at this stage. The relevant Articles on the delimitation of the SNT read as follows:

Territorial Sea

Article 13

1.   Where the coasts of two States are opposite or adjacent to each other, neither of the two States is entitled, failing agreement between them to the contrary, to extend its territorial sea beyond the median line every point of which is equidistant from the nearest points on the baselines from which the breadth of the territorial sea of each of the two States is measured. The provisions of this paragraph shall not apply, however, where it is necessary by reason of historic title or other special circumstances to delimit the territorial seas of the two States in a way which is at variance with this provision.

2.   The line of delimitation between the territorial seas of two States lying opposite to each other or adjacent to each other shall be marked on large-scale charts officially recognized by the coastal States.

Exclusive Economic Zone

Article 61

1.   The delimitation of the exclusive economic zone between adjacent or opposite States shall be effected by agreement in accordance with equitable principles, employing, where appropriate, the median or equidistance line, and taking account of all the relevant circumstances.

2.   If no agreement can be reached within a reasonable period of time, the States concerned shall resort to the procedures provided for in part . . . (Settlement of disputes).

3.   Pending agreement, no State is entitled to extend its exclusive economic zone beyond the median line or the equidistance line.

4.   For the purposes of this Article, 'median line' means the line every point of which is equidistant from the nearest points of the baselines from which the breadth of the territorial sea of each State is measured.

5.   In delimiting the boundaries of the exclusive economic zone, any lines which are drawn in accordance with the provisions of this article should be defined with reference to charts, and geographical features as they exist at a particular date, and reference should be made to fixed permanent identifiable points on the land.

6.   Where there is an agreement in force between the States concerned, questions relating to the delimitation of the exclusive economic zone shall be determined in accordance with the provisions of that agreement.

Continental Shelf

Article 70

1.   The delimitation of the continental shelf between adjacent or opposite States shall be affected by agreement in accordance with equitable principles, employing, where appropriate, the median or equidistance line, and taking account of all the relevant circumstances.

228

2.   If no agreement can be reached within a reasonable period of time, the States concerned shall resort to the procedures provided for in part . . . (Settlement of disputes).

3.   Pending agreement, no State is entitled to extend its continental shelf beyond the median line or the equidistance line.

4.   For the purposes of this article, 'median line' means the line every point of which is equidistant from the nearest points of the baselines from which the breadth of the territorial sea of each State is measured.

5.   In delimiting the boundaries of the continental shelf, any lines which are drawn in accordance with the provisions of this article should be defined with reference to charts and geographical features as they exist at a particular date, and reference should be made to fixed permanent identifiable points on the land.

6.   Where there is an agreement in force between the States concerned, questions relating to the delimitation of the continental shelf shall be determined in accordance with the provisions of that agreement.[39]

Settlement of Disputes
Article 18

. . .

2.   When ratifying the present Convention, or otherwise expressing its consent to be bound by it, a Contracting Party may declare that it does not accept some or all of the procedures for the settlement of disputes specified in the present Convention with respect to one or more of the following categories of disputes:

. . .

(*b*)   Disputes concerning sea boundary delimitations between adjacent States, or those involving historic bays or titles, provided that the State making such a declaration shall indicate therein a regional or other third-party procedure, entailing a binding decision, which it accepts for the settlement of these disputes; . . .[40]

C. 1976 – 1977: Revised Single Negotiating Text – RSNT (May 1976)
Informal Composite Negotiating Text – ICNT (July 1977)

The Fourth Session of UNCLOS was held in New York from 15 March to 7 May 1976. The discussions revolved around the Single Negotiating Text (SNT) prepared in Geneva in May 1975. The question of maritime delimitation was discussed in the Second Committee, which followed 'a rule of silence', whereby delegations would refrain from speaking on an Article of the SNT if they were essentially in agreement with it. No records were maintained of these informal discussions. The SNT was revised in May 1976 as the Revised Single Negotiating Text (RSNT). The new provisions of the RSNT on maritime delimitation, namely the territorial sea (Article 14), the exclusive economic zone (Article 62) and the continental shelf (Article 71) were basically the same as those of the SNT, except that the provision concerning interim arrangements (Article 62, para. 3 and Article 71, para. 3) replaced the corresponding provision of the SNT. The new provision which deleted reference to the median or equidistance line read as follows:

> Pending agreement or settlement, the States concerned shall make provisional arrangements, taking into account the provisions of paragraph 1.[41]

The Chairman of the Second Committee justified his retention of the basic provisions of the SNT, with the change made in paragraph 3 of Articles 62 and 71 of the RSNT, as follows:

> On the issue of delimitation of the exclusive economic zone and the continental shelf between adjacent or opposite States an extensive exchange of views took place. A close study of the discussion, bearing in mind the rule of silence, revealed broad support for the thrust of the article in the single negotiating text (Article 62). However, paragraph 3 of former Articles 61 and 70 posed a problem. Since the Conference may not adopt a compulsory jurisdictional procedure for the settlement of delimitation disputes, I felt that the reference to the median or equidistant line as an interim solution might not have the intended effect of encouraging agreements. In fact such reference might defeat the main purport of the article as set out in paragraph 1. Nonetheless, the need for an interim solution was evident. The solution was, in my opinion, to propose wording in paragraph 3 which linked it more closely to the principles in paragraph 1.[42]

Earlier, Stevenson and Oxman in their review of the 1975 Geneva Session, had also commented on paragraph 3 of the SNT in similar terms as follows:

> The viability of paragraph 3 as an interim rule is largely dependent upon the right of a State to resort to compulsory dispute settlement under paragraph 2 to determine that a reasonable period of time has elapsed and to resolve the issue; otherwise the party that prefers the median or equidistant line could simply refuse to agree on another line.[43]

The Fifth Session of UNCLOS was held in New York from 2 August to 17 September 1976. The provisions of the RSNT on the maritime boundary were reviewed informally in Negotiating Group No. 5 established by the Second Committee. This Group held only two meetings, and a smaller group established by it met only once. Although no records were maintained, the Chairman of the Second Committee reported about its deliberations to the Main Committee on 17 and 18 September 1976. He said the following:

> This discussion confirmed the fact that the central point at issue is the value to be attributed to the method involving the median or equidistant line in solving the problems connected with the delimitation of these marine

230

areas. Some delegations felt that this method should be given primary importance, while others thought that the problems should be solved in accordance with equitable principles. For my part, I continue to believe, after having listened to this debate, that paragraph 1 of Articles 62 and 71, which already appeared in the single negotiating text drawn up at Geneva, may well be the solution which could bring about general agreement since it does not overlook the method involving the median or equidistant line, but at the same time restricts its use to those cases in which it can produce results that are in accordance with equity.[44]

With regard to paragraph 3 of Articles 62 and 71, he said that 'even though opinions were again divided, it was possible to find a compromise formula', although an alternative text had not yet been found.[45]

1977: ICNT

The Sixth Session of UNCLOS was held in New York from 23 May to 15 July 1977, and the discussions around the RSNT continued. On 27 June 1977 the Conference decided that the Revised Single Negotiating Texts prepared by different Chairmen should now be consolidated into a composite text. Accordingly, at the end of the Sixth Session, on 15 July 1977, an Informal Composite Negotiating Text (ICNT), as prepared by the President jointly with the Chairmen of the three Main Committees, was distributed among delegations. No change was made in the provisions on maritime delimitation 'as it had not been possible to devise a formula which would narrow the differences between the opposing points of view. The issue would, therefore, remain open to further negotiations'.[46]

Thus, the ICNT contained identical provisions on the territorial sea (now Article 15), the exclusive economic zone (now Article 74), and the continental shelf (now Article 83), which were the same as Articles 14, 62 and 71 of the RSNT, respectively. No provision was made on maritime delimitation of the contiguous zone. The provision on settlement of disputes contained in Article 297 of the ICNT was also similar to Article 18 of the RSNT, except that disputes concerning claims to sovereignty or other rights with respect to continental or insular land territory were excluded and required the express consent of the parties for any reference to a compulsory dispute settlement procedure.

One might get the impression that since the provisions on maritime delimitation contained in the SNT, the RSNT and the ICNT were mainly identical, except for the change in the provision concerning interim arrangements, the provisions of the ICNT would be broadly acceptable to the Conference. Further developments showed that this was not so and that the question of maritime delimitation remained an outstanding issue which needed further consideration for developing a consensus on the subject. The centre of controversy remained, however, on delimitation critera and the balancing of 'equitable principles' on the one hand and 'equidistance' on the other. Articles 74 and 83 of the ICNT had, as in the earlier provisions, provided that the delimitation of the exclusive economic zone/continental shelf 'shall be effected by agreement in accordance with equitable principles, applying, where appropriate, the median or equidistance line, and taking account of all the relevant circumstances'. The main controversy related to the meaning of the words 'where appropriate' in relation to the median or equidistance line. The delegations supporting the equitable principles would interpret it to imply that the median line would be used where it was in accordance with equitable principles. The delegations supporting equidistance wanted equidistance to be recognised as a principe in itself, so that the delimitation criteria mentioned in paragraph 1 of Articles 74 and 83 should be a fair compromise between the two viewpoints rather than be tilted towards equitable principles.

D. 1978 – 1980: Negotiating Group 7 on Maritime Boundary; Revisions to Informal Composite Negotiating Text – ICNT/Rev.1 (April 1979) and ICNT/Rev.2 (April 1980)

The Informal Composite Negotiating Text (ICNT) having been prepared in July 1977, combining the separate Revised Single Negotiating Texts of the three Main Committees and of the informal plenary on the settlement of disputes into a single document, the next stage in UNCLOS was to build areas of agreement on contentious and outstanding issues before the ICNT could be developed into a basic proposal of the Conference for adoption of a Convention on the Law of the Sea.
    Between 1978 and April 1980 UNCLOS held its sessions as follows:
(1)   Seventh Session in Geneva from 21 March to 19 May 1978.
(2)   Resumed Seventh Session in New York from 21 August to 15 September 1978.
(3)   Eighth Session in Geneva from 19 March to 27 April 1979.
(4)   Resumed Eighth Session in New York from 19 July to 24 August 1979.
(5)   Ninth Session in New York from 3 March to 3 April 1980.
The identification of hard-core issues and the procedure for developing areas of agreement around them, as well as the time-table for the adoption of the Convention of the Law of the Sea, were dealt with at the Seventh Session of UNCLOS. On the recommendations of the General Committee, the Conference adopted the following decisions which are contained in document A/CONF.62/62 of 13 April 1978:[47]
    (1)   It identified seven hard-core issues, the seventh of which read as follows: 'Delimitation of maritime boundaries between adjacent and opposite States and settlement of disputes thereof'.
232

(2)   It established seven Negotiating Groups to deal with these hard-core issues. Negotiating Group 7 (hereafter referred to as NG7) was established under the chairmanship of E.J. Manner of Finland, to deal with the question of maritime boundary.

(3)   The following procedure was adopted concerning modifications in the ICNT:

> Any modifications or revisions to be made in the Informal Composite Negotiating Text should emerge from the negotiations themselves and should not be introduced on the initiative of any single person, whether it be the President or a Chairman of a Committee, unless presented to the Plenary and found, from the widespread and substantial support prevailing in Plenary, to offer a substantially improved prospect of a consensus.

> The revision of the Informal Composite Negotiating Text should be the collective responsibility of the President and the Chairmen of the main committees acting together as a team headed by the President. The Chairman of the Drafting Committee and the Rapporteur-General should be associated with the team as the former should be fully aware of the considerations that determined any revision and the latter should, ex-officio, be kept informed of the manner in which the Conference has proceeded at all stages.[48]

(4)   A time-table was adopted which involved revision of the ICNT during the week 8 to 12 May 1978, and consideration of the ICNT and its formalisation by the plenary between 15 and 19 May 1978. These dates were later changed. The formalisation of the ICNT as the official document of the Conference was finally completed in August 1981.

Negotiating Group 7

During 1978 and 1979, the major work on delimitation was done in Negotiating Group 7 whose reports were submitted to the Second Committee and the plenary, since they dealt both with the question of delimitation and with the settlement of disputes. NG7 held 51 meetings between 1978 and 1979 and produced 45 informal working papers, proposals or reports in the form of documents NG7/1-45. Of these NG7/1 contained the text of the relevant provisions of the ICNT on delimitation; NG7/12 was not issued; and NG7/35 and 36 were withdrawn. Of the remaining 41 documents, 16 contained concrete proposals or status reports by Chairman Manner. As heretofore, the discussion in NG7 was organised around three aspects of maritime boundary, namely (1) delimitation criteria, (2) interim or provisional arrangements, and (3) settlement of disputes. Proposals were made by delegations which dealt either with all these aspects or with particular aspects. The major proposals were by the two main interest groups, namely the group which emphasised the median or equidistance line as a general principle for delimitation (NG7/2 cosponsored by 22 delegations – popularly known as the equidistance group), and the group which emphasised equitable principles as the basic delimitation criteria (NG7/10-Rev.1 cosponsored by 29 delegations – popularly known as the equity group). These proposals read as follows:

NG7/2

1. The delimitation of the Exclusive Economic Zone/Continental Shelf between adjacent or opposite States shall be effected by agreement employing, as a general principle, the median or equidistance line, taking into account any special circumstances where this is justified.

2. If no agreement can be reached, within a period of . . . from the time when one of the interested parties asks for the opening of negotiations on delimitation, the States concerned shall resort to the procedures provided for in part . . . (settlement of disputes) or any other third party procedure entailing a binding decision which is applicable to them.

3. Pending agreement or settlement in conformity with Paragraphs 1 and 2, the parties in the dispute shall refrain from exercising jurisdiction beyond the median or equidistance line unless they agree on alternative interim measures of mutual restraint.[49]

NG7/10-Rev.1

1. The delimitation of the exclusive economic zone [or continental shelf] between adjacent or/and opposite States shall be effected by agreement, in accordance with equitable principles taking into account all relevant circumstances and employing any methods, where appropriate, to lead to an equitable solution.

2. If no agreement can be reached within a reasonable period of time, the States concerned shall resort to the procedures of settlement of disputes provided for in Part XV of this Convention or such other procedures agreed upon in accordance with Article 33 of the Charter of the United Nations Organization.

3. Pending agreement or settlement, the States concerned shall make provisional arrangements, taking into account the provisions of paragraph 1.

4. Where there is an agreement in force between the States concerned, questions relating to the delimitation of the exclusive economic zone [or continental shelf] shall be determined in accordance with the provisions of that agreement.[50]

The membership of the equidistance group and the equity group cut across the regional groups or groups of developed and developing countries. Some other delegations made compromise proposals, but the major negotiating groups remained the Group of 22 and the Group of 29.

234

The major documents of NG7, which reflected the course of negotiations in 1978 and 1979, were the four reports of Chairman Manner. These were as follows: NG7/21 of 17 May 1978 containing the report of the Chairman on the Seventh Session;[51] NG7/24 of 14 September 1978 containing the report of the Chairman on the Resumed Seventh Session;[52] NG7/39 of 20 April 1979 containing the report of the Chairman on the Eighth Session;[53] and NG7/45 of 22 August 1979 containing the report of the Chairman on the Resumed Eighth Session.[54] The report of Chairman Manner on the work of NG7 as a whole between 1978 and 1980 is contained in document A/CONF.62/L.47 of 24 March 1980.[55]

In these reports, concrete proposals on delimitation criteria, interim arrangements and the settlement of disputes were also made by Chairman Manner.

The other 12 proposals or reports of Chairman Manner are contained in documents NG7/9, 11, 22, 23, 25, 26, 33, 38, 41, 42, 43 and 44. Two of these documents contained survey statements (NG7/22, 25), one was the report of discussions in the inter-sessional meeting held in Geneva in February 1979 (NG7/26); two dealt with comprehensive proposals (NG7/9 and 11); one dealt with delimitation criteria (NG7/44), four with interim arrangements (NG7/23, 38, 42 and 43), and two with settlement of disputes (NG7/33 and 41). Neither these documents, nor the proposals made by other delegations in Negotiating Group 7 in 1978 and 1979, have been published in the official records of UNCLOS. The text of these documents will be available from the delegations to the Conference.

A broad picture of the discussions held in Negotiating Group 7 is, however, available from the four reports of Chairman Manner in NG/7/21, 24, 39 and 45 as well as in the final report in document A/CONF.62/L.47 of 24 March 1980 which have been published in the official records of UNCLOS, as indicated above.

The course of negotiations in Negotiating Group 7 between 1978 and 1980 and its outcome may be summarised as follows:

(1)   There was broad support for the provision on maritime delimitation of the territorial sea (Article 15 of ICNT) which embodied the equidistance-cum-special circumstances rule. Only some delegations, namely Turkey, Bangladesh and Venezuela, held reservations.

(2)   On the maritime delimitation of the exclusive economic zone and the continental shelf, identical provisions were made in all the proposals. Thus no distinction was made concerning delimitation of these zones. Nor was any distinction made between States with opposite or adjacent coasts.

(3)   The major area of controversy related to delimitation criteria. The Group of 29 (co-sponsors of NG7/10-Rev.1) emphasised equitable principles whereas the Group of 22 (co-sponsors of NG7/2) emphasised equidistance. The delegations of Mexico, Peru, the Ivory Coast and others tried to propose com-

promise proposals which, however, could not break the impasse.

Chairman Manner said in his report (NG7/24 of 14 September 1978) that for a compromise proposal on delimitation criteria, the main elements to be balanced would be the following: (1) delimitation to be effected by agreement, (2) a reference to all relevant or special circumstances to be taken into account in the process of delimitation, (3) in some form a reference to equity or equitable principles, and (4) in some form a reference to the median or equidistance line.[56] He indicated that there was full agreement on the first two elements. The real problem was as to how to balance the third and the fourth elements. He later suggested that perhaps the listing of these four elements in a non-hierarchical manner without indicating priority might resolve the question. This also was not found satisfactory. He then made a concrete proposal of his own in NG7/39 of 20 April 1979 relating equitable principles to a solution, which also did not gain acceptance.[57]

He then referred to the suggestion that the delimitation might be effected by agreement in accordance with international law. However, he found that this was not acceptable to the two sides.

In NG7/44 of 20 August 1979 he related equitable principles to an agreement and also proposed that perhaps a reference to 'equality of States in their geographical relation to the areas to be delimited' might introduce elements of appropriate equity and proportionality which have been emphasised by the International Court of Justice in the *North Sea Continental Shelf* cases, 1969. This also was not found acceptable.[58]

Finally, in his report NG7/45 of 22 August 1979, he reported the negative conclusions on delimitation criteria as follows:

> At the Chairman's meetings with the supporters of the two differing opinions, it became apparent that a consensus may not be based upon a 'non-hierarchical' formulation listing only the basic elements of delimitation, an alternative which earlier had seemed to have some support. Similarly, a concise formulation providing merely that the delimitation would be 'effected by agreement in accordance with international law' did not receive any particular sympathy from either side.[59]

Thus by the end of August 1979, no breakthrough had been achieved on the question of delimitation criteria.

(4) On interim arrangements, the concerns expressed during the negotiations were as follows: (a) interim arrangements should be in conformity with the delimitation criteria; (b) such arrangements should not prejudice the final outcome; (c) these should not impose a moratorium on exploitation of the area, although they may appeal for self-restraint; and (d) such arrangements should be freely agreed to by the parties without there being any legal obligations to do so. The main controversy was on points (a) and (c).

Intensive efforts were made to resolve these points in 1979 in the proposals made by India, Iraq and Morocco (NG7/32) and later modified by Chairman Manner (NG7/38, 42 and 43). Ultimately, by August 1979, Negotiating Group 7 had agreed to a compromise proposal which read as follows:

> Pending agreement as provided for in paragraph 1 the States concerned, in a spirit of understanding and cooperation, shall make every effort to enter into provisional arrangements of a practical nature and, during this transitional period, not to jeopardise or hamper the reaching of the final agreement. Such arrangements shall be without prejudice to the final delimitation.[60]

This was later embodied in the ICNT/Rev. 2 prepared in April 1980.

(5)   On settlement of disputes on which the views of delegations cut across their co-sponsorship of proposals, intensive preparatory work was done by a small group of experts under the chairmanship of Louis B. Sohn of the United States in 1978 and 1979. The group prepared a series of working papers which elaborated the various models and alternatives for delimitation disputes settlement procedures.[61] On the two extremes were the views of those delegations who did not want any such disputes to be referred to the compulsory settlement procedure without the express consent of the parties, and those who insisted that all unresolved delimitation disputes must be submitted to a compulsory third-party settlement procedure. Between these two extremes, the major areas of concern expressed were as follows:

(a)   that past disputes, that is, disputes which arose prior to the entry into force of the Convention, and disputes involving questions of sovereignty, as well as disputes which have already been settled or are agreed to be settled by a special procedure between the parties, should be excluded from the settlement procedure to be provided in the negotiating text;

(b)   that the parties should have autonomy to determine the contents of the reference for settlement, namely whether only applicable principles, circumstances or methods would be referred to a compulsory settlement procedure or whether the determination of the maritime boundary itself would be submitted to such a settlement procedure, and

(c)   that the type of compulsory settlement procedure itself should have flexibility.

On the first point, all three exceptions to a compulsory settlement procedure were agreed to in the course of the negotiations. On the second point, it was felt that the parties should have autonomy and that no provision should be made in this regard in the negotiating text. On the third point, the broader support emerged in favour of compulsory conciliation. If the dispute still remained unresolved, the parties should, by mutual consent, refer it to one of the compulsory settlement procedures specified in the negotiating text, unless the parties agreed otherwise. This compromise between compulsory conciliation and residual settlement by mutual consent was the combined effect of the compromise worked out in Negotiating Group 5 on the resolution of disputes in the exclusive economic zone and the proposal by Bulgaria in Negotiating Group 7.

On the basis of these developments, Chairman Manner reported the outcome in his report to the Second Committee and the plenary on 22 August 1979. This solution was later on embodied in the ICNT/Rev.2 prepared in April 1980.

It may be noted that, although discussions on the maritime boundary continued to be organised between 1978 and 1980 around interest groups emphasising equitable principles on the one hand and equidistance on the other, these interest groups cut across the various regional groups as well as the groups of developed and developing States. The countries having concrete delimitation interests, although belonging to the same region or economic interest, could be sponsors of opposite proposals, such as the United Kingdom and France, Colombia and Venezuela, and Chile and Argentina.

Similarly, although both interest groups broadly supported the need for compulsory third-party settlement procedures, some delegations made express reservations to their joint proposal on the subject, such as Venezuela, Argentina, Turkey and Vietnam, reserving their position on the provision on compulsory settlement of disputes in their joint proposal in NG7/10/Rev.1.

1980: ICNT/2-Rev.2 (11 April 1980)

It will thus be observed that by the end of the Resumed Eighth Session in August 1979, a broad area of agreement had been built around the questions of (1) interim arrangements, and (2) settlement of delimitation disputes. On the question of delimitation criteria, however, the controversy continued. The ICNT/Rev.1 prepared in April 1979 had maintained the delimitation provisions of the ICNT. In view of the progress made in other areas at UNCLOS, a further revision of the ICNT was under consideration.

Against this background, Chairman Manner continued intensive consultations with the interest groups at the Ninth Session of UNCLOS held in New York from 3 March to 4 April 1980, although without much visible success. He concluded that the present formulation of paragraph 1 of Articles 74 and 83 of the ICNT 'cannot be considered a text which could provide consensus on the issue'.[62] He revived his earlier view that a reference to international law in the delimitation criteria might bridge the gap between the equity and the equidistance groups which received some support.[63] Finally with his report (A/CONF.62/L.47 of 24 March 1980) to the Second Committee, which was also considered in the plenary, he enclosed a concrete proposal on delimitation criteria which read as follows:

> The delimitation of the exclusive economic zone/continental shelf between
> States with opposite or adjacent coasts shall be effected by agreement in

conformity with international law. Such an agreement shall be in accordance with equitable principles, employing the median or equidistance line, where appropriate, and taking account of all circumstances prevailing in the area concerned.[64]

In the debate in plenary, the new proposal was not approved by the equity group as the basis of further negotiation and they insisted that it should not be included in a second revision of the ICNT. F.M. Hayes of Ireland, Chairman of the equity group, wished to remind all delegations that

on a question which affected vital bilateral interests of States, the convention must realistically give expression to the current state of international law without changing it . . . The text must accurately state current international law . . . there were no grounds for revising the relevant provisions of the negotiating text.[65]

The United States delegation, which had joined the equity group, was non-committal. The leader of the US delegation said:

. . . his delegation had not advocated the proposed changes and had no objection to the existing text. That should not be understood to mean, however, that his delegation objected to a decision to include the amendments to Articles 74 and 83 in a second revision of the negotiating text.[66]

The inclusion of the new proposal in a second revision was generally supported by the equidistance group, the Eastern European States and some other delegations. Accordingly, the new proposals of Chairman Manner were included in the ICNT/Rev.2 by the President and his collegium in April 1980, despite the reservation by the Chairman of the Second Committee,[67] and the resentment of the equity group.[67a]

The changes made in the ICNT/Rev.2 on delimitation provisions had a dramatic effect. The provisions of the ICNT and the ICNT/Rev.1 and of the SNT and the RSNT before them, were tilted towards the equity principles; the provisions of the ICNT/Rev.2 were regarded by the equity group to be tilted towards equidistance. This strengthened the position of the equidistance group in further negotiations and appeared to put the equity group on the defensive.

E. 1980 – 1981: Draft Convention on the Law of the Sea – Informal Text (27 August 1980); Draft Convention on the Law of the Sea (formalised as A/CONF.62/L.78 on 28 August 1981)

With the shift in balance of the new provisions on maritime delimitation in the ICNT/Rev.2 in April 1980, the two main groups, namely the equity group and the equidistance group, could proceed with the work of further negotiations with great difficulty. Negotiating Group 7 having concluded its work in March/April 1980, the first hurdle was to decide about the new procedure for negotiations. At the Resumed Ninth Session of UNCLOS held in Geneva from 28 July to 29 August 1980, the two groups ultimately decided to establish a special group consisting of ten representatives each to hold face-to-face negotiations on areas of disagreement. The proceedings were to be conducted by two co-chairmen, one representing either side. E.J. Manner of Finland, Chairman of Negotiating Group 7, who was no longer presiding, watched these proceedings sitting at the back, and found greater support for his own proposal of March 1980 than he might have expected. Nevertheless, the disagreement continued. At the end of August 1980, a third revision of the ICNT was made, which was now entitled 'Draft Convention on the Law of the Sea (Informal Text)'.[68] The provisions on delimitation, namely Articles 15, 74 and 83 and 298(1)(a), remained the same as in the ICNT/Rev.2. In other words, the position favourable to the equidistance group continued. The only change made in the Draft Convention related to the question of reservations to the Convention. In view of the continuing differences on questions of maritime delimitation, it was felt that these questions might not ultimately be resolved by consensus. Accordingly, although Article 309 of the Draft Convention provided that no reservations or exceptions were allowed to this Convention unless expressly permitted by other Articles of this Convention, a footnote was added thereto which mentioned that on the question of delimitation of maritime zones 'the final solution might include provision for reservations'.[69]

Before turning to the next phase, reference may be made to the views expressed on the subject by Judge E.J. Manner in the keynote speech he delivered at the 5th International Ocean Symposium held in Tokyo on 26 and 27 November 1980. Excerpts from his statement are as follows:

The four main elements considered at the Conference with regard to the formulation of the draft articles on the delimitation of the exclusive economic zone and the continental shelf, are the following: (1) any measure of delimitation should be effected by agreement; there should be (2) a reference to equitable principles; and (3) a reference to equidistance line; and (4) all special (or relevant) circumstances should be taken into account.

The proposed provision that the delimitation should be effected by agreement, which originates from the 1958 Convention on the Continental Shelf, is as such a procedural rule, but, depending on its formulation, it may express the principle that every (new) delimitation must be an agreed delimitation, and consequently, that neither the equidistance line, nor any other line not effected by agreement (or by other settlement), can be substituted for an agreed delimitation.

. . . Elements 2, 3 and 4, stating the material criteria which are to form the basis for agreements, are more or less controversial.

. . . Although it is generally admitted that delimitation agreement should be concluded with the view of reaching an equitable solution, and the employment of the median or equidistance line often appears to be in accordance with equitable principles, the question which of those two principles should have priority has proved most difficult. Matters of terminology and wording have often been given more emphasis than the substance of the problems. The supporters of the principle of equidistance have objected to the word 'method' and would like to use the word 'principle' or 'rule'. They have pointed to state practice and to the provisions of the 1958 Conventions. On the other hand, a strict observance of the wording used in the Truman Proclamation or by the International Court of Justice in its Judgement in the North Sea Continental Shelf Cases is advocated by the supporters of equitable principles.

. . . Instead of emphasizing the differences between the two opposing opinions, it would be more constructive to underline such aspects of the principles concerned as are common to them and may lead to a generally acceptable solution.

The International Court of Justice stated in its North Sea Continental Shelf Cases Judgement, 'that it is necessary to seek not one method of delimitation, but one goal'. That meant that the goal or object of delimitation should have preference to any method or to any formulation of provisions. There is no doubt that the application of both the competing criteria aims at reaching an equitable delimitation.[70]

1981: New compromise proposal

The Tenth Session of UNCLOS was held in New York from March 9 to April 16, 1981. Due to the decision of the Government of the United States to review the provisions of the Draft Convention, and therefore to delay its adoption by UNCLOS, the Conference could not make substantive progress. On maritime delimitation, informal negotiations as well as face-to-face negotiations between the equity group and the equidistance group were held up to April 15, 1981. There appeared to be some agreement on a reference to international law in the delimitation criteria, but the question of its link with the delimitation agreement and with equitable principles could not be resolved. The other elements of the delimitation criteria could also not be appropriately balanced. The two co-chairmen (Ireland for the equity group and Spain for the equidistance group) reported about the inconclusive outcome of these negotiations separately to the President.[70a] Informal negotiations were also held by the chairmen of the two interest groups with the President of the Conference. These were continued at the Resumed Tenth Session of UNCLOS which was held in Geneva from August 3 to 28, 1981. An attempt was made to bridge the differences between the two groups through their negotiations *inter se*, when the equity group appeared to have indicated their readiness to accept a reference to international law in paragraph 1 of Articles 74/83 of the Draft Convention if the paragraph was redrafted to mention its two aspects as follows: (a) delimitation in accordance with international law, and (b) agreement in accordance with equitable principles. Such separation was, however, not acceptable to the equidistance group. Alternatively, it was suggested that the paragraph might provide that delimitation may be effected by agreement 'in accordance with international law relevant to delimitation between the parties'. The equity group also suggested the deletion of the words 'all' and 'prevailing in the area concerned' from the words 'and taking account of all circumstances prevailing in the area concerned' appearing at the end of Articles 74(1) and 83(1) of ICNT/Rev.2 prepared in April 1980.[70b] The discussions on these proposals remained inconclusive.

Ultimately, during the last week of the Resumed Tenth Session, at the initiative of President Tommy Koh, assisted by Satya Nandan of Fiji, a new compromise proposal was floated among the two main interest groups. Between August 25 and 27, 1981, the two interest groups held intensive consultations separately and broadly accepted the new proposal with minor amendments. On August 27, 1981, the proposal by the President was circulated as an informal document. On the delimitation criteria in Articles 74(1) and 83(1) the proposal read as follows:

> The delimitation of the exclusive economic zone/continental shelf between States with opposite or adjacent coasts shall be effected by agreement on the basis of international law, as referred to in Article 38 of the Statute of the International Court of Justice, in order to achieve an equitable solution.[71]

In addition, it was proposed that the footnote to Article 309 on reservations should be modified to delete reference to reservations relating to the delimitation of maritime zones. Similarly, the footnote to Article 74 concerning the definition of the median or equidistance line was also deleted.

The new formula was discussed in the plenary of the Conference on August 28, 1981, when some 29 delegations spoke. While introducing the proposal, the President stated that 'During his consultations, he had gained the impression that the proposal enjoyed widespread and substantial support in the two most interested groups of delegations, and in the Conference as a whole'.[72] He asked the chairmen of the two groups to confirm that there was indeed substantial support for the proposal in their respective groups.

The representative of Ireland, chairman of the equity group, said that 'he could confirm that the proposal did indeed enjoy widespread and substantial support in the group'.[73] Similarly, the representative of Spain, chairman of the equidistance group, said that he now fully supported the comments made by the representative of Ireland, and added that there was general support in his group for the President's proposal.[74]

242

Support for the President's proposal was also expressed by the delegates of the USSR, Bulgaria, Indonesia, the Syrian Arab Republic, the GDR, Peru, Malaysia, Colombia, Kenya, the Ukrainian SSR, Senegal, the Ivory Coast and Chile.

On the other hand, the delegations of the USA, China, the UAE, Libya, Portugal, Venezuela, Qatar, Iran, Oman, Kuwait, Egypt, Bahrain, Argentina and Israel expressed either reservations, or suggested postponement of the question and its non-inclusion in the further revision of the Draft Convention.

The representative of the United States said that 'the substance of delimitation disputes was essentially local and bilateral, and that such disputes could not therefore be resolved by a general convention on the law of the sea'. He also shared 'the doubts of others that a complex body of law could in any meaningful sense be reduced to a few lines of text'. He thought that the new text might have the effect of adding confusion to the law and added that 'It was not the time, either, to take action on a text that delegations on both sides privately viewed with embarrassment and whose effect on the future prospects for a widely acceptable convention was unknown; and it was not the time for the Collegium to make a precipitous move that raised doubts about the sensitivity of its procedures to the interests of States as determined by their own Governments'.[75]

The delegate of Libya, while welcoming the proposed amendment of the President in the interests of consensus and in a desire to conclude the long negotiations in the various groups concerned, also welcomed the inclusion of the words 'in order to achieve an equitable solution' in his proposal and added that 'such a solution would be possible only if legal norms and standards which took into account the principles of equity were applied'. He also further added that his delegation's attitude of principle in regard to the amendment 'should not be interpreted as the final attitude of Libya, or as an obstacle to any change of position'.[76]

The delegation of Venezuela said that it had 'received instructions from its Government to state that it considered that the inclusion of the proposed text in the convention would be premature, and that any decision on the matter should be deferred until the next session'.[77]

However, in view of the support given by the two principal groups concerned, namely the equity group and the equidistance group, and the support received in the plenary on August 28, 1981, the President and the Collegium decided to include the new proposal in the formalised Draft Convention on the Law of the Sea which was printed and distributed under the symbol A/CONF. 62/L.78 (28 August 1981). In the new text, therefore, apart from the change in Articles 74(1) and 83(1), the footnote to Article 309 regarding reservations was modified, deleting reference to reservations on the subject of maritime delimitation, and the footnote to Article 74 regarding the definition of the median or equidistance line was deleted.

On 28 August 1981, being the last day of the Resumed Tenth Session of the Conference, the Conference also agreed to a time-bound programme of work for the Eleventh Session, which was to be the final decision-making session of the Conference.[78]

Commenting on the new provisions on delimitation in the Draft Convention, Oxman wrote the following:

> The proposed text, worked out in secret by Ireland and Spain representing their respective groups, and Fiji representing the President, was available even in private only for a few days. Its hasty insertion in the Draft Convention was questioned publicly by Arab countries, Iran, Israel, the United States, and Venezuela, and privately by others.
>
> The main pressure for some change in the text came from the advocates of emphasis on equitable principles rather than equidistance.* Among other things, with this text they had achieved the elimination of any express reference to equidistance, and the limitation of the entire provision to a rule of delimitation by agreement that does not, as such, purport to lay down a normative rule to be applied in the absence of agreement. In return, they changed the reference to 'equitable principles' to a vaguer notion that agreements should achieve an equitable solution. One can hardly imagine that the parties would characterize their agreements otherwise.
>
> . . . one might have expected more than a text that says nothing of significance while, worse still, trying to give a contrary impression by introducing unnecessary language and avoiding recognised terminology associated with the jurisprudence and scholarship on the subject.
>
> . . . There is perhaps no better evidence of the failure of the conference to think about this text than the inclusion of an express cross-reference to Article 38 of the Statute of the International Court of Justice. That article contains the 60-year-old reference to 'civilized' nations that is regarded by some developing-country lawyers as a product of colonialist attitudes. Such an express cross-reference would surely have encountered difficulty if it had been closely scrutinized at a conference that even refused to use the word 'customary' to preface a reference to international law in the Preamble.
>
> If such inclusion in this text is illustrative of the lengths the conference is willing to go to appear to 'make progress', there is little ground for optimism about either the process or the result. One must hope it is an isolated aberration that will be corrected, and that will not be repeated.[79]

---

* In part because of the US policy review, and in part because of concerns regarding the Canadian reaction on the collegium, these advocates encouraged the appearance of distance between themselves and a US delegation sympathetic to their substantive attitudes.

My own comments on the new provisions, written in October 1981, were as follows:

> In a nutshell, it would appear that by the new proposal of the President, the controversy between the equity group and the equidistance group regarding the appropriate balancing of the basic elements of delimitation criteria has been resolved by making a reference to the applicable international law combined with the goal of delimitation, namely, an equitable solution. In general, the new formalisation should protect the interests of either group as well as any party to a concrete case of delimitation. It may, however, be contended that this reference to international law and equitable solution is too vague, and that the precise factors to be taken into account in delimitation and the value or effect to be given to them have not been specified or clarified. To that extent, it may be argued that the new proposal would not act as a practical guide either to negotiators or to teachers or researchers or even to arbitrators or judges concerned with delimitation questions.
>
> In the personal view of this writer, however, the solution proposed by President Tommy Koh and accepted by a large section of the Conference, although not perfect, is workable.[80]

Notes

1. For the list of subjects and issues, see *Report of the Committee on the Peaceful Uses of the Sea-Bed and the Ocean Floor Beyond the Limits of National Jurisdiction*, General Assembly, *Official Records*, Twenty-seventh Session, Supplement No. 21 (A/8721), 1972, pp. 5-8.
2. For text of these proposals, see *Report of the Committee on the Peaceful Uses of the Sea-Bed and the Ocean Floor Beyond the Limits of National Jurisdiction*, Vol. III, General Assembly, *Official Records*, Twenty-eighth Session, Supplement No. 21 (A/9021), 1973.
3. *Ibid.*, L.22/Rev.1, para. 4.
4. *Ibid.*, L.36, para. 2(d).
5. *Ibid.*, L.40, Article IX.
6. For text of these variants, see *Report of the Committee on the Peaceful Uses of the Sea-Bed and the Ocean Floor Beyond the Limits of National Jurisdiction*, Vol. IV, under items 2.3.1 (Question of the delimitation of the territorial sea), 5.3 (Question of the delimitation of the continental shelf between States), and 6.7.2 (Delineation of exclusive economic zone between adjacent and opposite States), at pp. 5-14, 67-69 and 120-121.
   For text of comparative tables, see *ibid.*, Vol. V.
   For text of consolidated texts, see *ibid.*, Vol. VI, pp. 26-27 and 91.
7. *Report of the Committee on the Peaceful Uses of the Sea-Bed and the Ocean Floor Beyond the Limits of National Jurisdiction*, General Assembly, *Official Records*, Twenty-seventh Session, Supplement No. 21 (A/8721), 1972, p. 71.
8. *Ibid.*, p. 74.
9. A/CONF.62/C.2/L.9, 14, 18, 22, 23, 25, 26, 27, 28, 31/Rev.1, 32, 34, 43, 62, 74 and 82. For text, see *Official Records*, Third United Nations Conference on the Law of the Sea (UNCLOS), Vol. III (1975).

10. A/CONF.62/C.2/WP.1 (15 October 1974). For text, see *Official Records*, UNCLOS, Vol. III, pp. 107-142. Main trends on maritime boundary were contained in the following provisions: 21 (territorial sea), 49 (contiguous zone), 82-84 (continental shelf), 116-117 (exclusive economic zone), and 241-243 (regime of islands).
11. A/CONF.62/C.2/L.9, 23, 24 (Turkey), 14, 18, 28, 43, 62, 74 and 82 respectively.
12. *Ibid.*, L.22, 25, 32 (Greece), 26, 27, 31/Rev.1.
13. *Ibid.*, L.43 (Ireland).
14. *Ibid.*, L.28 (Kenya and Tunisia), L.62 (Algeria and others), L.74 (France) and L.82 (Ghana and others).
15. *Ibid.*, L.22, 25 and 32 (Greece), L.31/Rev.1 (Japan).
16. *Ibid.*, L.25 (Greece).
17. *Ibid.*, L.26, 27.
18. *Ibid.*, L.14.
19. *Ibid.*, L.62.
20. *Ibid.*, L.18.
21. *Ibid.*, L.43.
22. *Ibid.*, L.22 and 25.
23. *Ibid.*, L.28.
24. *Ibid.*, L.74.
25. *Ibid.*, L.23 and 34.
26. See n. 5 above.
27. *Official Records*, UNCLOS, Vol. III, p. 126.
28. *Ibid.*, p. 242 (A/CONF.62/C.2/L.86).
29. *Ibid.*, Vol. IV, p. 26.
30. *Ibid.*, pp. 137-181 (A/CONF.62/WP.8).
31. *Ibid.*, Vol. V, pp. 111-124 (A/CONF.62/WP.9).
32. *Ibid.*, Vol. V, pp. 125-201 (A/CONF.62/WP.8/Rev.1 of 6 May 1976 and A/CONF.62/ WP.9/Rev.1 of 6 May 1976).
33. *Ibid.*, No. VIII (A/CONF.62/WP.10/Rev.1 of 15 July 1977 and Add. 1 of 22 July 1977).
34. A/CONF.62/WP.10/Rev.1 (28 April 1979).
35. A/CONF.62/WP.10/Rev.2 (11 April 1980).
36. A/CONF.62/WP.10/Rev.3 (27 August 1980) – Draft Convention on the Law of the Sea (Informal Text).
37. See n. 18 above.
38. *Official Records*, UNCLOS, Vol. V, p. 115. A/CONF.62/WP.9, Article 18.
39. *Ibid.*, Vol. IV, pp. 154, 162, 163.
40. *Ibid.*, Vol. V, p. 115.
41. *Ibid.*, pp. 164, 165.
42. *Ibid.*, p. 153.
43. John R. Stevenson and Bernard H. Oxman, 'The Third United Nations Conference on the Law of the Sea: The 1975 Geneva Session', *American Journal of International Law*, Vol. 69 (1975), at p. 781.
44. *Official Records*, UNCLOS, Vol. VI, p. 138.
45. *Ibid.*
46. *Ibid.*, Vol. VIII, p. 69 (Memorandum by the President of the Conference).
47. *Ibid.*, Vol. IX, p. 18; Vol. X, pp. 6-10.
48. *Ibid.*, Vol. X, p. 8.
49. The co-sponsors included the Bahamas, Barbados, Canada, Chile, Colombia, Cyprus, Democratic Yemen, Denmark, Gambia, Greece, Guyana, Italy, Japan, Kuwait, Malta, Norway, Portugal, Spain, Sweden, the United Arab Emirates, the United Kingdom, Yugoslavia.

50. The proposal was in fact co-sponsored by the following 30 delegations, although they continued to be known as the 'Group of 29': Algeria, Argentina, Bangladesh, Benin, Burundi, Congo, France, Iraq, Ireland, the Ivory Coast, Kenya, Liberia, Libyan Arab Jamahiriya, Madagascar, Maldives, Mali, Mauritania, Morocco, Nicaragua, Nigeria, Pakistan, Papua New Guinea, Poland, Romania, Senegal, the Syrian Arab Republic, Somalia, Turkey, Venezuela, Vietnam.

51. *Official Records*, UNCLOS, Vol. X, pp. 124-125.

52. *Ibid.*, pp. 170-172.

53. *Ibid.*, Vol. XI, pp. 59-60.

54. *Ibid.*, Vol. XII, pp. 107-108.

55. *Ibid.*, Vol. XIII, pp. 76-78.

56. *Ibid.*, Vol. X, p. 171.

57. The proposal read as follows: 'The delimitation of the exclusive economic zone (or of the continental shelf) between States with opposite or adjacent coasts shall be effected by agreement between the parties concerned, taking into account all relevant criteria and special circumstances in order to arrive at a solution in accordance with equitable principles, applying the equidistance rule or such other means as are appropriate in each specific case'.

58. The proposal read as follows: 'The delimitation of the exclusive economic zone (the continental shelf) between States with opposite or adjacent coasts shall be effected by agreement in accordance with equitable principles, taking into account the equality of States in their geographical relation to the areas to be delimited, and employing, consistent with the above criteria and subject to the special circumstances in any particular case, the rule of equidistance'.

59. *Ibid.*, Vol. XII, p. 107.

60. *Ibid.*, Vol. XII, p. 108.

61. NG7/20/Rev.1 (25 August 1978), NG7/27 (27 March 1979), NG7/31 (5 April 1979) and NG7/37 (12 April 1979).

62. *Official Records*, UNCLOS, Vol. XIII, p. 77.

63. *Ibid.*

64. *Ibid.*

65. *Ibid.*, Vol. XIII, pp. 14-15 (2 April 1980).

66. *Ibid.*, p. 43 (3 April 1980).

67. A/CONF.62/WP.10/Rev.2 (11 April 1980), Explanatory Memorandum by President, p. 21.

67a. The Chairman of the equity group wrote a letter to the President on 30 May 1980 denouncing this inclusion, which was read out by him in the plenary on 28 July 1980 at teh commencement of the resumed session: see *Official Records*, UNCLOS, Vol. XIII (130th Meeting), p. 8.

68. A/CONF.62/WP.10/Rev.3 (27 August 1980).

69. The footnote to Article 309 in the Draft Convention in ICNT/Rev.3 (28 August 1980) read as follows: 'This article is based on the assumption that the Convention will be adopted by consensus. In addition, it is recognised that the article can be regarded only as provisional pending the conclusion of discussions on outstanding substantive issues such as that relating to the delimitation of maritime zones as between adjacent and opposite States and to settlement of disputes thereon, where the final solution might include provision for reservations'.

70. *The Frontier of the Seas, The Problems of Delimitation* 1980, Proceedings of the 5th International Symposium, 26-27 November 1980, The Ocean Association of Japan, Tokyo, pp. 11-14.

70a. Documents DEL/1 and DEL/2 of 22 April 1981.

70b. See n. 67 above.

71. A/CONF.62/WP.11 (27 August 1981). Article 38 of the Statute of the International Court of Justice reads as follows:

> The Court, whose function is to decide in accordance with international law such disputes as are submitted to it, shall apply:

(a) International conventions, whether general or particular, establishing rules expressly recognised by the contesting States;

(b) international custom, as evidence of a general practice accepted as law;

(c) the general principles of law recognised by civilised nations;

(d) subject to the provisions of Article 59, judicial decisions and the teachings of the most highly qualified publicists of the various nations, as subsidiary means for the determination of rules of law.

2. This provision shall not prejudice the power of the Court to decide a case *ex aequo et bono*, if the parties agree thereto.

72. A/CONF.62/SR.154, p. 2, *Official Records*, UNCLOS, Vol. XV, p. 39.

73. *Ibid.*, pp. 39-40.

74. *Ibid.*, p. 40.

75. *Ibid.*, p. 40.

76. *Ibid.*, p. 40.

77. *Ibid.*, p. 40.

78. A/CONF.62/116 of 28 August 1981. *Official Records*, UNCLOS, Vol. XV, pp. 101-102.

79. Bernard H. Oxman, 'The Third United Nations Conference on the Law of the Sea: The Tenth Session (1981)', *American Journal of International Law*, Vol. 76, No. 1 (January 1982), pp. 1-23 at pp. 14-15.

80. S.P. Jagota, *Maritime Boundary*, The Hague Academy of International Law, *Recueil des Cours*, Vol. 171 (1981-II), p. 190.

CHAPTER 14

1982: Adoption of the United Nations Convention on the Law of the Sea

In Chapter 13, we have reviewed the consideration of the question of maritime boundary at the Third United Nations Conference on the Law of the Sea (UNCLOS) up to the end of 1981, and indicated how the provisions on maritime boundary contained in the Draft Convention on the Law of the Sea, which was formalised in August 1981, evolved. These related to the delimitation of the territorial sea, the exclusive economic zone, and the continental shelf between States with opposite or adjacent coasts, the question of islands, and the settlement of delimitation disputes.

Since no changes were made in these provisions in the United Nations Convention on the Law of the Sea, as finally adopted by UNCLOS, it will be useful to refer to these provisions, the text of which is contained in Annex III to this study. Attention is invited particularly to Articles 15 (territorial sea − which followed the provisions of the 1958 Convention on the Territorial Sea and the Contiguous Zone), 74 and 83 (exclusive economic zone and continental shelf, respectively, which contain identical provisions on delimitation criteria, as proposed by the President of UNCLOS on August 27, 1981, as well as on interim arrangements), 121 (islands), and 298(1)(a) (settlement of delimitation disputes).

In this Chapter, we will review the adoption of the Draft Convention on the Law of the Sea by UNCLOS in April 1982, and its being opened for signature at Montego Bay, Jamaica, on December 10, 1982, and indicate the views expressed and declarations made by the delegations concerning the question of maritime boundary in its various aspects.

The Eleventh Session of the Third United Nations Conference on the Law of the Sea (UNCLOS) was held in New York from March 8 to April 30, 1982. This was to be the decision-making session of UNCLOS, which had been meeting since December 1973. Accordingly, it proceeded meticulously in accordance with the time-table agreed to on August 28, 1981.[81] The first three weeks were spent on consultations and negotiations on pending issues. Time was allocated for general statements by delegations between March 30 and April 1, 1982. On

April 2, 1982, the President and the Collegium issued a Memorandum incorporating changes in the Draft Convention. Further informal negotiations continued. 31 formal amendments to the Draft Convention were proposed by 6:00 PM on April 13, as envisaged, which were moved and discussed in the plenary session of UNCLOS between April 15 and 17, 1982. On April 23, the Conference decided that all efforts for reaching decisions by consensus had been exhausted. By April 26, 1982, most of the formal amendments were either withdrawn or not pressed to vote. Two of them, including the one on reservations to the Convention, were put to the vote and lost. Further informal negotiations still continued between April 26 and 30, 1982. The final report of the President was submitted on April 29, 1982. Ultimately, at the initiative of the United States delegation, the Draft Convention on the Law of the Sea, as modified by the President's proposals, and the related four Resolutions, including those relating to the Preparatory Commission and the Preparatory Investment in Pioneer Activities Relating to Polymetallic Nodules, were put to the Conference for a recorded vote on the afternoon of Friday, April 30, 1982, and the package was adopted by a vote of 130 in favour, 4 against and 17 abstentions. Statements explaining the votes were made thereafter.

The Eleventh Session concentrated mainly on the questions relating to deep seabed mining including the protection of the interests of landbased producers of the same minerals, pioneer activities relating to deep seabed mining pending the entry into force of the Convention, the establishment, with necessary functions and powers, of a Preparatory Commission, participation of international organisations in the Convention, final clauses, and some other aspects of the law of the sea, including the passage of warships through the territorial sea and partial removal of offshore installations.

On the question of *maritime boundary*, with the compromise proposal made by the President of UNCLOS on August 27, 1981,[82] which was included in the Draft Convention with the approval of the two main contestant groups, namely the equity group and the equidistance group, there was an observable sigh of relief and a broad satisfaction over the compromise. Only a few delegations referred to these provisions in their general statements between March 30 and April 1, 1982. No formal amendments were made to the texts of these Articles by April 13, 1982, except the two amendments relating to Article 309 on reservations proposed by Venezuela and Turkey. Few observations were made on the subject in the concluding statements made by the delegations between April 26 and 30, 1982.

General statements: March 30 – April 1, 1982

The views of delegations, expressed in their general statements between March 30 and April 1, 1982, may be summarised as follows:

On March 30, 1982, the representative of *Venezuela* devoted the bulk of his statement to the provisions on maritime delimitation in the Draft Convention. His main fear was that in the absence of delimitation criteria in the new Articles 74 and 83, these would be interpreted like Article 15 dealing with the delimitation of the territorial sea, on which also his Government had entered reservations, and that the reference to Article 38 of the Statute of the International Court of Justice in the new Articles would reduce the value of judicial decisions on maritime delimitation. Excerpts from his statement are as follows:

> After reviewing the new draft of articles 74 and 83, Venezuela had concluded that it could not accept the solution provided by the joint consideration of articles 15, 74, and 83 of the draft Convention. Venezuela had recalled on numerous occasions, whenever the question of delimitation was considered, that it had entered reservations on articles 12 and 24, paragraphs 2 and 3 of the Geneva Convention of 1958 on the Territorial Sea and the Contiguous Zone and on article 6 of the Geneva Convention of 1958 on the Continental Shelf, when it had ratified those conventions. Since article 15 of the draft Convention was a virtual restatement of article 12 of the first of those Conventions, his delegation, at the plenary meeting of 28 August 1981, had expressed its reservations on the proposed new drafting of articles 74 and 83, and at the same time reiterated its consistent reservation on article 15 of the draft Convention.
>
> The wording of articles 74 and 83 adopted at the previous session did not specifically indicate the criteria or procedures to be followed by the States concerned in order to achieve an equitable solution, but merely referred to international law as defined in article 38 of the Statute of the International Court of Justice. As sources of international law, article 38 cited international conventions, whether general or particular, establishing rules expressly recognised by the contesting States; international custom, as evidence of a general practice accepted as law; the general principles of law recognised by civilized nations; and, as subsidiary means for the determination of rules of law, judicial decisions and the teachings of the most highly qualified publicists of the various nations. In the absence, then, of particular conventions the rules expressly recognised in general international conventions by the States parties to a dispute would necessarily apply, and, if those conventions contained a provision similar to article 15 of the draft Convention, it could be argued that, for lack of any other substantive provision, the criterion established in that regulation would apply by analogy not only to the delimitation of the territorial sea but also to the

delimitation of the exclusive economic zone and the continental shelf. In short, since article 15 as currently worded was totally unacceptable to his delegation, the mere possibility of such an interpretation compounded the difficulties.

The reference to article 38 of the Statute of the International Court of Justice, moreover, relegated judicial decisions, which had played such an important role in the development of law in that field, to the status of a subsidiary means for the determination of applicable rules. It was a well-known fact that both the jurisprudence and the practice of States had diverged considerably from the solutions espoused by the Geneva Conventions of 1958 because it was considered that their literal application could lead in many cases to inequitable situations.

Articles 15, 74 and 83 of the draft Convention were closely linked and, for that very reason, the intentionally neutral wording arrived at for Articles 74 and 83, though understandable, created additional difficulties for his delegation. Without wishing to reopen debate on a question which had been the object of long and difficult negotiations and yet wishing at the same time to be able to become a party to the Convention, Venezuela proposed that States should be specifically entitled to express reservations on articles 15, 74 and 83, as was done in the case of the corresponding provisions of the Geneva Conventions of 1958, or else that article 15 should be given the same wording as articles 74 and 83.

Regarding the question of the settlement of disputes over delimitation, article 298, paragraph 1(a)(ii) of the draft Convention should be taken to mean that States were in no way obliged to resort to other means of resolving disputes if they did not expressly agree to do so, when negotiations between the parties based on the report of the conciliation commission had not resulted in an agreement. In order to clarify the text as it stood, Venezuela proposed the following wording for that provision: '. . . the parties, unless they agree otherwise, may submit the issue, by mutual consent, etc. . . .'

. . . Regarding the regime of islands, he was again compelled to raise serious objections to article 121, paragraph 3 of the draft Convention. That provision was objectionable because it introduced a distinction between parts of a nation's territory, and that could not be justified on principle or on grounds of equity.

. . . He had on other occasions underscored the obscurity and ambiguity of each one of the three paragraphs of article 121, and he again asked where the subtle line would be drawn between the islands of paragraph 1 and the rocks of paragraph 3. Some States might recognise the right of a particular island to be considered as having an exclusive economic zone and a continental shelf; others might argue that it was only a rock, in accordance with paragraph 3 of article 121. Article 121 should therefore be deleted.[83]

On March 30, 1982, the representative of *Turkey* stated as follows:

... the drafting of article 15 (Delimitation of the territorial sea between States with opposite or adjacent coasts) did not take into account situations that a country might face in semi-enclosed seas and, for that reason, his country maintained its right to a reservation on the article.

With regard to articles 74 and 83 of the draft Convention, relating to the delimitation of the exclusive economic zone and of the continental shelf between States with opposite or adjacent coasts, Turkey was not bound by any convention or agreement and no international custom in the matter could be invoked as binding international rules in respect of Turkey. His country's view was that those issues in such seas could only be settled by agreements reached directly between the parties concerned on the basis of equity, and it therefore maintained its right to formulate reservations also on articles 74 and 83. It was evident that islands situated in such semi-enclosed seas presented problems for the same reasons. Article 121 (Regime of islands) was unacceptable in its present form and his country maintained its right to reserve its position on that too.[84]

On March 30, 1982, the representative of *Romania* accepted the delimitation provissions as follows:

With regard to the provisions relating to delimitation, his delegation had accepted the compromise formula devised at the previous session, on the understanding that the basic factors should be agreement between the States concerned and equitable principles. Uninhabited islets had no maritime spaces of their own and should not have negative effects on the maritime spaces belonging to the main coasts of the States concerned. Pending an agreement between the States concerned, no unilateral measures should be taken which would jeopardize an ultimate agreement.[85]

On March 31, 1982, the representative of *Bangladesh* stated as follows:

... on the issue of delimitation, the provisions of articles 15, 74 and 83 of the compromise text did not adequately define the methodology to be adopted in delimiting the maritime boundary and reaching an equitable solution, as demanded by the Convention. Clearly, as the representative of Venezuela had pointed out, article 38 of the Statute of the International Court of Justice had relegated established precedents to a secondary status. The need to identify the relevant circumstances that would determine the delineation of the line leading to an equitable solution had a particular bearing on the case. Moreover, there must be uniformity in the principles governing delimitation, and article 15, concerning overlapping jurisdiction in the territorial sea, must be brought into conformity with articles 74 and 83. Furthermore, the provisions covering the settlement of disputes should cover pending disputes as well as future situations.[86]

On April 1, 1982, the representative of *Algeria* stated as follows:

The compromise reached on articles 74 and 83 was a decisive step forward to achieve consensus within the Conference. The effect of the reference to international law as referred to in article 38 of the Statute of the International Court of Justice was to give pre-eminence to the principles of equity, something which was logical and natural in order to achieve the 'equitable solution' expressly mentioned in articles 74 and 83 of the draft Convention.

Given that the search for equity was at the root of the Conference, it was regrettable that the regime of islands resulted, in certain cases, in a situation which was not equitable. By giving all islands the same maritime space and advantages, without taking account of the harmful effects on the delimitation of sea borders with neighbouring States, article 121 ran contrary to the general spirit of the draft Convention. A distinction should be made between islands which were not affected by delimitation agreements and those which were. He stressed the contradiction in claiming equity in cases of delimitation *per se* while excluding it in the case of certain islands which created unacceptable distortions, particularly in narrow or semi-enclosed seas. He felt the Conference had been wrong to separate delimitation and the regime of islands, which were really two aspects of the same problem.[87]

In his statement of April 1, 1982, the representative of *Oman* expressed his reservations on articles 74 and 83, 'since they failed to lay down criteria for the delimitation of the exclusive economic zone and the continental shelf between States with opposite or adjacent coasts'.[88]

In his statement of the same date, the representative of *Qatar* said that 'he hoped that improvements could be made to the wording of articles 74 and 83, which were confusing and ambiguous'.[89]

In his statement of March 31, 1982, the representative of *Spain*, who was Chairman of the equidistance group at the Conference, said that he now accepted in a spirit of compromise the provisions on delimitation of maritime spaces in articles 74, 83 and 298, paragraph 1(a), of the Draft Convention, with a view to facilitating a final consensus.[90]

On March 30, the representative of *Guyana* stated as follows:

One of the most difficult issues of the Conference had been that of the delimitation of the exclusive economic zone and the continental shelf. Although articles 74 and 83 of the draft Convention did not fulfil all the expectations of his delegation, they nevertheless appeared to offer improved prospects for consensus.[91]

On April 1, 1982, the representative of *Colombia* stated as follows:

The final shape of articles 74, 83 and 298 had been accepted by his delegation with difficulty and as a last resort he would refrain from comment so as not to damage the fragile compromise achieved. However, his delegation continued to believe that compulsory and binding third-party settlement of disputes was the best guarantee for maintaining the rule of international law, disposing of disputes within a reasonable period and ensuring the equality of all States. In the event of any attempt to reduce the scope of the process of conciliation, in violation of the general compromise which had been achieved, it would insist on that procedure.[92]

Earlier, the delegation of the United Arab Emirates, speaking on March 30, 1982, stated as follows:

. . . his delegation believed that the draft Convention's solution to the delimitation of the continental shelf and the exclusive economic zone between States with opposite or adjacent coasts, in articles 83 and 74 respectively, was not clear enough and that a simple reference to Article 38 of the Statute of the International Court of Justice was insufficient. It therefore continued to believe that the best solution would be to adopt the median principle in such cases, because it was both clear and euqitable.[93]

Amendments proposed

Against the background of the afore-mentioned statements, only two formal amendments were made relating to Article 309 on reservations by the evening of April 13, 1982. Article 309 in the Draft Convention read as follows:

No reservations or exceptions may be made to this Convention unless expressly permitted by other articles of this Convention.

The footnote to this Article read as follows:

This article is based on the assumption that the Convention will be adopted by consensus. In addition, it is recognised that the article can be regarded only as provisional pending the conclusion of discussions on outstanding substantive issues.

Venezuela proposed that article 309 of the Draft Convention be replaced by the following:

No reservations, other than to articles 15, 74, 83 and 121, paragraph 3, may be made to this Convention nor any exceptions unless expressly permitted by other articles of the Convention.[94]

The other amendment was by *Turkey* which read as follows:

Delete article 309.[95]

Romania proposed to amend Article 310 on Declarations and Statements as follows:

Replace 'with a view, *inter alia*, to the harmonization of national laws and regulations with the provisions of this Convention, provided that such declarations or statements do not purport to exclude or to modify the legal effect of the provisions of this Convention in their application to that State Party'

by

'in conformity with international law'.[96]

The representative of *Venezuela*, while introducing his amendment on April 15, 1982, stated as follows:

His delegation had earlier explained why it felt that States should be allowed to make reservations with regard to articles 15, 74, 83 and 121, paragraph 3. Venezuela's position on the question of reservations had been consistent throughout the ninth and tenth sessions. Even earlier, during the first Conference it had specifically expressed reservations on article 12 and article 24 paragraph 3 of the 1958 Geneva Convention on the Territorial Sea and the Contiguous Zone, and article 6 of the 1958 Geneva Convention on the Continental Shelf.

Venezuela had also invariably maintained that questions regarding the delimitation of ocean and undersea spaces should be resolved by equitable agreement among the parties concerned. Delimitation of that kind had to take into account various questions of judgement and factors that varied from case to case. The practice of States showed that no single method but rather a combination of methods had been used to achieve an equitable solution in the majority of agreements on delimitation of ocean spaces. That approach had in the last three years produced satisfactory agreements between Venezuela and four neighbouring States, the United States, the Netherlands, the Dominican Republic and France, and those agreements covered more than 50 per cent of the areas that Venezuela had to delimit. It hoped that it could reach equitable agreements with the other neighbouring States. Venezuela's position was based upon the jurisprudence of the International Court of Justice and recent arbitral awards.

Essentially bilateral problems, which often affected vital interests and differed widely, were not always adequately solved by general provisions established in multilateral conventions. Venezuela believed that such conventions could well omit provisions establishing delimitation criteria but, if they did not include them, states which took issue with some of those criteria must be allowed to make reservations. Authorizing such reservations could not in any way affect the basic structure or the content of the draft Convention.

. . . When it was not possible to arrive at agreement by consensus other methods must be sought to allow States to become parties to the Convention without violating their rights and practices in defiance of their own interests. The problems at issue were bilateral. The groups representing special interests, such as the Group of 29 and the Group of 21, favoured one position or the other in such questions. In the circumstances, consen-

256

sus was not feasible. Dissenting States should be allowed to become parties to the Convention by entering reservations on the provisions they could not accept.[97]

The representative of *Turkey*, while introducing his amendment on April 15, 1982, stated as follows:

The present text of the Convention was clearly far from being the result of a consensus, and it was highly desirable that the Convention should be adopted by the largest possible number of States. The purpose of his delegation's amendment, therefore, was to allow States to formulate reservations in accordance with the provisions of article 19 of the Vienna Convention on the Law of Treaties, in other words, reservations which would be compatible with the aim and object of the future Convention on the Law of the Sea. His delegation did not agree with those who had said that the opportunity to formulate reservations would endanger the delicate balance of the Convention. It thought that the difficulties which a not inconsiderable number of States faced in regard to the Convention had not been taken seriously enough in the past. The general principles expressed in the draft Convention gave little scope in certain cases for resolving individual problems, which might assume alarming dimensions, perhaps even on the level of international relations world-wide. Some of those principles, for example, were not at all likely to lead to equitable solutions in the cases of smaller seas. For all those compelling reasons, his delegation desired and hoped that the Conference would be able to resolve the question of reservations in such a way as to permit all States to become parties to the Convention.[98]

Opposing these amendments, the representative of *Colombia* stated on April 16, 1982, as follows:

Reservations to articles 15, 74, 83 and 121, paragraph 3, could not be permitted. According to the preamble to the draft Convention, the area of the sea-bed and ocean floor which constituted the common heritage of mankind lay beyond the limits of national jurisdiction. Under the draft Convention, the delimitation of national jurisdiction was not a purely bilateral question. Ultimately, the area constituting the common heritage would be defined after delimitation of the areas referred to in articles 15, 74, 83 and 121 and of the outer edge of the continental margin referred to in article 76.

. . . Having refrained from submitting any amendments, his delegation now found that there was a proposal to allow reservations in respect of articles 74 and 83 as a whole (A/CONF.62/L.108 and Corr. 1). In both those articles, paragraph 2 stated that, if no agreement could be reached within a reasonable period of time, the States concerned should resort to the procedures provided for in part XV. The adoption of the Venezuelan amendment would enable States to evade the settlement procedure. Part XV should not be subject to reservations.

Colombia found it difficult to accept reservations in respect of article 74, paragraph 1, and article 83, paragraph 1. The question was whether the international community could accept a reservation to the provision that the delimitation of the exclusive economic zone and of the continental shelf should be effected by agreement on the basis of international law, as referred to in Article 38 of the Statute of the International Court of Justice. Furthermore, it would be inadmissible if, by reason of reservations to article 74, paragraph 3, and article 83, paragraph 3, States felt that they were not obliged to refrain from jeopardizing or hampering the reaching of the final agreement.

Reservations to article 15 could allow States to extend their territorial sea without limitation. That could have serious implications for enclosed or semi-enclosed seas in various regions.

The provisions contained in articles 15, 74, 83, and 121, paragraph 3, and in part XV, were not matters of bilateral concern; they were the key elements of a system built up over eight years of negotiation. Allowing reservations to those articles, deleting article 309 or article 121, paragraph 3, or amending article 310 would be incompatible with the Convention.[99]

The Turkish amendment was also supported by Brazil and Oman,[100] while amendments to the Article on reservations were opposed by the GDR, the USSR, the Republic of Korea, Belgium, Bulgaria, Iraq, Portugal and Madagascar.[101] Bulgaria stated as follows on April 16, 1982:

The amendments proposed to article 309, particularly that contained in document A/CONF.62/L.108, touched upon much broader issues than that of reservations and exceptions, for instance, the whole system of delimitation and the legal integrity of a comprehensive convention such as the Convention on the Law of the Sea. Problems of delimitation had always been considered a very important part of the Convention, as was demonstrated by the lengthy negotiations on the subject and the fact that agreement had been reached on a set of provisions only on the understanding that they would not be subject to reservations. The provisions of the draft Convention not only removed some of the uncertainties characterizing the 1958 Geneva Convention, but were also very flexible and general in order to provide a framework for viable and equitable bilateral arrangements with regard to problems of delimitation between neighbouring States. His delegation could not therefore support attempts to weaken the legal integrity and stability of the draft Convention in respect of delimitation.[102]

China supported the Venezuelan amendment on April 17, 1982,[103] while the representative of Pakistan suggested a harmonisation of the two proposals in the following words:

The proposal in document A/CONF.62/L.120 was too wide in its applica-

258

tion while that in A/CONF.62/L.108 was too restrictive. The two proposals should be harmonized in such a manner that reservations would be permitted but their scope circumscribed.[104]

After the debate, the President issued his report to the Conference on April 22, 1982, and with reference to the amendments concerning reservations stated as follows:

The President undertook consultations on the amendments submitted to articles 309 and 310.

As a result of these consultations, the President has come to the conclusion that there are no prospects of achieving a generally acceptable solution to these admendments.[105]

Thereupon the representative of *Venezuela* addressed a letter to the President of the Conference on April 24, 1982. He recalled his earlier statements of March 30 and April 15, 1982, and reiterated the position of his delegation as follows:

. . . The substantive consideration of the articles to which our amendment relates has now concluded and the desired consensus has not been reached. It is therefore appropriate and timely to consider now the amendment to article 309 so as to allow reservations to those provisions which present serious difficulties for some delegations.

It must be recalled, above all, that the power to make reservations is the rule and not the exception as regards multilateral conventions. This is clear from article 19 of the Vienna Convention on the Law of Treaties. Suffice it to read, for example, the multilateral conventions drawn up by the United Nations, or under its auspices, on questions previously studied by the International Law Commission. We shall observe that most of these conventions do not contain provisions concerning reservations and hence they allow them implicitly, in accordance with international law. In practice, as may be easily verified, many reservations have been made to these conventions.

Of these conventions, 11 in all, only three allow reservations solely to determined articles. These conventions include: the Geneva Convention of 1958 on the Continental Shelf, article 12, paragraph 1 of which states: 'At the time of signature, ratification or accession, any State may make reservations to articles of the Convention other than to articles 1 to 3 inclusive.'; the Convention on the Reduction of Statelessness of 1961, which states in article 17, paragraph 1, that: 'At the time of signature, ratification or accession, any State may make a reservation in respect of articles 11, 14 and 15' and in paragraph 2 of the same article that: 'No other reservations to this Convention shall be admissible.'; and finally the Convention on the Prevention and Punishment of Crimes Against Internationally Protected Persons, Including Diplomatic Agents, of 1973, which allows in article 13 reservations to the provision contained in paragraph 1 of this article.

. . . The experience of the Conference clearly shows that only a limited number of delegations have taken part in the discussions and negotiations on the question of delimitation. It is a well known fact that some 50 delegations participated actively in the two interest groups which were established to discuss this problem. If we examine the composition of these groups we may clearly identify the States with unsolved problems of delimitation and with divergent positions. As we have already pointed out these are essentially bilateral problems which interest only a limited number of States. The statements made against our proposal, some of them particularly vehement, show clearly that this is a question which is of special interest and direct concern to these States and not to the large majority of States participating in the Conference.

. . . If it is not possible to make these reservations or to change the wording of the articles to which our amendment refers, we shall not be able to become parties to the Convention. This would adversely affect the universality so desirable at a conference of this kind and, in the final analysis, no State would benefit because Venezuela would not be subject to provisions of a treaty of which it is not a party.[106]

The representative of *Turkey* also addressed a letter to the President on April 23, 1982, and enquired about the status of the footnote to Article 309 on reservations which had stated that the article was based on the assumption that the Convention would be adopted by consensus. The President answered that the collegium had met and decided the same morning to recommend to the Conference that under rule 37 of its Rules of Procedure, all efforts to achieve a consensus had been exhausted, and that the decision applied to all Articles including Article 309.

The Conference agreed with that recommendation on Friday, April 23, 1982.

The President then announced that in order to meet the requirements of the rules, April 24 and 25 (Saturday and Sunday) would be working days, and that the amendments would be put to the vote on Monday, April 26, 1982.[107]

On April 26, 1982, when the amendments came up for voting, the representative of *Turkey* pressed that his amendment for the deletion of Article 309 on reservations should be put to the vote. Chile and Colombia were opposed to his amendment. The representative of Venezuela said that in view of the Turkish amendment, which he would support, he would not press for a vote on his own amendment.

Accordingly, only the Turkish amendment to delete Article 309 was put to the vote and, in a recorded vote, was rejected by 100 votes to 18 with 26 abstentions.[107a]

Finally, as mentioned above, at the request of the United States Delegation, a recorded vote was taken by the Conference of the Draft Convention on the Law of the Sea and the related Resolutions as a whole, and the package was adopted on April 30, 1982, by 130 votes to 4, with 17 abstentions. Turkey and Venezuela voted against the Convention.

After the vote on April 30, 1982, the representative of *Turkey* said that he had at the 160th Plenary meeting (March 30, 1982) of the Conference explained the difficulties Turkey had with some of the provisions of the Draft Convention which would jeopardise Turkey's vital and legitimate interests, and with the defeat of their amendment to delete Article 309, his delegation had no option but to vote against the adoption of the Draft Convention.[108]

The representative of *Venezuela* explained his negative vote on the Draft Convention as follows:

> Venezuela's negative vote clearly and unequivocally placed on record that, since under article 309 of the draft Convention reservations were not permitted, Venezuela could not accept articles 15, 74, 83 and 121, paragraph 3, in so far as those provisions applied to the delimitation of maritime and underwater areas between States with opposite or adjacent coasts.
>
> In its statements at the plenary meetings on 30 March and 15 April, and in its letter to the President of the Conference (A/CONF.62/L.134), his delegation had stated the reasons why it could not accept those articles, to which should be added article 309.[109]

After the adoption of the Convention by the Conference on April 30, 1982, the Drafting Committee met in Geneva between July 12 and August 25, 1982, but did not deal with the provisions of the Convention on maritime delimitation.

The resumed Eleventh Session of the Conference was held in New York between September 22 and 24, 1982, when the text of the Final Act of the Conference was finalised and the Convention was named 'United Nations Convention on the Law of the Sea'. In view of the inability of Venezuela to host the concluding session in Caracas, the Conference decided to hold its final part of the Eleventh Session in Jamaica from December 6 to 10, 1982, when both the Final Act and the United Nations Convention on the Law of the Sea were to be opened for signature.

Montego Bay, Jamaica: December 6 – 10, 1982

The final part of the Eleventh Session of UNCLOS was held in Montego Bay, Jamaica, from December 6 to 10, 1982. The Conference had before it the text of the United Nations Convention on the Law of the Sea and the Final Act, both of which were to be opened for signature on December 10, 1982.[110]

The provisions of the Convention relating to maritime boundary, which are also contained in Annex III to this study, read as follows:

Article 15. Delimitation of the territorial sea between States with opposite or adjacent coasts

Where the coasts of two States are opposite or adjacent to each other, neither of the two States is entitled, failing agreement between them to the contrary, to extend its territorial sea beyond the median line every point of which is equidistant from the nearest points on the baselines from which the breadth of the territorial seas of each of the two States is measured. The above provision does not apply, however, where it is necessary by reason of historic title or other special circumstances to delimit the territorial seas of the two States in a way which is at variance therewith.

Article 74. Delimitation of the exclusive economic zone between States with opposite or adjacent coasts

1. The delimitation of the exclusive economic zone between States with opposite or adjacent coasts shall be effected by agreement on the basis of international law, as referred to in Article 38 of the Statute of the International Court of Justice, in order to achieve an equitable solution.

2. If no agreement can be reached within a reasonable period of time, the States concerned shall resort to the procedures provided for in Part XV.

3. Pending agreement as provided for in paragraph 1, the States concerned, in a spirit of understanding and co-operation, shall make every effort to enter into provisional arrangements of a practical nature and, during this transitional period, not to jeopardize or hamper the reaching of the final agreement. Such arrangements shall be without prejudice to the final delimitation.

4. Where there is an agreement in force between the States concerned, questions relating to the delimitation of the exclusive economic zone shall be determined in accordance with the provisions of that agreement.

Article 83. Delimitation of the continental shelf between States with opposite or adjacent coasts

1. The delimitation of the continental shelf between States with opposite or adjacent coasts shall be effected on the basis of international law, as referred to in Article 38 of the International Court of Justice, in order to achieve an equitable solution.

2. If no agreement can be reached within a reasonable period of time, the States concerned shall resort to the procedures provided for in Part XV.

3. Pending agreement as provided for in paragraph 1, the States concerned, in a spirit of understanding and co-operation, shall make every effort to enter into provisional arrangements of a practical nature and, during this transitional period, not to jeopardize or hamper the reaching of the final agreement. Such arrangements shall be without prejudice to the final delimitation.

4. Where there is an agreement in force between the States concerned, questions relating to the delimitation of the continental shelf shall be determined in accordance with the provisions of that agreement.

Article 121. Régime of islands

1. An island is a naturally formed area of land, surrounded by water, which is above water at high tide.

2. Except as provided for in paragraph 3, the territorial sea, the contiguous zone, the exclusive economic zone and the continental shelf of an isand are determined in accordance with the provisions of this Convention applicable to other land territory.

3. Rocks which cannot sustain human habitation or economic life of their own shall have no exclusive economic zone or continental shelf.

Article 298. Optional exceptions to applicability of section 2

1. When signing, ratifying or acceding to this Convention or at any time thereafter, a State may, without prejudice to the obligations arising under section 1, declare in writing that it does not accept any one or more of the procedures provided for in section 2 with respect to one or more of the following categories of disputes:

(a) (i) disputes concerning the interpretation or application of articles 15, 74 and 83 relating to sea boundary delimitations, or those involving historic bays or titles, provided that a State having made such a declaration shall, when such a dispute arises subsequent to the entry into force of this Convention and where no agreement within a reasonable period of time is reached in negotiations between the parties, at the request of any party to the dispute, accept submission of the matter to conciliation under Annex V, section 2; and provided further that any dispute that necessarily involves the concurrent consideration of any unsettled dispute concerning sovereignty or other rights over continental or insular land territory shall be excluded from such submission;

(ii) after the conciliation commission has presented its report, which shall state the reasons on which it is based, the parties shall negotiate an agreement on the basis of that report; if these negotiations do not result in an agreement, the parties shall, by mutual consent, submit the question to one of the procedures provided for in section 2, unless the parties otherwise agree;

(iii) this subparagraph does not apply to any sea boundary dispute finally settled by an arrangement between the parties, or to any such dispute which is to be settled in accordance with a bilateral or multilateral agreement binding upon those parties; . . .

Before the signing ceremony, opportunity was given to delegations to make statements between December 6 and 9, 1982, and 121 delegations spoke.

On the maritime boundary, the following statements were made, which are reproduced hereunder in a chronological order.

Ireland (December 6, 1982 – p.m.)

The delimitation of maritime zones was one of the last issues to be resolved at the Conference and the main difficulty arose in connection with setting out the criteria particularly for delimitation in the economic zone or on the continental shelf. And, while there was broad agreement that these should be as determined by relevant international law, several efforts to express that law in a provision failed to command support across the two groups representing most of the directly interested delegations. Finally this stalemate was broken by abandoning efforts to express the relevant law substantively and the vast majority of the interested delegations, including the Irish delegation, endorsed the provision which now appears in the Convention.

This provides that delimitation shall be effected on the basis of international law as referred to in Article 38 of the Statute of the International Court of Justice. We are satisfied that the relevant principles of international law thus referred to are as identified by the International Court of Justice in its decision on the North Sea cases in 1969 and as confirmed by subsequent judicial and arbitral decisions.[111]

The UAE (December 7, 1982 – a.m.)

The interests and political aspirations of the United Arab Emirates make it necessary for us to disagree somewhat with some of the provisions of the Convention, . . . (relating to) . . . the delimitation of maritime boundaries between adjacent, opposite or neighbouring States in connection with the exclusive economic zone and the continental shelf, under articles 74 and 83 of the Convention. In this respect, the United Arab Emirates believe that we should apply the principle of the median line and that the delimitation of the continental shelf should be carried out in such a way as not to exceed 200 nautical miles.[112]

Turkey (December 8, 1982 – a.m.)

I come next to article 15, entitled 'Delimitation of the territorial sea between States with opposite or adjacent coasts'. As the International Court of Justice stated in the fisheries case: 'The delimitation of sea areas has always an international aspect. It cannot depend merely upon the will of the coastal State as expressed in its municipal law'. Article 15, by accepting negotiations and agreement as the principal method of delimitation, concurs with the view expressed by the Court. Therefore, attempts to establish maritime boundaries regardless of the legal position of other States is contrary to recognised principles of international law.

Although the wording of article 15 is different from that of articles 74 and 83 concerning the delimitation of the economic zone and the continental shelf, the principle of equity is also the guiding principle in the delimitation of territorial waters, since it is inadmissible to think that the intention of the authors of this article was to permit an inequitable delimitation. The reference in the article to special circumstances, which is a means to arrive at an equitable result, also confirms this view.

The reference in the article to the median line does not give the median line method prominence over other methods. The median line can be applied only if it produces an equitable delimitation.

Articles 74 and 83, on the delimitation of the exclusive economic zone and continental shelf between States with opposite or adjacent coasts, are the result of prolonged negotiations and reflect a compromise between the divergent positions of the States. As such they should be interpreted in the light of developments in international law with regard to the delimitation of the continental shelf or economic zone. Articles 74 and 83 confirm the generally accepted view that the delimitation should be effected by agreement between States with opposite or adjacent coasts.

The only concrete guidance provided in those articles is that the ultimate goal of the negotiations between the parties should be 'to achieve an equitable solution'.

The Court's judgement of 1982 on the continental shelf case between Tunisia and the Libyan Arab Jamahiriya clarifies the concept of 'equitable solution' as follows: 'The result of the application of equitable principles must be equitable . . . It is, however, the result which is predominant. The principles are subordinate to the goal.'

The Court also indicates how, in practice, the equitable principles should be applied. The application of equitable principles involves, according to the Court, 'to balance up the various considerations which it (the Court) regards as relevant in order to produce an equitable result'.

The Court then examines the relevant circumstances which are to be taken into account in the application of equitable principles. In the Court's opinion, 'It is virtually impossible to achieve an equitable solution in any delimitation without taking into account the particular relevant circumstances of the area'.

It is thus clear that the term 'equitable solution' in articles 74 and 83 comprises the idea of applying equitable principles by taking into account all relevant circumstances with a view to arriving at an equitable result. As stated in the same judgement, the existence and position of the islands in the area to be delimited is certainly one of the most significant and relevant factors to be taken into consideration. That judgement of the Court is of particular importance since the Court took into full consideration the relevant articles of the Convention and, *inter alia*, articles 74 and 83.

The phrase in articles 74 and 83 'on the basis of international law, as referred to in Article 38 of the Statute of the International Court of Justice' is the product of a last-minute compromise and, in fact, does not have a different connotation from the concepts of 'equitable principles' or 'equitable solution'.

It is now generally recognised that equity is the rule of international law to be applied to the delimitation of the continental shelf or the exclusive economic zone. This principle is reflected in the 1969 North Sea continental shelf case, in the Arbitral Tribunal's decision in 1977 on the continental shelf between France and the United Kingdom and in the Tunisia – Libyan Arab Jamahiriya case of 1982. In the North Sea continental shelf case of 1969, the Court provides that '. . . in this field it [equity] is precisely a rule of law that calls for the application of equitable principles'. In the Tunisia – Libyan Arab Jamahiriya case, the Court stipulates that 'the legal concept of equity is a general principle directly applicable as law'.

Furthermore, the Court rules: 'The principles and rules of international law applicable for the delimitation . . . are as follows: The delimitation is to be effected in accordance with equitable principles and taking account of all relevant circumstances'.

Therefore, it is to be concluded that the words 'on the basis of international law' do not add any new element to articles 74 and 83 since, in the delimitation context, equity or equitable solution, which already exists in the articles, is the rule of law.

On the other hand, the reference to international law does not leave the door open to introducing the equidistance method or the median-line method as a rule of international law, nor does it lead to a presumption in favour of equidistance or median line in relation to other methods.

In the Tunisia – Libyan Arab Jamahiriya case, the Court provides that 'Treaty practice, as well as the history of article 83 of the draft convention on the law of the sea, leads to the conclusion that equidistance may be applied if it leads to an equitable solution. If not, other methods should be employed . . . since equidistance is not, in the view of the Court, either a mandatory legal principle or a method having some privileged status in relation to other methods'.

The same thinking is embodied in the North Sea continental shelf case and in the decision of the Court of Arbitration on the continental shelf between France and the United Kingdom.

Article 121, on the regime of islands, is in our opinion an article of a general nature which does not predetermine the maritime space to be allocated to the islands in delimitation. The presence of islands in the area to be delimited is, as I have already mentioned, one of the relevant circumstances to be taken into account in order to arrive at an equitable solution.

The maritime spaces of the islands situated in the areas to be delimited are determined by the application of equitable principles. Hence article 121 is not applicable to the islands located in the maritime areas which are subject to delimitation. That view . . . is also confirmed in the Arbitral Tribunal's decision on the continental shelf delimitation between France and the United Kingdom in which islands are given partial effect and channel islands belonging to the United Kingdom are enclaved by the French continental shelf, as well as in the Tunisia – Libyan Arab Jamahiriya case, in which one Tunisian island is completely disregarded and another is given half effect.

. . .

The Convention is silent on the delimitation of contiguous zones between States with opposite or adjacent coasts. By analogy, the provisions on the delimitation of exclusive economic zones and continental shelves should also be applicable to the delimitation of contiguous zones.

Furthermore, we should like to refer to and confirm our written statement contained in document A/CONF.62/WS/34 of 15 November 1982.

Finally, though an objective interpretation of the above-mentioned provisions of the law of the sea treaty can only be made as stated, we solemnly declare that this treaty can in no way be applied against Turkey, nor would Turkey be bound by any of its provisions, since such claims would have no juridical validity.

. . .

We should like further to reiterate that the delimitation of the economic zone and of the continental shelf in such semi-enclosed seas can be settled only through agreements to be reached directly between the parties concerned on the basis of equity.[113]

Colombia (December 8, 1982 – a.m.)

Article 15 establishes as a rule for the delimitation of the territorial sea that of the median line and establishes that no State will have the right, unless there are stipulations to the contrary, to extend its territorial sea beyond the median line. Exceptions are allowed only through agreement between the parties.

Articles 74 and 83 use the same text for the delimitation of the continental shelf and the economic zone and they have a relation to article 15. They establish that delimitation will be done preferably through agreement between the parties and exclude delimitation as a unilateral act by any State. The basis for the agreement is the international law contained in Article 38 of the International Court of Justice's Statute, which will have to apply. This stresses the predominant role of the Convention and gives only second place to customary law, as evidence of a practice generally accepted as law.

Articles 74 and 83 advocate the 'equitable solution' of disputes, which is substantially different from the use of 'equitable principles' as a procedure for delimitation.

If the States do not reach agreement, they will resort to part XV, which contains the obligation to settle disputes by peaceful means.

. . . Article 121 defines what is an island and the difference between islands and rocks. Islands have a right to a territorial sea, a continental shelf and an exclusive economic zone. Rocks are entitled only to a territorial sea since they cannot sustain human habitation or economic life of their own. This is logical. It is a 'package' which results from the view that these maritime spaces have been granted to benefit the inhabitants, with an economic concept. Any other interpretation would distort the concept.

The rules contained in the Convention on delimitation of the territorial sea agree with international custom. Whoever may wish to invoke the rights and the corresponding obligations has to accept the norms as a whole.[114]

Spain (December 8, 1982 − p.m.)

Apart from the questions to which I referred a moment ago, there are other provisions − such as delimitation and access by third parties to the resources of the exclusive economic zone, which are the result of difficult and lengthy negotiations in which the balance attained is in any event a compromise − which we can support since if they are correctly interpreted they protect our interests even though they may not be the precise regulations we desired.[115]

The Bahamas (December 9, 1982 − a.m.)

With regard to the provisions of the treaty in respect of the delimitation of the maritime spaces between opposite and adjacent States, which has been one of the key areas of difficulty for the Conference, my delegation is not entirely at ease. Our preference for a clear statement of the law that the median line should be mandatory is well known to the Conference, as is our preference for mandatory and binding dispute settlement procedures. Recognising the virtual impossibility of achieving these desires, we are, in the spirit of accommodation and compromise, prepared to accept the provisions on delimitation contained in the treaty.[116]

Venezuela (December 9, 1982 − p.m.)

Since reservations could not be entered with regard to articles 15, 74 and 83 and paragraph 3 of article 121, suffice it to say that to the extent that these apply to maritime and submarine areas of opposite and adjacent States, we were forced to register our objection to those articles and to state that had there been a separate vote we would not have voted in favour of them. We reiterate that position at this time.

With that understanding, Venezuela will sign the Final Act, which faithfully reflects the work of the Conference and does not contain, as is appropriate for documents of this nature, any value judgement on the results of that work. Venezuela cannot, however, sign the Convention itself.[117]

On Friday, December 10, 1982, the United Nations Convention on the Law of the Sea and the Final Act of the Conference were opened for signature. The Convention was signed by 117 States, apart from the Cook Islands and the Council for Namibia.[118] Of the States which had expressed strong sentiments and reservations on the provisions on the maritime boundary in the Convention, Venezuela, Turkey and Oman did not sign the Convention. Those who signed the Convention included Ireland, Bangladesh, Pakistan, China, Brazil, Portugal, Romania, Algeria and Guyana.

Fiji signed as well as ratified the Convention on December 10, 1982.

Since December 10, 1982, and by the end of 1983, the Convention has been signed by 131 States and ratified by 9 States.

The Final Act of the Conference was signed by 140 States and 9 other entities. The signatories included Venezuela and the USA. Turkey did not sign the Final Act. While signing the Final Act, *Venezuela* made the following declaration:

> Venezuela is signing the Final Act on the understanding that it is merely noting the work of the Confrence without making any value judgement about its results. Its signing does not signify, nor can it be construed as signifying, any change in its position with regard to articles 15, 74, 83 and 121, paragraph 3, of the Convention. For the reasons stated by the delegation of Venezuela at the plenary meeting on 30 April 1982, those provisions are unacceptable to Venezuela, which is therefore not bound by them and is not prepared to agree to be bound by them in any way.[119]

Under Article 308 of the UN Convention on the Law of the Sea, it will enter into force 12 months after the date of deposit of the sixtieth instrument of ratification or accession.

Summing up

In conclusion, the developments at the third United Nations Conference on the Law of the Sea on the question of the maritime boundary between 1973 and 1982 and leading to the adoption of the UN Convention on the Law of the Sea, 1982, and its opening for signature, may now be summed up as follows:

(1)   On the delimitation of the territorial sea, the position of the 1958 Convention on the Territorial Sea and the Contiguous Zone and customary international law has been retained in Article 15 of the UN Convention on the Law of the Sea, with minor drafting changes.

(2)   On the delimitation of the contiguous zone, no provision has been made.

(3)   On the delimitation of the exclusive economic zone and the continental shelf, identical provisions have been made which make no distinction between the two maritime zones or between States with opposite or adjacent coasts.

269

Only the term 'between adjacent or opposite States' was changed to 'between States with opposite or adjacent coasts' in April 1980 on the advice of the Drafting Committee. The delimitation criteria emphasise the need for an agreement, which is based on applicable international law and which leads to an equitable solution. They are not formulated to apply in the absence of an agreement. Since the Convention itself refers to international law, and identifies it with reference to Article 38 of the Statute of the International Court of Justice, which article itself refers to the sources of international law and includes international conventions, whether general or particular, establishing the rules expressly recognised by the contesting States, the standard or delimitation criteria may appear to be circular. In practical application, such reference will imply a greater emphasis on international custom as evidence of a general principle accepted as law, among other sources of international law, but supplemented always by the requirement to achieve an equitable solution. No direct reference has been made either to equitable principles or to equidistance in Articles 74 and 83. Again, although no specific reference has been made to islands or other special circumstances, these will be covered by reference to the applicable international law and the need for an equitable solution. It has also been provided that a rock which cannot support economic life of its own cannot have an economic zone or continental shelf of its own.

(4)   The provision on interim arrangements is so defined as to promote and not to prejudice the conclusion of an agreement in accordance with the aforementioned delimitation criteria.

(5)   Maritime delimitation disputes shall be resolved by negotiations, failing which by reference to compulsory conciliation. If the dispute still remains unresolved, it shall, by mutual consent, be referred to the compulsory third-party settlement procedures set out in the Convention, unless the parties otherwise agree.

Unsettled disputes concerning sovereignty or other rights over continental or insular land territory, disputes already finally settled between the parties, and disputes which are to be settled in accordance with a bilateral or multilateral agreement binding upon the parties have been excluded from the application of the settlement procedures set out in the Convention.

(6)   Finally, no reservations may be made to the maritime delimitation provisions of the Convention.

The answer to the question as to whether the provisions of the UN Convention on the Law of the Sea will remain as conventional rules, or whether they embody or will develop as the general rules of international law on maritime delimitation, both substantive and procedural, will depend upon the number of States parties to the Convention, subsequent State practice of the requisite quality, and the manner in which the Convention is interpreted and applied in concrete disputes concerning delimitation.

270

The conclusions reached from the present study as a whole, which covers the period up to the end of 1983, will be summed up in Part V below.

The text of the relevant Articles on the maritime boundary of the United Nations Convention on the Law of the Sea, 1982, namely Articles 15, 16, 74, 75, 83, 84, 121, and 298(1)(a), is contained in Annex III to this study.

Notes

81. A/CONF.62/116 at n. 78 above.
82. See n. 71 above.
83. A/CONF.62/SR.158, pp. 4-7.
84. A/CONF.62/SR.160, p. 5.
85. A/CONF.62/SR.159, p. 15.
86. A/CONF.62/SR.162, pp. 3-4.
87. A/CONF.62/SR.164, p. 13.
88. *Ibid.*, p. 31.
89. A/CONF.62/SR.166, p. 8.
90. A/CONF.62/SR.163, p. 23.
91. *Ibid.*, p. 20.
92. A/CONF.62/SR.165, p. 19.
93. A/CONF.62/SR.160, p. 6.
94. A/CONF.62/L.108 of 13 April 1982 and A/CONF.62/L.108/Corr.1 of 14 April 1982.
95. A/CONF.62/L.120 of 13 April 1982.
96. A/CONF.62/L.111.
97. A/CONF.62/SR.168, pp. 19-20.
98. A/CONF.62/SR.169, pp. 13-14.
99. A/CONF.62/SR.172, p. 10.
100. A/CONF.62/SR.170.
101. A/CONF.62/SR.170 and 171.
102. A/CONF.62/SR.171, p. 20.
103. A/CONF.62/SR.173, p. 4.
104. *Ibid.*, p. 17.
105. A/CONF.62/L.132 (22 April 1982), paras. 31 and 32.
106. A/CONF.62/L.134.
107. A/CONF.62/SR.174, pp. 9, 10, 13.
107a. For details of voting, see A/CONF.62/SR.176, pp. 7-8.
108. A/CONF.62/SR.182, pp. 17-18.
109. A/CONF.62/SR.182, pp. 23-24.
110. A/CONF.62/122 and Corr. 1-11 and A/CONF.62/121 and Corr. 1-8, respectively.
111. A/CONF.62/PV.186, p. 8.
112. A/CONF.62/PV.187, p. 76.
113. A/CONF.62/PV.189, pp. 63-70.
114. *Ibid.*, pp. 94-95.
115. A/CONF.62/PV.190, pp. 43-45.
116. A/CONF.62/PV.191, p. 26.
117. A/CONF.62/PV.192, p. 16.
118. For a list of States which signed the Convention, see C.N. 297, 1982, Treaties-1 (Depository

Notification), United Nations, 17 December 1982. See also *The Law of the Sea, United Nations Convention on the Law of the Sea*, United Nations, 1983, p. 190.

119. C.N.7.1983, Treaties-1 (Depository Notification), United Nations, 23 February 1983, Annex B, p. 16.

PART FIVE

Conclusions

CHAPTER 15

Conclusions

As indicated at the outset of this study, the subject of maritime boundary applies both to the seaward outer limits of maritime zones of coastal States as well as to the limits of maritime zones between States with opposite or adjacent coasts.

The outer limits of maritime zones, namely the territorial sea, the contiguous zone, and the continental shelf were reviewed, in their historical perspective, in Chapter 2 above. That Chapter also dealt with the baselines, normal, straight, archipelagic, as well as the bay-closing lines. Chapter 4 dealt with the technical aspects of maritime delimitation.

The rest of the study has concentrated on the delimitation of maritime boundary between States with opposite or adjacent coasts, or having features of both. It is this aspect which comes within the scope of maritime boundary, in common parlance.

The period of time covered in this study is between 1945 and 1983.

The study of the applicable principles and rules of international law relating to maritime delimitation, and their development, has concentrated on three main aspects, namely (a) State practice as reflected in treaties and agreements concluded between States, (b) judicial, arbitral and other decisions relating to maritime boundary between 1969 and 1982, and (c) development of the law relating to maritime boundary at the Third United Nations Conference on the Law of the Sea, 1973 – 1982. These three aspects have been dealt with in Parts Two, Three and Four above. The conclusions drawn therefrom have also been summed up at the end of each Part.

As to *State practice*, a sample of 100 Agreements from all regions of the world has been analysed in this study. Three-fourths of these Agreements were concluded after 1969, when the Judgment of the International Court of Justice in the *North Sea Continental Shelf* cases was delivered. Eighty-four of them deal with the continental shelf, seabed or maritime boundary, which may also be applicable to other maritime zones, such as the fishery zone and the exclusive economic zone; 12 agreements deal with the territorial sea boundary; and 4 establish joint or common zones, without settling the maritime boundary. Sixty-four of the agreements relate to States with opposite coasts, 36 relate to States with adjacent coasts. The Agreements have also been analysed with respect to the regions used in the practice of the United Nations and at the Third United Nations Conference on the Law of the Sea, namely Asia, Africa, Latin America, Western European and other States, and Eastern Europe (Socialist) States. Of the 100 Agreements, 74 were concluded among the States of these regions, 26 were inter-regional Agreements.

As to the delimitation criteria followed in these 100 Agreements, 64 followed the median or equidistance line (whether true or simplified), 18 adopted a modified median line, and 14 adopted another line or a negotiated line, which would include a latitude, a longitude, or some other line. In four Agreements a joint or common zone was established without settling the maritime boundary.

In these Agreements, the criteria applied have generally been the same whether the coasts were opposite or adjacent, although a maritime boundary between States with adjacent coasts extending to long distances may require special adjustments, or whether the boundary related to the territorial sea or to the continental shelf or other maritime zones. The Agreements restricting themselves to the territorial sea boundary have, however, mainly followed the median line, although there are exceptions.

Generally, a single maritime boundary has been developed whether it relates to the continental shelf or the fishery zone or the exclusive economic zone, although in the Agreement between Australia and Papua New Guinea, 1978, a dual boundary was established in the Torres Strait, one for fisheries and the other for seabed jurisdiction, although the treaty also established a Protected Zone for protecting traditional fishing rights.

The special circumstances prevailing in the delimitation area and leading to the adoption of a modified median line or a separate negotiated line have been (i) islands, particularly if title thereto is disputed or if they are located on or near the median line or across the median line, (ii) the concavity of the coastline, (iii) the comparative length of coasts in the delimitation area (Agreement between France and Spain, 1974), (iv) geomorphology, (v) location of resources and structures, and extent of existing licenses or contracts, and (vi) traditional rights or rights under an existing agreement.

The overall conclusion from a study of these 100 Agreements will be that in a large majority of cases States have been satisfied that the median or equidistance line leads to an equitable solution or result. They have also been ready to negotiate an equitable solution by modifying the median or equidistance line, or by adopting a separate line altogether, if special circumstances obtaining in the area so required it. In some cases, the parties have followed a principle of their own, like the boundary line along a latitude or a meridian, particularly among States adhering to the Santiago Declaration of 1952, and in some other regions also. In some cases, to promote goodwill and cooperation between the parties, particularly where they held different views on the principles of maritime delimitation, the Agreement has also established joint zones for exploitation, or provided for sharing of proceeds from specified structures or fields. In four cases, joint or common zones were established, without settling the maritime boundary.

State practice would thus support the conclusion that the applicable principles and rules of delimitation are that the maritime boundary between States with opposite or adjacent coasts should be settled by agreement in accordance with equitable principles and that the equidistance – special circumstances rule would generally lead to an equitable solution.[1]

As to *judicial, arbitral and other decisions*, six cases have been analysed in this study covering the period 1969 to 1982, three of which more intensively, namely the *North Sea Continental Shelf* case, 1969, the *Case concerning the Continental Shelf* (Tunisia – Libyan Arab Jamahiriya), 1982, both decided by the International Court of Justice, and the *Arbitration between the United Kingdom and the French Republic on the Delimitation of the Continental Shelf*, 1977 – 78, decided by the Court of Arbitration. These three cases have made the most significant contribution both to settling the disputes referred to them as well as to the development of international law on delimitation.

The basic principle and rule of delimitation, as set out by the International Court of Justice in the 1969 Judgment was that 'delimitation is to be effected by agreement in accordance with equitable principles, and taking account of all the relevant circumstances'. The implications of the principle were elaborated in the Judgment.

In the 1977 – 78 arbitration between the United Kingdom and France, the Court of Arbitration, while upholding the 'fundamental norm that the delimitation must be in accordance with equitable principles', also held that 'the equidistance-cum-special circumstances rule and the rules of customary international law have the same object – the delimitation of the boundary in accordance with equitable principles'. The equidistance – special circumstances rule should however be applied without an onus of proof on the party invoking the special circumstances.

In the case between Tunisia and Libya, both parties supported the equitable principles, and neither of them invoked the equidistance method which was regarded by both as leading to an inequitable solution. The 1982 Judgment of the International Court of Justice upheld the primacy of equitable principles as the applicable principles and rules of international law relating to delimitation, and said that 'equidistance may be applied if it leads to an equitable solution; if not other methods should be employed'. Equidistance was neither 'a mandatory legal principle', nor 'a method having privileged status in relation to other methods'. But the Court added that the attitude of the parties to the equidistance method would not prevent it from adopting an equidistance line if that would 'bring about an equitable solution of the dispute'.[2] The Court also gave a restrictive role to historical geology and geomorphology as aids to the determination of the limits of the continental shelf as the natural prolongation of the land territory of a coastal State and to the application of the principle of non-encroachment. It is the geographical configuration of the present-day coasts and the present-day seabed, which must be considered, not their evolution in the long distant past, the Court said.

As to the special circumstances considered in these cases, the 1969 Judgment was affected by the concavity of the coast of the Federal Republic of Germany. The decisions of 1977 – 78 in the arbitration case between the United Kingdom and France took into account the position of the British islands close to the French coast, the position of Eddystone Rock as a base-point, the position of the low-tide elevations, and the distorting effect of the Scillies. In the 1982 Judgment in the Tunisia – Libya case, the International Court of Justice relied on the conduct of the parties to determine an equitable line, and gave half-effect to the Kerkennah Islands, which was computed with reference to the change in the direction of the Tunisian coastline.

Thus the principles and rules of international law, as emerging from the judicial and arbitral decisions reviewed in this study, give a place of primacy to equitable principles, the application of which requires the assessment of all relevant circumstances prevailing in the area, with a view to reaching an equitable solution. The 1977 – 78 decision in the United Kingdom – France arbitration case gave a high value to the equidistance – special circumstances rule.

The Conciliation Commission in the Iceland – Jan Mayen (Norway) case, 1981, recommended the establishment of a joint development area, without establishing two separate boundaries, one for the exclusive economic zone and another for the continental shelf.[3]

The judicial and other decisions reviewed above took into account State practice and the developments in delimitation law at the Third United Nations Conference on the Law of the Sea. The latter were also influenced by these judicial, arbitral and other decisions.

As to the *developments at the Third United Nations Conference on the Law of the Sea*, which have been covered in Chapters 13 and 14 above, the proposals, discussions and negotiations on the question of maritime delimitation showed increasing polarisation between two interest groups, one emphasising equitable principles as the basic delimitation criteria, the other emphasising the median or equidistance line as the normal boundary. The subject of maritime boundary was considered under three main headings, namely delimitation criteria, interim arrangements pending a delimitation agreement, and settlement of delimitation disputes. In May 1975, the Informal Single Negotiating Text was prepared for focussing further negotiations at the Conference. Its provisions on maritime delimitation were a compromise between equitable principles, the median or equidistance line, and relevant circumstances. These provisions were continued in the Revised Single Negotiating Text (May 1976) and in the Informal Composite Negotiating Text (ICNT – July 1977), despite opposition from the equidistance group, which regarded them as tilted towards equitable principles, leading to a discretionary assessment of the relevant circumstances. In 1978, delimitation of maritime boundary was included in the list of seven outstanding issues for further negotiations, and a Negotiating Group (Negotiating Group 7) was established, which worked between 1978 and 1980 under the chairmanship of Judge E.J. Manner of Finland, when the position of the two interest groups became further polarised. In 1980, Chairman Manner proposed a new formulation which added a reference to 'agreement in conformity with international law' in the clause on delimitation criteria, despite the opposition of the equity group, which suspected that the reference to 'international law' in this context might be interpreted as giving a greater weight to State practice. The new clause was included in ICNT/Rev.2 in April 1980 and was maintained in ICNT/Rev.3 which was entitled 'Draft Convention on the Law of the Sea (Informal Text)' (August 1980). The position now appeared to have tilted in favour of the equidistance group. In August 1981, a further compromise was worked out by the President of the Conference, which made no reference either to the equitable principles or to the equidistance method, and which qualified the term 'international law' with reference to Article 38 of the Statute of the International Court of Justice. The redrafted clause on delimitation criteria read as follows:

> The delimitation of the exclusive economic zone/continental shelf between States with opposite or adjacent coasts shall be effected by agreement on the basis of international law, as referred to in Article 38 of the Statute of the International Court of Justice, in order to achieve an equitable solution'.

It will be observed that the delimitation criteria were identical for the exclusive economic zone boundary and the continental shelf boundary, and made no distinction between States with opposite or adjacent coasts.

The compromise proposal was accepted both by the equity group and by the equidistance group, although some delegations held reservations. The proposal was included in Articles 74(1) and 83(1) of the Draft Convention on the Law of the Sea, which was formalised as the official document of the Conference in August 1981, with the symbol A/CONF.62/L.78.

Apart from the delimitation criteria, the relevant Articles of the Draft Convention also included provisions concerning interim arrangements pending the conclusion of delimitation Agreements, and the settlement of delimitation disputes which provided for a reference to compulsory conciliation.

As to the territorial sea boundary, Article 15 of the Draft Convention maintained the application of the equidistance – special circumstances rule.

The Draft Convention was adopted by the Conference by vote on April 30, 1982. It was designated as the United Nations Convention on the Law of the Sea in September 1982, and opened for signature at Montego Bay, Jamaica, on December 10, 1982. It was signed by 117 States, apart from the Council for Namibia and the Cook Islands, which number has now increased to 134. The representatives of Venezuela and Turkey voted against the Draft Convention on April 30, 1982, and did not sign the Convention on December 10, 1982, primarily on account of their reservations on the delimitation provisions of the Convention. Excerpts from their elaborate statements have been given in Chapter 14 above.[4]

The references to the aforementioned concluding provisions on delimitation in the Draft Convention in the February 1982 Judgment of the International Court of Justice in the Tunisia – Libya case, including the dissenting opinion of Judge Oda, have already been given in Part Three (Chapter 12) above.[5]

Against the background of the above conclusions reached in the three main segments of this study, namely those relating to State practice, to judicial, arbitral and other decisions, and to the developments at the Third United Nations Conference on the Law of the Sea, the broad conclusions of this study on maritime boundary as a whole may now be summarised as follows:

(1)   The subject of maritime boundary, like the subject of land boundary, is a sensitive one and should be handled carefully and with understanding of the opposite or different viewpoints. The subject has assumed greater importance because of the developments in the law of the sea regarding the extent of a coastal State's jurisdiction in the 200-mile exclusive economic zone and the continental shelf, whose outer limits may under certain circumstances exceed 200 miles. In these zones, the coastal State enjoys sovereign rights over their resources, as well as exclusive jurisdiction and rights in other specified matters. These may include oil and gas, fisheries, energy, environmental control, and other uses of the sea. Accordingly, the delimitation of maritime zones of States has to be done with due regard to this sensitivity and in an equitable and fair manner. A single rule or method may not be automatically or mandatorily applicable in all circumstances, irrespective of the geographical and other facts. A maritime boundary Agreement, to be durable, must be a fair and equitable one and take into account the special circumstances in the area relevant to delimitation.

(2)   Maritime boundaries between States, to be secure and stable, have to be settled by agreement between them. In case of difficulty or a dispute, despite serious and meaningful negotiations, the parties may have to resort to some third-party conciliation, arbitration or judicial settlement procedure. In either case, the options available to the parties, or to a forum, within the applicable

principles and rules of international law, should be as clear as possible. The present study has indicated that State practice in Agreements has generally applied the equidistance method, modified by special circumstances. The Courts have emphasised the primary role for the application of equitable principles, taking into account all the relevant circumstances, although the Court of Arbitration in the 1977 – 78 decisions had also developed and applied the single equidistance – special circumstances rule along with equitable principles. Developments at the Third United Nations Conference on the Law of the Sea, leading to the adoption of the United Nations Convention on the Law of the Sea, 1982, provide for the application of the equidistance – special circumstances rule for the territorial sea boundary, and make no direct reference either to equitable principles or to the equidistance method for the exclusive economic zone or the continental shelf boundary. In the latter case, the delimitation Agreement shall be effected on the basis of international law, as referred to in Article 38 of the Statute of the International Court of Justice, in order to achieve an equitable solution.

How will these three trends, apparently divergent, be coordinated in State practice into an applicable delimitation law for guidance to the States, or by the Courts or other forums in resolving delimitation disputes? Will there be a merger or some form of a three-in-one solution?

As at the Conference, the controversy between the States which emphasise the equitable principles and those which support the equidistance method or line will continue, hopefully without much bitterness. Those who uphold equitable principles as the basic law will question the normative character of the equidistance line based simply on the number of Agreements applying it. For quantity to change into quality, and assume the character of a normative rule of customary international law, the test of *opinio juris* must apply. 'Not only must the acts concerned amount to a settled practice, but they must also be such, or carried out in such a way, as to be evidence of a belief that this practice is rendered obligatory by the existence of a rule of law requiring it', said the International Court of Justice in its 1969 Judgment.[6]

Short of this test, the equidistance method will neither be a mandatory rule nor have any precedence or priority for testing the equity of its application, it will be urged.

On the other hand, those who support the equidistance rule will cite widespread State practice as evidence of its being equitable, and criticise equitable principles *simpliciter* as leading to a discretionary assessment of the relevant circumstances and as amounting to 'the principle of non-principle', resulting in the distinction between a decision in accordance with international law and a decision *ex aequo et bono* becoming fuzzy.

The divergent stands and arguments will continue, although merging tendencies may also emerge.

Divergence may also continue between State practice and judicial and other decisions. State practice may continue to strengthen the equidistance trends, particularly where equidistance leads to an equitable solution, and in most cases it would. Such cases will therefore be resolved by agreement between the States concerned. It will obviously not be necessary for the parties to refer such cases to the Courts or tribunals or conciliation commissions. When the parties disagree as to how to proceed to delimitation, they may refer the dispute to a third-party settlement procedure. If the parties have partially agreed to the equidistance line in the delimitation area as a whole, the Court or tribunal may apply the equidistance – special circumstances rule in resolving the disagreement, as was done by the Court of Arbitration in the United Kingdom – France case in 1977. If the parties have disagreed even to the partial application of the equidistance line, or both regard the application of the equidistance method as leading to an inequitable solution in the delimitation area as a whole, or in relation to the area in dispute, the Court or the tribunal may determine any other line, based on the assessment of the relevant circumstances, which may lead to an equitable solution. It will still be up to the Court or the tribunal to examine the feasibility of applying the adjusted equidistance line in some form, if this may lead to an equitable solution. This will be the application of equitable principles, as was done by the International Court of Justice in its 1969 and 1982 Judgments mentioned above.

In either case, that is, in State practice or in judicial or other decisions, the options available to the parties or to the forum in resolving a controversy or a dispute, or in assessing the variety of special circumstances prevailing in the delimitation area, are many and have been elaborated in the literature on the subject. These options may be a median or equidistance line, simple or modified, a new or separate line, or in case of overlaps or continued disagreement, a common or joint zone.

The adoption of the appropriate method will have to be tested by the result, namely whether it leads to an equitable solution. The reasonableness could be verified by the test of proportionality between the length of the coastlines and the extent of the respective areas resulting from the delimitation line, without building up proportionality as the basis of the delimitation line, because in the latter case the alignment of the delimitation line may become secondary.

In fact that is how the delimitation provisions in the United Nations Convention on the Law of the Sea, 1982, may perhaps be interpreted and applied in State practice and by the Courts and other forums dealing with the delimitation of the exclusive economic zone and the continental shelf. These provisions make no mention of either equitable principles or the equidistance line. But the references to international law and to an equitable solution would imply reliance on the applicable principles and the assessment of the relevant circumstances. It is in this way that the aforementioned diverging trends in State practice, judicial and other decisions and at the Third United Nations Conference on the Law of the Sea, will need to be coordinated. In a judicial or other decision, this coordination will ensure that the decision is in accordance with international law and not *ex aequo et bono*, unless the parties have requested the latter.

(3) Assessment of the special or relevant circumstances prevailing in the area has been tied up as part of the delimitation criteria, whether the governing rule was equitable principles or the equidistance – special circumstances rule. In the flexible approach envisaged in point (2) above, assessment of the special/relevant circumstances will remain a part of applicable international law with a view to reaching an equitable solution.

Except in respect of the territorial sea boundary in Article 15, the delimitation provisions of the United Nations Convention on the Law of the Sea, 1982, concerning the exclusive economic zone or the continental shelf boundary do not refer to the taking into account of special or relevant circumstances. Nor was any list given in the earlier provisions, or in judicial decisions, although special circumstances have included the position of islands, the concavity or other configuration of the coastline, the geomorphology of the area, the location of known resources, the conduct of the parties, and so forth. Since these circumstances may vary, it is not possible to enumerate them exhaustively, or to assign effect or value to them. This will have to be done appropriately by the States negotiating a delimitation Agreement, or by a tribunal or forum settling a dispute, and in either case in such a manner as will result in an equitable solution.

(4) As mentioned above, the delimitation provisions of the United Nations Convention on the Law of the Sea, 1982, do not make any distinction between the delimitation of the exclusive economic zone or of the continental shelf boundary, nor between States with opposite or adjacent coasts.

In State practice, this has not caused much difficulty and single exclusive economic zone/continental shelf boundaries have been agreed upon between States with opposite or adjacent coasts.

In difficult cases, however, the special circumstances relevant to the continental shelf boundary may be different from those relevant for the exclusive economic zone boundary, such as the location of living or mineral resources in the area and the extent of direct economic dependence of the parties relating thereto. The value and effect to be attached to such circumstances may therefore also vary.

Again, as Judge Shigeru Oda has remarked in his dissenting opinion in the Tunisia – Libya case, the question may be considered whether the criterion of *distance*, namely the 200-mile exclusive economic zone and the 200-mile continental shelf for all States, 'ought not to play a role in the common delimitation of the area'.[7] This may imply a closer testing of the application of the equidistance – special circumstances rule to the single exclusive economic zone/continental shelf boundary, although it could be argued that the distance criterion refers to the outer limits of the maritime zones and not to the delimitation between States with opposite or adjacent coasts.

In some difficult cases, the question may also arise as to whether separate delimitation lines may not be established between the parties to a delimitation Agreement, namely one for the exclusive economic zone and another for the continental shelf. This was done in the Torres Strait in the Agreement between Australia and Papua New Guinea, 1978. It was not recommended by the Conciliation Commission in the case between Iceland and Jan Mayen (Norway), 1981. In both cases, however, joint zones were established for protecting specific interests.

If separate delimitation lines were neither desirable nor feasible, but the special circumstances vary, it may be useful to consider the establishment of a form of joint development zone either after, or without, establishing a single delimitation line in the area. Its practicability will depend upon its leading to an equitale solution of the controversy, or in any case its being regarded as not inequitable by either party.

In the field of common continental shelf/economic zone boundaries in difficult cases, a larger body of State practice and judicial and other decisions has yet to emerge.

Notes

1. For details of conclusions reached from State practice, and reference to the relevant Agreements, see pp. 121-124 above.
2. *ICJ Reports 1982*, paras. 109-110; see also p. 185 above.
3. For a more comprehensive summing up of the conclusions from the judicial, arbitral and other decisions reviewed in this study, see pp. 206-210 above.
4. For details on these developments, see summary at pp. 269-271 and Chapters 13 and 14.
5. See pp. 178 and 199-200 above.
6. *North Sea Continental Shelf* cases, *ICJ Reports 1969*, para. 77. See also p. 135 above.
7. *ICJ Reports 1982*, p. 249. See also p. 200 above.

PART SIX

Addendum

CHAPTER 16

Addendum

After completion of the manuscript of this study in April 1984, some additional materials relating to State practice have come to light and certain developments relating to maritime boundary have taken place. It is proposed to update this study until the end of November 1984 in this Addendum.

The Addendum will deal with the following:

A. *Treaties and Agreements*
   (1) Agreement between the United Kingdom and France relating to the continental shelf boundary, 1982.
   (2) Agreement between France and Fiji relating to the economic zone boundary, 1983.
   (3) Memorandum of Understanding between Indonesia and Australia concerning provisional fisheries surveillance and enforcement arrangement, 1981.
   (4) Other developments.
B. *Judicial, arbitral and other decisions*
   (1) Delimitation of the Maritime Boundary in the Gulf of Maine Area (Canada/USA): Judgment of ICJ Chamber — 12 October 1984.
   (2) Other developments.

A. Treaties and Agreements

In the main study, a total of 100 Agreements on maritime boundary were reviewed. To this list, 3 more Agreements may now be added. These are summarised below.

(1) Agreement between the United Kingdom and France relating to the continental shelf boundary, 1982[1]

The Agreement between the UK and France, which was signed on 24 June 1982 and which entered into force on 4 February 1983, delimits the continental shelf boundary between the two States in the area *east* of 30 Minutes West of the Greenwich Meridian. The boundary in the English Channel in the area *west* of 30 Minutes West up to the 1,000-metre isobath had been setled by the Court of Arbitration in its Decisions of 30 June 1977 and 14 March 1978.[2] Although the 1982 Agreement does not indicate the method of delimitation used, it appears to follow the median line. The coasts of the two States are opposite in the area. The boundary joins points 1 to 14, whose geographical coordinates have been given, by loxodromes. It will be extended beyond point 14 up to the trijunction point with Belgium later on, following the same method of delimitation (Article 2(2)).

(2) Agreement between France and Fiji relating to the economic zone boundary, 1983[3]

The Agreement between France and Fiji, which was signed on 19 January 1983 and does not appear to have yet been ratified by both parties, delimits the economic boundary between France (New Caledonia) and Fiji, and France (Wallis and Futuna) and Fiji, respectively. The Agreement is a brief one, and contains four Articles and an Annex. The preamble states that the parties have negotiated the Agreement by 'taking into account the work of the Third Conference of the United Nations on the Law of the Sea and the relevant principles of international law', and that the method of equidistance was proposed by Fiji for this delimitation, which was accepted by France as being, in the present case, in conformity with the application of equitable principles. Article 1 indicates that the line of equidistance, 'with certain minor divergencies for administrative convenience', was drawn from their respective specified baselines. The points of the boundary line, the geographical coordinates of which have been specified with reference to the World Geodetic System 1972 (WGS 72), will be joined by the arcs of geodesics. Article 3 provides that the Agreement is 'without prejudice to the sovereign rights of any neighbouring State in the areas to which it applies'.

(3) *Memorandum of Understanding between Indonesia and Australia*
concerning provisional fisheries surveillance and enforcement
arrangement, 1981[4]

The Memorandum of Understanding between Indonesia and Australia, which
was signed in Jakarta on 29 October 1981 and which was to come into force
on 1 January 1982, is a provisional one, and establishes a 'provisional fisheries
surveillance and enforcement arrangement' in areas of overlap between the respective economic or fishery zones. A provisional fisheries line has been drawn
joining the points with specified geographical coordinates. The arrangement relates to swimming fish. The sedentary fish will continue to be regulated by the
existing seabed arrangements between the two countries. The regime established by the provisional arrangement is that of abstention from jurisdiction by
either State over each other's vessels across the provisional fisheries line. Paragraph 2 epitomises this aspect of the arrangement as follows:
> (2)   It is understood that in areas of that overlap, and pending the perma-
> nent settlement of maritime boundaries between the two countries, neither
> Government will exercise jurisdiction for fisheries surveillance and en-
> forcement purposes beyond a provisional fisheries line in respect of swim-
> ming fish species against fishing vessels licensed to fish for such species by
> the authorities of the other country.

The provisional fisheries line appears to follow the median line in the extended
Arafura Sea and Timor Sea sector. In this sector, the Seabed Boundary Agreement of 9 October 1972 between them had established a negotiated boundary
line beyond the median line and closer to the deepest channel in the sea near
the Indonesian coast.[5] There will thus be two boundary lines in this sector.

(4) *Other developments*

In March 1984, India and Burma were reported to have initialled a maritime
boundary Agreement between the two States in the Andaman Sea and the Bay
of Bengal, the details of which have not yet been released.

   On 25 February 1982, Indonesia and Malaysia signed a comprehensive Treaty by which Malaysia recognised the legal regime of the archipelagic State established by Indonesia, and Indonesia accepted the continuation of the existing
rights and other legitimate interests of Malaysia in the territorial sea and the archipelagic waters, as well as in the air space above them, of Indonesia. The
Treaty established, *inter alia*, two corridors to enable ship navigation and com-
munication between East and West Malaysia, and a designated fishing area to
protect the traditional fishing rights of Malaysian traditional fishermen.[6]

Summing up

Summing up this part of the Addendum, the following features of the three Agreements on maritime boundary reviewed in points (1) to (3) above may be noted: all these Agreements relate to the post-1969 period, are between States with opposite coasts, and follow the median line; one Agreement deals with the continental shelf boundary, and two deal with the economic zone or fishery zone boundary; the provisional fisheries Agreement between Indonesia and Australia establishes a separate fishing line in one sector, namely separate from the seabed boundary line established by the Agreement of October 1972 between the parties — the situation thus becoming similar to the dual maritime boundary between Australia and Papua New Guinea in the Torres Strait;[7] and, finally, whereas one Agreement is between European States, two Agreements are inter-regional.

In view of these features, the contents and the tables in Chapters 5 and 11 of this study should be appropriately updated. The conclusions of these Chapters will, however, remain unaffected.

B. Judicial, arbitral and other decisions

In Part Three of the main study, six judicial, arbitral or other decisions relating to maritime boundary were analysed and reviewed, the last being the *Case Concerning the Continental Shelf* (Tunisia/Libyan Arab Jamahiriya), 1982. In this part of the Addendum, the Judgment of the International Court of Justice Chamber of 12 October 1984 relating to *Delimitation of the Maritime Boundary in the Gulf of Maine Area* between Canada and the United States of America will be analysed and reviewed.

(1) Delimitation of the Maritime Boundary in the Gulf of Maine Area (Canada/USA): Judgment of 12 October 1984

Background to Judgment, relevant maps

It may be useful to give at the outset a brief background to the dispute, and to indicate the outcome of the Judgment with reference to the relevant maps.

Prior to 1976, the dispute between Canada and the United States related to the delimitation of the continental shelf boundary in the Gulf of Maine area. In 1977, pursuant to their respective legislation or order in council, both the United States and Canada established their fishing zones extending up to 200 nautical miles from their respective coasts. The bilateral negotiations were con-

290

tinued and led in 1979 to the adoption of a package consisting of (1) a Fisheries Agreement concerning continued access to each other's fishing zone, making catch allocations, and providing for the settlement of disputes, and (2) a Treaty to submit to binding dispute settlement the delimitation of the maritime boundary in the Gulf of Maine area, along with a special Agreement to refer the dispute to a Chamber of the ICJ, failing which to a Court of Arbitration pursuant to another arbitration Agreement. The Fisheries Agreement was withdrawn from the US Senate due to difficulties in obtaining its ratification. Following an understanding on the severance of the package, the parties agreed to refer the dispute on the single maritime boundary to a Chamber of the ICJ. Accordingly the Special Agreement on the Gulf of Maine Boundary Dispute Settlement, which entered into force on 20 November 1981, was deposited in the Registry of the ICJ on 25 November 1981.

The ICJ Chamber delivered its Judgment on 12 October 1984.

Prior to the reference of the dispute to the ICJ Chamber and its Judgment, a number of articles appeared relating to the controversy between the USA and Canada.[8]

The written pleadings submitted to the ICJ Chamber in the form of Memorials, Counter-Memorials and Reply, and the oral proceedings held in April and May 1984, were comprehensive and voluminous. The written pleadings comprise 29 volumes. The oral pleadings comprise 4 volumes, and run into about 1750 typed pages, apart from 173 maps and graphics used by Canada, and 137 maps and graphics used by the United States, in support of their oral pleadings. The Judgment of the ICJ Chamber (12 October 1984) runs into 104 pages, besides the Technical Report, the Separate Opinion and the Dissenting Opinion, which take up another 44 pages.

This was the first case before the ICJ concerning a *single* maritime boundary for the continental shelf and the exclusive fishery zone. It was also the first case after the opening for signature of the United Nations Convention on the Law of the Sea, 1982, which had been signed by Canada but not by the United States, and which had not yet entered into force. It was the first case submitted to a five-member Chamber of the ICJ, which was established in consultation with the parties to the dispute. The parties had also requested the ICJ Chamber to itself delimit the course of the single maritime boundary between them in the light of the applicable principles and rules of international law, and had agreed to abide by its decision. The parties had also indicated that the single maritime boundary line should start from Point A, which was at a distance of 39 nautical miles from the international land boundary terminus between them, and terminate in an area of a specified triangle in the Atlantic Ocean area. The parties had also agreed to the Gulf closing line separating the inner sector of the Gulf of Maine from the outer sector facing the Atlantic Ocean.

The four Charts on the following pages illustrate the case. Chart 12A is a gen-

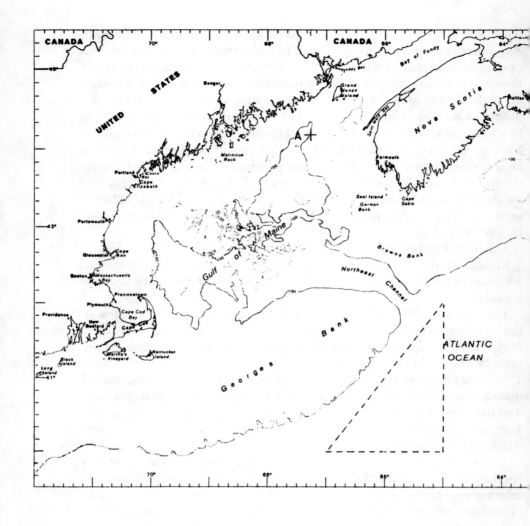

Chart 12A. Delimitation of the Maritime Boundary in the Gulf of Maine Area (Canada/USA):
General map of the region, showing the starting-point for the delimitation line and the area for its termination
Source: ICJ Reports, p. 269.

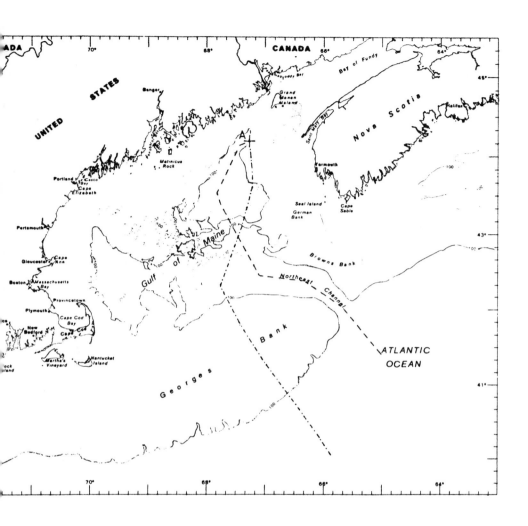

Chart 12B. Delimitation of the Maritime Boundary in the Gulf of Maine Area
(Canada/USA):
Limits of fishery zones and continental shelf claimed by the parties
at 1 March 1977 (see paras. 68-70)

United States line _ _ _ _ _ _ _ _ _ _
Canadian line _ . _ . _ . _ . _ . _ .

Source: ICJ Reports 1984, p. 285.

293

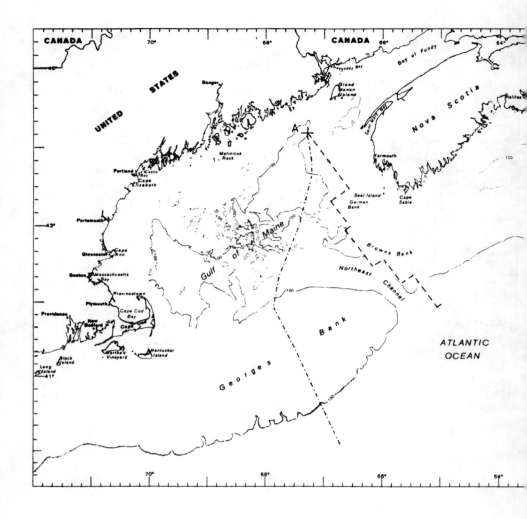

Chart 12C. Delimitation of the Maritime Boundary in the Gulf of Maine Area
(Canada/USA):
Delimitation lines proposed by the parties before the Chamber
(see paras. 71, 77-78)

United States line _ _ _ _ _ _ _ _ _ _
Canadian line _ . _ . _ . _ . _ . _ .

Source: ICJ Reports 1984, p. 289.

294

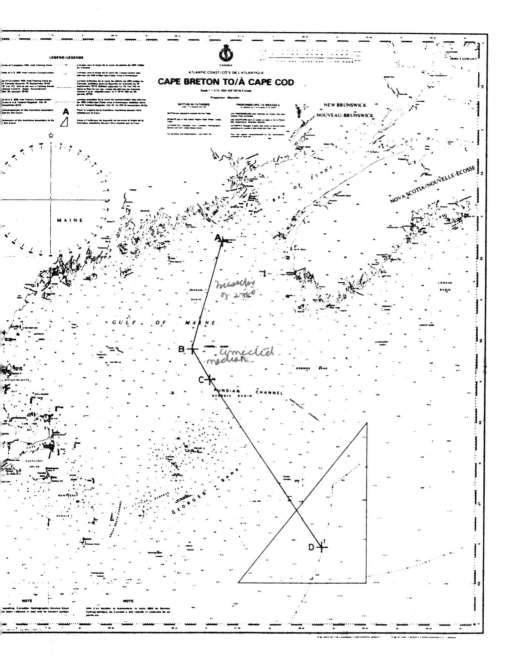

Chart 12D. Delimitation of the Maritime Boundary in the Gulf of Maine Area
(Canada/USA):
Delimitation line drawn by the Chamber
Source: ICJ Reports 1984, p. 346.

eral map of the region, showing the starting point (point A) for the delimitation line and the triangle area for its termination. Chart 12B shows the maritime boundary lines claimed by the parties up to 1 March 1977. The Canadian line is an equidistant line between the coasts of the parties. The US line follows the greatest depth of water in the Gulf of Maine and runs through the Northeast Channel to the Atlantic Ocean as a natural boundary. Chart 12C shows the maritime boundary lines claimed by the parties before the ICJ Chamber in their pleadings. Canada modified its earlier equidistance line in 1977 by ignoring Cape Cod and Nantucket Island off the northeast coast of Massachusetts, USA, and thus shifting the course of the boundary line towards the United States. The United States adopted a new maritime boundary line (September 1982) drawing a perpendicular to the general direction of the US coastline at point A and adjusting it in the coastal area opposite Nova Scotia to leave the fishing banks (German Bank and Browns Bank) wholly on the Canadian side, before reverting to the perpendicular line in the Atlantic Ocean area and moving it northeastward at the terminus.

Chart 12D shows the delimitation line drawn by the ICJ Chamber in its Judgment of 12 October 1984. This line passes through the Georges Bank, which was the heart of the controversy and places its northeastern part on the Canadian side.

We may now turn to the Judgment of the ICJ Chamber in the Canada/US case delivered on 12 October 1984, and summarise and analyse its contents. The ICJ Chamber consisted of Judge Ago as President, and Judges Gros, Mosler, Schwebel, and Judge *ad hoc* Cohen as Members. The vote for the Judgment was 4 to 1. A separate but concurring opinion was written by Judge Schwebel. Judge Gros wrote a dissenting opinion. The ICJ Chamber also appointed Commander Peter Bryan Beazley as a technical expert, pursuant to the Special Agreement between the parties, to assist the Chamber in respect of technical matters and in preparing the description of the maritime boundary and the charts. His Technical Report, presented to the Chamber, was appended to the Judgment.

Question before the ICJ Chamber

The ICJ Chamber was requested by the parties (Canada and the United States) to delimit a single maritime boundary between their respective continental shelf and the fishery zones in the Gulf of Maine area. The starting point (point A) as well as the area of termination (a triangle) of such a boundary line were specified by the parties with reference to their geographical coordinaties. Article II, paragraph 1, of the Special Agreement reads as follows:

296

The Chamber is requested to decide, in accordance with the principles and rules of international law applicable in the matter as between the Parties, the following question:

What is the course of the single maritime boundary that divides the continental shelf and fisheries zones of Canada and the United States of America from a point in latitude 44°11′12′′N, longitude 67°16′46′′W to a point to be determined by the Chamber within an area bounded by straight lines connecting the following sets of geographic coordinates: latitude 40°N, longitude 67°W; latitude 40°N, longitude 65°W; latitude 42°N, longitude 65°W?[9]

Submissions of parties

Canada. The formal submissions of Canada in the written and the oral proceedings concentrated on the alignment of the single maritime boundary in the delimitation area. The boundary should consist of geodesic lines connecting the following geographic coordinates of points, Canada submitted:

44°11′12′′N	67°16′46′′W
44°08′51′′N	67°16′20′′W
43°59′12′′N	67°14′34′′W
43°49′49′′N	67°12′30′′W
43°49′29′′N	67°12′43′′W
43°37′33′′N	67°12′24′′W
43°03′58′′N	67°23′55′′W
42°54′44′′N	67°28′35′′W
42°20′37′′N	67°45′36′′W
41°56′42′′N	67°51′29′′W
41°22′07′′N	67°29′09′′W
40°05′36′′N	66°41′59′′W[10]

This Canadian single maritime boundary line drawn accordingly was an equidistance line starting from point A and terminating in the triangle, and giving no effect to Nantucket Island and Cape Cod off the coast of Massachusetts, United States. Its alignment has been shown in Chart 12C above.

United States. The formal submissions of the United States of America in the written and oral proceedings were elaborate.[11] They dealt with the applicable law, the relevant circumstances, and the course of the delimitation line.

The *applicable law* highlighted 'the application of equitable principles, taking into account the relevant circumstances in the area, to produce an equitable solution'. The equitable principles to be applied in this case included (a) the principle of the relationship between the relevant coasts of the parties and the maritime areas lying in front of them, including non-encroachment, proportionality, and natural prolongation in the geographic sense, or coastal front extension, (b) conservation and management of the natural resources of the area, (c) minimisation of the potential for disputes, and (d) the taking into account of the relevant circumstances in the area.

The *relevant circumstances* were divided into three categories: the geographical circumstances, the environmental circumstances, and the circumstances relating to the predominant interests of the United States as evidenced by their activities in the area.

The geographical circumstances emphasised, *inter alia*, the extension of the coastal front of Maine and New Hampshire through the Gulf of Maine and beyond, the adjacency of the coasts of the US and Canada, the northeastern direction of the east coast of North America, the location of the international boundary terminus in the northern corner of the Gulf of Maine, the protrusion of the Nova Scotian (Canadian) coast, the concavity in the Gulf of Maine caused by the Nova Scotia peninsula and the curvature of the New England coast, the comparative length of the relevant coastlines of the parties, and the location of the Northeast Channel, Georges Bank, and Browns Bank and German Bank on the Scotian Shelf, as special features.

The environmental circumstances emphasised the existence of (a) three separate and identifiable ecological regimes associated with the Gulf of Maine basin, the Georges Bank, and the Scotian Shelf, and (b) the Northeast Channel as the natural boundary dividing the regimes of the Georges Bank and the Scotian Shelf and the fish stocks associated with them.

The circumstances relating to the predominant interests of the United States emphasised the duration and extent of the fishing activities of US fishermen 'since before the United States became an independent country', the sole development and, until recently, the almost exclusive domination of the Georges Bank fisheries by US fishermen, and other US activities relating to aids to navigation, search and rescue, defence, scientific research, and fisheries conservation and management in the area.

As to the *delimitation line* for a single maritime boundary, the United States submitted that 'the application of equitable principles taking into account the relevant circumstances in the area to produce an equitable solution' was best accomplished by drawing a perpendicular to the general direction of the coast in the Gulf of Maine area at point A, but adjusted during its course to avoid dividing German Bank and Browns Bank, both of which would be left in their entirety to Canada. The boundary line proposed by the United States consisted of geodetic lines connecting the following geographic coordinates:

	Latitude (North)	Longitude (West)
(a)	44°11′12′′	67°16′46′′
(b)	43°29′06′′	66°34′30′′

(c)	43°19'30''	66°52'45''
(d)	43°00'00''	66°33'21''
(e)	42°57'13''	66°38'36''
(f)	42°28'48''	66°10'25''
(g)	42°34'24''	66°00'00''
(h)	42°15'45''	65°41'33''
(i)	42°22'23''	65°29'12''
(j)	41°56'21''	65°03'48''
(k)	41°58'24''	65°00'00''

The United States' single maritime boundary line drawn accordingly has been shown in Chart 12C above.

It may be mentioned that although in the oral proceedings the United States had discussed other possible methods of delimitation of a single maritime boundary in the area, described as the 'Two-Sector Approach' (that is, separate boundary lines in the Gulf of Maine and in the Atlantic Ocean sectors), the 'One-Sector Approach' and the 'Two-Method Approach', which also emphasised the element of proportionality of the length of the respective coastlines,[13] their final submissions on 11 May 1984 concerning the delimitation line were not changed.

Nature of the dispute

After recording the submissions of the parties, the ICJ Chamber Judgment has been divided into eight sections, namely sections I to VIII, which are followed by the operative part.

Section I deals with the nature of the dispute. The Chamber notes, *inter alia*, that the parties have indicated the starting point of the boundary at point A and the terminal point in a triangle. The course of the boundary line between the international boundary terminus between Canada and the United States and point A will be determined by them directly, since the sovereignty over Machias Seal Island and North Rock located in this sector is in dispute between them. The parties have also agreed that the further extension of the boundary line from the triangle seaward, which involves the determination of the outer edge of the continental margin, will be dealt with by them by negotiations in the first instance, failing which this question may also be referred to the ICJ Chamber, although the Chamber's jurisdiction will in principle be determined by the Statute of the Court and its Rules.

The Chamber said that '. . . it must conform to the terms by which the Parties defined this task. If it did not do so, it would overstep its jurisdiction'.[14]

The Chamber noted that, unlike the cases concerning the *North Sea Continental Shelf*, 1969, and the *Delimitation of the Continental Shelf* (Tunisia/

Libyan Arab Jamahiriya), 1982, the task of the delimitation of the maritime boundary had been directly entrusted to the Chamber.

The Chamber had also been requested to delimit a *single* maritime boundary relating to both the continental shelf and the exclusive fishery zone. The parties had assumed that it would be possible, both legally and materially, to draw such a single boundary for two different jurisdictions. The Chamber said that 'there is certainly no rule of international law to the contrary, and, in the present case, there is no material impossibility in drawing a boundary of this kind'.[15]

The delimitation area

Section II of the ICJ Chamber Judgment deals with the identification of the delimitation area, which had not been defined in the Special Agreement between the parties. The delimitation area was distinguished by the Chamber from the 'Gulf of Maine Area' mentioned in the Special Agreement. The latter area was elaborated by the parties in the written and oral pleadings to include references to the 'coastal wings' extending in the case of Canada up to Lunenberg, Halifax or Cape Canso, and in the case of the United States up to Newport and Rhode Island, or even beyond. These extensions were intended to support their respective economic arguments relating to the delimitation area. 'It is easy to see from a map', the Chamber said, 'how these extensions tend to produce a shift towards one side or another when it comes to determining the central axis of the so-called "area".'[16]

The Chamber defined the delimitation area first in terms of *physical geography*. It noted that the inner zone or sector of the Gulf of Maine had roughly the shape of an elongated rectangle, bordered on three sides by straight lines. The short sides of the rectangle are those which join the tip of Cape Cod with Cape Anne on the US side, and the international boundary terminus with Brier Island and Cape Sable, the two extremities of Nova Scotia, on the Canadian side. These two short sides of the rectangle are 'quasi-parallel'.[17] The long side of the rectangle is formed by the line joining Cape Elizabeth in Maine (United States) and the international boundary terminus. This long side and the short side on the Nova Scotian side meet at the international boundary terminus at almost a right angle. The Chamber said:

> To sum up, the Gulf of Maine takes the form of a large, roughly rectangular indentation, bordered on three sides by land − except where the contiguous bays of Cape Cod/Massachusetts lie along the western side, and the Bay of Fundy opens out at the inner end of the eastern side − and on the fourth side open to the Atlantic Ocean.[18]

The open fourth side comprises the seaward 'closing line' of the Gulf of Maine. It joins Nantucket Island (US) and Cape Sable (Canada), and faces the Atlantic

300

Ocean. The area across the 'closing line' will thus constitute the outer zone or sector of the delimitation area, which includes the whole of Georges Bank, 'the main focus of the dispute'.[19]

Since the single maritime boundary is to terminate in a triangle located in this sector, 'one must logically deduce', the Chamber said, 'that the delimitation area comprises not only the sea areas surrounded by the coasts of the Gulf of Maine, but also those lying to seaward of, and over and against the Gulf, between bounds converging towards the outer edge of the triangle, for no delimitation by the Chamber may go beyond these bounds'.[20]

Earlier, referring to the correlation of the long and short sides of the rectangle in the Gulf of Maine, the Chamber cautioned that this should not be interpreted as espousal of the concept of 'primary' and 'secondary' coastal fronts with differential treatment for delimitation. Nor did the Chamber agree that certain geographical features are to be 'aberrant' by reference to the presumed dominant characteristics of an area, coast or even continent, such as the protrusian of the Nova Scotian peninsula or the location of Cape Cod.[21]

Turning to the other aspects of the delimitation area, the Chamber noted that 'both Parties recognise that the geological structure of the strata underlying the whole of the continental shelf of North America, including the Gulf of Maine area, is essentially continuous'.[22] Thus the *geological factors* were not significant in the present case. *Geomorphologically* also the Court supported the conclusion concerning the unity and uniformity of the whole seabed underlying the Gulf of Maine proper and the shelf up to the edge of the continental margin, despite the existence of some secondary characteristics resulting mainly from glacial and fluvial action. Even the Northeast Channel 'does not have the characteristics of a real trough marking the dividing-line between two geomorphologically distinct units'.[23]

As to the *water-column* of the delimitation area, the Chamber said that it was 'not . . . convinced of the possibility of discerning any genuine, sure and stable "natural boundaries" in so fluctuating an environment as the waters of the ocean, their flora and fauna'.[24] Nor could such a boundary be of equal relevance to the seabed for delimiting a single maritime boundary.

The Chamber thus considered that, in the present case, 'there are no geological, geomorphological, ecological or other factors sufficiently important, evident and conclusive to represent a single, incontrovertible natural boundary'.[25]

Nor were the *scio-economic* aspects, which were emphasised by the parties, so relevant to the delimitation of a single maritime boundary. These could be gone into in a decision *ex aequo et bono*, but not in a decision based on law, the Chamber said.[26]

History of dispute and claim lines of parties

Section III of the ICJ Chamber Judgment reviews the history of the dispute, and describes the boundary lines claimed by the parties with reference to Charts 12B and 12C given above.

Initially the differences between the parties related to the alignment of the *continental shelf* boundary. The United States claimed that the Truman Proclamation of September 1945, issued after consultation with Canada, had established the continental shelf limits of the United States up to 100 fathoms depth which applied to the Gulf of Maine area. Canada claimed jurisdiction on the basis of the equidistance line drawn pursuant to Article 6 of the Convention on the Continental Shelf, 1958, to which both the US and Canada were parties, asserted that it had engaged in activities in a part of the Georges Bank, and said that the US was aware of their position in the mid-1960s and had acquiesced therein. The Chamber, after reviewing the relevant facts, stated that:

> . . . it was at this stage − i.e., after the American diplomatic note of 5 November 1969 refusing to acquiesce in any authorization given by Canada to explore or exploit the natural resources of Georges Bank, and after Canada's reply of 1 December 1969, refusing *inter alia* to agree to any kind of moratorium − that the existence of the dispute became clearly established.[27]

The dispute, however, related only to the continental shelf at that time. The activity on either side in the disputed area continued until 1976, despite protests, but with elements of restraint on enforcement. In January 1974, the US informed Canada of their legislation concerning the American lobster, as a living resource of the shelf, and claimed exclusive jurisdiction along the 'lobster line' which followed the 100-fathom contour of Georges Bank, but in September 1974 it said that the law would not be enforced against Canadian fishermen.[28] Similarly, in December 1976 the US withdrew 28 tracts from the disputed area in Georges Bank from the proposed sale of leases, although the US rejected Canada's earlier protest.[29] No drilling activities were, however, authorised in the disputed area by either side. Negotiations were held between the parties between 1975 and 1976, without much success.

The *fisheries* aspect of the maritime boundary assumed importance from 1976 onwards, when both the United States and Canada, basing themselves on the consensus achieved at the Third United Nations Conference on the Law of the Sea, proceeded to establish a 200-mile fisheries zone off their coasts pursuant to their respective law and order in council, which came into force on 1 March 1977 and 1 January 1977, respectively.

The Canadian order defined the limits for the future Canadian zone, which were based on the equidistance line.

A notice in the United States *Federal Register* on 4 November 1976 stated the

302

limits of the US 200-mile fishery zone and continental shelf in areas bordering Canada, and this line followed the deepest water through the Gulf of Maine basin and the Northeast Channel, and was approximately equidistant between the 100-fathom depth contours there. It left Georges Bank on the side of the United States and Browns Bank on the Canadian side. (For illustration of these US and Canadian lines, see Chart 12B above).

From 1976 to 1979, negotiations were held between the US and Canada to continue and regulate trans-boundary fishing, but interim arrangements were suspended and on 2 June 1978 trans-boundary fishing ceased. Two inter-linked Agreements were, however, negotiated and signed on 29 March 1979, one the Treaty to Submit to Binding Dispute Settlement the Delimitation of Maritime Boundary in the Gulf of Maine Area, and the other the Agreement on East Coast Fisheries Resources concerning access to each other's fishing zone, catch allocations, and settlement of disputes by arbitration. The Fisheries Agreement had difficulties in obtaining ratification in the US Senate and was therefore withdrawn by the President of the United States on 6 March 1981. Later the parties agreed to separate the Boundary Settlement Treaty, which was ratified by both States on 20 November 1981. On 25 November 1981, the Special Agreement referring the dispute to a Chamber of the ICJ was notified to the Registry.

As to the *claim lines*, Canada reviewed its 1 November 1976 line, communicated it to the US Government by a diplomatic note on 3 November 1977, and published it in the *Canadian Gazette* on 15 September 1978. The second Canadian line gave no effect to Cape Cod and the islands of Nantucket and Martha's Vineyard, since these added to the marked protrusion of the US coastline southeast of Boston. This action was taken by Canada pursuant to the Decision of the Court of Arbitration in the Anglo-French Continental Shelf Delimitation case, 1977. The new Canadian claim line thus modified the equidistant line and moved it towards the United States coast by shifting the basepoint in this sector to the eastern end of the Cape Cod Canal.

The Canadian claim line was rejected by the United States by a Note of 2 December 1977, although in January 1978 the US also withdrew some tracts on Georges Bank from sale, pursuant to a request from Canada, without giving any recognition to the new Canadian position.[30]

The United States revised its claim line of 4 November 1976, which followed the deepest water channel, by a new claim line only after the present case had been submitted to the ICJ Chamber and the proceedings had begun in 1982. The new line was a perpendicular to the general direction of the coast, and drawn at point A. The perpendicular line was adjusted, 'in its resulting rather complicated course', by separating the 'ecological regimes' which the US regarded as distinct in respect of the fishery resources of the area.[31] The US claim line thus left Georges Bank on their side and German Bank and Browns Bank on the Canadian side. (For illustration of these revised Canadian and US lines, see Chart 12C above).

The claim lines of the parties were examined more intensively by the Chamber in section VI of the Judgment, which will be dealt with below.

Principles and rules of international law relating to maritime delimitation

In sections IV and V, the Chamber Judgment reviews the applicable principles and rules of international law relating to maritime delimitation.

At the outset, in section IV, the Chamber recalled that it had been requested to decide the question submitted to it 'in accordance with the principles and rules of international law applicable in the matter between the Parties'. The use of the words 'principles and rules' 'is no more than the use of a dual expression to convey one and the same idea'.[32] In its major task, the Chamber said that it would have to refer primarily to customary international law which could only provide 'a few basic legal principles, which lay down guidelines to be followed with a view to an essential objective', and the most appropriate criteria, and the method or methods most likely to yield a result consonant with the law 'can only be determined in relation to each particular case and its specific characteristics'.[33]

In the light of Article 38 of the Statute of the Court, the Chamber first looked at the general international conventions, where the principles and rules of general application could be identified, but which should be seen 'against the background of customary international law and interpreted in its light'.[34] It referred to Article 6 of the Convention on the Continental Shelf, 1958,[35] which dealt only with the continental shelf and not the fishery zone. Nor did the 1982 United Nations Convention on the Law of the Sea deal with the delimitation of a single maritime boundary, the Chamber said.[36] Article 6 of the 1958 Convention consisted of two aspects, one, a principle of international law, and two, an equitable criterion backed by a practical method to be used in certain circumstances for effecting the delimitation. The first aspect emphasised that the boundary should be determined by agreement between the States concerned, either by a direct agreement or by some other method based on consent. The Chamber added:

> To this one might conceivably add — although the 1958 Convention does not mention the idea, so that it entails going a little far in interpreting the text — that a rule which may be regarded as logically underlying the principle just stated is that any agreement or other equivalent solution should involve the application of equitable criteria, namely criteria derived from equity which — whether they be designated 'principles' or 'criteria', the latter term being preferred by the Chamber for reasons of clarity — are not in themselves principles and rules of international law.[37]

In contrast, these rules, namely, delimitation by agreement and the application of equitable criteria, the Chamber said, 'are principles already clearly affirmed by customary international law . . . valid for all States and in relation to all kinds of maritime delimitation'.[38] The Chamber supported this conclusion by reference to the decisions of the ICJ in the *North Sea Continental Shelf* cases, 1969, the *Case Concerning the Continental Shelf* (Tunisia/Libyan Arab Jamahiriya), 1982, and the Court of Arbitration Decision of 30 June 1977 in the case between the UK and France. It also referred to Articles 74 and 83 of the United Nations Convention on the Law of the Sea, 1982,[39] which contain identical provisions concerning the delimitation of the continental shelf and the exclusive economic zone, and said:

> It is thus limited to expressing the need for settlement of the problem by agreement and recalling the obligation to achieve an equitable solution. Although the text is singularly concise it serves to open the door to continuation of the development effected in this field by international case law.[40]

Referring to the respective positions of the parties on the question of the applicable law, the Chamber noted that both of them had agreed to the existence of a 'fundamental norm' governing maritime delimitation, although differently drafted by them, namely that the delimitation of a single maritime boundary should be in conformity with equitable principles, taking account of all relevant circumstances, in order to achieve an equitable result or solution.[41] This fundamental norm seemed to be 'closely related to the conclusion reached by analysis of international case law and also, in the end, to that arrived at by the Third Conference on the Law of the Sea', the Chamber said.[42]

Beyond the 'fundamental norm', the parties had differences. Canada pressed for geographic adjacency, proximity, and distance as the relevant rules for delimitation, and claimed the equidistance line as a concept endorsed by customary international law. The Chamber denied validity to these rules, and said that the 'boundary results from a rule of law, and not from any intrinsic merit in the purely physica fact' of adjacency, proximity, or distance.[43] Similarly, equidistance was 'a practical method that can be applied for the purposes of delimitation', and not a genuine rule of law.[44]

Nor did the Chamber agree to the US distinction between a 'primary' coast, which follows the general direction of the mainland coastline, and a 'secondary' coast, which deviates from that direction, for giving a preferential treatment to a 'primary' coast concerning its coastal front in relation to the coastal front of a 'secondary' coast, despite its proximity thereto.

The Chamber said: '. . . the *a priori* nature of these premises and these deductions is as patent as that of the thesis elaborated by the other Party. In both cases the outcome of the Parties' efforts can be said to have been preconceived assertions rather than any convincing demonstration of the extension of the rules that each had hoped to find established by international law'.[45]

The Chamber applied this observation to the Canadian argument advanced as a 'principle' that a single maritime boundary should ensure the preservation of the existing fishing patterns in the area concerned (Nova Scotia), or the US claimed 'principles' relating to the optimum conservation and management of living resources, reduction of the potential for future disputes, and the 'non-encroachment' and 'cut-off' effect of the seaward projection of the coasts of another State. These were not established rules endorsed by customary international law, although these might in given circumstances constitute equitable criteria in delimitation, the Chamber said.[46]

'Fundamental norm' of delimitation

The Chamber concluded section IV of the Judgment by giving a more precise reformulation of the 'fundamental norm' of delimitation, drawing also on the Court's Judgment in the *North Sea Continental Shelf* cases, 1969, which read as follows:

(1)   No maritime delimitation between States with opposite or adjacent coasts may be effected unilaterally by one of those States. Such delimitation must be sought and effected by means of an agreement, following negotiations conducted in good faith and with the genuine intention of achieving a positive result. Where, however, such agreement cannot be achieved, delimitation should be effected by recourse to a third party possessing the necessary competence.

(2)   In either case, delimitation is to be effected by the application of equitable criteria and by the use of practical methods capable of ensuring, with regard to the geographic configuration of the area and other relevant circumstances, an equitable result.[47]

Equitable criteria and practical methods of delimitation

In section V of the Judgment, the Chamber dealt with the equitable criteria and practical methods of delimitation, referred to in point (2) of the preceding paragraph, and also embodied in the second aspect of Article 6 of the 1958 Convention on the Continental Shelf, to which both Canada and the United States were parties. The Chamber noted that the 1958 Convention related only to the continental shelf and not to the water column or the fishery zone. It said that 'the maritime water mass overlying the continental shelf' was not 'a mere accessory of that shelf', nor could a method of delimitation applied for the 'water column' only and its resources be simply extended to the continental shelf.[48]

306

Article 6 of the 1958 Convention not applicable

To the Canadian argument that the equidistance – special circumstances method should be applied to the present case of a single maritime boundary, as treaty-law for the delimitation of the continental shelf component, and as a general norm for the delimitation of the adjacent fishery zone, the Chamber said that as treaty-law for the continental shelf the principle could be valid, but to accept the latter 'would amount to transforming the "combined equidistance – special circumstances rule" into a rule of general international law, and thus one capable of numerous applications, whereas there is no trace in international custom of such a transformation having occurred'.[49]

Referring to the Decision of the Court of Arbitration on the Delimitation of the Continental Shelf between France and the UK, 1977, the Chamber said:

. . . the finding of the Court of Arbitration clearly shows the different levels at which the various rules concerned are situated: the provisions of Article 6 of the 1958 Convention at the level of special international law, and, at the level of general international law, the norm prescribing application of equitable principles, or rather equitable criteria, without any indication as to the choice to be made among these latter or between the practical methods to implement them. The Chamber considers that such is the current state of customary international law.[50]

The Chamber then summed up the position on this point as follows:

The Chamber must therefore conclude in this respect that the provisions of Article 6 of the 1958 Convention on the Continental Shelf, although in force between the Parties, do not entail either for them or for the Chamber any legal obligation to apply them to the single maritime delimitation which is the subject of the present case.[51]

Conduct of parties

The Chamber then turned to the *conduct of the parties* to examine (a) whether this imposed a legal obligation, similar to that of consent or implied consent, by means of acquiescence or estoppel in favour of the application of a particular method of delimitation or precluding opposition thereto, (b) whether such conduct resulted in a *modus vivendi* or a *de facto* boundary based on such a method of delimitation, and (c) whether such conduct led to regarding a particular method of delimitation as equitable.

Canada had pleaded intensively in favour of the application of the equidistance method of delimitation, particularly in Georges Bank, and relied on the conduct of the US authorities concerning petroleum exploration in the area between 1965 and 1969 for the argument of acquiescence and estoppel, and their conduct between 1965 and 1972 for the argument of *modus vivendi*.

Reviewing the facts of the case, the Chamber noted that in the aide memoire of 5 November 1969 to Canada, the United States had specifically stated that they 'cannot acquiesce in any Canadian authorization of exploration or exploitation of the natural resources of the Georges Bank continental shelf'.[52]

The Chamber said that it

> . . . does not feel able to draw the conclusion that the United States acquiesced in delimitation of the Georges Bank continental shelf by a median line, setting aside for the moment both the fact that the platform of Georges Bank is only a limited portion of the continental shelf of the area to be delimited, and the fact that at the present time the continental shelf is only one of the two subjects of the delimitation requested of the Chamber.[53]

Nor did the Chamber agree that the conduct of the parties had established a *'modus vivendi* maritime limit' or a *'de facto* maritime limit' as a result of the alleged coincidence between the Canadian equidistance line on the one hand and the United States 'BLM (Bureau of Land Management) line' and those of the numerous US oil companies from 1965 to 1972 on the other. The US had denied the very existence of the 'BLM line'. In any case, the Chamber said that the period 'is too brief to have produced a legal effect of this kind', and the argument had also the same objections as those applicable to acquiescence.[54] Nor could conduct lead to the equidistance line being regarded as equitable *per se*, for the same reasons as given by the Chamber to the arguments of acquiescence, estoppel and *modus vivendi*.[55]

The Chamber then referred to the *US argument* that by its conduct, Canada had acquiesced in the delimitation of the continental shelf by agreement and in accordance with equitable principles, which was mentioned in the Truman Proclamation of September 1945, and which had been communicated to Canada five months prior to its issue. The US Proclamation and the communique issued relating thereto also claimed a boundary along the 100-fathom depth line. The US did not press the latter point for acquiescence. As to the former, the Chamber said that 'the United States position on that point merely refers back to the "fundamental norm" which Canada also relies on in the case'.[56] But this did not require a particular method for delimiting their respective maritime jurisdiction.

The Chamber thus concluded that the parties in the present case were not bound, by treaty law or other rule, 'to apply certain criteria or to use certain particular methods for the establishment of a single maritime boundary for both the continental shelf and the exclusive maritime fishing zone, as in the present case. Consequently, the Chamber also is not so bound'.[57]

Delimitation criteria

The Chamber then referred to some theoretical criteria, such as that the land dominates the sea, the equal division of the areas of overlap of the maritime and submarine zones appertaining to the respective coasts of neighbouring States, the non-encroachment or avoiding a cut-off, and the criterion relating to the inequalities of the relevant coastlines in the area of delimitation. A comprehensive list or a study of their comparative equitableness may not be useful. The equitableness of a criterion 'can only be assessed in relation to the circumstances of each case', the Chamber said.[58]

Practical methods

As to the *practical methods*, the Chamber said that different methods had been used in different delimitations settled by agreements between States, but added that 'in this connection statistical considerations afford no indication either of the greater or lesser degree of appropriateness of any particular method, or of any trend in favour thereof discernible in international customary law'.[59]

The Chamber referred to the question put by the President to the parties during the course of the oral hearings, namely 'in the event that one particular method, or set of methods, should appear appropriate for the delimitation of teh continental shelf, and another for that of the exclusive fishery zone, what they considered to be the legal grounds that might be invoked for preferring one or the other in seeking to determine a single line'. The reply of the United States was that the applicable principles and relevant circumstances should be considered as an integrated whole, and that the circumstances relevant to both the water column and the seabed should be given greater weight than circumstances relating to only one of them. The Canadian reply was that preference as to method should be dictated by the relevant circumstances of each of the two areas of delimitation.[60]

The Chamber said that it would select 'the criteria that it regards as the most equitable for the task to be performed in the present case, and the method or combination of practical methods whose application will best permit of their concrete implementation'.[61]

Claim lines of parties

In section VI of the Judgment, the Chamber examined the criteria and methods used by the parties in the four lines claimed by them.

The United States lines.　The *criteria* for the *first* United States delimitation line of 1976 (see Chart 12B above), were the natural factors of geomorphology and ecology of the area. The *method* adopted was to follow the line of the greatest depth of water in the Gulf of Maine, and later the Fundian Channel and the Northeast Channel up to the continental margin. The line remained more or less equidistant from the 100-fathom isobath. The main objective was to keep intact the unity of the ecosystems, namely the respective fishery banks on the Scotian Shelf and the Gulf of Maine area. This line was explained by the United States in the oral proceedings to be in conformity with Article 6 of the 1958 Convention, which was 'a courteous gesture', the Chamber said, because the 1976 US line was inspired 'by the objective of a distribution of fishery resources according to a "natural" criterion',[62] which was not the purpose of Article 6.

The *criteria* for the *second* United States delimitation line of September 1982 (see Chart 12C above) emphasise priority for the general direction of the coast, the distinction between the 'primary coast' which follows this general direction and the 'secondary coasts' which deviate therefrom, and the projection or coastal extension of the primary coastal front as its natural prolongation in the geographical sense. Additional equitable criteria relate to the avoidance of encroachment and cut-off, and to proportionality.

The practical *method* of delimitation, based on the treatment of the coast of Maine as a 'primary coast', is the vertical line perpendicular to the general direction of the coast drawn at point A, 39 miles from the international boundary terminus, 'for adaptation to the relevant circumstances of the area' since a perpendicular drawn at the terminus would intersect Grand Manan Island and the Nova Scotia peninsula of Canada. The perpendicular was later adjusted to deal with another relevant circumstance, namely the unity of the ecosystems or ecological regimes identified in the delimitation area. These adjustments left the two fishing banks (German Bank and Browns Bank) entirely on the Canadian side in application of the principle of a single State mangement, and kept Georges Bank on the US side. The line did not follow the *thalweg* of the Northeast Channel, as did the 1976 line, although it ran close to its north-eastern edge.

The Chamber had already disapproved of the ecological criteria, as well as of the 'primary' and 'secondary' coasts, which gave preferential treatment to the former.

As to the method of drawing perpendicular to the general direction of the coast in implementation of the criteria of the coastal front, the Chamber said:

> It is almost an essential condition for the use of such a method in a specific case that the boundary to be drawn in the particular case should concern two countries whose territories lie successively along a more or less rectilinear coast, for a certain distance at least. The ideal case, so to speak, would be one in which the course of the line would leave an angle of 90° on either side. On the other hand, it is hard to imagine a case less conducive to the

application of this method of delimitation than the Gulf of Maine case, in which the starting point of the line to be drawn is situated in one of the angles of the rectangle in which the delimitation is to be effected.[63]

. . . In a word, the method of delimitation by the perpendicular to the coast or to the general direction of the coast might possibly be contemplated in cases where the relevant circumstances lent themselves to its adoption, but is not appropriate in cases where these circumstances entail so many adjustments that they completely distort its character.[64]

The Canadian lines. The Chamber considered the two Canadian lines of 1976 (see Chart 12B above) and 1977 (see Chart 12C above) together. The *criterion* used for both was the equal division of the disputed area, the *method* was that of equidistance, the second line being a corrected equidistance line, which gave no effect to Cape Cod and Nantucket Island by taking into account the special circumstances of their protrusion into the delimitation area.

These lines were based on the application of Article 6 of the 1958 Convention. They applied to the continental shelf. The question still remained open as to whether they could be applicable to the fishery zone or a single maritime boundary. The Chamber had already stated that equidistance was not a mandatory rule of customary international law for a single maritime boundary, but this would not prohibit Canada from using this method in its proposal. 'The absence of an obligation to do something must not be confused with an obligation not to do it', the Chamber said. While so doing, either party had to meet two conditions: '(a) it must show that the use of the method chosen, while in no way mandatory, is nevertheless specially recommended by its equity and by its adaptability to the circumstances of the case; (b) it must ensure that the application of that method which is proposed in concrete terms has due regard to those circumstances and is, moreover, correctly carried out'.[65]

Applying these conditions to the Canadian *second* line, the Chamber noted that Canada ignored Cape Cod and Nantucket Island as a geographical anomaly but did not 'feel obliged also to displace the eastern basepoint for the calculation of the same line from Seal Island to the coast of Nova Scotia'. The new line affected the dividing line in Georges Bank: 'the effect is considerable, which does not mean it is justified'.[66]

Nor were the geography of the delimitation area and the proportionality of the length of their coastlines taken into account by Canada. As the Chamber had described the delimitation area, the short coastlines of the parties in the rectangular Gulf of Maine were quasi-parallel, and the long side of the Maine coast and the line joining the Nova Scotia coast with the land terminus were at a right angle to each other. The geographical relations of the coasts of the parties were therefore *adjacent* at the terminus and *parallel* later on. This major geographical distinction was ignored by Canada. 'In any event what had to be avoided was to draw, the whole way to the opening of the Gulf, a diagonal line dominated solely by the relationship between Maine and Nova Scotia, even where the relationship between Massachusetts and Nova Scotia should have predominated', the Chamber said.[67]

Earlier, on proportionality, the Chamber observed that it was niether a criterion nor a method of delimitation. It said that 'a maritime delimitation can certainly not be established by a direct division of the area in dispute proportional to the respective lengths of the coasts belongong to the parties in the relevant area, but it is equally certain that a substantial disproportion to the lengths of those coasts that resulted from a delimitation effected on a different basis would constitute a circumstance calling for an appropriate correction'.[68]

The Chamber noted that the length of the US coasts in the Gulf of Maine was considerably greater than that of the Canadian coast, even if part of the Bay of Fundy coasts was included in the calculation of this perimeter. 'This difference in length is a special circumstance of some weight, which, in the Chamber's view, justifies a correction of the equidistance line, or of any other line'.[69] This was not done by Canada in either of its claim lines.

Single maritime boundary determined by the Chamber

In section VII, the Chamber addressed itself to the final phase of the decision-making process, namely to determining the single maritime boundary, within the framework of the fundamental norm of maritime delimitation, the equitable criteria, the relevant circumstances of the case, an appropriate practical method or combination of methods for applying these criteria, and all this with a view to reaching an equitable result.

This was the first case of a *single* maritime boundary before the Court. The Chamber noted that with the gradual adoption of exclusive economic zones by the majority of maritime States, there will be an increasing general demand for single delimitation to avoid the disadvantages inherent in a plurality of separate delimitations. This will give preference to criteria which, because of their neutral character, are best suited for use in a multi-purpose delimitation.[70]

For the present case, the basic *criteria* selected by the Chamber related to the physical and political geography of the relevant coasts in the delimitation area, and the equal division of the areas of overlap. The Chamber said that '. . . in principle, while having regard to the special circumstances of the case, one should aim at an equal division of areas where the maritime projections of the coasts of the States between which delimitation is to be effected converge and overlap'.[71]

The special circumstances in the area might require the use of auxiliary criteria, such as the proportionality of the length of the respective coasts, the cut-off effect on one coastline, and the location of small islands.

312

The equitable nature of the selected criteria would become 'tangible', the Chamber said, in the drawing of the practical delimitation line.

The practical *methods* used by the Chamber for drawing the single maritime boundary delimitation line followed the Chamber's observations on the Canadian claim line, mentioned above. The Chamber decided to use only geometrical methods. It did not favour the equidistance method which, apart from not being mandatory for a single delimitation, would give undue importance to the islands, uninhabited rocks or low-tide elevations as basepoints for the drawing of a line intended to equally divide a given area. It might be desirable to have a constant course line, rather than a zig zag line, for the exploitation of the fishery resources of the sea. In the present case, the equidistant line could not start from point A because, first, point A was not equidistant from the coasts of the parties, and, secondly, an equidistance line 'would encounter the difficulty of the persistent uncertainty as to sovereignty over Machias Seal Island'.[72]

The geometrical methods used by the Chamber were for the entire delimitation area, namely the Gulf of Maine sector and the Atlantic Ocean sector, separated by the Gulf closing line. The Chamber recalled the geography of the Gulf of Maine and said that this demanded that in the segment near the international boundary terminus, 'whatever the practical method selected, the boundary should be a lateral delimitation line'. But, between the parallel short sides of the rectangle, the boundary should be a median line, corrected to the extent necessitated by the special circumstances of the area.[73]

Thus between point A and the Gulf closing line, the delimitation line could not be 'unidirectional'.[74]

Delimitation line determined by the Chamber

In the light of the above, the Chamber determined the single maritime boundary between Canada and the United States of America in three segments (the first two segments in the Gulf of Maine sector and the third segment in the Atlantic Ocean sector) as follows:

(1) In the Gulf of Maine, starting from point A in accordance with the Special Agreement between the parties, and having decided not to adopt the equidistance method for the reasons mentioned above, and there being no special circumstances standing in the way, the Chamber decided to adopt the method of a bisector of the reflex angle formed by perpendiculars drawn from point A to the long and short sides of the rectangle. This method would be more suited to the production of the desired result, namely the equal division of the area of overlap, the Chamber said. The Chamber described the method as follows:

. . . one may justifiably draw from point A two lines respectively perpendicular to the two basic coastal lines here to be considered, namely the line from Cape Elizabeth to the international boundary terminus and the line from that latter point to Cape Sable. These perpendiculars form, at point A, on one side an acute angle of about 82° and on the other a reflex angle of about 278°. It is the bisector of this second angle which the Chamber considers that it should adopt for the course of the first segment of the delimitation line.[75]

(2)   The terminus of the line starting from point A was determined by settling the location of the boundary line in the second segment in the Gulf of Maine sector, which although shortest, 'will certainly be the central and most decisive segment for the whole of the delimitation line'.[76]

In the second segment, the Chamber decided in favour of a median line 'approximately parallel to the approximately parallel lines of the two opposite coasts',[77] namely the Massachusetts coast (US) and the Nova Scotia coast (Canada).

The *location* of the median line was adjusted[78] taking into account the following:

(a)   the proportionality of the lengths of the respective coasts of the United States and Canada in the Gulf of Maine, including in the case of Canada the coast in the Bay of Fundy up to a point along New Brunswick 'off which there cease to be any waters in the bay more distant than 12 miles from a low-water line', then from that point across to the corresponding point on the Nova Scotian coast.[79] The length of the respective coasts was 284 nautical miles (USA) and 206 nautical miles (Canada), having a ratio of 1.38 to 1;[80] and

(b)   the half-effect of Seal Island, an inhabited island but located 9 miles off the Nova Scotia coast, to avoid its full south-westward effect on the coastline, thereby modifying the coastal ratio from 1.38 : 1 to 1.32 : 1.[81]

The intersection of the median line so drawn and located and the extension of the lateral bisector line coming from point A will constitute point B of the single maritime boundary. Similarly, in the southeastern direction, the intersection of the median line so drawn and located and the Gulf closing line will constitute point C of the single maritime boundary.

(3)   The precise location of point C and its extension in the third segment was of special concern to the Chamber in view of its impact on Georges Bank and the intensive pleadings of the parties. 'Indeed the Chamber has borne constantly in mind the problem of determining the final segment of the delimitation line when applying itself so meticulously to the task of establishing the previous segments', the Chamber said.[82]

From point C, which is thus not at the mid-point of the Gulf closing line, the single maritime boundary runs as a perpendicular to the Gulf closing line, which is in conformity with the general direction of the two coasts.[83]

314

(4)   The terminal point is point D, which is located within the triangle specified in the Special Agreement referring the dispute to the Chamber. 'It will . . .
coincide with the last point the perpendicular (from point C) reaches within the
overlapping of the respective 200-mile zones claimed by the two States and established from appropriate basepoints on their coastlines', the Chamber
said.[84]

In a nutshell, therefore, the single maritime boundary determined by the ICJ
Chamber, joining points A, B, C and D, is composed of three segments: the
line joining points A and B is a lateral line and is a bisector of the reflex angle
formed at point A with the coastal fronts of the parties in the area; the line joining points B and C is a median line, whose location has been adjusted in proportion to the length of the US and Canadian coasts in the Gulf of Maine and by
giving half-effect to Seal Island; and the line joining points C and D is a perpendicular to the Gulf closing line at point C. Point D is located in the triangle and
is a point 200 nautical miles from the nearest point of the low-water line of the
United States of America.

For the alignment of the single maritime boundary line, as determined by the
Chamber, see Chart 12D above. For details of its technical construction, see the
Technical Report enclosed with the Judgment.[85]

Equitable result of delimitation line tested

In section VIII, the Chamber tested the equitable result of the single maritime
boundary line determined by it. Such test was not necessary for the first two
segments of the line in the Gulf of Maine, where neither party had made any
special mention of fishery or petroleum resources and of their importance to
their economies. The question was, however, different for the third segment,
with reference to which both parties had made intensive pleadings. The Chamber did not agree with the relevance of the US arguments concerning the extent
of their historic and continuing activities in Georges Bank, the principles of the
single State conservation and management of fishery resources, and of avoidance of disputes. Nor did it approve of the Canadian arguments concerning the
socio-economic aspects of their fishing activities in Georges Bank, the dependence of the Nova Scotian communities on these fishing activities, or the need
to ensure the maintenance of the existing fishing patterns while settling the
single maritime boundary.

'The Chamber cannot adopt these positions of the parties', it said.[86] After
the adoption of the 'exclusive' fishery zones in the area, which was high seas
before and where even third States could and did fish, no historic activity or
preferential rights could be preserved for either side. Nor could such rights of
access to a State be ensured in delimitation. Nor could delimitation provide for

'a compensation equivalent to what it loses elsewhere'.[87] The Chamber said that

> . . . the respective scale of activities connected with fishing − or naviga-
> tion, defence or, for that matter, petroleum exploration and exploitation
> − cannot be taken into account as a relevant circumstance or, if the term
> is preferred, as an equitable criterion to be applied in determining the de-
> limitation line. What the Chamber would regard as a legitimate scruple lies
> rather in concern lest the overall result, even though achieved through the
> application of equitable criteria and the use of appropriate methods for
> giving them concrete effect, should unexpectedly be revealed as radically
> inequitable, that is to say, as likely to entail catastrophic repercussions for
> the livelihood and economic well-being of the population of the countries
> concerned.[88]

By applying this test the Chamber said that there was no reason to fear that any such damage would arise from the course of the delimitation line in the third segment. The line had left the greater part of the 'Northern Edge and Peak' of Georges Bank to the Canadian side, where the scallop resources lie, which have been and are of special interest to its fishermen. The interests of the US fishermen had also not been adversely affected, either in respect of scallop or lobster, or even free-swimming fish. So no serious economic repercussions would arise from the single maritime boundary determined by the Chamber.[89]

Nor would the boundary line affect the interests of the parties in the potential hydrocarbon resources of the area.[90]

Nor would the boundary line lead to 'any inevitable source of insurmountable disputes' between the parties, which with their tradition of friendly and fruitful cooperation in maritime matters they could not resolve.

The Chamber summed up this section as follows:

> In short, the Chamber sees in the above findings confirmation of its con-
> viction that in the present case there are absolutely no conditions of an ex-
> ceptional kind which might justify any correction of the delimitation line
> it has drawn. The Chamber may therefore confidently conclude that the
> delimitation effected in compliance with the governing principles and rules
> of law, applying equitable criteria and appropriate methods accordingly,
> has produced an equitable overall result.[91]

The operative part of the Judgment reads as follows:

> THE CHAMBER,
>
> By four votes to one,
>
> *decides*
>
> That the course of the single maritime boundary that divides the continen-
> tal shelf and the exclusive fisheries zones of Canada and the United States
> of America in the area referred to in the Special Agreement concluded by
> those two States on 29 March 1979 shall be defined by geodetic lines con-
> necting the points with the following co-ordinates:

316

	Latitude North	Longitude West
A.	44°11'12''	67°16'46''
B.	42°53'14''	67°44'35''
C.	42°31'08''	67°28'05''
D.	40°27'05''	65°41'59''

IN FAVOUR: *President* AGO; *Judges* MOSLER, SCHWEBEL; Judge *ad hoc* COHEN;

AGAINST: Judge GROS.

Done in French and in English, the French text being authoritative, at the Peace Palace, The Hague, this twelfth day of October one thousand nine hundred and eighty-four, in three copies, one of which will be placed in the archives of the Court and the others transmitted to the Government of Canada and the Government of the United States of America respectively.

(*Signed*) Roberto AGO
President of the Chamber
(*Signed*) Santiago Torres BERNARDEZ
Registrar[92]

Judge Schwebel wrote a separate opinion. Judge Gros wrote a dissenting opinion.

Separate opinion

In his separate opinion, *Judge Schwebel* agreed with the reasoning of the Judgment concerning the non-mandatory nature of the equidistance method of delimitation, the rejection of the 'distance principle', the non-acceptance of the concept of 'primary' and 'secondary' coasts, the application of the governing role of geography and the equal division of the area of overlap, and the division of Georges Bank, despite the American argument that the Georges Bank was 'as American as apple pie'.

He disagreed on the extent of the coasts of the Bay of Fundy to be taken into account for determining the proportionality between the coastlines of the parties, which had affected the placement of the dividing line. In his view, the Chamber had erred in this key respect, and the inclusion of the coasts of the Bay of Fundy up to 12 miles from the low-water mark had a distorting effect on measuring proportionality and was inequitable.

In his view, 'Canada should be credited in a calculation of proportionality with that portion of the coast of New Brunswick which, running from the international border, actually fronts upon the Gulf of Maine, as far, at least, as Point Lepreau, and, at most, as Saint John, together with the length of a closing line running from one of those points to Brier Island, Nova Scotia'.[93]

On the basis of measuring the coast of New Brunswick up to Saint John, and

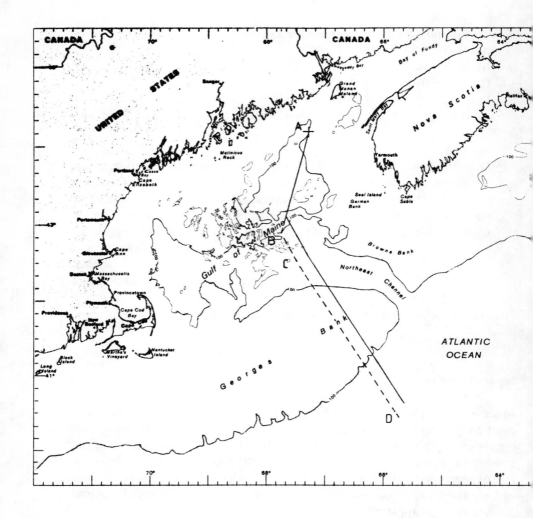

Chart 13. Delimitation of the Maritime Boundary in the Gulf of Maine Area
(Canada/USA):
Separate opinion Judge Schwebel

Chamber's line _ _ _ _ _ _ _ _ _ _ _
Judge Schwebel's line _____

Source: ICJ Reports 1984, separate opinion of Judge Schwebel, p. 359.

318

referring in this respect to Figure 171 presented by Canada in the oral proceedings, he prepared a chart which showed the alignment of the single maritime boundary differently from that determined by the Chamber (see Chart 13).

However, Judge Schwebel added the following:

> Despite the extent of the difference between the line of delimitation which the Chamber has drawn and the line which my analysis produces, I have voted for the Chamber's Judgment. I have done so not only because I am generally in agreement with its reasoning but because I recognize that the factors which have given rise to the difference between the lines are open to more than one legally − and certainly equitably − plausible interpretation.
>
> . . . the alternative approach which I propose is open to criticism on several counts, not least on the ground that the portion of the coasts of New Brunswick that 'faces' the Gulf of Maine is in some measure a matter of subjective perspective.
>
> On a question such as this, the law is more plastic than formed, and elements of judgment, of appreciation of competing legal and equitable considerations, are dominant. It is easier to criticize than to construct. . . . While I am convinced of the equity of my conclusion, nevertheless I am not prepared to maintain that the Chamber is necessarily wrong and that the line which its position on the test of proportionality has produced is inequitable.[94]

Dissenting opinion

In his dissenting opinion, *Judge Gros* elaborated the grounds of his disagreement with the Judgment and presented his own line of delimitation.[95] In his view, neither the parties nor the Chamber had examined the law applicable to a single maritime boundary. The concept of the continental shelf had been ignored and the concept of solely dividing the water had prevailed, presumably because of the developments at the Third United Nations Conference on the Law of the Sea, for no legally sound reasons. The present Judgment 'chimes with the standpoint taken by the Court in 1982', and had eroded rather than strengthened the law on maritime delimitation.[96] Referring to Articles 74 and 83 of the United Nations Convention on the Law of the Sea, 1982, Judge Gros said:

> It is difficult to discern any rule in such a formula: to say that due application of international law should give rise to an equitable result is a truism. Necessity for an agreement between the States concerned, application of international law, equity − yes, but by what means?[97]
>
> That is what lies enshrined in the two articles of the 1982 Convention

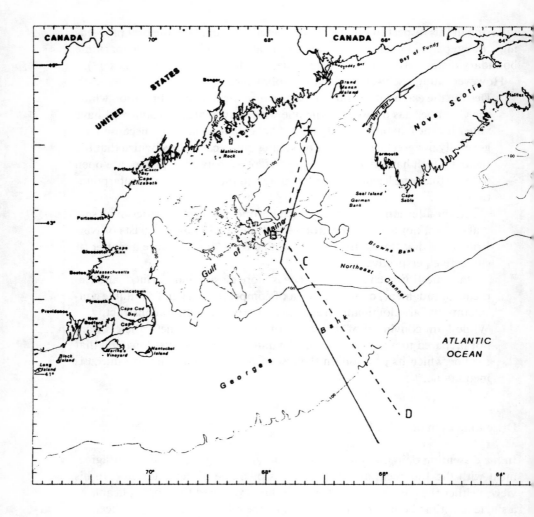

Chart 14. Delimitation of the Maritime Boundary in the Gulf of Maine Area
(Canada/USA):
Dissenting opinion Judge Gros

Chamber's line _ _ _ _ _ _ _ _ _ _
Judge Gros's line _____

Source: ICJ Reports 1984, dissenting opinion of Judge Gros, p. 390.

320

(Arts. 74 and 83), which open the way to arbitrariness by defining nothing, and it is likewise the reasoning of the Chamber's Judgment, founded as it is, like the 1982 Judgment, on those same articles . . .[98]

The Chamber took the request by the parties in their Special Agreement for delimitation of a single maritime boundary as a 'fact', 'special aspect' or a 'special circumstance', and had developed the concept of neutral criteria equally applicable to the continental shelf and the fishery zone, without elaborating the legal basis of that neutrality.

The essence of the delimitation law developed in the Chamber Judgment in the form of a 'fundamental norm' was 'agreement + equity', and the doctrine might be summed up as 'the result is equitable'.[99] The criteria of 'agreement' was of relevance to the States or parties and not to the Court. The concept of equity, as developed in the Judgment in the form of criteria, methods and result, promoted a decision by judicial discretion rather than a decision in accordance with the law, and the difference between a court of law and an amicable conciliator had been forgotten.

To quote Judge Gros:

In redefining the law of maritime delimitation on the basis of Articles 74 and 83 of the 1982 Convention the Chamber has exposed the disservice rendered international law by the Third United Nations Conference; I have summed up this formulation in two words: agreement – equity. As the concept of agreement has nothing to do with the work of judges, only equity remains. But if there is any legal concept to which each attaches his own meaning, it is equity.[100]

One must not narrow down the law of delimitation to two words, agreement plus equity, only to equate that equity with judicial discretion.[101]

Judge Gros also felt that the word 'criteria' developed by the Chamber was 'another word which can mean very different things'.[102]

As to the specific criteria applied by the Chamber in its Judgment, Judge Gros felt that the concepts of geography, equal division of overlap, and proportionality had not been properly applied. In fact, the Chamber, while defining the delimitation area in the Gulf of Maine as a rectangle, 'already interprets the geographical facts so as to prepare the treatment it will be giving them in its use of methods and in its corrections of a line . . .', such as a bisector of an angle at point A, the correction of the median line, and the drawing of a perpendicular subsequently. The Gulf was not such a rectangle, Judge Gros said.[103]

As to the equal division of the area of overlap, Judge Gros was of the view that the area of overlap should have been a limited one, 'which does not extend beyond an initial segment of the line as from point A, in the part where the two States had adjoining coasts',[104] and 'could be resolved simply by dividing it equally with the aid of any appropriate method, and equidistance in the first place'.[105] Proportionality should have been applied restrictively to this area of overlap.

Judge Gros also did not agree with the Judgment attributing distorting effect to Seal Island but not to Nantucket.[106]

He also noted that the resources aspects had been given a minor role at the end of the Judgment to test the equity of the line.

As to the practical method, he felt that the rejection by the Judgment of the application of Article 6 of the 1958 Convention, binding on both parties, was not well-founded. As to equidistance, he felt that although 'much-reviled', this method 'provided a reasonable solution to the Parties' request for the separation of their respective continental shelf and fishery zones'.[107]

Finally, Judge Gros proposed his own delimitation line (see Chart 14) which was based on equidistance from the mainland basepoints of the parties. Since point A was not an equidistant point, the line starting at point A follows a neutral course perpendicular to the coastal front of Maine until it intersects the equidistance line. In drawing this line no account is taken of Nantucket or the other islands and islets south of Cape Cod, or of Seal Island off Nova Scotia. The line turns to the south-east at a point a few miles south-east of a line between Cape Cod Elbow and Cape Sable. It crosses Georges Bank 14½ miles west of the Chamber delimitation line.[108]

Assessment or appraisal

By way of assessment or appraisal of the Judgment of the ICJ Chamber in the *Delimitation of the Maritime Boundary in the Gulf of Main Area* (Canada/USA) of 12 October 1984, the following observations may be made:

(1) This being the first case before an ICJ Chamber concerning a single maritime boundary extending up to 200 nautical miles in the sea, with emphasis on the fisheries aspects in the delimitation area, particularly in Georges Bank, and the first Judgment delivered after the opening for signature of the United Nations Convention on the Law of the Sea, 1982, its contribution to the law on maritime delimitation and its importance to the world community of States as a whole cannot be overemphasised. The voluminous pleadings, written and oral, and a reasoned Judgment, offer a gold mine of legal, scientific and technical information, and will be a sound legal and practical guide to those interested in the subject and affected by it. The trend towards a single maritime boundary is likely to be a global one, primarily for reasons of practical convenience and the avoidance of controversies, as contemplated in the present Judgment and as evidenced in increasing State practice. The exceptional situation in areas having conflicting geological, geomorphological, fisheries or other relevant circumstances may still require a dual maritime boundary, or some form of common zones, or a combination of a common zone with a single or dual maritime boundary, or some other form of an equitable solution. These aspects may be

322

dealt with in State practice or in future judicial, arbitral or other decisions.

(2)   As to the law applicable to the single maritime boundary, the Judgment has enunciated a flexible but hierarchical framework, namely that such a boundary shall be determined by the States concerned by agreement, failing which by reference to a third-party settlement, applying equitable criteria and an appropriate method relating thereto, taking account of relevant circumstances, and capable of ensuring an equitable result.

In the present case, the Judgment has applied the criteria of physical and political geography, and supplemented them by the auxiliary criteria of proportionality of the length of the relevant coastlines and avoiding the distorting effect of islands, with a view to dividing equally the area of overlap. No other criteria, principles or special circumstances advanced by the parties have been accepted as relevant.

(3)   The practical method of delimitation is a geometrical one, which has been applied in all the three segments of the line, namely a bisector of the reflex angle at point A, a corrected median line in the middle, and a perpendicular to the Gulf closing line for the Atlantic Ocean area. The preference was for simple continuous lines rather than zig zag ones.

The resulting line has been tested by the Chamber with reference to the socio-economic arguments pressed by the parties and its alignment in Georges Bank has been justified as equitable.

(4)   Looking at it objectively, the resulting line of the single maritime boundary determined by the Court Chamber is equitable, and may therefore serve as an inspiration and a guidance to delimitations in State practice and in future decisions.

As to the applicable law, the Chamber has, in continuation of the Court decision in the Tunisia/Libya case, 1982,[109] given a subordinate and residual role to the socio-economic argument for testing the equities of the result, although it had stated that the question was in its mind even while determining the location of the BC segment of the delimitation line and the precise location of point C for drawing the perpendicular to the Gulf closing line which would pass through Georges Bank. In State practice and in future decisions, it is possible that this aspect may be given a higher status, even that of a primary or auxiliary criterion. Even in the present case, one may reflect whether the resulting line would have been materially different, if the socio-economic argument had been given the status of an auxiliary criterion.

Nor is the practical geometrical method of delimitation adopted by the Chamber materially different from a simplified or modified equidistance line, despite the Chamber's sensitivity to the latter as a method or to the 'equidistance – special circumstances rule'. In fact, the bisector from point A has given to Canada in that segment an additional area of some 800 square nautical miles, which was not claimed by it when proposing the equidistance line.

Nor has the application of proportionality been tested with reference to the area delimited, perhaps in order to avoid giving proportionality the status of a sharing criterion, although the respective delimitation areas had been referred to by the Court in its 1982 Judgment in the Tunisia/Libya case.[110]

(5) The gains and losses to the parties from the Judgment will obviously be up to them to assess. In general terms, the parties had agreed to the 'fundamental norm' of delimitation, but differed substantially on the relevant equitable criteria and accordingly in their proposed claim lines. The Court appears to have inclined more towards the United States in terms of the applicable criteria, despite their rejection of the arguments of the coastal front, primary and secondary coasts, single State conservation and management of natural resources, avoidance of disputes, ecological regimes, and so forth, than towards Canada. But the method applied, and the course of the delimitation line determined by the Chamber, was more akin to that proposed by Canada, despite the reservations.

Even as to the method, there appears to be a coincidental similarity between the views expressed by the Deputy Agent of the United States in the oral proceedings of 13 April 1984 before the Chamber, and the method actually applied by the Chamber with some material modifications. The United States Counsel had stated as follows:

> An equitable boundary should divide the closest inshore area, perhaps generally by dividing the angle between the two coastal fronts with reference to the proportions of their lengths, and then would turn seaward perpendicular to the general direction of the coast.[111]

The Court Chamber applied a similar method, but introduced the points BC segment in the delimitation line as a corrected median line whose location was determined by the proportionality of the coastal fronts of the parties. It is on proportionality that the United States did not succeed: the US throughout calculated the proportionality as 3 to 1 or more, whereas the Chamber settled it at 1.32 to 1. This affected the precise location of point C for the drawing of the perpendicular to the Gulf closing line, which divided Georges Bank between the parties. The United States received a larger area of Georges Bank, with potential fisheries resources possibly higher than those which it might have received under the unratified Fisheries Agreement of 1979.

From the Canadian viewpoint, the introduction of the BC segment shifted the location of point C from the midpoint of the Gulf closing line, based on the full effect to the Massachusetts and Nova Scotia abutting coasts, towards Nova Scotia with its consequential effects.

But the Canadian gains included a significant area of Georges Bank with is fisheries and other natural resources, a significant part of the Bay of Fundy for computing proportionality, and the bonus in the first segment of the delimitation line arising from the bisector of the angle at point A.

324

(6)   Although this case did not directly invoke the provisions on maritime delimitation of the United Nations Convention on the Law of the Sea, 1982, which is not yet in force, the flexibility and neutrality of the delimitation criteria and the practical methods developed by the Chamber appear to be in conformity with the provisions of Articles 74 and 83 of that Convention. The text of these two Articles is identical. This may not necessarily support the concept of a single maritime boundary, although it is likely to be preferred in State practice. Hence this Judgment will promote the workability of these and related provisions of the Convention.

As to the impact of this Judgment on single maritime boundary (12 October 1984) on Part V (Conclusions) of this study, the above comments may be read in continuation of that Chapter (Chapter 15).

(2) Other developments

In October 1984, the mediation by the Pope in the Argentina – Chile controversy concerning the Beagle Channel region, which was referred to him by the Agreement of Montevideo signed between the parties on 8 January 1979, was successful. A Treaty between Argentina and Chile was initialled at the Vatican on 18 October 1984. In accordance with the decision of the Argentine Government, it was submitted to a referendum in Argentina on 25 November 1984 and received wide support. The Treaty was to be signed between the parties at the Vatican on 29 November 1984
    The Treaty acknowledges the sovereignty of Chile over the Islands of Picton, Lennox and Nueva south of the Beagle Channel, gives them a three-mile territorial sea and a specified area of the exclusive economic zone, endorses the bioceanic principle, namely the access of Chile and Argentina to the Pacific Ocean and the Atlantic Ocean, respectively, and establishes a maritime boundary between the two States accordingly. It also fixes the limits at the mouth of the Megallanes Strait, and regulates aspects of navigation.
    The text of the Treaty and the details of the developments since 1979 have not yet become available.

Notes

1. For the precise title of the Agreement, see Annex I, item 101 below.
2. See pp. 140-163 above.
3. For the precise title of the Agreement, see Annex I, item 103 below.
4. For the precise title of the Memorandum of Understanding, see Annex I, item 102 below.

5. See p. 89 above.

6. See in this connection pp. 33-34 and footnote 99 (Part One) above.

   For a background to this Treaty, see B.A. Hamza, 'Indonesia's Archipelagic Regime – Implications for Malaysia', *Marine Policy*, Vol. 8, No. 1 (January 1984), pp. 30-43.

7. For the Treaty between Australia and Papua New Guinea, 1978, see pp. 90-92 above.

8. See, for example, Sang-Myon Rhee, 'Equitable Solutions to the Maritime Boundary Dispute between the United States and Canada in the Gulf of Maine', *AJIL*, Vol. 75 (1981), pp. 590-628; Mark B. Feldman and David Colson, 'The Maritime Boundaries of the United States', *AJIL*, Vol. 75 (1981), pp. 729-763 at pp. 754-763; D.M. McRae, 'Adjudication of the Maritime Boundary in the Gulf of Maine', *The Canadian Yearbook of International Law*, Vol. XVII (1979), pp. 292-303; D.M. McRae, 'Proportionality and the Gulf of Maine Maritime Boundary Dispute', *The Canadian Yearbook of International Law*, Vol. XIX (1981), pp. 287-302; D.M. McRae, 'The Gulf of Maine Case: The Written Proceedings, *The Canadian Yearbook of International Law*, Vol. XXI (1983), pp. 266-283. For text of the 1979 fisheries and boundary dispute settlement Agreements and related documents, see 'Canada – United States: Treaty on Gulf of Maine Boundary Dispute Settlement', *International Legal Materials*, Vol. XX (1981), No. 6, pp. 1371-1390.

9. Delimitation of the Maritime Boundary in the Gulf of Maine Area (Canada/USA), *Judgment, ICJ Reports 1984*, p. 253.

10. *Ibid.*, p. 257.

11. *Ibid.*, pp. 261-263 (as presented at the close of the oral hearings on 11 May 1984). For the changes made at that hearing, see *ibid.*, Public Sitting of the Chamber, 11 May 1984, C 1/CR 84/26 at p. 66.

12. *Judgment*, n. 9, p. 263.

13. These alternatives for the delimitation of a single maritime boundary would start from point A either by drawing an equidistance line or a perpendicular to the general direction of the coast as computed by Canada, stop in the middle of the line joining point A with the midpoint of the Gulf closing line, and proceed therefrom (that is, from the stop point) as a perpendicular to the Gulf closing line up to the triangle in the Atlantic Ocean. For details, see Public Sitting of the Chamber, 10 May 1984, Verbatim Record, C 1/CR 84/25, pp. 62-78.

14. *Judgment*, n. 9, p. 266, para. 23.

15. *Ibid.*, p. 267, para. 27.

16. *Ibid.*, p. 272, para. 40.

17. *Ibid.*, p. 270, para. 32.

18. *Ibid.*, para. 34.

19. *Ibid.*, p. 272, para. 38.

20. *Ibid.*, para. 39.

21. *Ibid.*, p. 271, paras. 36 and 37.

22. *Ibid.*, p. 273, para. 44.

23. *Ibid.*, p. 274, para. 46.

24. *Ibid.*, p. 277, para. 54.

25. *Ibid.*, para. 56.

26. *Ibid.*, p. 278, para. 59.

27. *Ibid.*, p. 281, para. 64.

28. *Ibid.*, p. 282, para. 66.

29. *Ibid.*, para. 67.

30. *Ibid.*, p. 286, para. 74.

31. *Ibid.*, para. 73.

32. *Ibid.*, p. 288, para. 79.

33. *Ibid.*, p. 290, para. 81.

34. *Ibid.*, p. 291, para. 83.
35. For text of Article 6, see pp. 128, 130 above.
36. *Judgment*, n. 9, p. 291, para. 84.
37. *Ibid.*, p. 292, para. 89.
38. *Ibid.*, p. 293, para. 90.
39. For text of these Articles, see pp. 262-263 above.
40. *Judgment*, n. 9, p. 294, para. 95.
41. For the text of the Canadian and US definitions of the 'fundamental norm', see *ibid.*, p. 295, para. 99.
42. *Ibid.*, para. 100.
43. *Ibid.*, p. 296, para. 103.
44. *Ibid.*, p. 297, para. 106.
45. *Ibid.*, p. 298, para. 109.
46. *Ibid.*, p. 299, para. 110.
47. *Ibid.*, pp. 299-300, para. 112.
48. *Ibid.*, p. 302, para. 119.
49. *Ibid.*, para. 122. See also para. 118.
50. *Ibid.*, p. 303, para. 123.
51. *Ibid.*, para. 125.
52. Cited in *ibid.*, p. 307, para. 136.
53. *Ibid.*, para. 137. See also para. 148, which repeats this conclusion and refers to the non-application of both acquiescence and estoppel. The Chamber recognised that the conduct of the US revealed 'uncertainties and a fair degree of inconsistency', and delay in response, but this does not amount to acquiescence and estoppel. See *ibid.*, paras. 138-142. The Chamber reviewed briefly the precedents cited by Canada but concluded that these precedents were 'inconclusive'. See *ibid.*, paras. 143-148.
54. *Ibid.*, p. 311, para. 151.
55. *Ibid.*, para. 152.
56. *Ibid.*, p. 312, para. 154.
57. *Ibid.*, para. 155.
58. *Ibid.*, p. 313, para. 158.
59. *Ibid.*, pp. 313-314, para. 159.
60. *Ibid.*, p. 315, para. 161.
61. *Ibid.*, p. 312, para. 156.
62. *Ibid.*, p. 317, para. 167.
63. *Ibid.*, p. 320, para. 176.
64. *Ibid.*, para. 177.
65. *Ibid.*, p. 321, para. 180.
66. *Ibid.*, p. 322, para. 182.
67. *Ibid.*, p. 325, para. 189.
68. *Ibid.*, p. 323, para. 185.
69. *Ibid.*, p. 322, para. 184.
70. *Ibid.*, p. 327, para. 194.
71. *Ibid.*, para. 195.
72. *Ibid.*, p. 332, para. 211.
73. *Ibid.*, p. 331, para. 206.
74. *Ibid.*, para. 207.
75. *Ibid.*, p. 333, para. 213.
76. *Ibid.*, para. 214.
77. *Ibid.*, p. 334, para. 216.

78. The adjustment was necessitated by the geographical realities of the area. The international boundary terminus was not located in the middle of coast at the back of the Gulf, the Chamber said. The Chamber was also influenced 'only in some measure' by the US argument about the cut-off effect of the median line, but not by its argument on the 'concavity' of the US coast in the Gulf of Maine. See *ibid.*, paras. 217 and 219.

79. *Ibid.*, p. 336, para. 221.

80. For details, see *ibid.*, paras. 221 and 222.

81. For details, see *ibid.*, pp. 336-337, para. 222.

82. *Ibid.*, p. 338, para. 226.

83. For the Chamber's supporting arguments of simplicity, conformity with the views of the parties, and geography, see *ibid.*, pp. 337-338, paras. 224, 225 and 226.

84. *Ibid.*, p. 339, para. 228.

85. *Ibid.*, pp. 347-352.

86. *Ibid.*, p. 341, para. 235.

87. *Ibid.*, p. 342, para. 236.

88. *Ibid.*, para. 237.

89. For elaboration, see *ibid.*, p. 343, para. 238.

90. *Ibid.*, para. 239.

91. *Ibid.*, p. 344, para. 241.

92. *Ibid.*, p. 345.

93. *Ibid.*, Separate opinion of Judge Schwebel, p. 355.

94. *Ibid.*, p. 357.

95. *Ibid.*, Dissenting opinion of Judge Gros, pp. 360-390.

96. *Ibid.*, pp. 361-362, para. 3.

97. *Ibid.*, p. 365, para. 8.

98. *Ibid.*, p. 366, para. 10.

99. *Ibid.*, paras. 27, 29 and 47.

100. *Ibid.*, p. 377, para. 27.

101. *Ibid.*, p. 378, para. 29.

102. *Ibid.*, p. 383, para. 39.

103. *Ibid.*, pp. 379-380, para. 32.

104. *Ibid.*, p. 381, para. 35.

105. *Ibid.*, p. 382, para. 36.

106. *Ibid.*, p. 380, para. 33.

107. *Ibid.*, p. 386, para. 42.

108. For details of the delimitation line proposed by Judge Gros, see *ibid.*, p. 387, para. 45.

109. See p. 184 above.

110. See p. 189 above.

111. Gulf of Maine Case, ICJ, Oral Proceedings, Verbatim Record, 13 April 1984, C 1/CR 84/12, at p. 24.

Annexes

List of Agreements on maritime boundary

No. Title	Date of signature	Date of entry into force	Text published in
Asia: The Gulf			
1. Continental Shelf Boundary Agreement between Bahrain and Saudi Arabia	22 February 1958	26 February 1958	ST/LEG/SER.B/ 16, pp. 409-411 *Limits in the Seas*, No. 12 (1970)
2. Continental Shelf Boundary Agreement between Iran and Saudi Arabia	24 October 1968	29 January 1969	*Limits in the Seas*, No. 24 (1970)
3. Agreement for Settlement of Maritime Boundary Lines and Sovereign Rights over Islands between Abu Dhabi and Qatar	30 March 1969	30 March 1969	ST/LEG/SER.B/ 16, p. 403 *Limits in the Seas*, No. 18 (1970)
4. Agreement concerning the Boundary Line Dividing the Continental Shelf between Iran and Qatar	20 September 1969	10 May 1970	*Limits in the Seas*, No. 25 (1970)
5. Agreement concerning Delimitation of the Continental Shelf between Bahrain and Iran	17 June 1971	14 March 1972	*Limits in the Seas*, No. 58 (1974)
6. Agreement concerning Delimitation of the Continental Shelf between Iran and Oman	25 July 1974	28 May 1975	*Limits in the Seas*, No. 67 (1976)
7. Agreement concerning the Boundary Line Dividing Parts of the Continental Shelf between Iran and the United Arab Emirates	31 August 1974	Ratified by Iran on 15 March 1975	*Limits in the Seas*, No. 63 (1975)
8. Agreement between the State of Kuwait and the Kingdom of Saudi Arabia relating to the Partition of the Neutral Zone	7 July 1965	25 July 1966	*American Journal of International Law*, Vol. 60 (1966), pp. 744-749

No. Title	Date of signature	Date of entry into force	Text published in
Asia: India and the Neighbouring States			
9. Agreement between India and Sri Lanka on the Boundary in Historic Waters between the Two Countries and Related Matters	26/28 June 1974	8 July 1974	UN, National Legislation and Treaties relating to the Law of the Sea ST/LEG/SER.B/ 19 (1980), pp. 396-398 Lay, Churchill, Nordquist, *New Directions in the Law of the Sea*, Vol. V, pp. 326-328 (Oceana)
10. Agreement between India and Sri Lanka on the Maritime Boundary between the Two Countries in the Gulf of Manaar and the Bay of Bengal and Related Matters	23 March 1976	10 May 1976	ST/LEG/SER.B/ 19, pp. 402-406 *New Directions in the Law of the Sea*, Vol. VIII, pp. 99-101 *Limits in the Seas*, No. 77 (1978)
11. Supplementary Agreement between India and Sri Lanka on the Extension of the Maritime Boundary between the Two Countries in the Gulf of Manaar from Position 13 m to the Trijunction Point between India, Sri Lanka and the Maldives (Point T)	22 November 1976	5 February 1977	ST/LEG/SER.B/ 19, pp. 412-413 *New Directions in the Law of the Sea*, Vol. VII, pp. 97-98
12. Agreement between India, Sri Lanka and the Maldives concerning the Determination of the Trijunction Point between the Three Countries in the Gulf of Manaar	23/24 July 1976 (at Colombo), 31 July 1976 (at Male)	31 July 1976	ST/LEG/SER.B/ 19, pp. 415-416 *New Directions in the Law of the Sea*, Vol. VIII, pp. 102-103
13. Agreement between India and the Maldives on Maritime Boundary in the Arabian Sea and Related Matters	28 December 1976	8 June 1978	*Limits in the Seas*, No. 78 (1978)
14. Agreement between the Government of the Republic of India and the Government of the Republic of Indonesia relating to the Delimitation of the Continental Shelf Boundary between the Two Countries	8 August 1974	17 December 1974	*Limits in the Seas*, No. 62 (1975) *New Directions in the Law of the Sea*, Vol. V, pp. 265-267

No.	Title	Date of signature	Date of entry into force	Text published in
15.	Agreement between the Government of the Republic of India and the Government of the Republic of Indonesia on the Extension of the 1974 Continental Shelf Boundary between the Two Countries in the Andaman Sea and the Indian Ocean	14 January 1977	15 August 1977	*Limits in the Seas*, No. 93 (1981)
16.	Agreement between the Government of the Republic of India, the Government of the Republic of Indonesia and the Government of the Kingdom of Thailand concerning the Determination of the Trijunction Point and the Delimitation of the Related Boundaries of the Three Countries in the Andaman Sea	22 June 1978	2 March 1979	*Limits in the Seas*, No. 93 (1981)
17.	Agreement between the Government of the Republic of India and the Government of the Kingdom of Thailand on the Delimitation of the Seabed Boundary between the Two Countries in the Andaman Sea	22 June 1978	15 December 1978	*Limits in the Seas*, No. 93 (1981)

Asia: Other Agreements

South East Asia

No.	Title	Date of signature	Date of entry into force	Text published in
18.	Agreement between the Government of the Republic of Indonesia and the Government of Malaysia relating to the Delimitation of the Continental Shelves between the Two Countries	27 October 1969	7 November 1969	*Limits in the Seas*, No. 1 (1970)
19.	Treaty between the Republics of Indonesia and Malaysia on Determination of the Boundary Lines of the Territorial Waters of the Two Nations at the Strait of Malacca	17 March 1970	10 March 1971	*Limits in the Seas*, No. 50 (1973)
20.	Agreement between Thailand, Indonesia and Malaysia relating to the Delimitation of the Continental Shelf Boundaries in the Northern Part of the Straits of Malacca	21 December 1971	16 July 1973	*Limits in the Seas*, No. 81 (1978)

No. Title	Date of signature	Date of entry into force	Text published in
21. Agreement between Thailand and Indonesia relating to the Delimitation of a Continental Shelf Boundary between the Two Countries in the Northern Part of the Straits of Malacca and in the Andaman Sea	17 December 1971	16 July 1973	*Limits in the Seas,* No. 81 (1978)
22. Agreement between the Government of the Republic of Indonesia and the Government of the Kingdom of Thailand relating to the Delimitation of the Sea-Bed Boundary between the Two Countries in the Andaman Sea	11 December 1975	18 February 1978	*Limits in the Seas,* No. 93 (1981)
23. Agreement stipulating the Territorial Sea Boundary Lines between Indonesia and the Republic of Singapore in the Strait of Singapore	25 May 1973	Ratified by Indonesia on 3 December 1973 and by Singapore on 29 August 1974	*Limits in the Seas,* No. 60 (1974

The Gulf of Thailand

No. Title	Date of signature	Date of entry into force	Text published in
24. Memorandum of Understanding between Malaysia and the Kingdom of Thailand on the Delimitation of the Continental Shelf Boundary between the Two Countries in the Gulf of Thailand	24 October 1979	15 July 1982	
25. Memorandum of Understanding between the Kingdom of Thailand and Malaysia on the Establishment of Joint Authority for the Exploitation of the Reserves of the Seabed in a Defined Area of the Continental Shelf of the Two Countries in the Gulf of Thailand	21 February 1979	15 July 1982	

Burma – Thailand

No. Title	Date of signature	Date of entry into force	Text published in
26. Agreement on Delimitation of the Maritime Boundary between Burma and Thailand in the Andaman Sea	25 July 1980	12 April 1982	

334

No. Title	Date of signature	Date of entry into force	Text published in

Japan and the Republic of Korea

27. Agreement between Japan and the Republic of Korea concerning the Establishment of the Boundary in the Northern Part of the Continental Shelf Adjacent to the Two Countries — 30 January 1974 — Ratified by both States — *Limits in the Seas*, No. 75 (1977)

28. Agreement between Japan and the Republic of Korea concerning Joint Development of the Southern Part of the Continental Shelf Adjacent to the Two Countries — 30 January 1974 — Ratified by both States — *Limits in the Seas*, No. 75 (1977)

Africa

29. Exchange of Notes between France and Portugal regarding the Maritime Boundary between Senegal and Portuguese Guinea — 26 April 1960 — 26 April 1960 — *Limits in the Seas*, No. 68 (1976)

30. Agreement between the Government of the Republic of Gambia and the Government of the Republic of Senegal concerning the Delimitation of Maritime Boundaries in the North Atlantic Ocean — 4 June 1974 — 27 August 1976 — *New Directions in the Law of the Sea*, Vol. VIII, pp. 104-108 / *Limits in the Seas*, No. 85 (1979)

31. Exchange of Notes between Kenya and the United Republic of Tanzania concerning the Delimitation of the Territorial Waters Boundary between the Two States — Kenyan Note: 17 Dec. 1975; Tanzanian Note: 9 July 1976 — 9 July 1976 — ST/LEG/SER.B/ 19, pp. 406-408 / *Limits in the Seas*, No. 92 (1981)

32. Continental Shelf Boundary between Mauritania and Morocco — 14 April 1976

Latin America

33. Agreement between the Government of the United Kingdom of Great Britain and Northern Ireland and the Government of the United States of Venezuela relating to the Division of the Submarine Areas of the Gulf of Paria — 26 February 1942 — 22 September 1942 — *Limits in the Seas*, No. 11 (1970)

No. Title	Date of signature	Date of entry into force	Text published in
34. (a) Declaration of the Maritime Zone between Chile, Ecuador and Peru signed at the First Conference on the Exploitation and Conservation of the Maritime Resources of the South Pacific, Santiago, 28 August 1952 – Agreement between Chile and Peru	28 August 1952	Ratified by Chile and Peru	*Limits in the Seas*, No. 86 (1979)
(b) Agreement between Chile, Ecuador and Peru relating to a Special Maritime Frontier Zone	4 December 1954	Ratified by Chile and Peru	*Limits in the Seas*, No. 86 (1979)
35. Agreement between Peru and Ecuador pursuant to Declaration on the Maritime Zone, 1952	28 August 1952	Ratified by Peru and Ecuador (1955)	*Limits in the Seas*, No. 88 (1979)
36. Agreement on the Delimitation of Marine and Submarine Areas and Maritime Cooperation between the Republics of Ecuador and Colombia	23 August 1975	22 December 1975	*Limits in the Seas*, No. 69 (1976)
37. Treaty of Rio de Plata and its Maritime Limits between the Argentine Republic and the Oriental Republic of Uruguay	19 November 1973	12 February 1974	*Limits in the Seas*, No. 64 (1975)
38. Exchange of Notes constituting an Agreement on the Final Establishment of the Chuy River Bank and the Lateral Sea Limit between Uruguay and Brazil	21 July 1972	12 June 1975	*Limits in the Seas*, No. 73 (1976)
39. Agreement between the Government of the Republic of Colombia and the Republic of Panama Delimiting Maritime Boundaries in the Caribbean Sea and the Pacific Ocean	20 November 1976	30 November 1977	*Limits in the Seas*, No. 79 (1978)
40. Treaty on Delimitation of Marine and Submarine Areas and Maritime Cooperation between the Republic of Colombia and the Republic of Costa Rica	17 March 1977		*Limits in the Seas*, No. 84 (1979)
41. Treaty concerning Delimitation of Marine Areas and Maritime Cooperation between the Republic of Costa Rica and the Republic of Panama	2 February 1980	11 February 1982	*Limits in the Seas*, No. 97 (1982)
42. Agreement on Maritime Boundary between Mexico and Cuba	26 July 1976	26 July 1976	

No. Title	Date of signature	Date of entry into force	Text published in
43. Maritime Limits Agreement between Colombia and Haiti	18 February 1978		*New Directions in the Law of the Sea*, Vol. VIII, pp. 76-77
44. Agreement on the Declaration of Marine and Submarine Areas and Maritime Cooperation between the Dominican Republic and the Republic of Colombia	13 January 1978		*New Directions in the Law of the Sea*, Vol. VIII, pp. 78-79
45. Agreement between the Republic of Haiti and the Republic of Cuba regarding the Delimitation of the Maritime Boundaries between the Two States	27 October 1977		*New Directions in the Law of the Sea*, Vol. VIII, pp. 69-75
46. Treaty on Delimitation of Marine and Submarine Areas between the Republic of Venezuela and the Dominican Republic	3 March 1979	15 January 1982	*New Directions in the Law of the Sea*, Vol. VIII, pp. 80-83

West European and other States

The North Sea

No. Title	Date of signature	Date of entry into force	Text published in
47. UK – Norway: Agreement between the Government of the United Kingdom of Great Britain and Northern Ireland and the Government of the Kingdom of Norway relating to the Delimitation of the Continental Shelf between the Two Countries	10 March 1965	29 June 1965	*Limits in the Seas*, No. 10, Revised (1974)
48. Denmark – Norway: (a) Agreement between Denmark and Norway relating to the Delimitation of the Continental Shelf	8 December 1965	22 June 1966	*Limits in the Seas*, No. 10, Revised (1974)
(b) Exchange of Notes constituting an Agreement between the Government of Denmark and the Government of Norway amending the Agreement of 8 December 1965 concerning the Delimitation of the Continental Shelf	24 April 1968	24 December 1968	ST/LEG.SER.B/ 16, p. 412

No. Title	Date of signature	Date of entry into force	Text published in
49. UK – Netherlands: Agreement between the Government of the Kingdom of the Netherlands and the Government of the United Kingdom of Great Britain and Northern Ireland relating to the Delimitation of the Continental Shelf under the North Sea between the Two Countries	6 October 1965	23 December 1966	*Limits in the Seas*, No. 10, Revised (1974)
50. Netherlands – FRG: Treaty between the Kingdom of the Netherlands and the Federal Republic of Germany concerning the Lateral Delimitation of the Continental Shelf in the Vicinity of the Coast	1 December 1964	18 September 1965	*Limits in the Seas*, No. 10 (1970)
51. Denmark – FRG: Agreement between the Kingdom of Denmark and the Federal Republic of Germany concerning the Delimitation in the Coastal Regions of the Continental Shelf of the North Sea	9 June 1965	27 May 1966	*Limits in the Seas*, No. 10 (1970)
52. Netherlands – FRG: Treaty between the Kingdom of the Netherlands and the Federal Republic of Germany on the Delimitation of the Continental Shelf under the North Sea	28 January 1971	7 December 1972	*Limits in the Seas*, No. 10, Revised (1974)
53. Denmark – FRG: Treaty between the Kingdom of Denmark and the Federal Republic of Germany relating to the Delimitation of the Continental Shelf under the North Sea	28 January 1971	7 December 1972	*Limits in the Seas*, No. 10, Revised (1974)
54. FRG – UK: Agreement between the Federal Republic of Germany and the United Kingdom of Great Britain and Northern Ireland relating to the Delimitation of the Continental Shelf under the North Sea between the Two Countries	25 November 1971	7 December 1972	ST/LEG/SER.B/ 18, pp. 435-437 *Limits in the Seas*, No. 10, Revised (1974)
55. UK – Netherlands: Protocol between the United Kingdom and the Netherlands Amending the Agreement of 6 October 1965 concerning the Delimitation of the Continental Shelf under the North Sea between the Two Countries	25 November 1971	7 December 1972	*Limits in the Seas*, No. 10, Revised (1974)

338

No. Title	Date of signature	Date of entry into force	Text published in
56. UK – Denmark: Agreement between the Government of the United Kingdom of Great Britain and Northern Ireland and the Government of the Kingdom of Denmark relating to the Delimitation of the Continental Shelf between the Two Countries	25 November 1971	7 December 1972	*Limits in the Seas*, No. 10, Revised (1974)
57. Protocol supplementary to the Agreement of 10 March 1965 between Norway and the United Kingdom	22 December 1978	20 February 1980	

WEO: Other Agreements

58. Declaration between the Danish and Swedish Governments concerning the Boundaries in the Sound	30 January 1932	30 January 1932	*Limits in the Seas*, No. 26 (1970)
59. Agreement between Sweden and Norway concerning the Delimitation of the Continental Shelf	24 July 1968	18 March 1969	*Limits in the Seas*, No. 2 (1970)
60. Agreement between Finland and Sweden concerning the Delimitation of the Continental Shelf in the Gulf of Bothnia, the Aland Sea and the northernmost part of the Baltic Sea	29 September 1972	15 January 1973	*Limits in the Seas*, No. 71 (1976
61. Convention between France and Spain on the Delimitation of the Territorial Sea and the Contiguous Zone in the Bay of Biscay	29 January 1974	5 April 1975	*New Directions in the Law of the Sea*, Vol. V, pp. 1-4 *Limits in the Seas*, No. 83 (1979)
62. Convention between the Government of the French Republic and the Government of the Spanish State on the Delimitation of the Continental Shelves of the Two States in the Bay of Biscay	29 January 1974	5 April 1975	*New Directions in the Law of the Sea*, Vol. V, pp. 251-260 *Limits in the Seas*, No. 83 (1979)
63. Convention between Italy and Spain on Delimitation of the Continental Shelf between the Two States	19 February 1974	16 November 1978	*New Directions in the Law of the Sea*, Vol. V, pp. 261-264 *Limits in the Seas*, No. 90 (1980)

No. Title	Date of signature	Date of entry into force	Text published in
64. Agreement between Canada and France on their Mutual Fishing Relations. The Annex to the Agreement was a Declaration delimiting the Territorial Sea between the Canadian Province of Newfoundland and the French overseas territory of St.-Pierre and Miquelon	27 March 1972	27 March 1972	*Limits in the Seas*, No. 57 (1974)
65. Agreement between Canada and Denmark concerning the Delimitation of the Continental Shelf Boundary between Canada and Greenland	17 December 1973	13 March 1974	*Limits in the Seas*, No. 72 (1976)
66. Agreement on the Continental Shelf Boundary between Denmark and the Federal Republic of Germany (Baltic Sea)	9 June 1965	7 July 1977	
67. Agreement on the Continental Shelf Boundary between Italy and Greece	24 May 1977	12 November 1982	*Limits in the Seas*, No. 96 (1982)
68. Agreement between Portugal and Spain on the Delimitation of the Continental Shelf	12 February 1976		
69. Agreement between Norway and Denmark (Faroes)	15 June 1979	3 June 1980	
70. Agreement between Norway and Iceland	22 October 1981	2 June 1982	*International Legal Materials*, Vol. 21 (1982), pp. 12-22
71. Convention on Delimitation between France and Australia (Coral Sea and Indian Ocean)	2 October 1980	10 January 1983	*Law of the Sea Bulletin* (UN, New York), No. 3, March 1984

Eastern Europe

No. Title	Date of signature	Date of entry into force	Text published in
72. Poland – USSR: Protocol between the Government of the Polish People's Republic and the Government of the Union of Soviet Socialist Republics concerning the Delimitation of Polish and Soviet Territorial Waters in the Gulf of Gdansk of the Baltic Sea	18 March 1958	29 July 1958	*Limits in the Seas*, No. 55 (1973)
73. Poland – USSR: Treaty on the Course of the Boundary of the Continental Shelf in the Gulf of Gdansk and the southern Baltic Sea	28 August 1969	13 May 1970	*Limits in the Seas*, No. 55 (1973) ST/LEG/SER.B/ 16, pp. 414-416

340

No. Title	Date of signature	Date of entry into force	Text published in
74. GDR – Poland: Agreement between the German Democratic Republic and Poland concerning the Territorial Sea and Continental Shelf Boundaries	29 October 1968		*Limits in the Seas*, No. 65 (1975)

Inter-regional Agreements

(a) Analysed with Asian Agreements:

Sudan – Saudi Arabia (The Red Sea)

75. Agreement between Sudan and Saudi Arabia relating to the Joint Exploitation of the Natural Resources of the Sea-Bed and Sub-Soil of the Red Sea in the Common Zone	16 May 1974	26 August 1974	ST/LEG/SER.B/ 18, pp. 452-455

Australia – Indonesia – Papua New Guinea

76. Agreement between the Government of the Republic of Indonesia and the Government of the Commonwealth of Australia establishing Certain Seabed Boundaries	18 May 1971	8 November 1973	*Limits in the Seas*, No. 87 (1979)
77. Agreement between the Government of the Republic of Indonesia and the Government of the Commonwealth of Australia establishing Certain Seabed Boundaries in the Area of the Timor and Arafura Seas, Supplementary to the Agreement of 18 May 1971	9 October 1972	8 November 1973	*Limits in the Seas*, No. 87 (1979)
78. Agreement between Indonesia and Australia concerning Certain Boundaries between Indonesia and Papua New Guinea	12 February 1973	26 November 1974	*Limits in the Seas*, No. 87 (1979)
79. Treaty between Australia and the Independent State of Papua New Guinea concerning Sovereignty and Maritime Boundaries in the Area between the Two Countries, including the Area known as Torres Strait, and Related Matters	18 December 1978		*New Directions in the Law of the Sea*, Vol. VIII, pp. 215-282

Agreements in the South Pacific

80. Convention on Maritime Boundary between the Republic of France and the Kingdom of Tonga	11 January 1980	11 January 1980	

No. Title	Date of signature	Date of entry into force	Text published in
81. Treaty between the United States of America and the Cook Islands on Friendship and Delimitation of the Maritime Boundary between the United States of America and the Cook Islands	11 June 1980	8 September 1983	*Limits in the Seas*, No. 100 (1983)
82. Treaty between the United States of America and New Zealand on the Delimitation of the Maritime Boundary between Tokelau and the United States of America	2 December 1980	3 September 1983	*Limits in the Seas*, No. 100 (1983)

(b) Analysed with African Agreements:

83. Agreement between the Government of the Italian Republic and the Government of the Tunisian Republic relating to Delimitation of the Continental Shelf Boundary between the Two Countries	20 August 1971	6 December 1978	*Limits in the Seas*, No. 89 (1980)
84. Convention on Maritime Boundary between France and Mauritius	2 April 1980	2 April 1980	*Limits in the Seas*, No. 95 (1982)

(c) Analysed with Latin American Agreements:

85. Agreement between France and Brazil	30 January 1981	19 October 1983	
86. Treaty between the United States of America and Mexico on Territorial Sea Boundary	23 November 1970	18 April 1972	*Limits in the Seas*, No. 45 (1972)
87. Treaty on Maritime Boundaries between the United States of America and the United Mexican States	4 May 1978		*New Directions in the Law of the Sea*, Vol. VIII, pp. 63-65
88. Maritime Boundary Agreement between the United States of America and the Republic of Cuba	16 December 1977		*New Directions in the Law of the Sea*, Vol. VIII, pp. 66-68
89. Maritime Boundary Treaty between the United States of America and the Republic of Venezuela	28 March 1978	24 November 1980	*Limits in the Seas*, No. 91 (1980)
90. Agreement between Venezuela and the Netherlands (Netherlands Antilles)	30 March 1978	15 December 1978	

No. Title	Date of signature	Date of entry into force	Text published in
91. Agreement between France and Venezuela	17 July 1980		
92. Agreement between France and Saint Lucia	4 March 1981	4 March 1981	

(d) Analysed with WEO Agreements:

No. Title	Date of signature	Date of entry into force	Text published in
93. Agreements between Italy and Yugoslavia concerning the Delimitation of the Continental Shelf Boundary between the Two Countries	8 January 1968	21 January 1970	*Limits in the Seas*, No. 9 (1970)
94. Agreement between the Federal Republic of Germany and the German Democratic Republic concerning Maritime Boundary	29 June 1974	1 October 1974	*Limits in the Seas*, No. 74 (1976)
95. Agreement between the Kingdom of Sweden and the German Democratic Republic about Delimitation of the Continental Shelf	22 June 1978		

(e) Analysed with East European Agreements:

No. Title	Date of signature	Date of entry into force	Text published in
96. (a) Agreement between the Kingdom of Norway and the Union of Soviet Socialist Republics relating to the Division of the Continental Shelf in the Varangerfjord	15 February 1957	24 April 1957	*Limits in the Seas*, No. 17 (1970)
(b) Descriptive Protocol	November 1957	17 March 1958	*Limits in the Seas*, No. 17 (1970)
97. Agreement between the Government of the Republic of Finland and the Government of the Union of Societ Socialist Republics concerning the Boundaries of Sea Areas and of the Continental Shelf in the Gulf of Finland	20 May 1965	25 May 1966	*Limits in the Seas*, No. 16 (1970)
98. Agreement between the Government of the Republic of Finland and the Government of the Union of Soviet Socialist Republics concerning the Boundary of the Continental Shelf between Finland and the Soviet Union in the North-Eastern part of the Baltic Sea	5 May 1967	15 March 1968	*Limits in the Seas*, No. 56 (1973)

No.	Title	Date of signature	Date of entry into force	Text published in
99.	Protocol concerning the Territorial Sea Boundary between the Union of Soviet Socialist Republics and the Republic of Turkey in the Black Sea	17 April 1973	Soviet Union ratified the Protocol on 3 January 1974	*Limits in the Seas*, No. 59 (1974)
100.	Agreement between the USSR and Turkey regarding the continental shelf boundary in the Black Sea	23 June 1978	15 May 1981	

Agreements analysed in the Addendum

WEO: Other Agreements

101.	UK – France Agreement between the Government of the United Kingdom of Great Britain and Northern Ireland and the Government of the French Republic relating to the Delimitation of the Continental Shelf in the Area East of 30 Minutes West of the Greenwich Meridian	24 June 1982	4 February 1983	

Inter-regional Agreements

102.	Indonesia – Australia Memorandum of Understanding between the Government of the Republic of Indonesia and the Government of Australia concerning the implementation of a Provisional Fisheries Surveillance and Enforcement Arrangement	29 October 1981	1 January 1982	
103.	France – Fiji Agreement between the Government of the Republic of France and the Government of Fiji relating to the Delimitation of their Economic Zone	19 January 1983		

344

Text of Agreements on maritime boundary (sample)

1. Agreement between India and Maldives on the Maritime Boundary in the Arabian Sea and Related Matters

The Government of the Republic of India and the Government of the Republic of Maldives,

Desirous to strengthen the existing historical bonds of friendship between the two countries,

Recalling the Agreement between India, Maldives and Sri Lanka concerning the determination of the trijunction point (Point T) between the three countries in the Gulf of Manaar, which came into force on 31 July 1976, and

Desiring to establish the maritime boundary between the two countries in the Arabian Sea,

Have agreed as follows:

Article I

The maritime boundary between India and Maldives in the Arabian Sea shall be arcs of Great Circles between the following positions, in the sequence given below, defined by latitude and longitude:

Point No.	Latitude (North)	Longitude (East)
T	04°47′04′′	77°01′40′′
1	04°52′15′′	76°56′48′′
2	05°05′35′′	76°43′15′′
3	05°13′56′′	76°36′48′′
4	06°28′14′′	75°41′34′′
5	06°33′21′′	75°38′31′′
6	06°51′06′′	75°25′46′′
7	07°15′27′′	75°16′19′′

8	07°24'00''	75°12'06''
9	07°25'19''	75°11'18''
10	07°51'30''	74°56'09''
11	07°48'30''	74°29'45''
12	07°41'50''	73°38'34''
13	07°39'02''	73°19'38''
14	07°40'52''	73°03'23''
15	07°42'19''	72°49'30''
16	07°42'54''	72°42'26''
17	07°49'05''	72°03'45''
18	08°05'38''	70°15'08''
19	07°57'27''	69°35'45''

Article II

The coordinates of the positions specified in Article I are geographical coordinates and the straight lines connecting them are indicated in the chart annexed hereto, which has been signed by the officials duly authorised for the purpose by the two Governments respectively.

Article III

The actual location at sea and on the seabed of the positions specified in Article I shall be determined by a method to be mutually agreed upon by the two Governments respectively.

Article IV

(1)   Each Party shall have sovereignty over all islands falling on its side of the aforesaid boundary, as well as over the territorial waters and the airspace above them.

(2)   Each Party shall have sovereign rights and exclusive jurisdiction over the continental shelf and the exclusive economic zone as well as over their resources, whether living or non-living, falling on its own side of the aforesaid boundary.

(3)   Each Party shall respect rights of navigation through its territorial sea and the exclusive economic zone in accordance with its laws and regulations and the rules of international law.

Article V

If any single geological petroleum or natural gas structure or field, or any single geological structure or field of any mineral deposit, including sand or gravel, extends across the boundary referred to in Article I and the part of such structure or field which is situated on one side of the boundary is exploited, in whole or in part, from the other side of the boundary, the two countries shall seek to reach agreement as to the manner in which the structure or field shall be most effectively exploited and the manner in which the proceeds deriving therefrom shall be apportioned.

Article VI

The Agreement shall be subject to ratification. It shall enter into force on the date of exchange of instruments of ratification which shall take place as soon as possible

(*Signed*) Y.B. Chavan, for the Government of the Republic of India, New Delhi, 28 December 1976
(*Signed*) A. Hilmy Didi, for the Government of the Republic of Maldives, New Delhi

2. Memorandum of Understanding between the Kingdom of Thailand and Malaysia on the Establishment of a Joint Authority for the Exploitation of the Resources of the Sea-bed in a Defined Area of the Continental Shelf of the Two Countries in the Gulf of Thailand

The Kingdom of Thailand and Malaysia,

Desiring to strengthen further the existing bonds of traditional friendship between the two countries;

Recognizing that, as a result of overlapping claims made by the two countries regarding the boundary line of their continental shelves in the Gulf of Thailand, there exists an overlapping area on their adjacent continental shelves;

Noting that the existing negotiations between the two countries on the delimitation of the boundary of the continental shelf in the Gulf of Thailand may continue for some time;

Considering that it is in the best interests of the two countries to exploit the resources of the sea-bed in the overlapping area as soon as possible; and

Convinced that such activities can be carried out jointly through mutual cooperation,

Have agreed as follows:

Article I

Both Parties agree that as a result of overlapping claims made by the two countries regarding the boundary line of their continental shelves in the Gulf of Thailand, there exists an overlapping area, which is defined as that area bounded by straight lines joining the following coordinated points:

(A) N 6°50′.0   E 102°21′.2
(B) N 7°10′.25   E 102°29′.0
(C) N 7°49′.0   E 103°02′.5
(D) N 7°22′.0   E 103°42′.5
(E) N 7°20′.0   E 103°39′.0
(F) N 7°03′.0   E 103°06′.0
(G) N 6°53′.0   E 102°34′.0

and shown in the relevant part of the British Admiralty Chart No. 2414, Edition 1967, annexed hereto.

Article II

Both Parties agree to continue to resolve the problem of the delimitation of the boundary of the continental shelf in the Gulf of Thailand between the two countries by negotiations or such other peaceful means as agreed by both Parties, in accordance with the principles of international law and practice especially those agreed to in the Agreed Minutes of the Malaysia – Thailand Officials' Meeting on Delimitation of the Continental Shelf Boundary Between Malaysia and Thailand in the Gulf of Thailand and in the South China Sea, 27 February – 1 March 1978, and in the spirit of friendship and in the interest of mutual security.

Article III

(1)   There shall be established a Joint Authority to be known as 'Malaysia – Thailand Joint Authority' (hereinafter referred to as 'the Joint Authority') for the purpose of the exploration and exploitation of the non-living natural resources of the sea-bed and subsoil in the overlapping area for a period of fifty years commencing from the date this Memorandum comes into force.

(2)   The Joint Authority shall assume all rights and responsibilities on behalf of both Parties for the exploration and exploitation of the non-living natu-

348

ral resources of the sea-bed and subsoil in the overlapping area (hereinafter referred to as the joint development area) and also for the developments, control and administration of the joint developments area. The assumption of such rights and responsibilities by the Joint Authority shall in no way affect or curtail the validity of concessions or licences hitherto issued or agreements or arrangements hitherto made by either Party.

(3)   The Joint Authority shall consist of:
(a) two joint-chairmen, one from each country, and
(b) an equal number of members from each country.

(4)   Subject to the provisions of this Memorandum, the Joint Authority shall exercise on behalf of both Parties all the powers necessary for, incidental to or connected with the discharge of its functions relating to the exploration and exploitation of the non-living resources of the sea-bed and subsoil in the joint development area.

(5)   All costs incurred and benefits derived by the Joint Authority from activities carried out in the joint development area shall be equally borne and shared by both Parties.

(6)   If any single geological petroleum or natural gas structure or field, or other mineral deposit of whatever character, extends beyond the limit of the joint development area defined in Article I, the Joint Authority and the Party or Parties concerned shall communicate to each other all information in this regard and shall seek to reach agreement as to the manner in which the structure, field or deposit will be most effectively exploited; and all expenses incurred and benefits derived therefrom shall be equitably shared.

Article IV

(1)   The rights conferred or exercised by the national authority of either Party in matters of fishing, navigation, hydrographic and oceanographic surveys, the prevention and control of marine pollution and other similar matters (including all powers of enforcement in relation thereto) shall extend to the joint development area and such rights shall be recognized and respected by the Joint Authority.

(2)   Both Parties shall have a combined and coordinated security arrangement in the joint development area.

Article V

The criminal jurisdiction of Malaysia in the joint development area shall extend over that area bounded by straight lines joining the following coordinated points:

349

A	N 6°50'.0	E	102°21'.2
X	N 7°35'.0	E	103°23'.0
D	N 7°22'.0	E	103°42'.5
E	N 7°20'.0	E	103°39'.0
F	N 7°03'.0	E	103°06'.0
G	N 6°53'.0	E	102°34'.0

The criminal jurisdiction of the Kingdom of Thailand in the joint development area shall extend over that area bounded by straight lines joining the following coordinated points:

A	N 6°50'.0	E	102°21'.2
B	N 7°10'.25	E	102°29'.0
C	N 7°49'.0	E	103°02'.5
X	N 7°35'.0	E	103°23'.0

The areas of criminal jurisdiction of both Parties defined under this Article shall not in any way be construed as indicating the boundary line of the continental shelf between the two countries in the joint development area, which boundary is to be determined as provided for by Article II, nor shall such definition in any way prejudice the sovereign rights of either Party in the joint development area.

Article VI

(1) Notwithstanding Article III, if both Parties arrive at a satisfactory solution on the problem of the delimitation of the boundary of the continental shelf before the expiry of the said fifty-year period, the Joint Authority shall be wound up and all assets administered and liabilities incurred by it shall be equally shared and borne by both Parties. A new arrangement may, however, be concluded if both Parties so decide.

(2) If no satisfactory solution is found on the problem of the delimitation of the boundary of the Continental Shelf within the said fifty-year period, the existing arrangements shall continue after the expiry of the said period.

Article VII

Any difference or dispute arising out of the interpretation or implementation of the provisions of this Memorandum shall be settled peacefully by consultation or negotiation between the Parties.

Article VIII

This Memorandum shall come into force on the date of exchange of instruments of ratification.

Done in duplicate at Chiang Mai, the Twenty-first day of February in the year One thousand Nine hundred and Seventy-nine, in the Thai, Malay and English Languages.
In the event of any conflict among the texts, the English text shall prevail.

For the Kingdom of Thailand, General Kriangsak Chomanan, Prime Minister
For Malaysia, Datuk Hussein Onn, Prime Minister.

3. Agreement concerning the Boundary Line Dividing the Continental Shelf between Iran and Qatar, Done at Doha on 20 September 1969

The Imperial Government of Iran and the Government of Qatar, desirous of establishing in a just, equitable and precise manner the boundary line between the respective areas of Continental Shelf over which they have sovereign rights in accordance with international law,
    have agreed as follows:

Article 1

The Boundary Line dividing the Continental Shelf lying between the territory of Iran on the one side and that of Qatar on the other side shall consist of geodetic lines between the following points in the sequence given below:
    Point (1) is the westernmost point on the westernmost part of the northern boundary line of the continental shelf appertaining to Qatar formed by a line of geodetic azimuth 278 degrees 14 minutes 27 seconds west from Point 2 below.

	Lat. N	*Long. E*
Point (2)	27°00′35′′	51°23′00′′
Point (3)	26°56′20′′	51°44′05′′
Point (4)	26°33′25′′	52°12′10′′
Point (5)	26°06′20′′	52°42′30′′
Point (6)	25°31′50′′	53°02′05′′

Article 2

If any single geological petroleum structure or petroleum field, or any single geological structure or field of any other mineral deposit, extends across the Boundary Line set out in Article 1 of this Agreement and the part of such structure or field which is situated on one side of that Boundary Line could be exploited wholly or in part by directional drilling from the other side of the Boundary Line, then:

(*a*)   No well shall be drilled on either side of the Boundary Line as set out in Article 1 so that any producing section thereof is less than 125 metres from the said Boundary Line, except by mutual agreement between the two Governments;

(*b*)   Both Governments shall endeavour to reach agreement as to the manner in which the operations on both sides of the Boundary Line could be coordinated or unitized.

Article 3

The Boundary Line referred to in Article 1 herein has been illustrated on the British Admiralty Chart No. 2837 which is annexed to this Agreement.

The said Chart has been made in duplicate and signed by the representatives of both Governments each of whom has retained one copy thereof.

Article 4

Nothing in this Agreement shall affect the status of the superadjacent waters or airspace above any part of the Continental Shelf.

Article 5

A.   The present agreement will be ratified and the instruments of ratification will be exchanged as quickly as possible in Doha (Qatar).

B.   The present agreement will be implemented beginning with the date of the exchange of the instruments of ratification.

4. Exchange of Notes between the United Republic of Tanzania and Kenya concerning the Delimitation of the Territorial Waters Boundary between the Two States

I. *Kenyan note*

December 17th, 1975

Your Excellency,

I have the honour to refer to the meetings held between officials of the United Republic of Tanzania and of the Republic of Kenya on 8th May, 1972 at Mombassa, Kenya and from 6th to 8th August, 1975 at Arusha, Tanzania and on 4th September, 1975 at Dar-es-Salaam, Tanzania, on the delimitation of the territorial waters boundary between our two countries and to state that, as a result of the said meetings, the following points were agreed:

1. *Boundary:*
Base Lines:
(*a*) Ras Jimbo beacon – Kisite Island (rock)
(*b*) Ras Jimbo – Mwamba-wamba beacon
(*c*) Mwamba-wamba beacon – Fundo Island beacon (rock)
(*d*) Fundo Island beacon (rock) – Ras Kigomasha lighthouse
(*e*) Kisite Island (rock) – Mpunguti ya Juu-lighthouse.

2. *The description of the boundary:*
(*a*) *On the West:* The median line between the Ras Jimbo beacon – Kisite Island/Ras Jimbo – Mwamba-wamba beacon base lines to a point 12 nautical miles from Ras Jimbo up to a point hereinafter referred to as 'A', located at 4°49'56''S and 39°20'58''E;
(*b*) *On the East:* The median line derived by the Intersection of two arcs each being 12 nautical miles drawn from Mpunguti ya Juu lighthouse and Rs Kigomasha lighthouse respectively hereinafter referred to as point 'B', located at 4°53'31''S and 39°28'40''E and point C, located at 4°40'52''S and 39°36'18''E;
(*c*) *On the South:* An arc with the centre as the Northern Intersection of arcs with radii 6 nautical miles from point 'A' as described in paragraph 2(a) above and point 'B' which is the Southern Intersection of arcs from Ras Kigomasha lighthouse and Mpunguti ya Juu lighthouse.
(*d*) The eastward boundary from point C, which is the Northern Intersection of arcs from Ras Kigomasha lighthouse and Mpunguti ya Juu lighthouse as described under paragraph 2(b) above, shall be the latitude extending eastwards to a point where it intersects the outermost limits of territorial water boundary or areas of national jurisdiction of two States.

(e) The marine charts of 1:250,000 describing the co-ordinates of the above points shall form an integral part of this agreement.

3. *Fishing and fisheries:*
(a) It was agreed that indigenous fishermen from both countries engaged in fishing for subsistence, be permitted to fish within 12 nautical miles of either side of the territorial sea boundary in accordance with existing regulations.
(b) It was agreed that there be reciprocal recognition of fisheries licences, regulations and practices of either State applicable to indigenous fishermen aforesaid. The fishing within the area specified in paragraph 3(a).

After due consideration of the said points of agreement, including the attached map describing the co-ordinates of the boundary as delimited, the Government of the Republic of Kenya hereby confirms that it accepts the above recommendations having been fully convinced that they are for the mutual benefit of our two countries.

If the Government of the United Republic of Tanzania is of the same view, then it is suggested that this Note and your reply thereto in the affirmative shall constitute an Agreement for the territorial waters boundary between our two States and other related matters referred to above and the same shall enter into force on the date of the receipt of your said Note in reply.

Accept, Your Excellency, the assurances of my highest consideration.

Yours, Dr. Munyua Waiyaki, Minister for Foreign Affairs

H.E. Mr. Ibrahim Kaduma, M.P., Minister for Foreign Affairs,
United Republic of Tanzania, Dar es Salaam, Tanzania

II. *Tanzanian note*

9th July, 1976

Your Excellency,

I have the honour to acknowledge receipt of your letter Ref. No. MFA.273/430/001A/120 of 17th December, 1975 which reads as follows:

[See Letter I]

I have the honour to confirm that the foregoing is acceptable to the Government of the United Republic of Tanzania.

Please accept, Your Excellency, the assurances of my highest consideration.

Ibrahim M. Kaduma, Minister for Foreign Affairs

H.E. Dr. Munyua Waiyaki, Minister for Foreign Affairs,
Office of the Minister, Nairobi, Kenya

354

5. Treaty on Maritime Boundaries between the United States of America and the United Mexican States

The Government of the United States of America and the Government of the United Mexican States:

Considering that the maritime boundaries between the two countries were determined for a distance of twelve nautical miles seaward by the Treaty to Resolve Pending Boundary Differences and Maintain the Rio Grande and Colorado River as the International Boundary Between the United States of America and the United Mexican States, signed on November 23, 1970;

Taking note of the Decree adding to Article 27 of the Political Constitution of the United Mexican States to establish an Exclusive Economic Zone of Mexico outside the Territorial Sea, and of the Fishery Conservation and Management Act of 1976 establishing a fishery conservation zone off the coast of the United States;

Bearing in mind that, by an exchange of notes dated November 24, 1976, they provisionally recognized maritime boundaries between the two countries between twelve and two hundred nautical miles seaward in the Gulf of Mexico and the Pacific Ocean;

Recognizing that the lines accepted by the exchange of notes dated November 24, 1976, are practical and equitable, and

Desirous of avoiding the uncertainties and problems that might arise from the provisional character of the present maritime boundaries between twelve and two hundred nautical miles seaward,

Have agreed as follows:

Article I

The United States of America and the United Mexican States agree to establish and recognize as their maritime boundaries in the Gulf of Mexico and the Pacific Ocean, in addition to those established by the Treaty of November 23, 1970, the geodetic lines connecting the points whose coordinates are:

In the Western Gulf of Mexico

GM.W-1	25°58′30.57′′ Lat.N.	96°55′27.37′′ Long.W.
GM.W-2	26°00′31.00′′ Lat.N.	96°48′29.00′′ Long.W.
GM.W-3	26°00′30.00′′ Lat.N.	95°39′26.00′′ Long.W.
GM.W-4	25°59′48.28′′ Lat.N.	93°26′42.19′′ Long.W.

In the Eastern Gulf of Mexico

GM.E-1	25°42′13.05′′ Lat.N.	91°05′24.89′′ Long.W.
GM.E-2	25°46′52.00′′ Lat.N.	90°29′41.00′′ Long.W.
GM.E-3	25°41′56.52′′ Lat.N.	88°23′05.54′′ Long.W.

In the Pacific Ocean

OP-1	32°35′22.11′′ Lat.N.	117°27′49.42′′ Long.W.
OP-2	32°37′37.00′′ Lat.N.	117°49′31.00′′ Long.W.
OP-3	31°07′58.00′′ Lat.N.	118°36′18.00′′ Long.W.
OP-4	30°32′31.20′′ Lat.N.	121°51′58.37′′ Long.W.

The coordinates of the geodetic points referred to above were determined with reference to the 1927 North American Datum.

Article II

North of the maritime boundaries established by Article I, the United Mexican States shall not, and south of said boundaries, the United States of America shall not, claim or exercise for any purpose sovereign rights or jurisdiction over the waters or seabed and subsoil.

Article III

The sole purpose of this Treaty is to establish the location of the maritime boundaries between the United States of America and the United Mexican States.

The maritime boundaries established by this Treaty shall not affect or prejudice in any manner the positions of either Party with respect to the extent of internal waters, of the territorial sea, of the high seas or of sovereign rights or jurisduction for any other purpose.

Article IV

This Treaty shall be subject to ratification and shall enter into force on the date of exchange of instruments of ratification which shall take place in Washington, D.C. at the earliest possible date.

Done at Mexico, May 4, 1978, in the English and Spanish languages, both texts being equally authentic.

For the United States of America,
For the United Mexican States,

356

6. Convention between the Government of the French Republic and the Government of the Spanish State on the Delimitation of the Continental Shelves of the two States in the Bay of Biscay

The Government of the French Republic and the Government of the Spanish State,

Taking into consideration the Convention on the Continental Shelf, done at Geneva on April 29, 1958,

Having resolved to establish the dividing line between the portions of the continental shelf in the Bay of Biscay over which the two States exercise exploration and exploitation of their natural resources,

Have agreed on the following provisions:

Article 1

This Convention applies to the Bay of Biscay beyond the 12-mile limit, from the French and Spanish base line up to a line joining Cape Ortegal in Spain to Pointe du Raz in France.

Article 2

1. The dividing line between the two States' continental shelves is the line joining points Q, R, and T.

    (a) Point Q is the point defined in Article 2(1,a) of the Convention of January 29, 1974 between France and Spain on the delimitation of the territorial sea and contiguous zone in the Bay of Biscay.

The coordinates of point Q, according to the most recent surveys, are as follows:

Latitude: 43°35′43′′N.
Longitude: 1°48′08′′W. (GR)

    (b) Up to point R, defined below, the line QR is, in principle, the line whose points are all equidistant from the French and Spanish baselines. In application of the foregoing, line QR consists of the geodetic lines following the great-circle arcs joining the points having the following coordinates:

	Latitude N.	*Longitude W.* (GR)
Q1	43°39′40′′	1°51′30′′
Q2	43°43′59′′	1°55′30′′
Q3	43°48′00′′	2°02′40′′
Q4	43°53′25′′	2°11′25′′

Q5	44°00'00''	2°16'00''
Q6	44°06'30''	2°20'30''
Q7	44°13'00''	2°25'30''
Q8	44°19'10''	2°31'00''
Q9	44°24'40''	2°36'19''
Q10	44°30'00''	2°42'30''
Q11	44°35'45''	2°50'27''
Q12	44°39'50''	2°57'00''
Q13	44°45'25''	3°03'50''
R	44°52'00''	3°10'20''

(c) Point T is defined by the following coordinates:
Latitude: 45°28'30''N.
Longitude: 6°41'14''W. (GR)

Line RT is the geodetic line following the great-circle arc joining points R and T.

2. The dividing line is indicated, in conformity with the criteria and data given above, on French marine chart No. 5381 published in 1972, attached to this Convention (Annex 1).

Article 3

1. The contracting parties agree to apply the supplementary procedures provided in Annex II for the awarding of rights to prospect for and exploit natural resources in the zone defined by the geodetic lines joining the points having the following coordinates:

	Latitude N.	*Longitude W.* (GR)
Z1	45°30'00''	5°40'00''
Z2	45°30'00''	5°00'00''
Z3	45°00'00''	5°00'00''
Z4	45°00'00''	5°40'00''

2. The boundaries of this zone are indicated on the marine chart referred to in Article 2(2) of this Convention.

Article 4

1. If a deposit of a natural resource lies across the continental shelves' dividing line, and if the portion of the deposit on one side of the dividing line is whol-

358

ly or partially exploitable by means of installations located on the other side of the line, the Contracting Parties, acting in conjunction with the holders of the exploitation rights, if such exist, shall seek an agreement on terms for exploiting the deposit so that such exploitation may be as profitable as possible and in such manner that each of the Parties shall preserve all its rights over the natural resources of its continental shelf. This procedure is particularly applicable if the method for exploiting the portion of the deposit located on one side of the dividing line affects conditions for exploiting the other portion of the deposit.

2.   In the event that the natural resources of a deposit lying across the dividing line have already been exploited, the Contracting Parties, acting in conjunction with the holders of exploitation rights, if such exist, shall seek an agreement on appropriate compensation.

Article 5

1.   The Contracting Parties shall seek to settle any disagreement arising with regard to interpretation or application of this Convention as quickly as possible, through diplomatic channels.

2.   In the event that a disagreement is not settled within four months of notification by one Contracting Party of its intention to initiate the procedure referred to in the preceding paragraph, it shall be submitted to an arbitral court by request of either Party.

3.   The arbitral court shall be constituted in each instance as follows: Each Party shall appoint an arbiter and these two arbiters shall jointly appoint a third, who is not a national of either Party; the third arbiter shall preside over the arbitral court. If the arbiters are not appointed within two months following notification by one Contracting State of its intention to refer the matter to the court, or if the arbiters appointed by the two Parties do not reach an agreement, within one month of the appointment of the second of them, on the appointment of the third arbiter, either Party may request the President of the International Court of Justice to make the necessary appointments. If the President of the Court is a national of either Party, or is unable to act for any reason, the Vice President of the Court shall make the appointments. If the President is also a national of one of the two Parties, or is unable to act for any reason, the Court's senior judge who is not a national of either Party shall make the appointments.

4.   Each Contracting Party shall cover its arbiter's costs and one-half of all other costs. The arbitral court shall establish its own rules of procedure if the Parties do not establish them within two months following the appointment of the second arbiter.

5.   The arbitral court shall adopt decisions by majority vote. These decisions shall be binding upon the Parties.

6. The arbitral court may adopt precautionary measures at the request of either Party.

Article 6

None of the provisions of this Convention shall affect the rules governing superjacent waters and air space.

Article 7

The Contracting Parties shall attempt to prevent the explorations of the continental shelf of the Bay of Biscay and the exploitation of its natural resources from threatening the ecological balance and legitimate uses of the marine environment, and shall consult with each other to this end.

Article 8

In the event that a multilateral treaty which modifies the Convention on the Continental Shelf done at Geneva on April 29, 1958 and which would be capable of affecting the provisions of this Convention enters into force between the Contracting Parties, they shall consult with each other immediately with a view to agreeing on such amendments to the provisions of this Convention as appear necessary.

Article 9

Each Contracting Party shall notify the other of completion of the constitutional procedures necessary for the Convention's entry into force. The Convention shall enter into force upon the date of the final notification.

In witness whereof, the undersigned plenipotentiaries, duly authorized for this purpose by their respective Governments, have signed this Convention.

Done at Paris on January 29, 1974 in two copies, each in French and Spanish, both texts being equally authentic.

For the Government of the French Republic: J.P. Cabouat
For the Government of the Spanish State: A. Poch

Annex II. Provisions applicable to the zone defined in Article 3 of this Convention

1.   The Contracting Parties encourage exploitation of the zone conducive to equal distribution of its resources.

2.   Consistent with this principle, each Contracting Party, acting in accordance with its mining regulations, undertakes to encourage agreements between companies applying for prospecting rights in the zone in order to permit companies having the nationality of the other Party to participate in such prospecting on an equal partnership basis, with financing of operations proportional to each company's interest.

3.   To this end, any application for prospecting rights in one Contracting Party's sector must be communicated to the other Party. The latter Party shall have six months in which to designate one or more companies of its nationality to participate in the rights-awarding procedure with the other applicants.

4.   If the applicant companies do not reach an agreement within one year following their designation, the Contracting Party with jurisdiction over the sector in question shall consult with the other Contracting Party before making any decision to award rights.

5.   Companies holding prospecting and exploitation rights and linked by partnership agreements concerning the zone must notify the Parties of any changes they may make in these agreements. In this instance, and at the request of one of them, the Parties would confer in order to examine the significance of the change and its effects on the objective referred to in Paragraph 1 of this Annex.

6.   Any draft amendment of the rights granted by one Contracting Party for prospecting and exploitation of its sector of the zone shall be communicated to the other Contracting Party, which shall have three months in which to submit comments and proposals, if it so desires. In the event of disagreement on the proposed amendment, the Parties may have recourse to the procedures provided for in Article 5 of this Convention.

7.   The Contracting Parties shall agree on appropriate procedures for encouraging the partnership agreements referred to in Paragraph 2 above, and also on the system for exporting to one Party the products obtained from the exploitation in the other Party's sector by the company or companies designated by the first Party.

Paris, January 29, 1974

To His Excellency Antonio Poch, Minister Plenipotentiary, Head of the Spanish Delegation in the negotiations on the delimitation of the Spanish and French continental shelves, Madrid.

Your Excellency:

Article 2(b) of the Convention signed on this date by the Government of the Spanish State and the Government of the French Republic on the delimitation of the continental shelves of the two States in the Bay of Biscay stipulates that 'line QR is, in principle, the line whose points are all equidistant from the French and Spanish baselines.' It is in application of this principle that the same article of the Convention lists the coordinates of a certain number of points located along this equidistant line between points Q and R.

In the course of our negotiations we acknowledged that the geodetic and cartographic data and techniques utilized to establish the points listed in Article 2(b) of the Convention might be improved in the future. We nevertheless agreed that, even should this occur, and subject to a later agreement between the Parties on a different solution, the dividing line between the Spanish and French continental shelves between points Q and R would continue to be determined by the geodetic lines following the great-circle arcs joining the points whose coordinates are listed in the Convention.

If the foregoing meets with your approval, I propose that this note and your reply constitute an Agreement between our two Governments on the interpretation of Article 2(b) of the Convention. This Agreement shall take effect from the date of your reply.

Accept, Excellency, the assurances of my very distinguished consideration.

J.-P. Cabouat, Minister Plenipotentiary, Head of the French Delegation in the negotiations on the delimitation of the French and Spanish continental shelves

Paris, January 29, 1974

To Mr. J.-P. Cabouat, Head of the French Delegation in the negotiations on the delimitation of the French and Spanish continental shelves, Ministry of Foreign Affairs, Paris

Excellency:

I have the honor to acknowledge receipt of your note of this date, the translation of which reads as follows:

[The three substantive paragraphs of this note are the same as those of the French note, dated January 29, 1974, translated above.]

I have the honor to inform you that the Spanish Government is in agreement with the foregoing.

Accept, Excellency, the assurance of my very high consideration.

Antonio Poch y Gutierrez de Caviedes, Head of the Spanish Delegation

7. Treaty between the United States of America and the Cook Islands on Friendship and Delimitation of the Maritime Boundary between the United States of America and the Cook Islands

The two governments,

Desiring to strengthen the existing bonds of friendship between their countries and in particular between the peoples of the Cook Islands and American Samoa,

Noting the Territorial Sea and Exclusive Economic Zone Act of 1977 of the Cook Islands,

Noting the Fishery Conservation and Management Act of 1976 of the United States of America,

Desiring to establish a maritime boundary between the United States of America and the Cook Islands,

Noting that the United States of America has maintained a claim to sovereignty over the islands of Pukapuka (Danger), Manihiki, Rakahanga and Penrhyn,

Noting further that this claim has not been recognized by the Cook Islands,

Have agreed as follows:

Article I

The maritime boundary between the United States of America and the Cook Islands shall be determined by the geodetic lines connecting the following coordinates:

Latitude (South)	Longitude (West)
17°33'28''	16°38'35''
16°45'30''	166°01'39''
16°23'29''	165°45'11''
16°18'30''	165°41'29''
16°08'42''	165°34'12''

15°44'58''	165°16'36''
15°38'47''	165°12'03''
15°14'04''	165°18'29''
15°00'09''	165°22'07''
14°03'30''	165°37'20''
13°44'56''	165°58'44''
13°35'44''	166°09'19''
13°21'25''	166°25'42''
13°14'03''	166°34'03''
13°11'25''	166°37'02''
12°57'51''	166°52'21''
12°41'22''	167°11'01''
12°28'40''	167°25'20''
12°01'55''	168°10'24''
11°43'54''	168°27'58''
11°02'40''	168°29'21''
10°52'31''	168°29'42''
10°12'49''	168°31'02''
10°12'44''	168°31'02''
10°01'26''	168°31'25''

Article II

The geodetic and computational bases used are the World Geodetic System, 1972 (WGS 72) and the following charts and aerial plans:

Rose Island – U.S. Chart Nos. 83484, 6th ed., March 26/77, 1:80,000 – local datum;

Manua Islands – U.S. Chart Nos. 83484, 6th ed., March 26/77, 1:80,000 – corrected for WGS 72, 1980;

Swains Island – U.S. Chart Nos. 83484, 6th ed., March 26/77, 1:40,000 – astro datum 1939;

Palmerston Atoll – Aerial Plan No. 1036/8H (N.Z. Lands & Survey), 1:50,400, 1976 – local datum;

Suwarrow (Suvorov) Atoll – Aerial Plan No. 1036/8E (N.Z. Lands & Survey), 1:50,400, 1975 – local datum;

Nassau Island – Aerial Plan No. 1036/8B (N.Z. Lands & Survey), 1:148,000, 1974 – local datum;

Pukapuka (Danger) Island – Aerial Plan No. 1036/8D (N.Z. Lands & Survey), 1:28,800, 1975 – local datum;

364

Niue – British Admiralty Chart BA 968, 16th ed., March 1979, 1:150,000, corrections to 1979 – local datum;

Fakaofo Atoll – Aerial Plan No. 1036/7C (N.Z. Lands & Survey), 1:18,000, 1974 – local datum.

Article III

On the side of the maritime boundary adjacent to the Cook Islands, the United States of America shall not, and on the side of the maritime boundary adjacent to American Samoa the Cook Islands shall not, claim or exercise for any purpose sovereign rights or jurisdiction over the waters of the seabed and subsoil.

Article IV

The maritime boundary established by this Treaty shall not affect or prejudice in any manner any government's position with respect to the rules of international law concerned with the exercise of jurisdiction over the waters or seabed and subsoil or any other matter relating to the law of the sea.

Article V

The United States of America recognizes the sovereignty of the Cook Islands over the islands of Penrhyn, Pukapuka (Danger), Manihiki and Rakahanga.

Article VI

The Government of the United States of America and the Government of the Cook Islands, in the spirit of peace and friendship existing between the two governments and peoples, agree to cooperate with a view to promoting social and economic development in the Cook Islands, and to work toward the advancement of the South Pacific region as a whole. To these ends, they shall promote discussions between their peoples and appropriate government entities, in particular between the peoples of the Cook Islands and American Samoa.

Article VII

This Treaty shall be subject to ratification and shall enter into force on the date of the exchange of instruments of ratification.

DONE in duplicate, in the English and Maori languages, of which English shall be the authentic text, at Rarotonga this eleventh day of June 1980.

For the Government of the United States of America:
For the Government of the Cook Islands:

8. Treaty between the Union of Soviet Socialist Republics and the Polish People's Republic concerning the Boundary of the Continental Shelf in the Gulf of Gdansk and the South-Eastern Part of the Baltic Sea, Done at Warsaw on 28 August 1969

The Presidium of the Supreme Soviet of the Union of Soviet Socialist Republics and the Council of State of the Polish People's Republic,

Desiring to intensify and expand the friendly, good-neighbourly relations existing between the Union of Soviet Socialist Republics and the Polish People's Republic,

Desiring to define the boundary of the continental shelf between the Union of Soviet Socialist Republics and the Polish People's Republic in the Gulf of Gdansk and the south-eastern part of the Baltic Sea,

Having regard to the provisions of the Geneva Convention on the Continental Shelf of 29 April 1958,

Reaffirming the principles set out in the Declaration on the Continental Shelf in the Baltic Sea signed in Moscow on 23 October 1968, by the Governments of the Union of Soviet Socialist Republics, the Polish People's Republic and the German Democratic Republic,

Have decided to conclude this Treaty . . .

. . .

Article 1

The boundary of the continental shelf between the Union of Soviet Socialist Republics and the Polish People's Republic in the Gulf of Gdansk and the south-eastern part of the Baltic Sea shall, with slight variations, be a line equidistant from the nearest points of the baselines from which the breadth of the territorial waters of each Contracting Party is measured.

The said line shall begin at the point at which the outer limit of Polish territorial waters intersects the line delimiting the territorial waters of the USSR and the Polish People's Republic established in the Protocol of 18 March 1958 between the Government of the Union of Soviet Socialist Republics and the Government of the Polish People's Republic concerning the delimitation of Soviet

and Polish territorial waters in the Gulf of Gdansk of the Baltic Sea; it shall follow the line of the boundary of the territorial waters of the USSR to its terminal point and shall then continue in the same direction to point A, whose geographical co-ordinates are 54°40.2′ north latitude and 19°18.9′ east longitude, thence through the points whose geographical co-ordinates are the following:
B – 54°48.9′ north latitude, 19°20.7′ east longitude,
C – 55°20.8′ north latitude, 19°03.8′ east longitude,
D – 55°51.00 north latitude, 18°56.2′ east longitude,
and then up to the point of intersection of the boundaries of the continental shelf appertaining to the Union of Soviet Socialist Republics, the Polish People's Republic, and the Kingdom of Sweden.

Article 2

The boundary of the continental shelf between the Union of Soviet Socialist Republics and the Polish People's Republic defined in article 1 is indicated on chart No. 1150, issued in 1966 by the Hydrographical Department of the Ministry of Defence of the USSR, which is annexed to this Treaty and constitutes an integral part thereof.

All the geographical co-ordinates referred to in this Treaty conform to the system employed in the Chart.

Article 3

The provisions of this Treaty shall in no way affect the legal status of the waters of the high seas superjacent to the continental shelf or that of the airspace above those waters.

Article 4

This Treaty shall be registered with the Secretariat of the United Nations in accordance with Article 102 of the Charter of the United Nations.

Article 5

This Treaty is subject to ratification and shall enter into force on the date of exchange of the instruments of ratification, which shall take place at Moscow as soon as possible.

DONE at Warsaw on 28 August 1969, in duplicate in the Polish and Russian languages, both texts being equally authentic.

United Nations Convention on the Law of the Sea, 1982 (Text of Articles)

A. Text of Articles on outer limits of maritime zones

Article 3. Breadth of the territorial sea

Every State has the right to establish the breadth of its territorial sea up to a limit not exceeding 12 nautical miles, measured from baselines determined in accordance with this Convention.

Article 4. Outer limit of the territorial sea

The outer limit of the territorial sea is the line every point of which is at a distance from the nearest point of the baseline equal to the breadth of the territorial sea.

Article 33. Contiguous zone

1.   In a zone contiguous to its territorial sea, described as the contiguous zone, the coastal State may exercise the control necessary to:
(a) prevent infringement of its customs, fiscal, immigration or sanitary laws and regulations within its territory or territorial sea;
(b) punish infringement of the above laws and regulations committed within its territory or territorial sea.
2.   The contiguous zone may not extend beyond 24 nautical miles from the baselines from which the breadth of the territorial sea is measured.

Article 57. Breadth of the exclusive economic zone

The exclusive economic zone shall not extend beyond 200 nautical miles from the baselines from which the breadth of the territorial sea is measured.

Article 76. Definition of the continental shelf

1.   The continental shelf of a coastal State comprises the sea-bed and subsoil of the submarine areas that extend beyond its territorial sea throughout the natural prolongation of its land territory to the outer edge of the continental margin, or to a distance of 200 nautical miles from the baselines from which the breadth of the territorial sea is measured where the outer edge of the continental margin does not extend up to that distance.

2.   The continental shelf of a coastal State shall not extend beyond the limits provided for in paragraphs 4 to 6.

3.   The continental margin comprises the submerged prolongation of the land mass of the coastal State, and consists of the sea-bed and subsoil of the shelf, the slope and the rise. It does not include the deep ocean floor with its oceanic ridges or the subsoil thereof.

4.   (a) For the purpose of this Convention, the coastal State shall establish the outer edge of the continental margin wherever the margin extends beyond 200 nautical miles from the baselines from which the breadth of the territorial sea is measured, by either:
(i)   a line delineated in accordance with paragraph 7 by reference to the outermost fixed points at each of which the thickness of sedimentary rocks is at least 1 per cent of the shortest distance from such points to the foot of the continental slope; or
(ii) a line delineated in accordance with paragraph 7 by reference to fixed points not more than 60 nautical miles from the foot of the continental slope.
(b) In the absence of evidence to the contrary, the foot of the continental slope shall be determined as the point of maximum change in the gradient at its base.

5.   The fixed points comprising the line of the outer limits of the continental shelf on the sea-bed, drawn in accordance with paragraph 4(a)(i) and (ii), either shall not exceed 350 nautical miles from the baselines from which the breadth of the territorial sea is measured or shall not exceed 100 nautical miles from the 2,500 metre isobath, which is a line connecting the depth of 2,500 metres.

6.   Notwithstanding the provisions of paragraph 5, on submarine ridges, the outer limit of the continental shelf shall not exceed 350 nautical miles from the baselines from which the breadth of the territorial sea is measured. This

paragraph does not apply to submarine elevations that are natural components of the continental margin, such as its plateaux, rises, caps, banks and spurs.

7. The coastal State shall delineate the outer limits of its continental shelf, where that shelf extends beyond 200 nautical miles from the baselines from which the breadth of the territorial sea is measured by straight lines not exceeding 60 nautical miles in length, connecting fixed points, defined by co-ordinates of latitude and longitude.

8. Information on the limits of the continental shelf beyond 200 nautical miles from the baselines from which the breadth of the territorial sea is measured shall be submitted by the coastal State to the Commission on the Limits of the Continental Shelf set up under Annex II on the basis of equitable geographical representation. The Commission shall make recommendations to coastal States on matters related to the establishment of the outer limits of their continental shelf. The limits of the shelf established by a coastal State on the basis of these recommendations shall be final and binding.

9. The coastal State shall deposit with the Secretary-General of the United Nations charts and relevant information, including geodetic data, permanently describing the outer limits of its continental shelf. The Secretary-General shall give due publicity thereto.

10. The provisions of this article are without prejudice to the question of delimitation of the continental shelf between States with opposite or adjacent coasts.

ANNEX II.
COMMISSION ON THE LIMITS OF THE CONTINENTAL SHELF

Article 1

In accordance with the provisions of article 76, a Commission on the Limits of the Continental Shelf beyond 200 nautical miles shall be established in conformity with the following articles.

Article 2

1. The Commission shall consist of 21 members who shall be experts in the field of geology, geophysics or hydrography, elected by States Parties to this Convention from among their nationals, having due regard to the need to ensure equitable geographical representation, who shall serve in their personal capacities.

2. The initial election shall be held as soon as possible but in any case within

18 months after the date of entry into force of this Convention. At least three months before the date of each election, the Secretary-General of the United Nations shall address a letter to the States Parties, inviting the submission of nominations, after appropriate regional consultations, within three months. The Secretary-General shall prepare a list in alphabetical order of all persons thus nominated and shall submit it to all the States Parties.

3. Elections of the members of the Commission shall be held at a meeting of States Parties convened by the Secretary-General at United Nations Headquarters. At that meeting, for which two thirds of the States Parties shall constitute a quorum, the persons elected to the Commission shall be those nominees who obtain a two-thirds majority of the votes of the representatives of States Parties present and voting. Not less than three members shall be elected from each geographical region.

4. The members of the Commission shall be elected for a term of five years. They shall be eligible for re-election.

5. The State Party which submitted the nomination of a member of the Commission shall defray the expenses of that member while in performance of Commission duties. The coastal State concerned shall defray the expenses incurred in respect of the advice referred to in article 3, paragraph 1(b), of this Annex. The secretariat of the Commission shall be provided by the Secretary-General of the United Nations.

Article 3

1. The functions of the Commission shall be:
(a) to consider the data and other material submitted by coastal States concerning the outer limits of the continental shelf in areas where those limits extend beyond 200 nautical miles, and to make recommendations in accordance with article 76 and the Statement of Understanding adopted on 29 August 1980 by the Third United Nations Conference on the Law of the Sea;
(b) to provide scientific and technical advice, if requested by the coastal State concerned during the preparation of the data referred to in sub-paragraph (a).

2. The Commission may co-operate, to the extent considered necessary and useful, with the Intergovernmental Oceanographic Commission of UNESCO, the International Hydrographic Organization and other competent international organizations with a view to exchanging scientific and technical information which might be of assistance in discharging the Commission's responsibilities.

Article 4

Where a coastal State intends to establish, in accordance with article 76, the outer limits of its continental shelf beyond 200 nautical miles, it shall submit particulars of such limits to the Commission along with supporting scientific and technical data as soon as possible but in any case within 10 years of the entry into force of this Convention for that State. The coastal State shall at the same time give the names of any Commission members who have provided it with scientific and technical advice.

Article 5

Unless the Commission decides otherwise, the Commission shall function by way of sub-commissions composed of seven members, appointed in a balanced manner taking into account the specific elements of each submission by a coastal State. Nationals of the coastal State making the submission who are members of the Commission and any Commission member who has assisted a coastal State by providing scientific and technical advice with respect to the delineation shall not be a member of the sub-commission dealing with that submission but has the right to participate as a member in the proceedings of the Commission concerning the said submission. The coastal State which has made a submission to the Commission may send its representatives to participate in the relevant proceedings without the right to vote.

Article 6

1. The sub-commission shall submit its recommendations to the Commission.
   2. Approval by the Commission of the recommendations of the sub-commission shall be by a majority of two thirds of Commission members present and voting.
   3. The recommendations of the Commission shall be submitted in writing to the coastal State which made the submission and to the Secretary-General of the United Nations.

Article 7

Coastal States shall establish the outer limits of the continental shelf in conformity with the provisions of article 76, paragraph 8, and in accordance with the appropriate national procedures.

Article 8

In the case of disagreement by the coastal State with the recommendations of the Commission, the coastal State shall, within a reasonable time, make a revised or new submission to the Commission.

Article 9

The actions of the Commission shall not prejudice matters relating to delimitation of boundaries between States with opposite or adjacent coasts.

FINAL ACT

ANNEX II. STATEMENT OF UNDERSTANDING CONCERNING A SPECIFIC METHOD TO BE USED IN ESTABLISHING THE OUTER EDGE OF THE CONTINENTAL MARGIN

The Third United Nations Conference on the Law of the Sea
    Considering the special characteristics of a State's continental margin where: (1) the average distance at which the 200 metre isobath occurs is not more than 20 nautical miles; (2) the greater proportion of the sedimentary rock of the continental margin lies beneath the rise; and
    Taking into account the inequity that would result to that State from the application to its continental margin of article 76 of the Convention, in that, the mathematical average of the thickness of sedimentary rock along a line established at the maximum distance permissible in accordance with the provisions of paragraph 4(a)(i) and (ii) of that article as representing the entire outer edge of the continental margin would not be less than 3.5 kilometers; and that more than half of the margin would be excluded thereby;
    Recognizes that such State may, notwithstanding the provisions of article 76, establish the outer edge of its continental margin by straight lines not exceeding 60 nautical miles in length connecting fixed points, defined by latitude and longitude, at each of which the thickness of sedimentary rock is not less than 1 kilometre,
    Where a State establishes the outer edge of its continental margin by applying the method set forth in the preceding paragraph of this statement, this method may also be utilized by a neighbouring State for delineating the outer edge of its continental margin on a common geological feature, where its outer edge would lie on such feature on a line established at the maximum distance permissible in accordance with article 76, paragraph 4(a)(i) and (ii), along which the

374

mathematical average of the thickness of sedimentary rock is not less than 3.5 kilometres,

The Conference requests the Commission on the Limits of the Continental Shelf set up pursuant to Annex II of the Convention, to be governed by the terms of this Statement when making its recommendations on matters related to the establishment of the outer edge of the continental margins of these States in the southern part of the Bay of Bengal.

Article 121. Régime of islands

1.   An island is a naturally formed area of land, surrounded by water, which is above water at high tide.

2.   Except as provided for in paragraph 3, the territorial sea, the contiguous zone, the exclusive economic zone and the continental shelf of an island are determined in accordance with the provisions of this Convention applicable to other land territory.

3.   Rocks which cannot sustain human habitation or economic life of their own shall have no exclusive economic zone or continental shelf.

B. Text of Articles on baselines

Article 5. Normal baseline

Except where otherwise provided in this Convention, the normal baseline for measuring the breadth of the territorial sea is the low-water line along the coast as marked on large-scale charts officially recognized by the coastal State.

Article 6. Reefs

In the case of islands situated on atolls or of islands having fringing reefs, the baseline for measuring the breadth of the territorial sea is the seaward low-water line of the reef, as shown by the appropriate symbol on charts officially recognized by the coastal State.

Article 7. Straight baselines

1.   In localities where the coastline is deeply indented and cut into, or if there is a fringe of islands along the coast in its immediate vicinity, the method of

straight baselines joining appropriate points may be employed in drawing the baseline from which the breadth of the territorial sea is measured.

2. Where because of the presence of a delta and other natural conditions the coastline is highly unstable, the appropriate points may be selected along the furthest seaward extent of the low-water line and, notwithstanding subsequent regression of the low-water line, the straight baselines shall remain effective until changed by the coastal State in accordance with this Convention.

3. The drawing of straight baselines must not depart to any appreciable extent from the general direction of the coast, and the sea areas lying within the lines must be sufficiently closely linked to the land domain to be subject to the régime of internal waters.

4. Straight baselines shall not be drawn to and from low-tide elevations, unless lighthouses or similar installations which are permanently above sea level have been built on them or except in instances where the drawing of baselines to and from such elevations has received general international recognition.

5. Where the method of straight baselines is applicable under paragraph 1, account may be taken, in determining particular baselines, of economic interests peculiar to the region concerned, the reality and the importance of which are clearly evidenced by long usage.

6. The system of straight baselines may not be applied by a State in such a manner as to cut off the territorial sea of another State from the high seas or an exclusive economic zone.

Article 8. Internal waters

1. Except as provided in Part IV, waters on the landward side of the baseline of the territorial sea form part of the internal waters of the State.

2. Where the establishment of a straight baseline in accordance with the method set forth in article 7 has the effect of enclosing as internal waters areas which had not previously been considered as such, a right of innocent passage as provided in this Convention shall exist in those waters.

Article 9. Mouths of rivers

If a river flows directly into the sea, the baseline shall be a straight line across the mouth of the river between points on the low-water line of its banks.

376

Article 10. Bays

1. This article relates only to bays the coasts of which belong to a single State.

2. For the purposes of this Convention, a bay is a well-marked indentation whose penetration is in such proportion to the width of its mouth as to contain land-locked waters and constitute more than a mere curvature of the coast. An indentation shall not, however, be regarded as a bay unless its area is as large as, or larger than, that of the semi-circle whose diameter is a line drawn across the mouth of that indentation.

3. For the purpose of measurement, the area of an indentation is that lying between the low-water mark around the shore of the indentation and a line joining the low-water mark of its natural entrance points. Where, because of the presence of islands, an indentation has more than one mouth, the semi-circle shall be drawn on a line as long as the sum total of the lengths of the lines across the different mouths. Islands within an indentation shall be included as if they were part of the water area of the indentation.

4. If the distance between the low-water marks of the natural entrance points of a bay does not exceed 24 nautical miles, a closing line may be drawn between these two low-water marks, and the waters enclosed thereby shall be considered as internal waters.

5. Where the distance between the low-water marks of the natural entrance points of a bay exceeds 24 nautical miles, a straight baseline of 24 nautical miles shall be drawn within the bay in such a manner as to enclose the maximum area of water that is possible with a line of that length.

6. The foregoing provisions do not apply to so-called 'historic' bays, or in any case where the system of straight baselines provided for in article 7 is applied.

Article 11. Ports

For the purpose of delimiting the territorial sea, the outermost permanent harbour works which form an integral part of the harbour system are regarded as forming part of the coast. Off-shore installations and artificial islands shall not be considered as permanent harbour works.

Article 12. Roadsteads

Roadsteads which are normally used for the loading, unloading and anchoring of ships, and which would otherwise be situated wholly or partly outside the outer limit of the territorial sea, are included in the territorial sea.

Article 13. Low-tide elevations

1.   A low-tide elevation is a naturally formed area of land which is surrounded by and above water at low tide but submerged at high tide. Where a low-tide elevation is situated wholly or partly at a distance not exceeding the breadth of the territorial sea from the mainland or an island, the low-water line on that elevation may be used as the baseline for measuring the breadth of the territorial sea.

2.   Where a low-tide elevation is wholly situated at a distance exceeding the breadth of the territorial sea from the mainland or an island, it has no territorial sea of its own.

Article 14. Combination of methods for determining baselines

The coastal State may determine baselines in turn by any of the methods provided for in the foregoing articles to suit different conditions.

Article 47. Archipelagic baselines

1.   An archipelagic State may draw straight archipelagic baselines joining the outermost points of the outermost islands and drying reefs of the archipelago provided that within such baselines are included the main islands and an area in which the ratio of the area of the water to the area of the land, including atolls, is between 1 to 1 and 9 to 1.

2.   The length of such baselines shall not exceed 100 nautical miles, except that up to 3 per cent of the total number of baselines enclosing any archipelago may exceed that length, up to a maximum length of 125 nautical miles.

3.   The drawing of such baselines shall not depart to any appreciable extent from the general configuration of the archipelago.

4.   Such baselines shall not be drawn to and from low-tide elevations, unless lighthouses or similar installations which are permanently above sea level have been built on them or where a low-tide elevation is situated wholly or partly at a distance not exceeding the breadth of the territorial sea from the nearest island.

5.   The system of such baselines shall not be applied by an archipelagic State in such a manner as to cut off from the high seas or the exclusive economic zone the territorial sea of another State.

6.   If a part of the archipelagic waters of an archipelagic State lies between two parts of an immediately adjacent neighbouring State, existing rights and all other legitimate interests which the latter State has traditionally exercised in

such waters and all rights stipulated by agreement between those States shall continue to be respected.

7. For the purpose of computing the ratio of water to land under paragraph 1, land areas may include waters lying within the fringing reefs of islands and atolls, including that part of a steep-sided oceanic plateau which is enclosed or nearly enclosed by a chain of limestone islands and drying reefs lying on the perimeter of the plateau.

8. The baselines drawn in accordance with this article shall be shown on charts of a scale or scales adequate for ascertaining their position. Alternatively, lists of geographical co-ordinates of points, specifying the geodetic datum, may be substituted.

9. The archipelagic State shall give due publicity to such charts or lists of geographical co-ordinates and shall deposit a copy of each such chart or list with the Secretary-General of the United Nations.

C. Text of Articles on delimitation of maritime zones between States with opposite or adjacent coasts

Article 15. Delimitation of the territorial sea between States with opposite or adjacent coasts

Where the coasts of two States are opposite or adjacent to each other, neither of the two States is entitled, failing agreement between them to the contrary, to extend its territorial sea beyond the median line every point of which is equidistant from the nearest points on the baselines from which the breadth of the territorial seas of each of the two States is measured. The above provision does not apply, however, where it is necessary by reason of historic title or other special circumstances to delimit the territorial seas of the two States in a way which is at variance therewith.

Article 16. Charts and lists of geographical co-ordinates

1. The baselines for measuring the breadth of the territorial sea determined in accordance with articles 7, 9 and 10, or the limits derived therefrom, and the lines of delimitation drawn in accordance with articles 12 and 15 shall be shown on charts of a scale or scales adequate for ascertaining their position. Alternatively, a list of geographical co-ordinates of points, specifying the geodetic datum, may be substituted.

2. The coastal State shall give due publicity to such charts or lists of geographical co-ordinates and shall deposit a copy of each such chart or list with the Secretary-General of the United Nations.

Article 74. Delimitation of the exclusive economic zone between States with opposite or adjacent coasts

1.   The delimitation of the exclusive economic zone between States with opposite or adjacent coasts shall be effected by agreement on the basis of international law, as referred to in Article 38 of the Statute of the International Court of Justice, in order to achieve an equitable solution.

2.   If no agreement can be reached within a reasonable period of time, the States concerned shall resort to the procedures provided for in Part XV.

3.   Pending agreement as provided for in paragraph 1, the States concerned, in a spirit of understanding and co-operation, shall make every effort to enter into provisional arrangements of a practical nature and, during this transitional period, not to jeopardize or hamper the reaching of the final agreement. Such arrangements shall be without prejudice to the final delimitation.

4.   Where there is an agreement in force between the States concerned, questions relating to the delimitation of the exclusive economic zone shall be determined in accordance with the provisions of that agreement.

Article 75. Charts and lists of geographical co-ordinates

1.   Subject to this Part, the outer limit lines of the exclusive economic zone and the lines of delimitation drawn in accordance with article 74 shall be shown on charts of a scale or scales adequate for ascertaining their position. Where appropriate, lists of geographical co-ordinates of points, specifying the geodetic datum, may be substituted for such outer limit lines or lines of delimitation.

2.   The coastal State shall give due publicity to such charts or lists of geographical co-ordinates and shall deposit a copy of each such chart or list with the Secretary-General of the United Nations.

Article 83. Delimitation of the continental shelf between States with opposite or adjacent coasts

1.   The delimitation of the continental shelf between States with opposite or adjacent coasts shall be effected by agreement on the basis of international law, as referred to in Article 38 of the Statute of the International Court of Justice, in order to achieve an equitable solution.

2.   If no agreement can be reached within a reasonable period of time, the States concerned shall resort to the procedures provided for in Part XV.

3.   Pending agreement as provided for in paragraph 1, the States concerned, in a spirit of understanding and co-operation, shall make every effort to enter

into provisional arrangements of a practical nature and, during this transitional period, not to jeopardize or hamper the reaching of the final agreement. Such arrangements shall be without prejudice to the final delimitation.

4. Where there is an agreement in force between the States concerned, questions relating to the delimitation of the continental shelf shall be determined in accordance with the provisions of that agreement.

Article 84. Charts and lists of geographical co-ordinates

1. Subject to this Part, the outer limit lines of the continental shelf and the lines of delimitation drawn in accordance with article 83 shall be shown on charts of a scale or scales adequate for ascertaining their position. Where appropriate, lists of geographical co-ordinates of points, specifying the geodetic datum, may be substituted for such outer limit lines or lines of delimitation.

2. The coastal State shall give due publicity to such charts or lists of geographical co-ordinates and shall deposit a copy of each such chart or list with the Secretary-General of the United Nations and, in the case of those showing the outer limit lines of the continental shelf, with the Secretary-General of the Authority.

Article 298. Optional exceptions to applicability of section 2

1. When signing, ratifying or acceding to this Convention or at any time thereafter, a State may, without prejudice to the obligations arising under section 1, declare in writing that it does not accept any one or more of the procedures provided for in section 2 with respect to one or more of the following categories of disputes:

(a) (i) disputes concerning the interpretation or application of articles 15, 74 and 83 relating to sea boundary delimitations, or those involving historic bays or titles, provided that a State having made such a declaration shall, when such a dispute arises subsequent to the entry into force of this Convention and where no agreement within a reasonable period of time is reached in negotiations between the parties, at the request of any party to the dispute, accept submission of the matter to conciliation under Annex V, section 2; and provided further that any dispute that necessarily involves the concurrent consideration of any unsettled dispute concerning sovereignty or other rights over continental or insular land territory shall be excluded from such submission;

(ii) after the conciliation commission has presented its report, which shall state the reasons on which it is based, the parties shall negotiate an agreement on the basis of that report; if these negotiations do not result in an agreement, the parties shall, by mutual consent, submit the question to one of the procedures provided for in section 2, unless the parties otherwise agree;

(iii) the subparagraph does not apply to any sea boundary dispute finally settled by an arrangement between the parties, or to any such dispute which is to be settled in accordance with a bilateral or multilateral agreement binding upon those parties; . . .

Bibliography

Part One. Scope, limits of maritime zones, technical aspects (Chapters 1-4)

Alexander, Lewis M., 'Baseline Delimitations and Maritime Boundaries', *Virginia Journal of International Law*, Vol. 23, No. 4 (Summer 1983), pp. 503-536.

Boggs, S. Whittemore, 'Delimitation of the Territorial Sea', *American Journal of International Law*, Vol. 24 (1930), pp. 541-555.

Boggs, S. Whittemore, 'Delimitation of Seaward Areas under National Jurisdiction', *American Journal of International Law*, Vol. 45, No. 2 (April 1951), pp. 240-266.

Bowett, D.W., 'The Second United Nations Conference on the Law of the Sea', *International and Comparative Law Quarterly*, Vol. 9 (July 1960), pp. 415-435.

Brown, E.D., 'The Continental Shelf and the Exclusive Economic Zone: The Problem of Delimitation at UNCLOS III', *Maritime Policy Management* (1977), pp. 377-408. (For outer limits of continental shelf.)

Colombos, C. John, *The International Law of the Sea*, 6th ed., 1967.

Dean, Arthur H., 'The Geneva Conference on the Law of the Sea: What was Accomplished', *American Journal of International Law*, Vol. 52 (1958), pp. 607-628.

Dean, Arthur H., 'The Second Conference on the Law of the Sea: The Flight for the Freedom of the Seas', *American Journal of International Law*, Vol. 54 (1960), pp. 751-789.

Fitzmaurice, Sir Gerald, 'Some Results of the Geneva Conference on the Law of the Sea – Part I – The Territorial Sea and Contiguous Zone and Related Topics', *International and Comparative Law Quarterly*, Vol. 8 (1959), pp. 73-121.

Gardiner, Piers R.R., 'Reasons and Methods of Fixing the Outer Limit of the Legal Continental Shelf beyond 200 Nautical Miles', *Geological Survey of Ireland* (Dublin) (January 1978), pp. 1-24.

Gutteridge, J.A.C., 'The 1958 Geneva Convention on the Continental Shelf', *The British Year Book of International Law* (1959), pp. 102-123.

Hedberg, Hollis D., 'Relation of Political Boundaries on the Ocean Floor to the Continental Margin', *Virginia Journal of International Law*, Vol. 17, No. 1 (Fall 1976), pp. 57-75.

Hedberg, Hollis D., 'A Critique of Boundary Provisions in the Law of the Sea Treaty', *Ocean Development and International Law*, Vol. 12 (1983), pp. 337-342.

Hodgson, Robert D. and Smith, Robert W., 'The *Informal Single Negotiating Text* (Committee II): A Geographical Perspective', *Ocean Development and International Law*, Vol. 3, No. 3 (1976), pp. 225-259.

Hodgson, Robert D. and Cooper, John, 'The Technical Delimitation of a Modern Equidistant Boundary', *Ocean Development and International Law*, Vol. 3 (1976), pp. 361-388.

Hodgson, Robert D., 'International Ocean Boundary Disputes', *Oceans Policy Study Series*, 1978.

Hodgson, Robert D. and Smith, Robert W., 'Boundary Issues Created by Extended National Marine Jurisdiction', *Geographical Review* (January 1979), pp. 423-433.

Hollick, Anne L., 'U.S. Oceans Policy: The Truman Proclamations', *Virginia Journal of International Law*, Vol. 17, No. 1 (1976), pp. 23-55.

Hudson, Manley O., 'The First Conference for the Codification of International Law', *American Journal of International Law*, Vol. 24 (1930), pp. 447-466.

Hunter-Miller, 'The Hague Codification Conference', *American Journal of International Law*, Vol. 24 (1930), pp. 674-693.

Hurst, Sir Cecil, 'Whose is the Bed of the Sea?', *The British Year Book of International Law* (1923-24), pp. 34-43.

Kapoor, D.C., 'The Delimitation of the Exclusive Economic Zones', *Maritime Policy and Management*, No. 4 (1977), pp. 255-263.

The Law of the Sea, United Nations Convention on the Law of the Sea, United Nations, New York 1983. (For text of the United Nations Convention on the Law of the Sea, 1982, and the Final Act of the Third United Nations Conference on the Law of the Sea.)

Misra, K.P., 'Territorial Sea and India', *The Indian Journal of International Law*, Vol. 6 (1966), pp. 465-482.

Mouton, R.W., *The Continental Shelf*, 1952.

Oda, Shigeru, *International Control of Sea Resources*, Leiden: Sijthoff, 1963.

Oda, Shigeru, 'International Law of the Resources of the Sea', Académie de Droit International, *Recueil des Cours*, 1969 (II), pp. 355-484.

Oda, Shigeru, *The International Law of the Ocean Development*, Basic Documents, Volumes I and II, Leiden: Sijthoff, 1972 and 1975 (updated).

Reeves, Jesse S., 'The Codification of the Law of Territorial Waters', *American Journal of International Law*, Vol. 24 (1930), pp. 486-499.

Shalowitz, Aaron L., *Shore and Sea Boundaries*, US Department of Commerce, Vol. I (1962), pp. 212-255; Vol. II (1964), pp. 365-383. (For technical aspects of construction of boundary line.)

Smith, Robert W., 'A Geographical Primer to Maritime Boundary-Making', *Ocean Development and International Law*, Vol. 12 (1982), pp. 1-22.

Study on the Future Functions of the Secretary-General Under the Draft Convention and on the Needs of Countries, Especially Developing Countries, for Information, Advice and Assistance under the New Legal Regime, A/CONF.62/L.76 (18 August 1981), *Third United Nations Conference on the Law of the Sea, Official Records*, Vol. XV, pp. 153-171.

United Nations Conference on the Law of the Sea, 1958, *Official Records*, Vols. II and III.

Second United Nations Conference on the Law of the Sea, 1960, *Official Records*, Vols. I and II.

Third United Nations Conference on the Law of the Sea, 1973 – 1982, *Official Records*, United Nations, New York, Vols. I to XV (up to end of August 1981).

Waldock, C.H.M., 'The Anglo-Norwegian Fisheries Case', *The British Year Book of International Law* (1951), pp. 114-171.

Whiteman, Marjorie M., 'Conference on the Law of the Sea: Convention on the Conti-

nental Shelf', *American Journal of International Law*, Vol. 52 (1958), pp. 629-659.
Whiteman, Marjorie M., *Digest of International Law*, Vol. 4 (1965), pp. 903-917.
The Work of the International Law Commission, United Nations, New York, 3rd ed. (1980). (For text of Articles of the Conventions on the Law of the Sea, 1958).
Year Book of the International Law Commission, 1950 to 1956, Vol. II.

Part Two. Treaties and Agreements (Chapters 5-11)

Amin, S.H., 'Customary Rules on Delimitation of the Continental Shelf: The Gulf State Practice', *Journal of Maritime Law and Commerce*, Vol. 2, No. 4 (July 1980), pp. 509-526.
Amin, S.H., 'Law of the Continental Shelf Delimitation: The Gulf Example', *Netherlands International Law Review* (1980), pp. 335-346.
Bastianelli, Fabrizio, 'Boundary Delimitation in the Mediterranean Sea', *Marine Policy Reports* (College of Marine Studies, University of Delaware, Newark, USA), Vol. 5, No. 4 (February 1983).
Burmester, H., 'The Torres Strait Treaty: Ocean Boundary Delimitation by Agreement', *American Journal of International Law*, Vol. 76, No. 1 (April 1982), pp. 321-349.
Churchill, R., Nordquist, M. and Lay, H., *New Directions in the Law of the Sea*, Documents, Vol. V (1977); Nordquist, M. and Lay, H., Vol. VIII (1980).
Feldman, Mark B. and Colson, David, 'The Maritime Boundaries of the United States', *American Journal of International Law*, Vol. 75, No. 4 (October 1981), pp. 729-763.
International Boundary Study, Limits in the Seas, US Department of State, Office of the Geographer, Nos. 1-100.
International Legal Materials, American Society of International Law, Vols. I to XXII.
Maritime Boundaries in the Western Indian Ocean Region, Research Memorandum No. 1/252 (81), October 1981, Office of National Assessment, Canberra.
National Legislation and Treaties relating to the Law of the Sea, United Nations Legislative Series, ST/LEG/SER.B/16 (1974); B/18 (1976); B/19 (1978).
Nweihed, Kaldone G., 'Venezuela's Contribution to the Contemporary Law of the Sea', *San Diego Law Review* (1974), pp. 603-632.
Nweihed, Kaldone G., 'EZ (Uneasy) Delimitation in the Semi-Enclosed Caribbean Sea: Recent Agreements between Venezuela and Her Neighbours', *Ocean Development and International Law*, Vol. 8, No. 1 (1980), pp. 1-33.
Oda, Shigeru, 'The Delimitation of the Continental Shelf in Southeast Asia and the Far East', *Ocean Management*, Vol. I (1973), pp. 327-346.
Oda, Shigeru, 'The Continental Shelf Agreement between Japan and the Republic of Korea 1974', *The Law of the Sea in Our Time — I. New Developments 1966 – 1975*. Leiden: Sijthoff, 1977, pp. 250-264.
Oda, Shigeru, *The International Law of the Ocean Development*, Basic Documents, Volumes I and II, Leiden: Sijthoff, 1972 and 1975 (updated).
Park, Chi Young, 'The Continental Shelf between Korea, Japan and China', *Marine Policy Reports* (University of Delaware, Newark, USA), Vol. 4, No. 5 (June 1982).
Prescott, J.R.V., *Maritime Jurisdiction in Southeast Asia: A Commentary and Map*, Research Report No. 2, East-West Environment and Policy Institute, East-West Centre, Honolulu, Hawaii, January 1981.
Rhee, Sang-Myon, 'Sea Boundary Delimitation between States before World War II', *American Journal of International Law*, Vol. 76, No. 3 (July 1982), pp. 555-588.

Sayed M. Hosni, 'The Partition of the Neutral Zone', *American Journal of International Law*, Vol. 60 (1966), pp. 735-749.

Smith, Robert W., 'The Maritime Boundaries of the United States', *The Geographical Review*, Vol. 71, No. 4 (October 1981), pp. 395-410.

Smith, Robert W., 'A Geographical Primer to Maritime Boundary-Making', *Ocean Development and International Law*, Vol. 12 (1982), pp. 1-22.

Vallat, Francis A., 'The Continental Shelf', *British Year Book of International Law* (1946), pp. 333-336.

Young, Richard, 'Equitable Solutions for Offshore Boundaries: The 1968 Saudi Arabia – Iran Agreement', *American Journal of International Law*, Vol. 64 (1970), pp. 152-157.

Part Three. Judicial, arbitral and other decisions (Chapter 12)

Aegean Sea Continental Shelf, Judgment, ICJ Reports 1978, p. 3.

Arbitration between the United Kingdom of Great Britain and Northern Ireland and the French Republic on the Delimitation of the Continental Shelf, Decisions of the Court of Arbitration dated 30 June 1977 and 14 March 1978, London, 1979, *Cmnd.* 7438.

Bowett, D.W., 'The Arbitration Between the United Kingdom and France concerning the Continental Shelf Boundary in the English Channel and South-Western Approaches', *British Year Book of International Law* (1978), 1979, pp. 1-29.

Brown, E.D., 'The North Sea Continental Shelf Cases', *Current Legal Problems*, Vol. 23 (London, 1970), pp. 187-215.

Case Concerning the Continental Shelf (Tunisia/Libyan Arab Jamahiriya), *Judgment, ICJ Reports 1982*, p. 18.

Colson, David A., 'The United Kingdom – France Continental Shelf Arbitration', *American Journal of International Law*, Vol. 72, No. 1 (1978), pp. 95-112.

Colson, David A., 'The United Kingdom – France Continental Shelf Arbitration Decision of March 1978', *American Journal of International Law*, Vol. 73, No. 1 (1979), pp. 112-120.

Controversy concerning the Beagle Channel Region (Chile/Argentina), Decision of Court of Arbitration dated 18 February 1977 – Award dated 2 May 1977.

Ely, Northcutt, 'Seabed Boundries between Coastal States: The Effect to be Given Islets as "Special Circumstances"', *International Observer*, Vol. 6, No. 2, pp. 219-256.

Feldman, Mark B., 'The Tunisia – Libya Continental Shelf Case: Geographic Justice or Judicial Compromise?', *American Journal of International Law*, Vol. 77, No. 2 (April 1983), pp. 219-238.

Friedmann, Wolfgang, 'The North Sea Continental Shelf Cases: A Critique', *American Journal of International Law*, Vol. 64, No. 2 (1970), pp. 229-240.

Goldie, L.F.E., 'The International Court of Justice's "Natural Prolongation" and the Continental Shelf Problem of Islands', *Netherlands Year Book of International Law* (1973), pp. 237-261.

Goldie, L.F.E., 'Delimiting Continental Shelf Boundaries', *Limits to National Jurisdiction over the Sea,* University Press of Virginia, 1974, pp. 3-74.

Grisel, Etienne, 'The Lateral Boundary of the Continental Shelf and the Judgment of the International Court of Justice in the North Sea Continental Shelf Cases', *American Journal of International Law*, Vol. 64, No. 3 (1970), pp. 562-593.

Gross, Leo, 'The Dispute between Greece and Turkey concerning the Continental Shelf in the Aegean', *American Journal of International Law*, Vol. 71, No. 1 (1977), pp. 31-59.

Johnson, D.H.N., 'The North Sea Continental Shelf Cases', *International Relations* (London), Vol. 3 (1969), pp. 522-540.

Karl, Donald E., 'Islands and the Delimitation of Continental Shelf: a Framework for Analysis, *American Journal of International Law*, Vol. 71, No. 4 (1977), pp. 642-673.

McRae, D.M., 'Delimitation of the Continental Shelf between the United Kingdom and France: the Channel Arbitration', *Canadian Yearbook of International Law*, Vol. 15 (1977; published in 1978), pp. 173-197.

Merills, J.G., 'The United Kingdom – France Continental Shelf Arbitration', *California Western International Law Journal* (Spring 1980), pp. 314-364.

North Sea Continental Shelf, Judgment, ICJ Reports 1969, p. 3.

Report and Recommendations to the Governments of Iceland and Norway of the Conciliation Commission on the Continental Shelf Area Between Iceland and Jan Mayen, June 1981, pp. 1-60.

Rhee, Sang-Myon, 'Sea Boundary Delimitation between States before World War II', *American Journal of International Law*, Vol. 76, No. 3 (July 1982), pp. 555-588.

Part Four. Maritime boundary at the Third United Nations Conference on the Law of the Sea (Chapters 13-14)

Adede, A.O., 'Toward the Formulation of the Rule of Delimitation of Sea Boundaries Between States with Adjacent or Opposite Coasts', *Virginia Journal of International Law*, Vol. 19, No. 2 (1979), pp. 207-255.

Adede, A.O., 'Streamlining the System of Settlement of Disputes under the Law of the Sea Convention', *Pace Law Review*, Vol. 1, No. 1 (1980), pp. 44-45.

Brown, E.D., 'The Continental Shelf and the Exclusive Economic Zone: the Problem of Delimitation of UNCLOS III', *Maritime Policy Management* (1977), pp. 377-408.

Irwin, Paul C., 'Settlement of Maritime Boundary Disputes: An Analysis of the Law of the Sea Negotiations', *Ocean Development and International Law*, Vol. 8, No. 2 (1980), pp. 105-148.

Jagota, S.P., 'Maritime Boundary', Académie de Droit International, *Recueil des Cours*, Vol. 171 (1981-II), pp. 85-223.

McDorman, Ted L., Beauchamp, Kenneth P. and Johnston, Douglas M. (eds.), *Maritime Boundary Delimitation: An Annotated Bibliography*, Lexington, Massachusetts and Toronto: Lexington Books, 1983.

Oxman, Bernard H., 'The Third UNCLOS: The 1976 New York Session', *American Journal of International Law*, Vol. 71, No. 2 (1977), pp. 247-269; 'The Third UNCLOS: 1977 New York Session', *American Journal of International Law*, Vol. 72, No. 1 (1978), pp. 57-83; 'The Third UNCLOS: The Seventh Session (1978)', *American Journal of International Law*, Vol. 73, No. 1 (1979), pp. 1-41; 'The Third UNCLOS: The Eighth Session (1979)', *American Journal of International Law*, Vol. 74, No. 1 (1980), pp. 1-47; 'The Third UNCLOS: The Ninth Session (1980)', *American Journal of International Law*, Vol. 75, No. 2 (1981), pp. 211-256; 'The Third UNCLOS: The Tenth Session (1981)', *American Journal of International Law*, Vol. 76, No. 1 (1982), pp. 1-23.

Report of the Committee on the Peaceful Uses of the Sea-Bed and the Ocean Floor beyond the Limits of National Jurisdiction, *General Assembly Official Records*, 28th Session (1973), Supplement No. 21 (A/9021), Vols. III, IV and VI (for proposals before the UN Seabed Committee, 1973).

Third United Nations Conference on the Law of the Sea, Official Records, Vol. III (for text of proposals made in 1974), Vol. IV (for text of Informal Single Negotiating Text at pp. 137-181), Vol. V (for text of Revised Single Negotiating Text at pp. 125-185), Vol. VIII (for text of Informal Composite Negotiating Text − ICNT, at pp. 1-63).

Informal Composite Negotiating Text/Rev. I: for text see A/CONF.62/WP.10/Rev.1 (28 April 1979); *ICNT/Rev. 2*, see A/CONF.62/WP.10/Rev.2 (11 April 1980); *Draft Convention on the Law of the Sea (Informal Text)*, see A/CONF.62/WP.10/Rev.3 (27 August 1980); and *Draft Convention on the Law of the Sea*, see A/CONF.62/L.78 (28 August 1981), published in *Third United Nations Conference on the Law of the Sea*, Official Records, Vol. XV, pp. 172-240.

Negotiating Group 7: For text of proposals in NG7 between 1978 and 1980, see documents NG7/1-45. For Report of the Chairman on the work of Negotiating Group 7, see A/CONF.62/L.47 (24 March 1980), published in *Third United Nations Conference on the Law of the Sea, Official Records*, Vol. XIII, pp. 76-78.

Stevenson, John R. and Oxman, Bernhard H, 'The Preparation for the law of the Sea Conference', *American Journal of International Law*, Vol. 68, No. 1 (1974), pp. 1-32; 'The Third United Nations Conference on the Law of the Sea: The 1974 Caracas Session', *American Journal of International Law*, Vol. 69, No. 1 (1975), pp. 1-30; 'The Third United Nations Conference on the Law of the Sea: The 1975 Geneva Session', *American Journal of International Law*, Vol. 69 (1975), pp. 763-797.

United Nations Convention on the Law of the Sea, 1982 and Final Act of the Third United Nations Conference on the Law of the Sea: for text see *The Law of the Sea, United Nations Convention on the Law of the Sea*, United Nations, New York, 1983.

Part Six. Addendum (Chapter 16)

'Canada − United States: Treaty on Gulf of Maine Boundary Dispute Settlement', *International Legal Materials*, Vol. XX (1981), No. 6, pp. 1371-1390 (for text of the 1979 fisheries and boundary dispute settlement Agreements and related documents).

Cuyvers, Luc, 'Maritime Boundaries: Canada vs. United States', *Marine Policy Reports* (University of Delaware, Newark, USA), Vol. 2, No. 1 (February 1979).

Delimitation of the Maritime Boundary in the Gulf of Maine Area (Canada/USA), *Judgment, ICJ Reports 1984*, p. 253.

Feldman, Mark B., and Colson, David, 'The Maritime Boundaries of the United States', *American Journal of International Law*, Vol. 75 (1981), pp. 729-763, at pp. 754-763.

Hamza, B.A., 'Indonesia's Archipelagic Regime − Implications for Malaysia', *Marine Policy*, Vol. 8, No. 1 (January 1984), pp. 30-43.

McRae, D.M., 'Adjudication of the Maritime Boundary in the Gulf of Maine', *The Canadian Yearbook of International Law*, Vol. XVII (1979), pp. 292-303.

McRae, D.M., 'Proportionality and the Gulf of Maine Maritime Boundary Dispute', *The Canadian Yearbook of International Law*, Vol. XIX (1981), pp. 287-302.

McRae, D.M., 'The Gulf of Maine Case: The Written Proceedings', *The Canadian Yearbook of International Law*, Vol. XXI (1983), pp. 266-283.

Rhee, Sang-Myon, 'Equitable Solutions to the Maritime Boundary Dispute between the United States and Canada in the Gulf of Maine', *American Journal of International Law*, Vol. 75 (1981), pp. 590-628.